Double Shift

Transforming Work in Postsocialist and Postindustrial Societies

A U.S.–Post-Soviet Dialogue

Edited by
Bertram Silverman, Robert Vogt,
and Murray Yanowitch

M.E. Sharpe
ARMONK, NEW YORK
LONDON, ENGLAND

Translations © 1992 by M. E. Sharpe, Inc.,
first published in *Sociological Research*, September–October 1992,
and *Problems of Economic Transition*, September 1992.

Library of Congress Cataloging-in-Publication Data

Double shift : transforming work in postsocialist and postindustrial societies /
edited by Bertram Silverman, Robert Vogt, and Murray Yanowitch.
p.   cm.—(U.S.–post-Soviet dialogues)
Revised versions of some papers presented at two symposia held in Moscow,
June 2–8, 1991 and in New York, March 12–15, 1992 and jointly organized by
Hofstra University's Center for the Study of Work and Leisure and the Russian
Institute of Sociology and the Institute of Employment Studies and the Academy
of Labor and Social Relations.
Includes bibliographical references and index.
ISBN 1-56324-205-2 (C).—ISBN 1-56324-206-0 (P)
1. Labor policy.
2. Labor policy—Former Soviet republics.
3. Labor policy—United States.
4. Post-communism. 5. Capitalism.
6. Full employment policies. 7. Work.
I. Silverman, Bertram. II. Vogt, Robert C.
III. Yanowitch, Murray. IV. Series.
HD4904.D68   1993
331.1—dc20
93-9482
CIP

Printed in the United States of America

The paper used in this publication meets the minimum requirements of
American National Standard for Information Sciences—
Permanence of Paper for Printed Library Materials,
ANSI Z 39.48-1984.

♾

BM (c) 10   9 8 7 6 5 4 3 2 1
BM (p) 10   9 8 7 6 5 4 3 2 1

Contents

Part 2
**Postsocialist Marketization and Privatization:
Western Views**

Part 3
Labor Strategies in a Postindustrial Society

Preface

The wealth of a nation, as Adam Smith understood, depends on the productivity of labor. To improve work performance and thus raise living standards and reduce social instability, both the former Soviet Union and the United States must address the difficult task of restructuring work and worker–management relations as well as reforming education and labor-market practices. A growing number of scholars in the United States and abroad believe that economic performance in today's rapidly changing global economy depends on constructing more equitable and democratic ways of organizing human resources. Ray Marshall, one of the contributors to this volume, calls this newly evolving stage "human resource" capitalism.

Restructuring labor-market institutions is a time-intensive process not easily accomplished by rapid doses of the "shock therapy" that has been recommended by some United States economists seeking a quick transition to a market system. Enterprises, both public and private, need time to absorb, implement, and adjust to the changing rules, procedures, practices, and outcomes of labor-market reforms. Special attention must also be given to those groups whose work life is disrupted during the transition period. For unless assistance is given to losing groups, social and political stability will be threatened, undermining the reform process. Institutional innovation of this sort requires greater (not less) cooperation among business, labor, government, and community-based institutions.

The transformation of work in the former Soviet Union is particularly problematic. The former Soviet republics face a double shift: marketization and postindustrialism. Marketization requires the restructuring of labor-market institutions so that managers, workers, and trade unions can respond more effectively to market signals rather than to centrally administered commands. But in reorganizing work, the former Soviet Union must also take account of the information and communications revolution that is transforming the production structure of advanced industrial economies.

This book seeks to explore the labor dimension of this double shift. All the authors were participants in one or both of two symposia on New Directions in Worker–Management Relations, which took place June 2–8, 1991, in Moscow and March 12–15, 1992, in New York. Their essays were revised for publication in this volume. The conferences were jointly sponsored by Hofstra University's Center for the Study of Work and Leisure and by the Russian Institute of Sociology, the Institute of Employment Problems, and the Academy of Labor and Social Relations. Some of the papers prepared for these symposia were published in another book in this series, *Labor and Democracy in the Transition to a Market System: A U.S.–Post-Soviet Dialogue* (1992).

Unfortunately, we could not publish many of the important essays and reports presented at the symposia. Some have been published in other scholarly journals and books. We would especially like to acknowledge the contribution of the following individuals from the former Soviet Union: Marat V. Baglai, Vice-Chancellor, Academy of Labor and Social Relations; Iurii A. Boldyrev, Member of the Donetsk Regional Workers' Committee; Aleksandr V. Buzgalin, Deputy Head, Department of Economics, Moscow State University; K.D. Krylov, Secretary of the Council, Federation of Independent Trade Unions of Russia; Vladimir Kusmenok, Deputy President, General Confederation of Trade Unions; Vladimir Magun, Senior Research Associate, Institute of Sociology; Nikolai P. Popov, Director, Political Survey Department, Center for Public Opinion and Market Research; Leonid Z. Solomin, Leader, Kazakhstan Independent Trade Union "Birlesu"; Victor Utkin, People's Deputy, Supreme Soviet, Russian Republic; and from the United States: Barbara Bergmann, Professor of Economics, American University; Fred Feinstein, Legal Counsel, Labor–Management Relations Subcommittee, U.S. House of Representatives; William Gould, Professor of Law, Stanford University; Samuel Kaynard, Professor of Law, Hofstra University; Eugene Eisner, Labor Attorney, Eisner, Levy, Pollack & Ratner; Douglas Fraser, Past President, United Automobile, Aerospace and Agriculture Implement Workers; Joe Layman, Director of Corporate Industrial Relations, Xerox Corporation; Vickie Saporta, Director of Organizing, International Brotherhood of Teamsters; Eric Schmertz, Professor of Law, Hofstra University; Jack Sheinkman, President, Amalgamated Clothing and Textile Workers Union; John Ullmann, Professor of Management, Hofstra University; and Alfred Warren, Past Vice-President, Strategic Labor Issues, General Motors Corporation.

For permission to include some of the essays which have been or are scheduled to be published elsewhere, we would like to thank the editors of *Dissent*, *Economic and Industrial Democracy*, and the University of Chicago Press.

Hofstra University has been particularly generous in supporting this project. We would especially like to thank President James M. Shuart, Alexej Ugrinsky and the Cultural Center Staff, and Phyllis Droessler, Secretary of the Center for the Study of Work and Leisure.

We would like to express our special appreciation for the financial support provided by the Carnegie Corporation of New York, as well as the Slant Fin Foundation of Roslyn, New York, and the Soros Foundation.

Our publisher has worked closely with us on this project. We would especially like to thank Patricia Kolb, Executive Editor at M.E. Sharpe and a specialist on post-Soviet affairs.

Introduction

The Transformation of Work in Postsocialist and Postindustrial Societies

Bertram Silverman and Murray Yanowitch

No road map exists to guide the successor states of the former Soviet Union (SSSU) in their difficult journey to a market economy. Their quest is made more difficult because there are many possible roads they can travel. Market systems differ among successful capitalist countries, and many of them are undergoing dramatic transformations of their economic and social structures. The central question the SSSU face, then, is not only how to make the transition to a market economy but what kind of market system to construct.

The economic disintegration of the Soviet Union in the late 1980s and pressures to introduce the market rapidly have also tended to oversimplify our understanding of the marketization process. The emphasis given to price liberalization, monetary policy, and macroeconomic stabilization, all of which are assumed to have universal applicability rooted in principles of economics, downplays the institutions, rules, and customs through which those policies must be filtered. Without restructuring economic institutions, managers of enterprises may respond in ways that distort economic reforms, undermining economic performance and creating new forms of privilege and inequalities. Such outcomes produce resistance to marketization. It is, of course, easier to liberalize prices, reduce government spending, and restrain monetary growth than to deal with the complex problems of restructuring production and work relations. But these are precisely the issues that are addressed by the contributors to this book. In examining the place of labor in the transformation of contemporary postsocialist and capitalist economies, they challenge traditional ideas about how market systems work.

Postsocialist Labor Relations: Problems and Mixed Signals

Given the volatility of the economic and political situation in the former Soviet Union, the absorption with continuing the radical reform of the old system, there is little point in searching for the emergence of anything approximating a stable new pattern of labor relations. Clearly, such a quest would be premature at this point. However, a model or vision of a future labor market, one in which "postsocialist" labor relations will prevail, has been repeatedly proclaimed as a goal by intellectuals associated with the labor movement (in both its recently emerged "independent" sectors as well as its reformed "traditional" sectors) and by representatives of the Russian government responsible for labor policy. What are the principal features of this model? How do its adherents see the "normal" functioning of labor markets and labor relations following the implementation of the monetary, pricing, and privatization reforms currently in progress? What are some of the principal problems associated with making the transition to the new model? In the course of answering these questions, it will become clear that this transition process will require reliance on continuities as well as breaks with the "economic culture" and traditions of the past.

"Normal" Labor Relations in the Future Economy

In the new vocabulary that emerged in the social-science literature of the former Soviet Union in 1991–92, it was not uncommon for democratically oriented intellectuals to characterize the type of system that they hoped would replace the Soviet version of state socialism by such unusual—in the Soviet context—terms as a "mixed economy," a "social market economy," or even a "socialized" capitalism. While the precise institutional characteristics implied by such terms were rarely, if ever, spelled out in detail, those who relied on the new language made no attempt to conceal that they had in mind the kinds of societies and economies commonly found in the more economically advanced, predominantly capitalist Western countries. When the Russian authors of these works did specify the principal institutional characteristics of such societies, they almost invariably included a market economy, a strong private-property sector, political democracy, and reliable "social guarantees" or "social protection" for workers.[1]

This was also the broad institutional framework within which "civilized" or "humanized" or "normal" labor markets and labor relations would eventually emerge in the reformed domestic economy.[2] Perhaps the most critical feature (certainly the most frequently cited feature) of such markets was that they reflected the interactions of three essentially independent groups or agencies: representatives of (a) workers (whether in the form of trade unions or other types of workers' organizations), (b) employers (whether in the form of owners of productive property or economic managers), and (c) government authorities. This model of the tripartite framework of future labor relations was commonly elaborated in the literature in a manner that stressed its fundamental departure from the pattern of traditional Soviet labor relations. The latter, after all, also included participants who were allegedly representatives of workers and employing organizations, but these were in no sense independent market agents, nor could the typical "employer" under state socialism be regarded as anything other than a unit of the state's economic structure. All of the parties involved in the old system of industrial relations were "completely subordinate" to the directives of the same party–state apparatus (see the Gordon paper in this volume). Hence, in contrast with the "unipartite" and strictly "vertical" nature of labor relations under state socialism, the new model stresses the independence of all the parties involved in the future tripartite framework and the special role of state agencies functioning as "neutral intermediaries" and thus helping to resolve disputes between representatives of workers and employers. In this "civilized" mechanism of labor relations, the latter two groups have "equal rights," and although they may be adversaries, they are also—together with the appropriate state agencies—collaborators or "social partners," i.e., groups that commonly reach voluntary agreements through negotiation and compromise. The strike weapon remains legal in this vision of a "tripartite social partnership" but is used comparatively infrequently.

None of the serious literature of 1991–92 projecting this vision of labor relations claimed that more than the very first steps required for its realization had already been accomplished. Perhaps the most obvious signs of the initial stages of such a transition were the appearance of a labor movement independent of party and state authorities and the emergence of nonstate (mainly cooperative) enterprises employing a small minority of the nonagricultural work force. In this sense, it could be said that labor relations had already lost their former strictly vertical, command-like, and unipartite character. But at the beginning of 1992, the overwhelming bulk of employers or entrepreneurs did not yet function as labor-market agents who were distinct from state authorities. In the words of the former minister of labor of the Russian Republic (published early in 1992), "the interests of the employer and the interests of the state are to a large extent still represented by the same persons."[3] Or put somewhat differently, some members of the government performed the role of employers or entrepreneurs, while others—associated with the very same government—performed the kind of state functions commonly associated with the ministries of finance, labor, justice, etc. At best, this provided the basis for what might be characterized as a bipartite framework for industrial relations, a necessary transitional stage on the path toward the model of a tripartite social partnership. In the view of at least some intellectual sympathizers with the new labor movement, the attainment of the latter model now required, "above all," the mass privatization of productive property.[4] This would not only help break the dependence of enterprise managers and business executives on state authorities, thereby helping transform employers into independent market agents, but also encourage these groups (who would then function as owners or representatives of owners) to resist the inflationary wage demands of workers and their unions.

In addition to the institutional and organizational framework sketched above, the effective functioning of the "civilized" labor market that Russian reformers have in mind also presumes the transformation of the "economic culture" or traditional modes of thought on labor issues, particularly among workers. The nature of the problem may best be illustrated by noting how some Russian scholars characterize the "lumpen mentality" fostered by decades of state socialism. Perhaps its most obvious elements are "a feeling of total dependence on the state's authority structures," a tendency to identify "social justice" with an egalitarian distribution of income, intolerance of dissent, and a hypersensitivity to the dangers posed by "enemies"—whether internal or external.[5] Thus the state-dependent worker relies on the state not only as the natural source of employment but also as the agency that properly decides which incomes are too low and which are too high, and which views on broader issues of social and economic policy are the "correct" views. Little wonder that the current literature commonly describes the typical Soviet worker of the past as characterized by a reluctance to take risks, to display initiative, to assume responsibility, to make independent decisions[6]—that is, to display a market mentality.

Of course, the turbulence of recent years—in particular, the emergence of an independent labor movement and the associated strike waves—suggests that the "lumpen mentality" described above has been substantially weakened. But the habits of thought on labor issues built up over decades can hardly be expected to dissipate in a few years. Thus, however sketchy and idealized the vision of reformed, tripartite ("normal" or "civilized") labor relations presented earlier, the more serious Russian scholars are clearly aware that the implementation of such a model requires that a new "economic culture" accompany and reinforce the necessary changes in political, economic, and property institutions (see, in particular, the essays in this volume by Iadov, Gimpel'son, and Rakitskii). While the precise content of this "economic culture" remains to be spelled out, we would expect that—from the standpoint of workers and their organizations—it would encourage such traits as the capacity for self-organization, autonomy, initiative, and the readiness to question state authority. Clearly, such traits are the very opposite of those embodied in the "lumpen mentality."

Problems and Paradoxes in Reformist Thought on Labor Issues

All of the material considered thus far stresses the institutional and cultural break with the past that is expected to accompany the establishment of the model of postsocialist labor relations described above. But some of the arguments invoked to justify policies allegedly necessary to attain this vision of the future draw on the kind of reasoning that surely has a familiar ring to citizens of the former Soviet Union. Moreover, some of the attitudes on labor issues in the Russian reformist literature are quite at odds with views commonly associated with Western labor movements and "enlightened" or "prolabor" policies in the more economically developed market economies. Of course, given the nature of the system being transformed and its stage of economic development, it should come as no surprise if some of the attitudes and policies defended by Russian reformers and labor spokesmen seem "conservative" or "neoconservative" when considered in a Western, "postindustrial" context. The points that follow should serve to illustrate these propositions.

(a) The Russian government's position that a decline in workers' living standards is an unavoidable social cost associated with the transition to a market economy has been accepted—in some cases implicitly, in others explicitly—by leading intellectuals associated with diverse wings of the labor movement. Among the more forthright statements in support of such a proposition was that by Marat Baglai, rector of the Academy of Labor and Social Relations. Baglai seemed certain that the newly emerging system of labor relations would eventually ensure just and adequate levels of income for workers ("an equivalent exchange between labor power and its payment"). But for the moment the principal task in the area of labor relations was to ensure "the acquiescence of the working people to the lowering of the living standard necessary for the transition to a market economy."[7] An essentially similar position was accepted by Leonid Gordon, an industrial sociologist whose writings had repeatedly stressed the positive role of independent unions (including the strikes conducted by them prior to the August 1991 coup attempt) in promoting economic and political reforms. In Gordon's view, a temporary decline in workers' living standards was an inevitable accompaniment of the transition to a market system, "a prerequisite" for economic expansion in the future. True, some workers did not understand this, but fortunately most of the new unions recognized "the necessity of some sacrifice and the destructive nature of strike anarchy in the critical period of transformations."[8] (It was not clear whether Gordon's reference to new unions here included some of the transformed "official" unions or only the recently organized "independent" unions.)

It should be noted that these affirmations of the inevitability of temporary reductions in workers' living standards were made on the heels of two successive years (1990 and 1991) of declines in workers' real incomes and shortly following the Russian government's implementation of "price liberalization" early in 1992. It would be an oversimplification, of course, to equate these appeals for current "sacrifices" in the name of a bountiful future with analogous appeals commonly found in the Soviet labor literature of earlier years. Certainly Gordon's view that workers should retain the strike weapon and be prepared to rely on "balancing-on-the-brink-of-a-strike" tactics while recognizing the need for certain "sacrifices" differentiates his position from those who unquestioningly accepted any government labor policies in the past. But it would also be a mistake to fail to recognize elements of continuity between the arguments of Baglai and Gordon cited above and the logic invoked to justify very different policies in the past. Clearly, these arguments marked a reversion to familiar traditions. Whether or not a decline in workers' living standards is really avoidable in the course of the transition from an "administrative-command system" to a market economy, persuading workers of its inevitability undoubtedly facilitated the government's marketization reforms and promoted a process that some Russian scholars have characterized—perhaps with some justification—as the "primitive accumulation of capital" (see paper by Galina Rakitskaia below).

(b) One of the principal messages repeatedly conveyed in the Russian literature on labor problems in 1991–92 was that the marketization process would necessarily bring with it a significant rise in unemployment. While there were substantial differences in estimates of its probable magnitude, it seemed clear that the reduction in state subsidies, the elimination of state-fixed production targets, and the privatization of state property would require confronting what had long been celebrated as a nonproblem in the Soviet past. What was now regarded as the "redundant employment" inherent in the earlier socialist economy seemed to make the emergence of open unemployment unavoidable during the market transition. Studies of public opinion in the early nineties also pointed to the growing acceptance by the Russian population of the "permissibility and inevitability" of unemployment (see the paper by Vladimir Gimpel'son below).[9] Leading labor scholars like Gimpel'son welcomed such sentiments as indicators of an emerging "promarket mentality" and as signifying the liberation of society from the "illusions and myths" of the past. Along with the increased recognition that some unemployment was inherent in the market-reform process, these studies also documented an increasing "fear" among workers that their jobs would be threatened by this process. But for scholars like Gimpel'son, such "fear" also performed a positive function in the given historical context. It heightened people's sense of "personal responsibility for their own fate," thereby contributing to the healthy transformation of the state-dependent worker.

Of special interest is the selective manner in which some Russian labor scholars and government officials invoked the Western experience in formulating their own responses to the anticipated growth of unemployment. The views of Aleksandr Shokhin, former minister of labor of the Russian Republic, may serve as an illustration.[10] There was no question but that the state had to ensure some level of "material support" for the unemployed (along with measures to finance job retraining and encourage part-time work and self-employment). However, Shokhin seemed particularly concerned to stress the dangers of excessive unemployment benefits. The experience of countries with a "very comfortable system of social protection against unemployment," i.e., countries with relatively generous levels of assistance that remain in effect for extended periods, tended to generate an unhealthy "dependency mechanism" among their workers. "This is why specialists throughout the entire world recommend that when a person becomes unemployed, he should feel it" (*dolzhen eto pochuvstvovat'*). Shokhin's reading of the U.S. and West European experience with unemployment benefits seemed to suggest that the more "liberal" the level and duration of such benefits, "the higher is the unemployment."[11] Thus, whatever the precise mix of policies adopted in response to the forthcoming unavoidable (and substantial) rise in the number of laid-off workers, a prime objective must be to stimulate the latter to seek and find alternative sources of employment as rapidly as possible. The principal "value" for the unemployed worker must be obtaining alternative employment, not the receipt of unemployment compensation. Shokhin's reiteration of this theme, like Gimpel'son's view of the potentially positive impact of the growing "fear" of unemployment, appear rooted in a common concern—the urgency of overcoming the "lumpen mentality" of the state-dependent worker, thereby facilitating the transition to a market economy. But is it presumptuous or premature to suggest that Russian labor scholars (and their readers) might also benefit from confronting those Western studies that stress the positive impact job security may have on productive performance in the context of a market system (see, for example, the papers by Harry Katz et al. and Ray Marshall below)?

(c) If there is anything that seems to conflict with the new economic culture required by a market economy, it is the heritage of egalitarianism and wage leveling. Although such sentiments and practices were frequently denounced during the years of Soviet rule as being in conflict with the socialist principle of distribution, they are now commonly regarded as having been inherent in the ideology and economic institutions of Soviet state socialism. The current absorption with overcoming this heritage is apparent in the frequent attacks in the recent labor literature on phenomena variously characterized as the "egalitarian psychology" or the "mass leveling mentality."[12] The target of these attacks is not simply a wage system that had a negative impact on work incentives by failing to provide meaningful rewards for improved work performance, but also a set of attitudes toward one's colleagues and the role of the state that reflected the presumably unhealthy influence of egalitarian stereotypes. Some illustrations of the latter cited in the recent anti-egalitarian literature include the following: a tolerant attitude toward obviously "redundant" workers, the assumption that those who "live so much better than others" must be "making money by dishonest means," the view that the state has the responsibility of ensuring that "some people do not earn too much while others earn too little." While some critics focused on the residual negative impact of these Soviet-era attitudes toward inequality, others (Iurii Volkov, for example) elaborated the theme of the market mechanism as "the most reliable instrument" for assessing the relative contributions to output of the various participants in the production process, and thus for ensuring "social justice" in the distribution of income.[13] No model of the economy, noted Volkov, could ensure an absolutely just income distribution, but even the "wildest" forms of Western capitalism—aided by the market and appropriate "social regulations"—distributed income more justly than the old Soviet Union.

The exaltation of the market as an income-differentiating mechanism was almost invariably accompanied by acknowledgement of the need for special "social protection" for low-income groups, especially under the conditions of the price inflation prevailing in 1991–92. But the dominant view among specialists in this area was that, given the ongoing transition to a market, only a "minimum" program of "social protection" for such groups was possible, i.e., income supplements for low-income strata must not grow more rapidly that the earnings of the more "active" and productive groups of the population. After all (as an article in the comparatively liberal journal *Svobodnaia mysl'* noted), if the economy was to be pulled out of its current crisis, it would not be mainly through the efforts of relatively low-paid groups but by those "who even today must be relatively well paid."[14] The point seemed to be that protection for the "weak" must not cut excessively into the incomes of the "strong."

(d) One of the principal controversies of the early 1990s in the Russian economic literature—and in the political sphere at large—centered on the issue of denationalization and privatization of state property. This is a large theme and deserves separate examination—but not here. What is of special interest in the context of our discussion, however, is the distinctly critical attitude of some of the leading intellectuals associated with the labor movement toward proposals to transfer ownership and control of state enterprises to their work collectives. Thus for Leonid Gordon such proposals, in the guise of promoting "collective owner- ship" and "collective management," represented one more misguided attempt to implement the socialist idea (see Gordon's paper below). Historical experience, including the Yugoslav case as well as the Soviet *kolkhoz*, surely demonstrated that a collective form of economic organization "is far less efficient than a private one." Moreover, it seemed clear to Gordon that only a small minority of workers was interested in substantial participation in managerial decision making (in "striving to become real masters of production"). Thus Gordon cited with obvious approval the views of some miners' union leaders that the reformed economy needed "real businessmen" with whom unions could struggle over issues involving wages and working conditions. An essentially similar view is conveyed in the writings of Iurii Volkov of the Academy of Labor and Social Relations, an organization long associated with what are now characterized as the "official" unions of the Soviet era. For Volkov, the transfer of state enterprises to their work collectives would threaten to reduce further their productive efficiency and create pressures to divert a firm's net earnings into increased workers' current money income rather than capital investment. Although the views of Gordon and Volkov on these issues are by no means unanimously accepted in the Russian labor literature,[15] their position is clearly a common—and perhaps the dominant— one. Writings in defense of worker ownership, or worker self-management, or simply "strategic participation" by workers in management decisions are now as likely to appear in the U.S. labor literature as in the Russian (see the papers below by Weisskopf, Marshall, and Katz).[16] One reason is surely the continuing absorption of most Russian labor scholars with shedding the slogans, as well as the reality, of state socialism.

Clearly, there are certain tensions or conflicts between the somewhat idyllic vision of future labor relations projected in the reformist literature reviewed earlier and the more immediate steps required to transform this vision into reality. On the one hand, the commonly accepted objective is to make the transition to "the same kind of market-democratic model of society that exists in most indus- trially developed countries."[17] But the attainment of this model, when the transi- tion is being made *from* state socialism, appears to require workers to accept—temporarily, but for an indeterminate period—a decline in real income, a substantial rise in unemployment, and in all probability an increase in income inequality, while leaving the bulk of productive property and managerial decision making in the hands of some combination of the old *nomenklatura* and the newly emerging "real businessmen." These features of the economic environment, as well as the absence of a strong political party associated with an experienced mass labor movement, do not seem conducive to the rapid emergence of "civilized" labor relations or a tripartite "social partnership." The latter, after all, require something approximating equality of bargaining power. In the short run, however, there may be no alternative to the kind of market transition that some Western observers characterize as "Wild West capitalism and a growing gulf between rich and poor,"[18] a situation that in the vocabulary of some Russian scholars may be translated as approximating "the primitive accumulation of capital." But the resistance of workers and their unions to the rapid pace of the market transition, and to continuing appeals for "sacrifice," contributes to social policies that may reduce the social costs of change and, as a consequence, may help create the rules and practices commonly embedded in more "civilized" labor markets.[19]

Labor Relations and Work Organization in Postindustrial Society

In some ways the recent post-Soviet reformist literature parallels an earlier defense of capitalism by economists trained in the tradition of classical economics. They, too, saw the social disruptions and destructive aspects of the market as a necessary part of a process that would eventually ensure the superiority of capitalism.[20] But their defense obscured the relational and tie-forming aspects of markets that had been so transparently a part of premarket economic relations.[21] In wishing the market well, mainstream economists have continued to present a picture of market systems free from close affective connections. Their claim for the market's allocational efficiency was based on the theory that self-seeking and rationally informed individuals guided by competitive pressures will act in ways that enhance the general welfare of a nation.

The most important message conveyed by the U.S. contributors to this and an earlier volume is that this idealization of the market ignores the special role that rules and regulations imposed by customs and law have on market outcomes. They join a growing number of economists who recognize the significance of market imperfections and therefore the widespread existence and need for trust, cooperation, and responsibility among buyers and sellers in both product and resource markets. The social norms and rules that regulate those tie-forming interactions influence perceptions of fairness that have consequences for work performance and democratization. The quality of work relations that evolve during the post-Soviet transition period is therefore critically important to the success of market and democratic reform. As Richard Freeman notes, labor accounts for the bulk of gross national output and "mistakes in the labor area can generate strikes, wage inflation, and political instability in addition to inefficiencies, shortages of skilled workers, unemployment, and the like. Because labor institutions have long lives, moreover, a country that develops a flawed labor-relations system may suffer from labor conflict and poor economic performance for decades."[22]

But no single model of industrial relations now exists toward which post-socialist economies must inevitably move. During the heyday of American economic ascendancy, many social scientists assumed that in the long run most countries would adopt some variant of the United States model of industrial relations. With the recent decline of U.S. economic power and the success of alternative labor-relations systems in Japan and Germany, that argument is no longer compelling. As Harry Katz and his colleagues stress in this volume, greater emphasis is now placed on the "cross-national diversity of stable industrial-relations patterns" and the need to transform the mass-production system pioneered in the United States.[23]

These changes have motivated social scientists to look more closely at the special characteristics of labor markets and work systems in order to understand their successes or limitations. Departing from traditional ideas of "Homo economicus" in which notions of a natural and inevitable market are rooted, some labor economists suggest that labor markets are cultural as well as economic institutions and as such encourage certain types of behavior and discourage others.[24] Individualism and competitiveness grow not out of human nature but rather from market rewards and punishments. If individual self-interest is considered necessary to encourage work effort, then unregulated competitive markets may be seen as necessary and inevitable economic arrangements. If, on the other hand, trust, cooperation, and loyalty are seen as necessary for greater efficiency, new rules ensuring greater economic security and democratic participation may be required.

The 1970s and 1980s witnessed significant changes in labor-market patterns and industrial-relations systems. Increased international competition, intensified by rapid technological innovations and slower economic growth (following the oil crisis), has pressured governments and businesses to modify industrial relations and government policies that have regulated market behavior since the 1940s. As mass-production industries moved to newly developing low-wage economies, new industrial-relations models in Japan and Germany calling for more flexible work relations suggested more productive ways of organizing work. But for some advocates of the free market, greater flexibility was a code word for increasing wage and employment competition and reducing government regulation and social programs. The Soviet system of centralized planning has sometimes been identified with government control and regulation in the West. Consequently, as Michael Piore has argued, "the collapse of the Soviet system is being interpreted as supporting the case for deregulation and the curtailment of the welfare state."[25]

While some dismantling of the welfare state and declining trade-union density in the United States and many European countries has occurred, it would be a mistake to see this development as a triumph of free-market economics. First, the SSSU should take note of some of the consequences of diminishing government protection and support. Persistent unemployment has reached levels that would have been politically unthinkable a few decades ago. The incidence of poverty has increased significantly, and the divisions between the working and nonworking poor and the remainder of society have sharpened. Middle-income jobs of the semiskilled blue-collar worker are diminishing, and as a result the income gap between the less educated and the more educated is widening.[26] Nor have declining real wages of workers stemmed the movement of basic industries to newer industrializing nations. While the evidence is still incomplete, the free-market strategy may have contributed to greater social divisions and inequalities and declining U.S. economic power rather than promoting higher living standards and competitiveness.

Second, Japan and Germany, the most successful countries making the transition to more flexible work organization and work relations, have imposed greater constraints by public and private associations on individual economic activities than the United States. Therefore, in seeking to compete effectively in the changing international division of labor, the critical challenge is not to choose between a regulated and an unregulated market system but rather to identify those work practices and public policies that best reflect the requirements of the postindustrial era.

From Mass-Production to Flexible-Production Systems

In the United States the industrial system of labor relations reflected the demands of mass production. These included large investments in highly specialized capital equipment requiring a detailed division of work tasks, narrowly trained workers, and central control of information and planning. The mass production of standardized products depended on stable and growing mass markets. The 1930s made clear the need for additional institutional support to sustain domestic demand and social stability. The social-insurance system, protection of trade unions, macroeconomic stabilization, and monetary policies created conditions to sustain domestic purchasing power and reduce labor conflict. America's unique economic position after the Second World War reinforced the success of the industrial system.

But by the end of the 1960s, domestic markets could no longer support the mass-production systems of the major capitalist countries, and no institutional framework existed to stabilize and expand international markets. Fluctuations in energy, food, and raw-material prices and exchange rates intensified economic uncertainty. In the face of this instability, new patterns of more flexible production and work practices emerged most successfully in Japan, Germany, and central

Italy. The United States is a follower rather than a leader in the development of these new postindustrial production systems.

The reports in this and a previous volume deal more fully with the characteristics of mass-production and flexible-production methods. We will focus on what caused the mass-production system to erode and on the implications that a postindustrial model has for transforming labor and work relations. First, the recipe for producing goods and services, usually referred to as technology, changed. Mass production is based on the processing of natural resources through heavy investment in fixed capital and narrowly defined labor tasks. The new technology, based on the computer and communications revolution, substitutes knowledge and information for physical resources of all kinds to improve efficiency and production. Postindustrial production does not change the importance of manufacturing, but it does change how we produce things. In the mass-production system based on large investments in fixed and specialized capital, economies of scale were a key element in reducing costs and increasing efficiency.[27] In the new technology, size no longer provides any advantages. Information technology makes smaller economic units and decentralized decision making a more effective way of enhancing productivity.

The information and communications revolution also contributed to the growth of the global economy. Technology based on information and knowledge rather than natural resources and physical capital cannot be restricted to national borders. The postindustrial economy is therefore international in scope and is not as easily subject to national economic policies. This poses difficult problems for nations if they wish to avoid wage competition, which inevitably leads to lowering living standards. Postindustrial labor policies will require new ways of promoting international labor standards, but they will also increase the importance of developing national work systems that enhance what former labor secretary Ray Marshall calls a high-performance, high-wage strategy. A high-wage labor market is possible in an economy that is based on the production of customized quality goods. Competing in quality and productivity rather than around the production of low-priced standardized goods is, as Ray Marshall suggests, the "only way to command the high prices that alone can support a high wage economy."[28]

What are some of the requirements of a new postindustrial labor strategy, and what are some of its potential problems? First, a high-performance, high-wage strategy changes the objectives of labor-relations policies. When workers perform relatively unskilled tasks with limited control over decisions, the major goal of industrial relations is to reduce labor turnover, absenteeism, and work resistance. Industrial engineering and human relations focuses on increasing worker morale and job satisfaction. In a well-known critical essay, Daniel Bell called such techniques "cow sociology."[29] In a high-performance system, workers undertake a wider range of tasks because information and work decisions are more decentralized, giving workers greater control over their work activities.

The quantity and quality of work depends more on what workers know and on their sense of fairness. Work performance and work equity are now the primary concerns of "human resource management."[30]

Such a strategy is in sharp contrast with more traditional economic analysis. A growing number of labor economists now recognize that there is a social dimension to labor markets and work places that requires that an economy do more than "get prices right" if it is to operate efficiently. For example, providing a small wage premium may reduce labor turnover and training costs and enhance loyalty and work effort. Therefore, some labor economists suggest that paying workers more than a market clearing wage may be perfectly rational if it reduces labor costs and conflicts and enhances work motivation.

Moreover, wage structures also reflect workers' perceptions of fairness and justice rooted in rules and customs that resist attempts by markets to undermine them. This structure of wages is formed as part of a system of "coercive comparisons" and "wage contours" on which perceptions of fairness and equity are constructed.[31] Writing in a period when the U.S. economy was subject to considerable regulation and planning, the War Labor Board warned in 1943 that "there is no single factor in the whole field of labor relations that does more to break down morale, create individual dissatisfaction, encourage absenteeism, increase labor turnover, and hamper productivity than obviously unjust inequalities paid to different individuals in the same labor group within the same plant."[32] As Robert Solow observed, wage rates and jobs are not like other prices and quantities. The old trade-union slogan "A fair day's wage for a fair day's work" recognizes the link between wages and productivity, as does the Soviet workers' satirical barb "They pretend to pay us, and we pretend to work." It is therefore necessary to take account not only of technological and budget constraints but also of the "constraints arising from social norms."[33]

A second element in the new postindustrial labor strategy links work performance and work equity to how the enterprise is governed. In the mass-production system, where planning and thinking are done by management and workers are supposed to do what they are told, collective bargaining has provided the institutional mechanism to promote greater equality, democracy, and work discipline. But in the United States the system has discouraged work flexibility because rigid job classifications and job ladders are used by trade unions to protect workers against arbitrary managerial authority. The new industrial relations break down sharp divisions between managers and workers and reduce the protective work rules, giving workers greater flexibility in planning and organizing work. New forms of participation in management, including quality circles, work teams, and work councils,[34] reduce the centrality of collective bargaining as the instrument of worker influence. These new methods of work-place governance suggest that cooperation rather than conflict is the best way to conduct labor relations and challenge traditional ideas of an inherently adversarial relationship between workers and managers.

But labor markets are political as well as economic institutions that can encourage democratic as well as authoritarian relationships.[35] The persistence of unemployment creates inequalities between workers and managers because it increases the cost of leaving a job. In the idealized free competitive market, as Sam Bowles notes, "it is costless for any market participant to walk away from any transaction—the same deal can be struck across the street."[36] However, since those who work usually live better than those who are unemployed, the power of exit to improve the quality of one's work is limited. As U.S. workers have recently learned, the fear of job loss can also be a powerful inhibitor on exercising opposition to managerial objectives. In the absence of policies ensuring greater job security, a competitive market may encourage more authoritarian work relations,. But such arrangements, as some contributors to this volume note, may be counterproductive to economic efficiency.

A third element of the new industrial relations turns to the importance of education and training and to the use of positive rather than negative incentives to encourage skill development. A high-wage economy requires continuing on-the-job training and the sharing of knowledge and innovation. To encourage such behavior, in some firms employment security is given to a core group of workers, and profit sharing and bonuses are used to connect work effort to an organization's economic performance. Employment and wage competition are rejected because they undermine cooperation and increase resistance to technological innovation and change in work rules and customs. Why would a journeyman train an apprentice if the new worker might underbid him for his or her job? Moreover, while productivity depends on individual effort, it also requires teamwork that is learned through on-the-job experiences, cooperation, and, as Lester Thurow observes, "a substantial period of practice working together."[37] Skills are learned by sharing knowledge on the job. Workers learn from doing, and they learn from working together.

Much of this analysis therefore suggests that there is a degree of indeterminacy in setting wage and employment policies. If productivity depends on the group rather than the individual, how are wages to be determined? What kind of wage structure is consistent with a worker's sense of fairness? What form of employment and wage flexibility is compatible with encouraging innovation and work effort? What role will trade unions play in the new industrial relations?

These questions suggest that workers face new risks as well as potential benefits in this new work system. Flexibility is designed to reduce total labor costs by making wages and fringe benefits a more variable cost of production. Consequently, the firm's work force is divided into two groups: core workers are granted employment security, while a more peripheral and contingent work group of part-time, temporary, and subcontracted workers fluctuates with changing market and production needs. But even the compensation of the core workers fluctuates, because their income partly depends on the business's economic performance.

The new work relations pose significant challenges and problems for trade unions. Management has taken the lead in introducing these new work practices. But if management seeks to change its relationship with workers so that, according to Charles Heckscher, "every employee is seen as a manager, involved in decisions and contributing intelligently to the goal of the corporation," why, asks David Brody, should workers join a union?[38]

The contributors to this book reject the view that the new industrial relations eliminate the distinction between managers and workers, thereby ending adversarial relations and equalizing power and authority. Greater democratic participation encourages cooperation and improves the quality of work. But without an independent voice provided by trade unions, management will assert its power during periods of adversity and conflict. This will undermine the trust and cooperation so essential in making the new system work.

But how can trade unions provide such a voice? The decentralization of business and divisions between core and contingent workers potentially increase wage and work segmentation. Do unions need to organize differently to reduce those divisions? How shall unions represent contingent workers who have less organic links to their enterprises? How can unions sustain workers' solidarity in a system that encourages workers to behave like managers? Who should or should not be represented by the union if managers are included in work teams? While cooperation and teamwork rather than individualism and competition are encouraged, workers are still rewarded and punished as individuals. How do unions represent workers' rights within the team system?

As in the SSSU, transitional problems make trade unions suspicious of managerial strategies to transform work relations. Flexibility can be used as a means to prevent unionization and escape restrictions on managerial authority.[39] For these managers, as Michael Piore notes, "there is really no new 'model,' only the binding constraints of the old, and the survival of American business is to be had at the expense of the gains which unions have made through collective bargaining and legislation since the 1930s."[40] Nor does the new information technology insure greater decentralization of authority; it may be used to control and regulate the work process more effectively. In fact, technological innovation and flexibility may cover a wide range of policies that fall short of the high-wage, high-performance model outlined by Ray Marshall.

Both the evolution of new work patterns and increasing managerial resistance to trade unions in the United States are weakening the power of unions within the enterprise. Conflicting views exist about what unions should do. On the basis of historical experiences, David Brody argues in this volume that unions should continue to remain job centered and adversarial, seeking to defend workers' dignity and rights at work. While not denying this important function, Michael Piore, Alice Kessler-Harris, and Bertram Silverman suggest that unions need to look beyond the work place to overcome worker divisions and address the changing needs of a diverse work force and a changing social structure.[41] Such a strategy involves trade unions in the construction of new social and industrial policies that redefine the social responsibility of the corporation and address quality-of-life issues that are central to working men and women and their families.

The shift from mass production to "flexible specialization" creates a greater variety and quality of consumer goods. But postindustrialism also entails an increase in the production and consumption of services. The quality of life increasingly depends on the quality of education, health, income security, and a variety of family and community services. Government necessarily will continue to play a major role in the delivery of those services. Just as in the new work place, the production and delivery of those services depend on interpersonal skills and cooperation and trust among workers and consumers. How to improve the quality of those services and distribute them fairly is a major task for postindustrial society. As Kessler-Harris and Silverman suggest, in organizing and representing workers around these concerns, trade unions can play a central role in reducing divisions and inequalities and improving workers' quality of life, and in doing so, they can reflect the interests of the larger society.

These transitional problems in the United States may seem remote and irrelevant to the construction of a market economy in the SSSU. But the development of a new system of production and work relations is as important as introducing the market institutions that will regulate the economy. The free market in some respects undermines this transformation. As many of the U.S. participants in this volume argue, if the organizational and technological revolution depends on fostering values of cooperation and trust, competitive labor markets may weaken loyalty and create resistance to change.

The administrative-command system failed in its effort to promote loyalty and cooperation because workers and citizens were excluded from the decision-making process. When neither voice nor exit are available to improve the quality of one's work or nonwork life, apathy and resignation or other forms of covert resistance undermine economic performance and social responsibility. Private life becomes the only authentic source of involvement and satisfaction. A "free" market may also undermine trust and cooperation if loyalty is sold to the highest bidder and the fear of unemployment increases workers' powerlessness and resistance to change.

Constructing the organizational forms that promote greater economic security, fairness, and democracy rather that any simple transition from planning to the market is what connects the journeys of the SSSU and the United States. In dealing with the social costs of the transition, market economies cannot ignore what Isabel Sawhill identifies as the first principle of policy making: "to compensate the losers."[42] For the SSSU and the United States, this will entail developing government policies and a labor-relations system that are viewed even by the losers as fair and reasonable and that provide opportunities for workers to participate in the reform process, giving losing groups ways to defend their interests.[43] In this sense our transitions may provide new opportunities for shared learning and cooperation.

Notes

1. See, for example, T.I. Zaslavskaia, "Socialism, *Perestroika*, and Public Opinion," *Sotsiologicheskie issledovaniia*, 1991, no. 8, pp. 3–21; L.A. Gordon and E.V. Klopov, "Labor Relations: Toward Tripartite Social Partnership," *Polis*, 1992, no. 1–2.

2. This section draws largely on an interview with A.N. Shokhin, "We Do Not Yet Have a Labor Market," *Obshchestvennye nauki i sovremennost'*, 1992, no. 1, pp. 5–14, also in *Problems of Economic Transition*, vol. 35, no. 7 (November 1992), pp. 40–54; Gordon and Klopov, "Labor Relations"; and the paper by L.A. Gordon in this volume.

3. Shokhin, "We Do Not Yet Have a Labor Market," p. 6.

4. Gordon and Klopov, "Labor Relations," p. 172.

5. See the paper by V.A. Iadov in this volume.

6. See the paper by V.E. Gimpel'son in this volume. Also V. Zaslavskii, "Russia on the Path to the Market: State-Dependent Workers and Populism," *Polis*, 1991, no. 5, pp.65–79.

7. M.V. Baglai, "The Creation of a New System of Labor Relations in Russia," *Problems of Economic Transition*, vol. 35, no. 5 (September 1992), pp. 42–49.

8. See Gordon's paper in this volume.

9. See also the paper by T.I. Zaslavskaia and V.L. Kosmarskii in *Labor and Democracy in the Transition to a Market System*, ed. B. Silverman, R. Vogt, and M. Yanowitch (Armonk, NY: M.E. Sharpe, 1992).

10. We rely here mainly on the interview with Shokhin, "We Do Not Yet Have a Labor Market." See also A.N. Shokhin and V.L. Kosmarskii, "The Labor Market in the USSR in the Transition Period," *Problems of Economic Transition*, vol. 35, no. 1 (May 1992), pp. 6–15.

11. Shokhin, "We Do Not Yet Have a Labor Market," p. 8.

12. We rely here mainly on the paper by V.E. Gimpel'son below and N.N. Popov, "Labor Relations in Soviet Public Opinion," *Sociological Research*, vol. 31, no. 5 (September–October, 1992), pp. 33–42.

13. Iu. Volkov, "The Market Economy and Ensuring Social Justice in the Sphere of Labor Relations," *Problems of Economic Transition*, vol. 35, no. 5 (September 1992), pp. 50–62.

14. See M. Mozhina, "The Poor: What is the Boundary Line?" *Problems of Economic Transition*, vol. 35, no. 6 (October 1992), pp. 65–75.

15. See the paper in this volume by G. Rakitskaia as well as E. Rudyk and J. Vanek, "Labor and Democracy in the Transition Period to a Market Economy: Problems in the Selection of Management Systems," *Problems of Economic Transition*, vol. 35, no. 5 (September 1992), pp. 24–41.

16. For a defense of worker ownership by John Simmons and John Logue, see *Rabochaia tribuna*, May 22, 1992, p. 2. The authors noted that in twenty years of work on problems of privatization and worker ownership, "we have never confronted such an abundance of arguments based on so few facts as we observed in Russia last year."

17. Gordon and Klopov, "Labor Relations," p. 168.

18. Marshall D. Shulman, "The Human Side of Revolution," *Columbia*, Summer 1992, pp. 42–43.

19. Karl Polanyi, *The Great Transformation: The Political and Economic Origins of Our Time* (Boston: Beacon Press, 1957), chap. 3.

20. Albert O. Hirschman, "Rival Interpretations of Market Society: Civilizing, Destructive, or Feeble?" *Journal of Economic Literature*, December 1982.

21. Ibid. See also Polanyi, *The Great Transformation*, and Robert L. Heilbroner, *Behind the Veil of Economics: Essays in the Worldly Philosophy* (London: W.W. Norton & Company, 1988).

22. Richard B. Freeman, "Getting Here from There: Labor in the Transition to a Market Economy," in *Labor and Democracy*, ed. Silverman, Vogt, and Yanowitch, pp. 139–57.

23. See Harry Katz et al. in this volume.

24. Samuel Bowles, "Markets: Indispensable Servants, Cruel Masters," in *Labor and Democracy*, ed. Silverman, Vogt, and Yanowitch, pp. 159–70.

25. Michael J. Piore, "The Limits of the Market and the Transformation of Socialism," in *Labor and Democracy*, ed. Silverman, Vogt, and Yanowitch, p. 173.

26. McKinley L. Blackburn, David E. Bloom, and Richard B. Freeman, "The Declining Economic Position of Less Skilled American Men," in *A Future of Lousy Jobs? The Changing Structure of U.S. Wages*, ed. Gary Burtless (Washington DC: The Brookings Institution, 1990).

27. A more exaggerated form of mass production than existed in the United States was introduced in the Soviet Union in part because the problem of excess demand imposed no limit on this technology.

28. Ray Marshall and Marc Tucker, *Thinking for a Living: Education and the Wealth of Nations* (New York: Basic Books, 1992), p. 57.

29. Daniel Bell, "Work and Its Discontents: The Cult of Efficiency in America," in *The End of Ideology* (New York: The Free Press, 1965), p. 250.

30. See George T. Milkovich's essay in this volume.

31. John T. Dunlop, "Wage Contours," and Arthur G. Ross, "Orbits of Coercive Comparison," in *Unemployment and Inflation: Institutional and Structuralist Views*, ed. Michael J. Piore (White Plains, NY: M.E. Sharpe, 1979).

32. Cited in Robert M. Solow, *The Labor Market as a Social Institution* (Cambridge, MA: Basil Blackwell, 1990), p. 9.

33. Ibid., pp. 23–24.

34. Work councils are not part of the U.S. industrial-relations system.

35. Bowles, "Markets"; Albert O. Hirschman, *Exit, Voice and Loyalty: Responses to Decline in Firms, Organizations and States* (Cambridge, MA: Harvard University Press, 1970); and Richard Freeman and James L. Medoff, *What Do Unions Do?* (New York: Basic Books, 1984).

36. Bowles, "Markets," p. 166.

37. Lester C. Thurow, *Dangerous Currents: The State of Economics* (New York: Random House, 1983), p. 204.

38. See David Brody's essay in this volume.

39. See Ruth Milkman's essay in this volume.

40. Michael J. Piore, "The Future of Unions in Industrial Countries," in *The State of the Unions*, ed. George Strauss, Daniel G. Gallagher, and Jack Fiorito (Madison, WI: Industrial Relations Research Association, 1991).

41. Ibid., and Alice Kessler-Harris and Bertram Silverman's essay in this volume.

42. *The New York Times*, August 20, 1992, p. D2.

43. See Richard Freeman's essay in this volume.

Part 1

The Emergence of Post-Soviet
Labor Relations: Russian Views

Russia on the Road to New Industrial Relations

From Unipartite Commands to Tripartite Partnership via Bipartite Conflicts and Bargaining

Leonid A. Gordon

In the initial stages of *perestroika*, the essence of our labor movement was, first, an economic struggle for improvement in working conditions and in pay and, second, an ever-clearer conscious political struggle for one or another type of social development, for the complete overthrow of state socialism or its restoration. It is natural that until now—the winter of 1991–92—the main thing that has been achieved by the labor movement has been in the sphere of politics and has signified that the mass of ordinary people has become involved in public life. It played a decisive role in staving off attempts by national-Bolshevik fundamentalists in the winter and spring of 1991 to turn back the clock on our whole social development, and it helped to crush the revolt in August 1991.[1]

At the same time, it is becoming increasingly clear that the labor movement has had other outcomes—outcomes that were not a conscious aim earlier and, perhaps, that do not now have such decisive significance as the political outcomes of the workers' struggle but that are in themselves fairly substantial. One of these outcomes has been the change in the system of labor relations in the economy, i.e., the system of everyday interactions of conflicts, compromises, collaboration between labor, especially wage labor, and institutions, groups, people, managers of industry—all that is meant today in the West by such concepts as "industrial relations," "industrial conflicts," "tripartite social partnership," "social collaboration," etc. And although today, to all appearances, this is not the main thing in the labor movement, tomorrow—when and if the phase of revolutionary changes comes to an end and the transition to a market-democratic society becomes irreversible—the establishment of one or another type of labor relations will be one of the most important factors in the effective (or ineffective) functioning of the new social system. This makes it all the more important to focus on changes in this sphere now.

The author is a department head at the Institute of Employment Problems, Russian Academy of Sciences.

1. The General Character of Labor Relations. The Combination of World Trends and Postsocialist Characteristics

Both general systems universal the world over and specific processes characteristic of our country and possibly of several other states in Eastern Europe are becoming apparent in post-Soviet labor relations. The former (i.e., general) patterns are linked to the fact that an attempt is being made in our country to change over to the same market-democratic model of society that exists in the majority of industrially advanced countries. As far as the second processes (specific to us) are concerned, they are determined by the fact that the movement toward democracy and a social market economy (i.e., to a mixed economy and socially responsible society, which to all intents and purposes has developed in the West) is happening in our society not from a position of early capitalism with uncontrollable market forces and bourgeois, landed-gentry–type rule but from state socialism, from universal "statization" and the complete absence of any kind of sociopolitical initiative. In other words, in our society (and in Eastern European countries), it is not classical tried-and-tested capitalism that is taking place but—almost for the first time in the world—postsocialist development.[2]

The combination of a general market-democracy orientation of social development and its postsocialist character is becoming transparently obvious in the field of labor relations. Under state socialism labor relations had an extremely specific character, fundamentally different from the systems of industrial relations that were characteristic of countries with market economies and democratic political systems. Industrial relations in the latter countries now represent the interaction of three relatively independent forces: (1) the labor movement, represented by trade unions and other organizations of wage laborers; (2) employers and economic management; and (3) the state and its bodies.

Nominally, the three types of social institutions also existed in state socialist countries, and their representatives often appeared at international forums and organizations on behalf of these three separate elements. Nevertheless, industrial relations in Russia and other state socialist countries have until recently been qualitatively different from those in other countries, and the heart of the difference lay in the fact that, in contrast to market-democratic countries, the participants in industrial relations—trade unions, employers, and the state—were not independent of one another in our society. They were, so to speak, pseudo-participants. In fact they were all elements of a single economic-political system and were completely subordinate, even in small ways, to the directives and the leaders of one and the same supreme party–state bodies.

Industrial relations, in the sense of conflicts and collaboration of various forces relatively independent of one another, simply did not exist in state socialist society. In reality, those relations connected with wages and working conditions that did exist in Soviet industry had a command-unipartite character. The activities of all institutionalized, organized participants in these relations were, in the main, indivisible and were directed toward the subordination of labor to state authority and the state plan. As a result, the main issues of labor relations and labor conflicts were the maintenance of discipline and the settlement of comparatively small-scale, secondary matters, such as the improvement of pay and working conditions. Not having any independent organizations of their own, workers could not raise any fundamental issues, and pseudo–trade unions, fused with the state, did not feel the need to do so either.

The command-unipartite nature of labor relations, the subordination of trade unions to the state, and the absence of any real labor organization led precisely to unequal forms and methods predominating in these relations. For trade unions and party, state, and economic institutions, the main forms of their interrelations with workers consisted in determining the mood among workers, making decisions on issues that were considered pressing, publishing appropriate orders, directives, and decisions, and organizing their subsequent implementation for workers. The only basic forms of labor relations, besides carrying out orders, were complaints to higher authorities (most often anonymous complaints), letters to newspapers, from time to time critical speeches at meetings, and occasionally spontaneous protest statements (usually directly suppressed with the help of administrative and punitive measures).

In general, when talking about state socialism it is more appropriate to talk not about labor relations in industry but about a vertical, hierarchical system of the management and organization of labor. As an object, labor (industrial) relations were not separate from the social sphere as a whole. Housing issues, day-to-day issues outside the sphere of production, and service areas were all dealt with in state socialist countries at the enterprise level as an organic part of pay and working conditions. Moreover, ideology in these societies was also a necessary condition of social and economic management and was therefore also drawn into the sphere of social-labor relations. This situation was further strengthened by the dependent position of wage labor in its relations with the state and the party, who declared that, more so than the workers themselves, they were better able to understand and express workers' interests.

The development of *perestroika*, which has grown into a fundamental social and political transformation of Soviet society, will lead to the collapse of the vertical command-unitary system of labor relations. In the market-democratic system, which will replace state socialism (unless present development is halted by another reactionary coup), industrial relations characteristic of a market economy should develop.

The first shifts, the first signs of movement toward this general system are already evident in current Russian society. Participants in labor relations are beginning to appear more and more clearly, disputes are occurring between them as in the rest of the world, and exactly the same forms of resolving disputes are being used. Labor movements are forming independently of the state, along with general movements of employed workers. The embryos of independent employers' organizations are appearing. The prospect of state institutions developing that are not involved in management and are capable of occupying a more or less independent, neutral position in relation to disputes between workers and management is beginning to be realized. Laws on the "destatization" and privatization of property are being passed.

Moreover, the most influential executive bodies of power—the USSR government (until August 1991) and the Russian government (after August 1991)—have considered it expedient to create a mechanism of tripartite social partnership based on agreements among state bodies, owners' representatives (unions and associations of entrepreneurs), and trade unions.

The task of creating such tripartite mechanisms was proclaimed already in May 1991 in the documents signed by the government of the then USSR and by the governments of most constituent republics.[3] After the crushing defeat of the August putsch, the disintegration of the Soviet Union, and Russia's initiation of radical economic reforms, its authorities began to demonstrate more clearly their commitment to the policy of social partnership.

The issue of the tripartite interaction to be developed among workers, employers, and the state was advanced by President Yeltsin as a separate point in the program of reforms that he presented at the Congress of People's Deputies of the Russian Federation (October 1991). To implement this point, in November Yeltsin issued a special decree "On Social Partnership and the Settlement of Labor Disputes."[4] It defines the organizational and legal forms of the tripartite mechanisms to settle conflicts and to regulate relations in the sphere of labor. Starting from January 1992, practical measures were taken to set up institutions that would implement the tripartite interaction. The Ministry of Labor and Employment approved the documents that outline the range of work and the membership of tripartite commissions. It shaped the first organizations of mediation and reconciliation in the sphere of social-labor relations.

Although the general direction of development is important and the legal acts that serve as a legislative provision for such development are significant, it is not enough to characterize them alone for drawing an overall picture of the present state of labor relations in Russia. It is obvious that labor relations have already lost their vertical and command-unipartite character, that they are evolving toward tripartite social partnership. But such partnership has not yet been secured. It takes time to establish legal norms that will define the component parts and modes of action of the tripartite mechanisms. The issuance of the appropriate documents does not mean at all that such mechanisms have begun to work. Labor relations in Russia today are not yet a system of developed tripartite partnership but only a specific intermediate stage of the transition to such a system. Normal labor relations of the market-democratic type are still under formation in Russia. Today, transitional relations prevail, wherein free-market elements are mixed with very powerful remnants of state socialism.

Therefore, alongside normal industrial disputes, general social conflicts—

linked to the struggle for one or another path of transition to the market and democracy and even for the preservation or abolition of the state socialist system itself—acquire decisive significance in labor relations. These are the conflicts that are related to such problems as the following: in what way, how fast, and by what methods a transition from state socialism to the market and democracy will be implemented; and whether this will happen at all or whether the administrative-command economy will be restored again. As they move away from the "ideologization" of the totalitarian system and develop in the direction of a relatively autonomous sphere with a clearly defined purpose (pay and working conditions), industrial relations will for a time remain even more closely linked to basic social and political relations and will become an organic part of them.

In connection with the latter point, a description of the present state of labor relations in our country involves showing how the general market-democracy direction in which they are moving is linked at every level with specific processes that are peculiar to the transitional stage of this evolution in Russia. In other words, the question is how this link is manifested in:

—the composition of labor-relations participants;

—the aims of labor relations and the nature of typical industrial disputes;

—the prevailing forms of relations and ways of settling industrial disputes.

2. New Participants in Industrial Relations.
Trade Unions and Workers' Social Movements

The most significant evidence of the fundamental changes taking place in labor relations in modern Russian society is the development of an independent labor movement and genuine trade unions. In this way, a new labor-relations participant, absent from state socialism, is emerging in the country—i.e., organizations that really do represent the interests of workers. Under postsocialist development, the distinctiveness of this process lies in the fact that workers' organizations, which do represent workers' genuine interests, are developing not in a vacuum but in a society where sham, pseudo–workers' organizations have existed for many years (and have covered all wage employees). In reality, the latter organizations were representatives, not of the workers, but of the party–state system (hence such justifiable popularity of the use of the term "independent" in the labor movement). The development of workers' organizations independent of the state can come about in two ways. First, in a direct, natural way, through the formation of new organizations and movements that have no connection with the state. Second, through the transformation, renewal, and revival of old organizations, especially trade unions, that in the past were pseudo–workers' organizations.

The events of 1989–92 show that both of these scenarios are taking place in social practice. Despite the onerous burden of the tradition of subordination to party–state power, a certain number of the former "official" trade unions are clearly trying to carry out genuine trade-union functions. Already, the actual dissolution of the AUCCTU [All-Union Central Council of Trade Unions] and the formation of the General Confederation of Trade Unions (GCTU) in its place shows that the influence of these elements is leading to tangible results. This is particularly evident in the activity of some people inside those organizations that in the past belonged to the AUCCTU but that in 1990 created the Federation of Independent Trade Unions of Russia (FITUR). In the spring of 1991 it demonstrated its attempt to become a real spokesman and defender of workers' interests by supporting, in word and deed, workers' mass political and economic positions. The evolution of the FITUR has continued after the August coup. At times this evolution has brought it to the brink of populism, but at any rate the link between the Federation and the state has become less and less distinct.

The changes in the FITUR became even more important when the influence of the GCTU began to decline with the disintegration of the USSR. In December 1991 the GCTU announced its intention of becoming an International Trade-Union Center of the independent states (the former USSR republics). Even if this intent is realized, such a Trade-Union Center would evidently play a secondary role in comparison with national trade-union associations. Thus the FITUR, which up to then was an autonomous organization yet subordinate to the GCTU, is today becoming the main center of the old trade unions in Russia. It may be presumed that the number of the industry unions within the FITUR (29 unions at the end of 1991) can grow during 1992 out of interrepublic unions, which up to the present time entered the GCTU directly and had no Russian departments as members of the FITUR.[5] Naturally, it would be totally incorrect to state that the signs of changes in the FITUR show that the old trade unions linked with it have already made a complete break with their past. In any event, it will take them years to finally get rid of the rest of their servile habits, formed by decades of domination by state socialism. (Not without reason do many workers' activists of the new wave call them "state trade unions.") Moreover, a significant number of groups and organizations remain that neither want nor are capable of change.

Under such circumstances, the formation of completely new trade unions in no way connected with old structures is as typical a trend of changing labor relations as are attempts to renovate the old ones. The new trend is most clearly seen in those strata of the working class that form the cradle and the avant-garde of the reviving labor movement. On the actual initiative and influence of the strike (workers') committees, in 1990 the first and second miners' congresses created the Independent Miners' Union (IMU), which up to now remains the most influential and militant of the recently formed professional associations.[6]

It is significant that the IMU has continued as a unified interrepublic organization even after the disintegration of the USSR. At the end of 1991 independent miners' trade unions of Russia, the Ukraine, Kazakhstan, and Belorussia were formed. However, these unions did not break with each other but held a special congress in December 1991 to affirm the solidarity of miners and to express the readiness of the republic unions to stay as organic and constituent parts of the common independent miners' trade union. The congress even decided not to add to the name of the union the word "interstate," thus stressing their adherence to the traditions of unity among republic unions. In the chaos of the rivalry among the republics that emerged on the ruins of the former USSR, miners are trying to preserve an ability to combine the autonomy of trade unions with mutual support and mutual assistance.

It is extremely important to emphasize that it is not just the miners who are creating new trade unions but that this is a general trend embracing the most diverse groups of workers. The new civil-aviation unions—the Federation of Flight Personnel, and the Association of Air Controllers—have demonstrated their capacity for energetic and diverse activities, which have brought major successes. Both unions are notable for the fact that their membership criteria function on the basis of whether employees work in a particular profession and not, as is the practice with the old Soviet trade unions, based on which industry they work in. However, the aviation unions often work together in the campaigns for their demands.

Nonindustry and interindustry amalgamations are also making an appearance. As a rule these usually include both workers and intelligentsia. In this respect, the Association of Socialist (as it originally called itself) or Social (as its leaders now say) Trade Unions—*Sotsprof*—is very significant. Moreover, the first stage of postsocialist development—the defense of economic interests above all—requires a struggle against the excessive role of the state. Basic differences of interests at the moment lie not between workers and employers but between the most diverse participants in industry and powerful state monopolies and departments. In these circumstances it is becoming possible for some unions to take into their membership both hired workers and cooperative workers and even small businessmen.

The Confederation of Amalgamated Trade Unions of Russia, for instance, or the union "Birlesu," which operates in Kazakhstan, are of this type. At the same time that it operates as a trade union, "Birlesu" also conducts successful business activity. On the other hand, here and there, particularly in St. Petersburg and the Urals, small interindustry unions of a syndicalist kind, which accept only manual workers as members, have appeared.

It is worth mentioning that strike committees came into being at dozens and maybe hundreds of enterprises in Russia during the last months of 1991 and at the beginning of 1992. Sometimes elections of such committees were organized by the old or new trade-union leaders. But more often than not strike committees were set up by independent groups of workers who had received more or less wide support by work collectives. It is important to stress that such independent strike committees were not always formed to begin a strike or at least to threaten a strike action. Quite often independent strike committees (at least at the end of 1991 and in early 1992) appeared as standing workers' organizations to defend the interests of their enterprises' workers in the most different forms. In fact, they are the embryos or the cells of new independent trade unions that are only using the name of a "strike committee," which already bears the new glory of miner's strikes, instead of the "trade-union" concept, which has discredited itself in the workers' consciousness. Miners also initially set up the strike committees in 1989, and then both such sociopolitical organizations as Workers' Committees (to be discussed below) and the Independent Miners' Union were founded based on them.

At the moment, naturally, the membership of old and new unions is highly uneven. Formally, a hundred times more workers belong to the old unions than to the new ones. Whatever the possible tricks of official union statistics, which include many "dead souls," there can be no doubt that at least 135–140 million workers, pensioners, and students—including 50–70 million in Russia itself—pay membership dues to the old unions in all states that in the past belonged to the USSR. As far as the number of workers who have become members of new unions is concerned, this is measured not in tens of millions but in tens of thousands.[7]

However, with all the stormy and rapid changes society has experienced at the beginning of its postsocialist development, formal membership numbers can in no way be an indicator of the real influence of these or any other trade unions or trade-union centers. From 30 to 70 percent of miners, not just 5 or 10 percent of miners (which more or less corresponds to the official number of IMU members), took part in different weeks of the March–April 1991 strikes, which were led by strike committees together with the IMU and which the old miners' union opposed. Moreover, the political and economic demands of the miners were supported by millions of people who took part in peaceful acts of solidarity, collections for miners, and so on. Toward the end of the strike (in April), hundreds of thousands of workers from other industries joined in directly, even from those industries where only official unions exist.

It is also significant that some FITUR leaders who, as mentioned above, want to overcome the resistance of their own bureaucratic apparatus try to do it based on the support of independent strike committees and some new trade unions. In December 1991, I. Klochkov, the FITUR chairman, called a meeting of such organizations and asked them for help in the struggle against the conventional trade-union bureaucracy. With the same purpose in mind, the representatives of strike committees were invited to the Plenary Session of the FITUR. Judging from what they said, they did not demonstrate either a lot of respect for the official trade unions or a lot of confidence in the possibility that they would change.[8] However, an evident desire to support new organizations of workers (in spite of the embryonic level of their development) testifies to the considerable prestige they enjoy among workers.

Thus the real strength of the new unions (as distinct from the size of their membership) is comparable to the traditional influence of the old unions, if not surpassing it.

The diversity of trade unions is not the only manifestation of labor-market pluralism or pluralism of the entire range of organizations that represent workers in the industrial-relations system. It is also quite natural that in the early period of postsocialist evolution, until the problem of liquidating state socialism has been finally resolved and while general social problems continue to play an enormous role in labor relations, the labor movement is inevitably going beyond a purely trade-union framework and is almost certainly acquiring a distinct socio-political orientation. In these circumstances, it is extremely unlikely that there will be an emergence in contemporary conditions of purely political mass organizations among workers or of mass workers' political parties reminiscent of the social-democratic parties of the first half of the twentieth century.

Theoretical considerations and actual experience in Russia and Eastern Europe suggest otherwise: the politization of the labor movement and industrial relations in postsocialist countries is manifested not so much by the appearance of workers' parties, in the pure sense of the word, as by the formation of broad multifunctional movements. In contrast to pure trade unions or pure parties, these latter movements combine the defense of workers' current interests (trade-union functions) with the campaign for this or that path of development for society as a whole (semiparty, sociopolitical functions) and the support of a particular ideology (cultural-ideological functions). The classic example of this kind of multifunctional organization was the Polish "Solidarity" of the 1980s (not of the 1990s), which, although calling itself an autonomous trade union, was of course something much larger than just a trade union.

In Russia and other republics of the former USSR, however (in contrast to Poland), multifunctional workers' social and political organizations have arisen as independent formations not formally fused with unions.

Chronologically, the first of this type of organization to appear was the United Front of Workers (UFW), which initially appeared in the autumn of 1989. Party apparatus cadres and professional ideologists (university lecturers who had joined the so-called Association of Scientific Communism) played a large part in its formation, attempting by these means to strengthen their influence among workers.

As the UFW did not enjoy popularity, the Russian Communist Party in the summer of 1991 began to set up new organizations of a similar type, so-called Unions of Workers (UW). At the end of 1991 and in early 1992, facing the difficulties of the transfer to the market, the UW–UFW, jointly with communists and nationalists, comprised the nucleus of the movement "Labor Russia," which opposed the market-oriented line of the Russian government.

In the spring of 1990 the second of the above-mentioned organizations—the Confederation of Labor—was formed. Its membership comprises miners' workers' (strike) committees. These are joined by workers' clubs from many towns and also by unions of working people of the Kuzbass, Karaganda, and Vorkuta, which blue- and white-collar workers from these regions join, irrespective of industry. (To emphasize the role of workers' committees in the Confederation of Labor, we will use the abbreviation WC–CL.)

In the autumn of 1990, the third all-Union workers' organization was formed—the Union of Work Collectives (UWC), representing an amalgamation of councils of work collectives from a number of enterprises, including such large enterprises as the Volga Automobile Factory. These councils appeared at enterprises in pre-*perestroika* times in accordance with the legislation at that time. In the majority of cases they had the same formal-bureaucratic character as the official unions had. However, in the years of *perestroika*, especially after the 1989 strikes, several of them became genuine workers' bodies. Thus both bureaucratic councils subordinate to management and really independent councils are represented in the UWC.

All the organizations listed above, both in their charter documents and in their practical activities, represent actual multifunctional bodies and not purely political or purely trade-union bodies. They take part in political campaigns at the same time as striving for improved conditions at the work place; they endeavor to become the proponents of current workers' demands and at the same time actively support one or another variant of social development as a whole. However, the sociopolitical orientations of the WC–CL, the UFW, the UWC, and the UW are very different from one another, if not even opposites.

The majority of the organizations that have joined the WC–CL, as documents and the activities of 1990–92 bear witness, hold a consistent line on the development of political democracy and a market economy. In August 1991 the WC led political strikes in support of the campaign for democracy and for Boris Yeltsin against the putschists. Of course the WC–CL stands for the comprehensive development of social-protection mechanisms.

But this social protection does not originate from the negation of the market and democracy. On the contrary, the WC–CL unambiguously emphasize their commitment to the policy of reforms even in the difficult conditions of price liberalization.

It is true that among the members of the WC–CL there are both supporters of democratic capitalism and those who hope for the possibility of creating a democratic and humanitarian variant of socialism. In any case, however, all of them oppose state socialism, the power of the CPSU, and universal statization.

On the other hand, the UFW and the UW are against the market and parliamentary democracy, putting forward their main aim as the defense of socialism. In point of fact, what is meant by the term 'socialism' here is state-planned organization of the economy and the leading role of the CPSU in political life. Insofar as both of these phenomena have been greatly compromised in peoples' minds, there is an attempt to "ennoble" them with ideas of Russian nationalism and to contend that only state property and the Communist Party can preserve the dignity and distinctive character of Russia. In this sense, this type of orientation can be called "national-Bolshevik." However, vulgar internationalist terminology is also used by the UFW and especially the UW. In this way, the idea of a single, indivisible Russia is put forward as an internationalist idea. During the August putsch, the Moscow Union of Workers openly supported the plotters.

In the winter of 1991–92, when liberalization of prices and some mistakes of the government produced discontent among a considerable part of the population, the UW–UFW undertook open and deliberate action to frustrate market reforms (they instigated demagogic rallies and demonstrations and called for strikes).[9]

The UWC, as many of its documents bear witness, occupies an intermediate position. On politics, it is for the consistent overthrow of the authoritarian, partocratic regime, but at the same time it lays particular emphasis on the special political role of work collectives, of direct and delegatory democracy. On the economy, acknowledging a diversity of forms of ownership, the UWC believes that workers in any kind of enterprise should have the option of owning it. However, it is not quite clear whether such ownership presupposes real "destatization" and real competition, or whether the transfer of enterprises to work collectives would mean that state support would be maintained. On the whole, the social and political aims of the UWC resemble yet another attempt to create the ideal socialist system—a society in which direct democracy would prevail in political life and in the economy, managing to combine state planning with a commodity market but without a full-fledged market system. Up to now such attempts (including those in Yugoslavia) have always reverted to authoritarian state socialism. However, after the events of August 1991 this kind of mood has weakened in the UWC. The possibility is not excluded that with time this organization will turn out to be some kind of representative of blue- and white-collar workers in the military-industrial sector (where the position of the UWC is particularly obvious).

Up to now (end of 1991–beginning of 1992) the democratic wing of the labor movement, represented by workers' committees and partly by the Confederation of Labor, has enjoyed the greatest relative influence among workers. It is hoped that the prevailing democratic trend will remain characteristic of the Russian labor movement in the future as well. However, there are no absolute guarantees of this. Objective conditions create possibilities for the growth of various labor movements and for their coexistence. But all the rest depends on a combination of a great number of factors (sometimes chance factors) and, of course, on the ability and selflessness of activists in each movement.

A tendency toward fusion between trade unions and workers' social movements is leading toward a certain regrouping of forces within the latter because trade unions are less politicized than the social movements. In addition, the entire situation changed dramatically in the country after August 1991. The decision to make the transition to a market has been adopted. Accordingly, such questions as what to do in the process of such a transition and how to implement it are in the focus of attention.

There are two approaches to defining the goals of the present reforms in the democratic branch of the workers' movement (WC–CL, new trade unions).

Recent congresses of the miners' union (the Russian in November and the interrepublic in December 1991) have shown these two approaches quite clearly. The first is oriented toward a consistent movement to socioeconomic solutions similar to the ones in the West, whatever name they may have—democratic capitalism, mixed economy, or anything else. To cite a view of one of the miners' leaders: "We need to struggle for real businessmen to appear in our economy. And then, or rather simultaneously, to fight with these businessmen over real wages and worthy conditions." The second approach is related to the intention to continue searching for a special way to preserve the foundations of socialism even after the transition to a market. In this approach, now that the old socialism has been discredited, priority is passing to the conception of work collectives' ownership, management, and disposition of the output at any enterprise of their own.

The supporters of transferring enterprises to the work collectives' ownership point out (and they are right here) that this facilitates democratic control over destatization. However, in these views the lessons of social practice are ignored (in particular, Yugoslav ones, not to speak of our own).

And these lessons indicate that a *"kolkhoz"* (collective-farm) type of organization in industry as well as in agriculture is far less efficient than a private one. Besides, collective ownership usually is linked with the concentration of real power in the hands of a limited group of administrators rather than its even distribution among all members of a work collective. In general, judging by world experience, only a minor proportion of workers are striving to become real masters of production; the majority prefer to work honestly, getting paid well for their work, and to concentrate their main interests on family life, leisure, hobbies, amateur activities, etc. And as is evident from history, the establishment of a collective organization of economic activity formally, but which in fact actually involves management by small groups, threatens to transform the labor movement into a force remote from democracy. Thus the intensification of the role of work collectives during the privatization period to some extent would be favorable, but the total transfer of enterprises to work collectives is unlikely to help in establishing a market system and democracy.

3. Employers' Organizations and State Bodies as Possible Participants in Labor Relations

The interaction of general market-democratic tendencies, and especially of postsocialist factors, also has an effect upon other industrial-relations participants—economic organizations, employers, and state institutions. It must be said that the formation of independent employer and state participants in industrial relations is proceeding much more slowly than the formation of an independent labor movement. In Russia employers and the state still remain virtually one and the same. In any case, until the beginning of 1992, managements of the overwhelming majority of enterprises in the Russian Federation continued to act as a more or less organic part of a state-economic structure. In these circumstances state mediation bodies inevitably turn out to be not unbiased and neutral mediators but specific elements in this structure. The whole position of state mediation bodies has been much closer to that of state enterprise managements (as is still the case in the overwhelming number of plants, factories, buildings, and institutes) than to that of workers.

Of course, it does not follow from the above that in this respect nothing is being achieved. The last two or three years have seen the first signs of the destatization of the economy. Enterprises have appeared in the economy that either are not dependent on central governmental institutions or are less dependent on them than in the past.

Until 1992 a significant degree of independence was achieved by cooperatives, of which a significant part (around one-third) are really small private enterprises that employ workers. Moreover, cooperatives represent the fastest growing sector of the nonstate economy. By early 1991 the number of working cooperatives had reached almost 250,000, and 6.1 million people, or more than 4 percent of the employed population, were working in them.[10] However, in the overwhelming majority of cases, cooperatives represent the smallest enterprises and do not influence very strongly the character of industrial relations as a whole.

From a long-term point of view, the growth of leased enterprises, joint-stock companies, combined state-cooperative businesses, small businesses, and so on is of greater significance. By the beginning of 1991 there were more than 2,000 such firms, at which 2–3 million people were employed.[11]

On a much larger scale, the unregulated destatization of industry is going (or, more accurately, was going until 1992) along a path in which former economic management bodies such as ministries, central directorates [glavki], and trusts, which have amalgamated their lower enterprises into associations and concerns, declare themselves to be independent. The founding bodies of new concerns and associations take charge of them and give themselves the authority to take charge of state enterprises and their production activity. In 1991 alone, 126 concerns, 54 special bodies, and around 500 similar associations were created in Soviet industry. According to some statistics, up to half the number of industrial enterprises have been taken over by them.[12]

A certain kind of independence from higher levels of state administration is sometimes evident here. However, the lawless nature of this type of destatization (in fact, privatization) means that the new owners will never become civilized, open participants in industrial relations. On the contrary, the indistinct and unstable position of the new managers fosters a desire in them to raise the level of exploitation in every way possible and at the same time camouflage their real position in industrial relations by hiding behind the government's back.

As distinct from those groups that carry out secret and unlawful "destatization," the formation of legal, independent alliances of enterprises should be seen as the real prerequisite for the growth of entrepreneur–manager participants in industrial relations. This kind of alliance, for instance, is found in the amalgamations of cooperative members and lessees, which cover thousands of small and medium-sized cooperatives and enterprises. Organizations of larger private entrepreneurs began to appear during the last months of 1991. Many of them have united into the Congress of the Business Community. Yet so far the representatives of trading and intermediary-type firms, banks, exchanges, and similar enterprises, i.e., those that are not directly connected with the main sectors of employment, are dominant in the Congress. It is true that among Congress members is the Union of Industrialists, but it is relatively small and plays a secondary role in the Congress. From this point of view the formation of the Scientific Industrial Union (SIU), comprising 1,500 of the country's large-scale enterprises and 40 associations with hundreds of members, could perhaps be considered even more important. In all, around two-thirds of industrial output in the summer of 1991 was produced by enterprises linked to the SIU.[13]

Early in 1992 the Scientific Industrial Union (SIU) was transformed into the Russian Union of Industrialists and Entrepreneurs (RUIE). Now both state and nonstate firms can enter it.

But the whole process of the freeing of real participants who will constitute the employers in industrial relations, separate from the government, is now only at a very early stage. Of these participants, those that have become really independent and have actually broken away from the government (cooperatives and certain private and joint-stock enterprises) have dealings with a very small number of employees (evidently less than 10 percent of industry, construction, and transport workers). Those, such as RUIE, that have dealings with spheres of production employing a significant number of hired workers are all still a long way from being independent and from being completely separate from the government.

Apart from anything else, this nonseparation in conjunction with the already-completed breakaway of labor organizations as independent participants characterizes the current stage of the formation of a tripartite system of social partnership.

Gradually, directives and commands are being replaced by competition between workers and employers, by conflict, dialogue, and compromise. Yet the formation of employers as distinct agents in industrial relations is only at its very beginning. Up to now, in most cases employers act as state structures that have not yet become independent entrepreneurial organizations fully separated from the state's sociopolitical institutions. It is no surprise that the presidential decree on social partnership envisages that at present the interests of entrepreneurs in their negotiations with trade unions on industry agreements will be represented primarily by so-called industry associations and concerns. The latter at the present transitional period fulfill many of the functions of former ministries and remain to a large extent a part of the state apparatus.

Hence this is a replacement of command-unipartite labor relations not by a developed tripartite partnership but mainly by bipartite industrial relations. These are relations in which not three but only two main, organized subjects participate: workers' organizations on the one hand, and employers on the other, who in most cases have not yet been separated from state institutions.

The growth of independent labor organizations signifies the end of the former command-unipartite labor relations, where all organized social institutions (including pseudo–labor organizations) opposed unorganized labor.

4. The Objectives of Labor Relations. The Nature of Disputes

In a postsocialist situation, even those economic conflicts that arise for reasons common to labor relations in every industrial society acquire a specific character. Among these, for example, are wage disputes.

Under state socialism wages have been at a much lower level than in market-democratic conditions. State monopoly in the final analysis limited the growth of productivity so that gross national product per capita was several times lower here than in market economies. Moreover, state monopoly—along with the absence of free trade unions—meant that the state could extract a much larger part of what workers created. Not only were less goods produced in the state socialist economy; wages paid to workers were also a much smaller share of the product. The rest was spent on military needs or squandered on other socially ineffective capital investments. This resulted in the distribution of output being much less favorable to workers.

Therefore, from the beginning of the development of a new trade-union movement, the most important basis of wage disputes was not so much a gradual increase in take-home pay as a substantial alteration in the real wage level and its share in value added. In the draft of the General Wage Agreement worked out by the Independent Miners' Union, the discussion was about raising miners' wages two or three times. In March 1991 (at the height of the strike) the former USSR Council of Ministers essentially agreed to their demand, promising to increase miners' wages by 100 percent within a year. Civil aviation pilots are putting forward demands of a similar magnitude.

Apart from disputes that are, so to speak, the consequence of the normal functioning of state socialism, an even greater role is now beginning to be played by problems that arise out of factors engendered by attempts to make the transition from a nonmarket (or distorted market) economy to a developed market economy. Such a crisis results in inflation occurring in a society where there are no mechanisms to compensate for the rise in prices at all. Inflation in these circumstances acts like an infection in an organism suffering from AIDS that is deprived of immune defense mechanisms. As a result, the most important topic of disputes is now becoming the issue of creating an indexation system and the basic principles of compensation in general. Characteristic of this is the fact that in the autumn of 1991 the decision of the new Russian government to move directly to decisive market reforms gave rise in the labor movement to the slogan "Market wages for market prices!"

The situation in Russia and some other republics in the winter of 1991–92 was aggravated by the fact that state regulation of prices ended before the processes of destatization and privatization had begun to develop. It is not proper to discuss now whether this happened as a result of the government's error, which could have been avoided, or whether it was the result of infinite vacillations by the predecessors, who had left no other choice. One way or another, in January 1992 the liberalization of prices began while competition was absent and the monopoly positions of most producers remained in effect. Hence, during the first few days of January prices soared by almost 5–10 times. Accordingly, the subject of labor conflicts became demands not to double or triple wages but to increase them manyfold. For example, low-paid hospital personnel already at the end of 1991 demanded an increase in minimum wages from 150–200 rubles to 1,000 rubles a month. Meanwhile, miners who received about 1,000–2,000 rubles a month in 1991 began to demand wages of 15,000–17,000 rubles. Realizing the depth of the economic crisis, they did not insist on the full satisfaction of their demands: the miners of Karaganda stopped the strike they had begun in December 1991 after they won monthly wages of 4,000–7,000 rubles. In January, more or less the same wages (5,000–10,000 rubles) were achieved by other miners. In other words, they agreed to a wage increase that was much less than the rise of prices.

To link wages with the rise in prices is not the only aspiration in the conditions of the crisis that developed out of the transition to a market. Even more important is the fact that due to the crisis numerous commodity shortages have developed. The destruction of the former production and distribution system is proceeding much faster than the development of market ties and the market regulation of the economy. It is followed by a decline in production and a breakdown in supplies that lead to a lack of most day-to-day goods. Very often such a lack of goods cannot be compensated by any increase in earnings. Money has stopped working. Consequently, there is a completely unusual type of labor conflict in Russia today when, for example, a part of money wages is paid in kind.

In some cases such conflicts are focused on the demand to provide through centralized means a set of basic day-to-day goods to an enterprise, a city, or a region. In other cases, enterprises or regions demand the right to retain part of their output at their disposal so as to use it for making barter transactions or to sell it abroad for hard currency, etc. Miners, for instance, both at the Congress of the IMU (December 1991) and when the representatives of the Kuzbass met B. Yeltsin and E. Gaidar (January 1992) insisted on getting disposition of some 15–20 percent of extracted coal for these purposes. Similar proposals were advanced by other groups of workers. Even the employees of the Center for Space Flights

Control declared a strike action to get (like the miners) the right to handle 10 or 15 percent of the resources of the Mir space station for a certain period of time.

It is evident that generally the demands for rationing or "wages in kind" have an exclusively antimarket character. However, in the extreme conditions of the disintegration of economic links and runaway inflation, such an approach can promote social stability. At a certain stage of economic stabilization, however, such practices must be stopped; otherwise they will begin to obstruct the process of marketization proper.

Finally, a specific feature of labor disputes in the early stages of postsocialist development seems to be that such conflicts very often develop into sociopolitical, or just purely political, clashes. Properly speaking, the actual prevalence of state ownership, maintained in our society up to now, leads to a situation where the smallest of labor disputes takes the form of a clash of workers with the government and with its economic and administrative-political bodies.

But what is very important, of course, at the present stage of the postsocialist evolution of Russia is that the critical question of its sociopolitical development has not yet been solved: whether market and democratic transformations will be implemented successfully, whether they will become irrevocable, or whether a restoration of the state-socialist order will take place in one form or another.

The fate of all other issues depends on the answer to this question. And labor activists—as the experience of the miners' movement shows, for example—with time begin to understand that the resolution of specific disputes directly concerning them (pay, leave, health, and safety) depends on which road the country takes. Therefore, disputes that begin by revolving around pay and working conditions swiftly develop into campaigns for a particular kind of social and economic organization of industry—for the autonomy of enterprises, for them to be handed over to work collectives, or, on the other hand, for the rehabilitation of directive management and state subsidies.

The politization of labor disputes (like the politization of labor organizations) is an organic and inevitable process in contemporary circumstances. Therefore, the major labor conflicts in Russia today almost always go beyond industrial relations proper. Their content is determined not only by the concrete subject of the dispute but also by the way the conflicting sides relate the dispute to their general sociopolitical position. Theoretically, three positions are possible from the viewpoint of the workers' movement.

The first is the combination of a fight for the improvement of labor conditions and wages with support for market and democratic reforms leading toward destroying state socialism and establishing a basically similar system and order as in the West.

The second is the combination of the protection of immediate economic interest with the struggle against democratic reforms aimed at restoring state socialism.

The third position is an attempt to achieve nothing more than labor protection without holding any constant attitude with respect to reforms.

In fact, all three conceptions exist in the real labor movement. Naturally, the distinctions are as usual not absolutely clear in society. One can find individuals agreeable to any of these attitudes everywhere in the labor movement. Nevertheless, various labor organizations stick to a definite position, and it is precisely this fact that explains the social role of a particular branch of the labor movement.

Thus, the most active new labor movements—workers' committees of the Kuzbass, *Sotsprof*, the majority of Belorussian strike committees—merge current economic demands with support for a transition to the market and democracy. It is significant that more and more often they demand to be given an increasing part of production to sell, and for the benefit of collectives. Irrational under normal conditions, during the next few months of crisis this demand will allow the achievement of labor protection not by strikes but by increasing production through the integration of enterprises into the market system that is being born.

Of course the democratic wing of the workers' movement is very much against shifting the entire burden of the transition to the market onto workers' shoulders alone. At the same time, it exposes the demagogy of some old trade unions, which advance unfeasible demands. In each concrete case democratic workers' organizations try to explain to the workers which burdens are inevitable and which are the result of the employers' egoism or incorrect governmental policy. In this respect the actions of workers' committees and the IMU in the Kuzbass in December 1991–January 1992 are significant. They resorted to the most decisive measures against a surprising lightmindedness of the authorities who were responsible for the cash deficit in the biggest industrial center of Russia for some months. There was no money to pay workers their wages, and, what is more, this happened at a time when prices shot up. But at the same time the IMU stressed its support in principle for the reforms and convinced workers (at least in January 1992) to postpone a strike and to allow authorities to correct the situation.

Alongside the new trade unions, some leaders of the Federation of Independent Trade Unions of Russia really began inclining toward reforms as well. In many cases the statements of I. Klochkov during the autumn and winter events have illustrated a combination of demands for increasing wages with support for reforms.

On the other hand, the labor organizations under the influence of Stalinists and nationalists, e.g., the United Front of Workers, regional workers' unions founded by the Communist Party not long before the August events that supported the coup, and the remnants of interfronts, declare that the protection of labor interests is inseparable from the restoration of state socialism or its national-socialist and national-Bolshevik variants. In fact, neo-Stalinism is the essence of these organizations, since they consider it impossible to achieve any current improvement in the situation of working people without the restoration of socialism.

Finally, there are some groups in the labor movement that adhere to the attitude that the organizations of workers should aim for a growth of wages in proportion to the growth of prices, not allowing any decrease in living standards whatever the consequences for the economy may be and not holding any active position with regard to reforms. This is actually the conception of many old trade unions and of a considerable part of their leaders. This policy threatens to appear hostile toward the reforms rather than neutral under the present reality.

The slogan demanding "market wages for market prices" is valid and progressive if it means establishing an expanded market economy and a fair distribution of incomes obtained by independent enterprises in the market. But if the question is not of increasing the proportion of wages in the cost of net production but of a mere increase in all wages by the state irrespective of the output performance of each enterprise in the market, then it is pure demagogy. And it may result only in a further deepening of the crisis and growing inflation.

It must be stressed that depending on the particular circumstances, the politization of labor relations might take any number of directions. The campaign to speed up market-democratic reforms (as in the activities of the WC–CL up to now) might win out, or political activities of a diverse character might be brought together. But one way or another, in the near future labor relations will in practice become fused with the sociopolitical conflicts that are tearing at our society.

5. Forms of Labor Relations. The Special Role of Strikes and Balancing on the Brink of Strikes

The nature of the present stage of postsocialist development determines not just the specific content of industrial relations and labor disputes but also the basic forms of their resolution. In this connection it is equally important to note that, owing to the current primarily bipartite (but not tripartite) nature of industrial relations and partly also as a result of the sociopolitical tendencies of many disputes, strikes and the threat of taking strike action play an increased role.

Data concerning the strike waves that hit the country between 1989 and 1991 support this conclusion. In 1989 more than 7.3 million man-days were lost in strike action; in 1990, 10.3 million; and in the first six months of 1991, 4.2 million.[14] This is not a great deal by Western standards, but in comparison with the past in our country these figures are enormous.

In general, from the point of view of strike dynamics, the situation in Russia and other states of the former USSR is substantially different from the situation of labor relations in many other developed industrial societies where the social market economy functions stably and where a democratic system prevails. As we know, effective tripartite social-partnership mechanisms have in recent years enabled the bulk of labor disputes to be resolved there without resorting to strike action. But although the number of strikes is reduced in these countries, they are not completely eradicated in social practice and are not prohibited by law. This situation is vitally important to us because it reminds us that the freedom to take strike action is, in principle, one of the factors that in the majority of cases makes its practical application unnecessary.

Such a position has been achieved in the West after long years of development, in which, at earlier stages, strikes formed a daily part of labor relations. Our country, albeit for somewhat different reasons, is going through a similar phase at the moment, where strikes are proving to be an integral element of labor relations. Some of the reasons for this are the following:

1. Under the crisis conditions that accompany a transition to market relations, the sharp and swift character of decline in the standard of living does not allow workers to understand its inevitability and to realize that a temporary aggravation of their life conditions is, in a given case, a prerequisite for an economic improvement in the future. Moreover, in real life the inevitable burdens are complemented by those that could have been avoided if authorities had conducted a more reasonable and more democratic policy, if they had listened more attentively to the voice of independent workers' and entrepreneurial organizations.

2. The persistence of the psychology and tradition of a command-unipartite approach to labor relations and labor conflicts in which state, public, and economic interests are always regarded as higher than the interest of the individual work collective or members of the profession. Such attitudes are unfortunately typical not only for old bureaucrats but for many new government officials, too.

3. The bipartite structure of labor relations, the absence of really independent managers' organizations and really neutral state mediation; really effective tripartite collaboration mechanisms are a thing of the future.

The transitional character of the sociopolitical situation in general and the revocability of reforms make possible the most varied types of development—both a transition to the market-democratic type of society and a return to state socialism. Under such circumstances social forces strive to use the ability to strike in critical situations, and they expect support from the workers' movement. The workers themselves, as noted above, become aware of the fundamental character of transformations, their organic link with labor conflicts, and therefore more and more often they are ready to put all the might of their organization on the scales.

The fact that sharp forms of settling labor conflicts are often dominant and that there is always a high probability of strikes does not signify at all that this tendency deserves a positive assessment and support in all cases. Unilateral conclusions are not possible here, and such assessments depend both on the general situation in the country and on a principled attitude to the prospects of its development.

Before the final months of 1991, before the reins of power in Russia passed to the groups that dared to begin radical reforms, very often strikes were one of the most effective methods of pushing the reform process forward and staving off attempts to turn back social development. At the same time, the strikes of 1989–91, including those of March–April 1991 and those conducted during the August coup, show that they were a relatively nonviolent means, one that allowed us to avoid open civil war and bloodshed. It is a significant fact that in the regions of the most intensive strikes—the Kuzbass, the Donbass, Belorussia—there were no pogroms, street riots, or bloody conflicts. At the same time, however, such conflicts did flare up very often in exactly those places where workers were not organized and were not on strike. This is by no means only true of regions with a long history of conflicts between nationalities but also of the central parts of Russia.

Even in the economic sense proper, for someone who is convinced of the necessity of market reforms, the strikes of workers in 1986–91 were a lesser evil than their total absence. Strikes—at least the kind we have had up to now—have accelerated economic and political reform. To retain the existing economic system would be incomparably more destructive for society. Strikes (including nationalist strife, which in essence is not part of the labor movement but due to the incompleteness of statistics is counted together with it) from 1989 to 1991 caused an annual loss of about 10 million man-days. Days lost due to absenteeism, days off, idle days, etc.—all permanent features of state socialism—led to a situation where in the last few decades no less than 80–100 million man-days were lost annually.[15]

It is natural that before August 1991 strikes had a very different meaning for those who were interested in preserving state socialism or at least in delaying its dismantling as long as possible. The opponents of reforms tried to preserve all possible elements of the pre-*perestroika* (or the early stage of *perestroika*) order and those elements of state socialism that had been destroyed in the years of *perestroika*. They believed that strikes could have a positive meaning only in those regions where the center was losing power, including the Baltic region, Moldavia, and the Transcaucasian region. They supported strikes there (which, strictly speaking, were manifestations of national conflicts rather than of the workers' movement). As for the Russian Federation, both the old trade unions and the United Front of Workers (UFW) always opposed strikes until the end of 1991. The situation changed drastically after the defeat of the August revolt, the disintegration of the center, and the coming to power of the Russian government, which started implementing market reforms. In their opinion such reforms mean only a disaster to society. Accordingly, many representatives of the old trade unions, the UFW, workers' unions, and political organizations that considered themselves successors of the CPSU (whose activities ceased in Russia) are now ready to use the most extreme forms of struggle: the worse it is in the country, the better it is for them. National-Bolsheviks who before had angrily rejected strikes, now do their best to take advantage of the peculiarities of the present-day situation in which labor disputes are easily transformed into strikes.

The position of the democratic branch of the workers' movement today is much more complicated. The majority of the new trade unions and the social-political movements support the reforms that have been started by the Yeltsin government and realize the necessity of some sacrifice and the destructive nature of strike anarchy in the critical period of transformation. At the same time, they are aware of mistakes that are being made by the central and local authorities and realize that in the state apparatus technocratic elements are strong enough and are ready to shift to the working people's shoulders not only the inevitable but absolutely all the burdens of reform. Judging by statements in the press, there are quite a number of economic advisers of the government who admire the Chilean version of stabilization. Moreover, the democratic organizations should, if at all possible, take into account the sentiments of ordinary workers whose desperate situation sometimes makes them lose reason and resort to extreme forms of settling labor disputes in situations in which one can theoretically do without them. Workers' leaders sometimes follow the majority, because the loss of confidence of the majority would be a more serious mistake than using the wrong methods of struggle.

All these circumstances require a certain policy in relation to strikes by democratic trade unions and democrats in general. Nowadays, after the change of power, they tend to resort to strikes much less frequently than they did before the August events. At the same time, they do not want to and cannot reject the strike struggle completely. (Moreover, it is practically impossible to do so.) In the near future it seems that leaders of the democratic workers' movement should follow some sort of balancing-on-the-brink-of-a-strike tactic, maintaining a high level of readiness to strike, using not so much the strike itself as the threat to resort to it if necessary. No doubt the acuteness of social labor conflicts, and the role of strikes if such tactics are to be used, remain much more significant than occurs in a normal economic situation and under the conditions of developed three-sided cooperation. At least this provides the hope of avoiding the most catastrophic option. As for a policy of completely rejecting strikes under present-day conditions, it is simply impossible. The practical possibility of a successful balancing on the brink of a strike is confirmed by the above-mentioned actions of Workers' Committees and the Kuzbass Independent Miners' Trade Unions in December 1991–January 1992. Having seen the essential shortcoming in the preparation for and, later, in conducting the liberalization of prices in the Kuzbass, the WC and the IMU resolutely demanded that they should be eliminated. These demands were supported by real preparations for a strike, such as the reestablishment of an extensive network of strike committees, a declaration of the readiness to strike, etc. Under the pressure of workers (the reality of a threat to strike), the authorities made all the concessions that could be made without undermining the essence of reforms. The WC and the IMU also refrained from a strike.[16]

The events of early 1992 give hope that other organizations of working people, including some old trade unions, will also be able to use the balancing-on-the-brink-of-a-strike tactic. Having used the preparation for a strike and a protest march, the Moscow Trade-Union Federation came to an agreement with the government of Moscow. According to that agreement, Moscow authorities committed themselves to regularly publish information concerning changes in the value of the mini-mum consumer budget and, in accordance with those changes, to provide for the indexing of salaries of white-collar workers and of budgetary benefits. In return, the Federation promised not to organize any more strikes on those grounds. The All-Russian Trade Union of Medical Workers, which had also been preparing for a strike since the middle of last year, agreed to call it off after receiving President Yeltsin's promises. The FITUR canceled its appeal for a general two-hour strike planned for 27 January 1992 after the meeting of various trade-union representa-tives with Vice-Premier G. Burbulis. It must be admitted that the official trade unions did not implement the balancing-on-the-brink-of-a-strike tactic as suc-cessfully as the IMU did. Many FITUR activists, especially the Moscow Trade-Union Federation (the anarchists' stronghold) from time to time shifted to demagogy that bordered on the full rejection of reforms and on direct support of the UW, "Labor Russia," and other national-Bolshevik organizations. In December the leaders of the Moscow official trade unions threatened to march on the White House (Russian Supreme Council headquarters). Here the balancing on the brink of a strike could be transformed into the very strike anarchy that it was designed to prevent. Fortunately, this did not happen in January 1992, but one should never forget the reality of such a threat.

Not only workers' organizations but also the authorities should not forget this threat. For the success of balancing on the brink of a strike depends on the former no less than on the latter. The January compromise with the Kuzbass miners became possible, *inter alia*, because the government not only agreed to meet the workers' claims but also clearly expressed its respect for them. The IMU representatives were received by the president and the vice-premier of Russia. Boris Yeltsin had a long and respectful talk with them.[17] The same goodwill attitude played a big role in talks with medical workers and Moscow trade unions.

6. Conclusion. Stages of Evolution of Industrial Relations

In conclusion, we emphasize that a realistic appraisal of the current state and future development of labor relations in Russia can be given only by taking into account the stages of postsocialist development.

At the current initial stage of the overthrow of state socialism, the former vertical command-unipartite system of labor relations has been undermined—a system in which the state and economic administration, public organizations, state trade unions, etc., played the role of a single organizer and director of industrial relations. In its place, the essential conditions for conflictual (adversarial) bipartite industrial relations have emerged, in which the interaction of workers and employers—conflict, dialogue, compromise, cooperation—takes place more or less on an equal footing.

It is particularly important that the participants in such bipartite relations—

new and renewed workers' organizations—confront the government and the employers. By their very nature these relations are now linked not only to the resolution of problems associated with the position of workers today but also to the campaign for a radical transformation of the very foundations of the industrial and sociopolitical system. Accordingly, labor relations have a sufficiently clear conflictual and politicized character. At the current stage this character may be toned down but not fundamentally changed.

At the same time there are as yet unformed, just emerging elements of tripartite industrial relations—the prerequisites of a mature tripartite social partnership. The main thing here is that employers are not yet separate from the government either organizationally or, even less so, psychologically or ideologically. The real option of broad tripartite social partnership will come about only when a greater part of the economy has been separated from direct state administration, i.e., when the process of destatization and privatization embraces the really significant spheres of the economy. Moreover, this will happen when the "breakaway" of the economy from the state is acknowledged in the public mind and when a significant proportion of the bosses and bureaucrats understand that the interests of labor are no less relevant than the notorious interests of the state.

In other words, a transition to a really modern form of industrial relations will only be possible at the next stage, when democratic and market changes embrace a more significant part of society and become irreversible. Only then will labor and industrial relations, so to speak, sail to the shore and become detached from political relations. Only then will all three parties of the modern kind of normal industrial relations be formed: independent trade unions, independent economic organizations and entrepreneurs, and neutral state mediation bodies. The interrelationship of these three will enable the creation of a full-fledged mechanism of tripartite social partnership.

How long the transition will take from the current stage to the next stage may vary greatly—from several years to several generations. Predictions are hardly appropriate here. However, one can assert with certainty that the more clearly the nature of the current stage is understood, the less of an attempt will be made to subordinate the labor movement to state bodies, to suppress it by extreme measures, and the easier and quicker will be the road to the next stage—the stage where labor relations in our country become more or less the same as they are in other democratic industrial societies.

Diagram 1

Basic Labor Organizations of the Russian Federation

Primary sociopolitical orientation of organizations and movements	General character and functional trends of organizations and movements		Old dependent and semidependent organizations
	New organizations and movements independent of official structures		
	Semi-political movements	Trade unions	
1. Democratic orientation (democratization and market economy)	—Workers' (strike) committees; —Confederation of Labor	—Independent Miners' Union; —Federation of Flight Personnel; —Association of Air Controllers; —"Sotsprof"	Several groups belonging to the Federation of Independent Trade Unions of Russia
2. Conservative, neo-Stalinist, or national-Bolshevik orientation (neither democratization nor market reforms)	—Workers' unions in Moscow and some other cities; —United Front of Workers; —"Labor Russia"	—	Basic groups belonging to former General Confederation of Trade Unions
3. Orientation toward genuine, "true" socialism (democratization without a market economy)	—Basic groups in the Union of Work Collectives	—Anarcho-syndicalist trade unions (Equality, "Independence," etc.)	Several groups in the Federation of Independent Trade Unions of Russia
4. Orientation toward authoritarian modernization (market economy without demo-cratization)	—	—	Several groups in the General Confederation of Trade Unions

Diagram 2

Modes of Industrial (Labor) Relations in Russia, 1980s–1990s

	Command unipartite industrial relations	Conflictual bipartite industrial relations	Tripartite industrial partnership
	1	2	3
Social conditions favoring a given model	State socialism, general statization (1930–1970)	Society in transition from state socialism to a market economy (1990s)	Democratic society with a (social) market economy (possible situation in the early twenty-first century)
Essence of the model, typical relations	Command and submission	Conflict	Social partnership
Basic parties (main subjects) of the relations in a given model	State economic institutions, pseudo–trade unions, managers, etc., all subordinate to the same higher party–state leadership	Genuine trade unions and other independent organizations on the one side, managers and state institutions, acting together, on the other side	Genuine trade unions and independent labor organizations, independent employer organizations, and neutral state institutions (mediators)
Main objects and fields of industrial conflicts	Minor problems of labor conditions, wages, housing, everyday life, etc.	Major, fundamental problems of labor conditions and problems associated with changes in property, socioeconomic organization of society	Major and minor problems of labor conditions, wages, equitable distribution of profits and power
Main (effective) forms of workers' protest actions	Complaints, sporadic spontaneous protests	Strikes, threats of strikes, bargaining	Tripartite consultations, negotiations, bargaining
Extent of link between industrial and other social relations	Middle (industrial relations connected with other aspects of everyday life and ideology)	High (main problems of labor directly connected with changes in the political and social systems)	Low (industrial relations are relatively autonomous)

Notes

1. The famous words, in this respect, of Boris Yeltsin, who emphasized that the March–April strikes were an answer to the "winter attack" of right-wingers and that, completely owing to "the democratic movement, labor movement, and strikers' movement, the 23 April meeting was held and the famous 9 + 1 agreement came about" (*Izvestiia*, 23 May 1991).

2. The author's ideas on postsocialist development are contained in articles published in the journals *Politicheskie issledovaniia*, 1991, no. 1, and *Kommunist*, 1991, no. 10.

3. See "The Program of Joint Action of the Cabinet of Ministers of the USSR and the Governments of the Sovereign Republics on Leading the Country's Economy out of the Crisis," *Izvestiia*, 10 June 1991; "Boris Yeltsin's Speech at the USSR Congress of People's Deputies," *Izvestiia*, 27 October 1991.

4. See "Decree of the President of Russia on Social Partnership and Labor Disputes," *Kuranty*, 15 November 1991.

5. *Trud*, 6 December 1991.

6. See *First USSR Miners' Congress, 11–15 June 1990 (Collected Materials)*, pts. 1 and 2 (Donetsk, 1990); *Workers' Shorthand Notes of the Second Miners' Congress (22–26 October 1990)* (Donetsk, 1990).

7. The membership of official trade unions is regularly published in state statistical and trade-union publications. See, for example, *The Social Development of the USSR. Statistical Collection* (Moscow, 1990), p. 66; *The Nineteenth Congress of Trade Unions. Informational Bulletin*, no. 7. Data on other trade unions are based on the estimates of their leaders; in a number of cases the author, having been called in as a consultant by various new unions, has had the opportunity to amend these estimates.

8. *Trud*, 7 December 1991; 11 January 1991.

9. *Trud*, 24 December 1991.

10. *Statistical Press Bulletin*, 1991, no. 12, p. 44.

11. *The Economy of the USSR in 1990—A Statistical Annual* (Moscow, 1990), pp. 51–55.

12. According to data presented at the 28 June 1991 Meeting of the Supreme Soviet of the USSR (see *Izvestiia*, 29 July 1991).

13. According to data provided by A. Volskii, president of the Scientific Industrial Union (see *Izvestiia*, 28 June 1991).

14. *The Social Development of the USSR, 1989 (Statistical Collection)* (Moscow, 1991), p. 80; press release of USSR *Goskomstat*, no. 135 (29 April 1991), no. 218 (26 July 1991).

15. See *The Social Development of the USSR*, 1989, pp. 78–79.

16. *Nasha gazeta*, 23 January 1992; 4 February 1992.

17. *Nasha gazeta*, 25 January 1992.

The Formation of Working-Class Consciousness Under Conditions of Social Crisis and the Developing Market Economy in Russia

Vladimir Iadov

The beginning of *perestroika* in the USSR, *glasnost'*, the criticism of ideological dogmas and the reassessment of the historical past, the economic and social crises, ethnic and national conflicts, and the disintegration of the USSR have entirely destroyed the old political and ideological mentality among all social strata. This is also seen in people's loss of their previous social identity. They no longer know which social groups and communities they belong to and which of them protects their interests.

It is important to consider the fact that post-totalitarian society is predominantly antitotalitarian in nature [1]. While it decisively and unanimously rejects the social institutions, structures, and ideologies of the past, it is by no means unanimous in developing new social structures and values.

The totalitarian society of state socialism ignored all manner of specific aspects of the particular social interests of different communities and groups, and equated citizens' interests with the interests of the state, which were depicted as common [*obshchenarodnye*] interests. The top-level bureaucracy essentially appropriated the right to express these "common" interests.

In the classical Marxist paradigm, the working class is the gravedigger of capitalism and the leading force behind revolutionary transformations. Communist parties considered it their most important task to make the working class conscious of its historic mission. The practical implementation of state-socialist transformations in the USSR revealed the exact opposite.

While the working class acquired the formal status of a dominant class, it became the *de facto* tool of the party bureaucracy for suppressing all dissent and personal initiative.

With the establishment of totalitarian state socialism, the development of the self-image of the working class as an active social force in the first years of the October Revolution gave way to a process of creation of a lumpen mentality. The main features of this mentality are: a feeling of total dependence on the state's authority structures, intolerance of dissent and free-thinking, the constant

The author is director of the Institute of Sociology, Russian Academy of Sciences.

feeling of being threatened by external and internal enemies, the predominance of consumerist orientations coupled with modest demands, and the affirmation of the values of social justice as synonymous with egalitarian distribution.

We have analyzed the formation of social strata on the basis of certain objectivized indicators derived from sample nonrepresentative surveys conducted in Russia and the Ukraine. These indicators, however, were obtained on the basis of questionnaires concerning various aspects of social status and conditions of occupational (labor) activity. The questions were of an informational rather than an evaluational nature—so-called factual questions.

The results were as follows [2].

Low-skilled and semiskilled workers, collective farmers, and state farmers had the lowest ratings in the "work autonomy" indicator. Highly skilled workers, along with engineering and technical personnel ranked in the middle (managers, entrepreneurs, and members of the creative intelligentsia ranked still higher).

For the indicator of "potential for vertical mobility," all workers regardless of their skill level, collective farmers, engineers, and employees [*sluzhashchie*] were in the same low-rated stratum. Professionals in nontechnical specialties and new enterpreneurs rated high in this indicator.

Low-skilled workers ranked lowest in "quality of life," on a par with rural dwellers and semiskilled employees. Highly skilled workers and engineers occupied a more favorable position in this type of stratification. Next came middle managers, nontechnical intelligentsia, and at the very highest level—top-level executives and new social strata of entrepreneurs.

Here we must call attention to the existence of two entirely different substrata of the working class in the old system of social stratification that was characteristic of society during the years of absolute dominance of the planned economy and the state-bureaucratic system of management: low-skilled and semiskilled workers (with minimum potential mobility and work autonomy, but high earnings) and, on the other hand, highly skilled workers who enjoyed virtually the same position in the social structure as engineering and technical personnel (in terms of work autonomy, material well-being, and their relatively privileged position in the production management system).

The present social situation *objectively* equalizes workers with strata of low social mobility, sharply differentiates subgroups with low and relatively higher work autonomy, and reduces the entire working class to the lowest level of "quality of life."

A new social identity in post-totalitarian society evolves primarily in the form of special interests (ethnic-national, corporate, group, class, etc.) that *stand opposed* to the common social interest. The formation of a new social identity therefore assumes a highly conflict-ridden character. Nor is there any kind of social institution or ideological conception that could act as an arbitrator of conflicting interests.

For the working class, the most important component of the new social identity is

Table 1

Strikers' Demands (in %)

Directed at	1989	1991
Central and republic authorities	8.8	29.1
Local authorities	91.2	70.9
	100.0	100.0

the awareness of the unity of interests of wage labor, of the owners of one's own labor power in a market economy. Because of the absence of real market relations and the dominance of the state's monopoly on property, this process acquires primarily the character of a protest against state structures and central and republic authority.

An analysis of strikers' demands (by Vorkuta miners in 1989–91) indicates a decline in the share of demands made on local authorities and a corresponding increase in the share of demands addressed to central authorities [see Table 1] [3].

At the same time, there were also changes in the content of the miners' demands: the share of political and economic demands (the deepening of the economic crisis) increased, the share of social demands remained stable, and the share of technical, technological, and organizational demands declined [see Table 2].

Meanwhile, social self-identification processes in the working class (as in other strata of the population) are proceeding slowly, are unstable, and are complicated by the tendency to identify with a certain social-propertied stratum (according to the "rich"– "poor" criterion) on the one hand and with political and ideological preferences on the other.

The profound economic crisis is impoverishing vast numbers of people, and, in combination with the loss of belief in a socially just society, it is forming the consciousness of a society with deepening contradictions between rich and poor and is stimulating self-identification with a certain social stratum on the scale of success in life.

Statistics on the decline of the population's living standard cannot be accurate because of mounting hyperinflation, the decline in production (up to 10 percent in the principal branches of industry at the beginning of 1992), the imbalance in the consumer market, and the shortage of food staples and the prime necessities. General trends in the state of mass consciousness are more indicative. For example, according to representative polls conducted in the USSR by T. Zaslavskaia's All-Union Center for the Study of Public Opinion, at the beginning of 1990 about 40 percent of the population indicated that they were worse off than before; at the beginning of 1991, 70 percent; at the beginning of 1992, over 90 percent. Given the generally modest demands on the level of well-being as a national character trait, at the end of the eighties up to 90 percent of the country's population indicated that they were "basically satisfied with their material well-being," but

Table 2

Content of Strikers' Demands

Demands	1989	1991
Economic	26.8	41.8
Social	61.9	45.5
Political	0.5–0.8	9.4
Organizational	8.1	2.3
Ecological	2.1	0.6
Technical-organizational	1.1	0.4
	100.0	100.0

according to polls conducted in mid-1991, this share declined to one-third. In February 1992, 6 percent of Russia's population reported that they "were not experiencing material difficulties." Of course, a large role is played here by *glasnost'*, by the possibility of comparing living standards in the countries of the former [Soviet] Union with Western countries, by the publication of the ruble–dollar exchange rate (people realize that by Western economic standards they are worse off than the unemployed in the developed countries of the world).

But in order to understand the processes underlying the formation of social identity, we must take into account not only changes in the scale of the general public's self-assessment of the growing poverty of this country's people in comparison with the people of other countries but also the way they identify with and consider themselves part of a more or less affluent social stratum in "their own" society.

Polls based on nonrepresentative samples in Russia and the Ukraine provide rough empirical data on such self-assessments [2]. These data from mid-1991 point to a single but very important parameter of social stratification—social-propertied stratification—as the dominant component. Less than 10 percent of the population classified themselves among the "above average," highest, and even "elite" strata; up to 50 percent classified themselves among the "middle stratum"; up to 30 percent, among the "below average" and "lowest" strata; and up to 10 percent were unable to assign themselves to a particular propertied stratum. The general configuration of social strata based on gradations of affluent–nonaffluent [*blagopoluchie–neblagopoluchie*] in a socially heterogeneous society that already accepts the conception of social inequality now looks approximately as follows: 1 : 5 : 3 : 1. This means roughly the following: 10 percent of the citizens consider themselves quite well-off, one-half identify themselves with the deprived majority—"like everyone," one-third consider themselves completely infringed upon [*ushchemlennye*], and about 10 percent regard themselves as marginals [*marginaly*].

The second important component of the emerging new social identity is the value orientation and politico-ideological component. The crisis of totalitarian society's value system has first of all taken the form of the erosion of notions of a socially just society and the decisive rejection of communist ideals.

More than half of the persons polled in different regions believe that the country would have been better off if there had been no October Revolution in 1917. More than one-third of all Muscovites believe that Marxism is utopian, and more than half of them reject Leninism. More than half of the population in all regions, republics, and ethnic-national communities also believe that the past history of the USSR is a chain of tragic mistakes. According to an all-Russian poll at the beginning of 1991, less than 20 percent of the population still believe in socialist ideals [4].

According to L. Gordon [5], three political currents have emerged in the working class. The most highly organized miners' movement (Donbass, Vorkuta) supports market reforms and at the same time demands a higher share in the distribution of profits based on the sale of part of the product in foreign markets; a movement that is connected with socialist ideals, opposes market reforms, and calls for a return to the planned economy and distributive state socialism (United Front of Workers, etc.) is growing stronger; and, finally, there is the most sizable segment of workers, those who do not support any political orientation but demand better working conditions and higher pay.

A representative survey in Russia (in mid-1990) found that about 40 percent of workers were "progressives" (advocates of economic and political freedom) and that 20–25 percent were "conservatives," i.e., inclined to reject both economic and political freedom. Among the peasantry, the latter comprise up to 65 percent. Among predominantly technical specialists, the distribution among these indicators was very close to the distribution among workers [6].

According to another survey that was representative for Russia (January–May 1991), there are certain differences between unskilled and skilled workers' attitudes toward a market economy on the one hand, while there is substantially less enthusiasm for a market economy among workers than among specialists, and especially among managers and entrepreneurs, on the other [see Table 3] [7].

Judging by this table, an awareness of the status of the working class as the owner of labor power in a market economy is beginning to emerge. Nevertheless, this process is not so noticeable if we judge by its "positive" component (speeding up the reforms), but it is quite clear cut if we look at the conservative component (a return to a planned economy). Specialists, managers, and entrepreneurs definitely hold a negative position on the latter issue; workers and employees are substantially more restrained in their criticism of the state-monopoly economy's planning and egalitarian distribution system. We also note that the positive-negative assymmetry in people's minds when they are faced with new perceptions carries more information specifically in the negative zone—the zone in which there is the feeling of danger. Workers are substantially more afraid of entering the market than skilled specialists, managers, and entrepreneurs.

Summary

The working class's awareness of itself as an active social force is presently in a formative stage. This is a contradictory process that is further complicated by the fact that particular social interests in a post-totalitarian society confront one

Table 3

Responses to the Question: "Should market reforms be speeded up or slowed down?" (in %)

	Low-skilled workers	Skilled workers	Employees (clerks)	Specialists	Managers and entre-preneurs
Reforms should be decisively accelerated	18.4	31.7	25.6	47.6	48.1
We should move "step by step"	46.8	39.5	46.8	41.6	47.5
We do not need a market economy; the planning system should be strengthened	24.7	21.3	24.7	5.8	3.2
Did not answer	10.0	7.6	12.0	4.9	1.3
Number of respondents	299	635	367	466	158

another in the absence of an arbiter of common national interest or of constitutional authority structures that might inspire confidence in the majority of the population. Hence the acute conflict situation that exists among various social forces (ethnic-national, class, and social-group).

The slow development of actual market relations makes it difficult for hired workers to develop an awareness of themselves as the owners of their own labor power. The profound economic and social crisis pushes criteria of inequality in property and identification with a certain property stratum based on the "rich"–"poor" criterion into the forefront. Social identification with socio-occupational and social-class formations is weak and unstable and is being pushed into the background compared with the criterion indicated above.

The crisis of the old ideologies and systems of values in the course of formation of new social ideals and values leads to the differentiation of political and ideological orientations in the working class. On the one hand, there emerge strata of workers quite well organized as a result of the experience of the strike movement that support market reforms, while on the other hand these are opposed by currents that favor the restoration of state socialism with its distributive relations. The majority of workers remain outside active politics and pressure all authority structures to improve their material condition by lowering prices, raising wages, and improving working conditions. They are restrained in their attitude toward economic reforms.

The stabilization of the economic and sociopolitical situation in countries of the former Soviet Union will inevitably entail the ordering of relations between wage labor and employers, including the state sector of the economy. The strengthening of legality and the formation of a civil society are the necessary conditions of this process.

Cooperation between the labor movement in the CIS [Commonwealth of Independent States] countries and trade unions in Western countries is an extremely important factor in making our trade unions more sophisticated in their negotiations with employers, in concluding collective contracts, in making professional assessments of the state of the economy in branches of industry, and in evaluating the fair distribution of profits between labor and capital with due regard for the entire complex of economic and social conditions in society and in a given region, in a given branch of production, which will be a decisive factor in the formation of the social identity of the working class.

References

1. Dahrendorf, R. *The Modern Social Conflict*. London, 1988.
2. Data of E. Igitkhanian. Institute of Sociology, Russian Academy of Sciences (RAN).
3. Data of I. Kiseleva. Institute of Sociology, RAN.
4. Data of A. Demidov. Institute of Sociology, RAN.
5. Gordon, L. *Nezavisimaia gazeta*, 10 January 1992.
6. Data of N. Lapin and V. Kolbanovskii (research project of the Institutes of Philosophy and Sociology, RAN).
7. From a preprint by L. D. Nelson (Virginia Commonwealth University) and L. Babaeva and R. Babaev (Institute of Sociology, RAN).

Economic Consciousness and Reform of the Employment Sphere

Vladimir Gimpel´son

The transition to a market economy is closely connected with profound changes in the economic consciousness and economic culture of the entire population. The discussion in Russia today concerns not only the formation of an entrepreneurial class with the ethic characteristic of this social group, but also involves the formation of a full-fledged wage-earning class. The myth of the "Soviet worker–manager of production" that existed during the years of "developed socialism" was transformed during *perestroika* into the idea that the Soviet worker was merely a wage laborer. This idea is also divorced from reality. The definition of this worker as "state-dependent,"[1] with an essentially traditionalist work ethic, seems more accurate. In his definition of this concept ("state-dependent worker"), Victor Zaslavsky wrote that it

> on the one hand . . . relates to a complex of specific work habits and to a production ethic based more on the avoidance of work than on discipline and productivity, on a general scorn for work in the state sector of the economy, on the inability and reluctance to take risks and display initiative. The state-dependent worker always values guarantees more than success and views guarantees more as the absence of a threat than as the existence of a prospect for the satisfaction of his needs. On the other hand, the production and distribution of goods and services based on state-directive management are directly related to this type of worker.[2]

The type of work ethic described above is not an invention of socialism. It is quite well known and has been described in the sociological literature as traditionalistic. This type of work ethic, which is characteristic of cheap labor power, was one of the circumstances that held back the development of capitalism when the transition to forms of production requiring intensive labor began.

Max Weber noted that

> in all cases when there is a need for skilled labor, when expensive machines requiring careful and skilled handling, and in general a sufficient degree of attention and initiative are the point at issue . . . it is absolutely necessary that there be not only a developed sense of responsibility, but also a way of thinking that, if only during work, would exclude the invariable question of how to

The author is affiliated with the Institute of Employment Problems, Russian Academy of Sciences.

preserve one's customary earnings with a maximum of convenience and a minimum of exertion: a way of thinking that makes labor an absolute end-in-itself, a "calling." However, such an attitude toward labor is not a property of human nature.[3]

In Weber's view, it can develop only as a result of long-term education.

One of the key problems in creating a developed market economy in our country is overcoming the state-socialist model of the traditional work ethic, strengthening an economic culture that is new for Russian society, and replacing entirely the prevailing models of work behavior.

In the present paper I would like to discuss only certain aspects of the economic consciousness and behavior of workers as they apply to the employment sphere:

(1) the problem of unemployment in mass consciousness;

(2) the problem of redundant employment;

(3) forced mobility and the price of stability;

(4) a typology of workers in terms of their attitude toward different models of work behavior.

Unemployment in the Consciousness of the Working Masses

Until the end of the 1980s unemployment problems did not occupy a serious place in people's consciousness. Earlier job-reduction campaigns had generally been of a provisional nature: either vacant positions were eliminated or someone was retired on pension or someone was moved from one chair to another. This had no relationship to unemployment nor did it affect the largest detachment of those employed in industry. It is not by chance that even during the years of *perestroika* many respondents in sociological polls did not show anxiety over the possible loss of their jobs.

The situation began to change rapidly in 1988. The beginning of a reduction of the work force in the state sector was accompanied by change in public opinion regarding unemployment.

Society's attitude toward unemployment as a key indicator of the state of the employment sphere developed along two interconnected lines. *First,* society moved toward the recognition of the inevitability or the permissibility of unemployment. The opinion began to form that while this is a serious illness, it is not fatal. In early 1990, 33 percent of those polled by the All-Union Center for the Study of Public Opinion in an all-Union sample believed that unemployment was either useful or permissible (54 percent rejected this view).[4] By the end of the same year this relationship changed to 47 percent compared to 39 percent (for a comparable group).[5] Moreover, young educated males in regions where reforms were proceeding at a faster pace (Estonia, for example) were most tolerant of unemployment. It can be assumed that the recognition of the permissibility of unemployment is becoming one of the key characteristics of the "promarket orientation" in the economic consciousness of the masses.

The growing understanding of unemployment as an inevitable socioeconomic

Table 1

Distribution of Opinions on the Permissibility and Inevitability of Unemployment (in % of the number of respondents)*

Question: "Many believe that the transition to the market will inevitably be accompanied by mass unemployment. What do you think?" (*n* = 600)

	Average for sample	Engineers	Workers	Males	Females
–Mass unemployment is inevitable; nothing can be done about it	13	17	11	16	11
–Mass unemployment is inevitable but it can and must be reduced	45	44	45	46	43
–It is by no means inevitable; it must be avoided	41	37	43	38	44

*See description of sample on p. 42.

phenomenon is also confirmed by our research, for example, by the findings of a sociological poll conducted in Taganrog in August 1991 [see Table 1].

More than half of the workers we polled in the city of Taganrog agreed with the thesis that unemployment is inevitable. Moreover, this figure is very stable and fluctuates only slightly between workers and engineers, and males and females. Incidentally, male engineers show the greatest tolerance for it. (We shall subsequently show that the admission of the possibility of unemployment belongs to the nucleus of "promarket" views and is strongly correlated with other elements of the orientation toward reform of the employment sphere.)

The perception of unemployment as an inevitable socioeconomic phenomenon during the period of transition to a market economy is also growing in other East European countries. In Poland, for example, unemployment is viewed as inevitable by 40–50 percent of workers and 80 percent of management's representatives. The majority of respondents regard it as a factor that is instrumental in surmounting economic difficulties and as a means of strengthening labor discipline.[6]

Second, there is now a fear of unemployment that did not exist before. Incidentally, the word "fear" probably does not reflect the essence of the matter with total precision. For many, this is more a sober understanding of the prospects than a state of psychological depression. According to data of the All-Union Center for the Study of Public Opinion, in December 1990, 65 percent of the population believed that the "fear of losing one's job has increased."[7] At the beginning of 1992, 30 percent of respondents expressed the fear that they might become unemployed in 1992.[8] The fear of unemployment is rising primarily among those who support far-reaching reforms: among the intelligentsia and engineering-technical personnel. This is not surprising because it appears that unemployment begins first of all with this group and employees with higher education (as well as in regions that are leading in the implementation of economic reforms). It would seem that both of these trends are positive in our concrete historical context. If the former attests to our society's increased understanding of market relations in all their complexity and a certain liberation from illusions and myths, the latter indicates that people are seriously reflecting on their future, on their personal responsibility for their own fate.

From Redundant Employment to Open Unemployment

It is known that hidden unemployment or redundant employment, which is the socialist economy's natural and inevitable accompaniment, is one of the most important sources of open unemployment during the period of transition. Until recently, redundant employment was perceived by many workers and managers as a positive factor because it led to a reduction of the overall work load per worker, served as a reliable reserve for contingencies—for example, for periodically recurring crash programs at the end of plan periods—and also as insurance against the need for various kinds of diversions from work.

With the introduction of market conditions and rigid budget constraints, a considerable volume of underutilized live labor is transformed into redundant workers who are doomed to be dismissed. Of course, some of the "redundant" workers may be kept employed at these enterprises as a result of the expansion of production. However, the potential for this is limited, and overemployment is enormous. The "redundancy" problem is beginning to be recognized by workers as concerning everyone personally, as directly affecting their vital interests.

Let us turn to the opinions of the industrial workers themselves. The investigation of the views of industrial workers on redundant employment and labor mobility was one of the points in a sociological research program conducted in 1988–91 by associates of the Institute of Employment Problems (who at that time worked at the Institute of the International Labor Movement, USSR Academy of Sciences) together with V. Magun (Institute of Sociology, USSR Academy of Sciences).

All respondents can be divided into four subgroups: (1) workers at one of Taganrog's large machine-building enterprises ($n = 290$) who were questioned in April 1989; (2) 196 persons representing two state enterprises in Moscow (December 1988); (3) workers at a cooperative enterprise in Moscow who were questioned in December 1988 ($n = 219$) and in January–February 1990 ($n = 290$); (4) 600 workers and engineers at two Taganrog industrial enterprises (August 1991). There was a total of approximately 1,600 persons.

We note first of all that the great majority (80–90 percent) of the workers polled in Taganrog believe that there are "redundant" workers at their enterprise and in their shop.

The figures are quite stable: their variation among sociodemographic groups is negligible. Unanimity is evident in all age groups up to 50 years. Only in the older cohort (over 50 years) is there an observable trend toward a decline in the share of those who acknowledge intraplant overemployment manifested in the existence of a considerable number of redundant jobs and redundant workers.

More modest assessments of employment redundancy may be observed at nonstate enterprises operating under tight budget constraints. There is also an increased differentiation in the scale of redundancy in the views of representatives of different sociodemographic groups. Women are more sensitive to increases in physical and psychological burdens, for example. A part of the previously unutilized internal reserves at enterprises that have become state-owned has already been activated and the intensity of labor here has increased.

As a result, certain groups of workers who were working below capacity yesterday are clearly aware of the exhaustion of their potential for giving anything more today. This is connected not only with the intensity of the work and the need to devote increasing physical effort to it. No less important are the new psychological demands and the necessity of adapting to constant changes of a social, economic, and in some places, a technological nature. Older women with low skill levels are the first to encounter difficulties in making such an adaptation.

At every step of the changes there is a further differentiation and restructuring of collectives that were relatively homogeneous in the past. Among the supporters of the incipient reforms, a growing stratum finds itself among the new "victims" of the reforms as a result of a number of circumstances (including sociodemographic and occupational-skill circumstances). In our case this means that those who supported radical reforms yesterday may be fired and become unemployed tomorrow. This leads to a smaller base of support and to increased resistance. Such an inevitable process in the change of orientation must be borne in mind.

Respondents at all enterprises noted the existence of redundant personnel considerably more frequently at the enterprise as a whole than in their shop. The tendency to make a lower assessment of work effort with an increase in social distance is an indicator of group self-centeredness. Strong antimanagement and antibureaucratic sentiments also make themselves known here, since most enterprise managers are concentrated not in shops but in offices.

Many persons in managerial work at enterprises not only prove to be redundant but also demonstrate their total incompetence and lack of readiness to work under conditions of economic independence. The real situation in this sphere, when refracted in the workers' consciousness, reinforces the already firm image of the manager as a "bureaucrat" and an "enemy of *perestroika*." The focused attribution of responsibility characteristic of mass consciousness in our country is concretized here in the fact that a considerable part of the blame for basic flaws in the system is assigned to the plant manager.

Social tensions between the managers and the managed depend only slightly on the type of enterprise and the real socioeconomic situation prevailing there. This is confirmed by our studies at enterprises that are leaders of the reform, have independently chosen radical models of management, and are successfully realizing them. Even the fact that changes are supported and approved by workers and initiated by enterprise management does little to reduce these tensions.

Until recently, many of those employed in management structures were still inclined to think that there are no redundant workers at their enterprises. What is more, in their opinion there is a need for more working hands. An insufficient knowledge of reality, the conviction that there will always be a chronic shortage of personnel, the fear of crash programs that usually recur at the end of every month, the desire to protect themselves against various external influences and to guarantee the fulfillment of plan targets by any means have become an integral part of the consciousness of many middle-level plant managers. Even under appreciably altered conditions the old views are abandoned slowly and with great effort.

Workers inevitably project a possible reduction in employment, even if it affects others, onto their own career, which forces them to evaluate proposed measures in terms of their own fate. It is necessary to choose: either a material raise for oneself tomorrow, or a dangerous precedent that may work the day after tomorrow, all the more so because a possible wage hike is threatened by devaluation as a result of inflation. For some categories of workers, the possible monetary gain resulting from an increase in the intensity of labor may become the limit beyond which it will be very difficult to compensate the physical efforts that are made. All this, when refracted through the prism of prevailing values and the work ethic in the workers' consciousness, and also depending on objective sociodemographic and socio-occupational characteristics, may determine people's positions toward radical economic reforms.

Notwithstanding the widespread recognition of hidden forms of unemployment (in the form of overemployment), workers do not support sanctions against those ordinary workers whom they are prone to consider redundant. The most "humane" are those workers who have limited possibilities for substantially adding to output on their jobs. This includes, in the first place, workers at enterprises that have already attained a substantial intensification of work activity, and second, women and workers in older age groups, i.e., those whose energy reserves are relatively more modest and who would find it difficult to restore fully their expended strength in the event of a significant additional increase in their work efforts.

One-fourth of male workers and one-third of female workers polled in Taganrog in 1989 opposed any measures that would hurt workers in any way and influence their status. Half of the respondents would permit mild sanctions. The prevailing opinion in this group was that order had to be established in the reckoning of real work performed, and when this was done those who were redundant would leave of their own accord. Pay cuts had the support of only 2–4 percent of respondents. Finally, one-fourth of males and one-fifth of females favored discharging redundant workers. At Taganrog enterprises in August 1991 (including the one at which the poll was conducted in 1989), practically the same percent of respondents voted against imposing sanctions against redundant workers as was recorded two years earlier. However, support for strict sanctions increased slightly as a result of the decline in the popularity of mild sanctions. As many as one-third of male respondents and one-fourth of female respondents "voted" to fire redundant workers.

Workers at enterprises at which the intensity of labor has increased as a result of privatization subscribe to a "milder" position than workers in the traditionally functioning state sector. The share of those who are opposed to any kind of sanctions is higher here, and only 10 percent support the idea of firing obviously redundant workers.

As we see, the consciousness of the mass of workers is highly tolerant of those whom it acknowledges as being redundant in production. Workers are more inclined to tolerate them, essentially giving them part of their own pay, than they are to subject them to sanctions for bad work. This is one of the manifestations of the egalitarian psychology that is nurtured by the lack of confidence in one's own strength, by an insufficient feeling of responsibility for oneself, and by uncertainty about the morrow. There is an increasing probability that such sentiments will be manifested among older workers and among workers with low skill levels. This is not so much a matter of "proletarian solidarity" as the fear of finding oneself in such a situation.

Tolerance toward redundant workers is connected with the recognition of overemployment. Increasing acknowledgment of overemployment is accompanied by higher, statistically significant demands for sanctions. The strictness of the sanctions supported is also connected with the orientation toward higher earnings. The more a worker is oriented toward higher earnings, the "harder" he is prepared to be toward potential redundant workers.[9]

The psychology of indifference is fed by the constantly reproduced social experience that an increase in work contribution (which should be the natural consequence of terminating those who have become dead weight) is not accompanied by a corresponding increase in pay. As before, workers continued to express the feeling that, whatever happened, they would not be paid more than a certain amount. The continuing "ceiling" and administrative restrictions on wages have not only undermined incentives for fuller personal involvement in work but have also reinforced such aspects of the work ethic as leniency and tolerance toward the poor work of others. The existing situation is fraught with difficult-to-predict consequences for the disintegration of the labor sphere in the life of society. For various reasons, material incentives malfunction seriously, the intrinsic value of high-quality, conscientious labor has been consigned to the distant periphery of work morality, the level of individual responsibility is traditionally low, while the prevailing (and strengthening!) standards of group interrelations do not prevent the erosion of the work ethic.

There is yet another danger. The common stereotypes of the work ethic include more than a calm, tolerant attitude toward ineffective work. There is the danger that those who will be dismissed will be by no means the worst workers in the work collectives (even with the most democratic procedures). According to V. Kosmarskii's data, more than 50 percent of the respondents link dismissal primarily with the character references of those who are dismissed rather than the kind of work they perform. And here, those with negative character references (the negligent, the unskilled, the undisciplined) and those with positive character references (those who are socially active) find themselves in the same boat. Almost one person in four names socially active workers who are inconvenient for the administration as the principal candidates for dismissal.[10]

Such fears are understandable. After all, in the 1970s and 1980s, dismissal was widely practiced in the USSR as a way of dealing with those workers who did not wish to remain indifferent to prevailing procedures. This applied not only to representatives of the intelligentsia but also to ordinary workers whose struggle for their rights, for better working conditions, for the introduction of technical innovations and inventions (to say nothing of political activity) gave way to stiff sanctions from enterprise management and the party leadership.

Forced Mobility and the Price of Stability

It would be extremely important to know how workers themselves picture the principal directions of the structuring of their working life in the event of their dismissal. This applies not only to those who may become redundant at a flourishing enterprise. As a result of structural transformations and the activation of market mechanisms, entire enterprises will inevitably be forced to terminate their production activity for one reason or another. What are the possible paths of readjustment of terminated workers? How do these directions of labor mobility appear to the workers themselves?

Responses to the question "What would be your preference if your enterprise were to close down tomorrow for one reason or another?" permit us to conclude that the intensification of economic changes at enterprises (the interconnected growth of pay and work load noted by workers in sociological polls may be taken as their indicators) is accompanied by a substantial redistribution of preferred spheres of employment. We note first of all an increase in the share of those who would like to work in the nonstate sector.

In an all-Union survey by the USSR State Committee for Statistics in October 1990, 60 percent against 15 percent of the respondents opted for the nonstate sector (25 percent of the respondents considered this immaterial or had difficulty answering). We may observe that the nonstate sector is becoming more attractive and that prejudice against it is waning. In this regard, we may note one more important point: the same survey recorded a higher share of those who agree to the role of a wage laborer in the private sector than those who choose the role of

Table 2

Respondents' Characterizations of Working Conditions and Wages in State and Nonstate Sectors

State sector		Nonstate sector	
1. Egalitarianism	93%	1. Competition	86%
2. Impossibility of high earnings	85%	2. High earnings	86%
3. Social benefits	84%	3. High intensity of labor	82%
4. Possibility of "taking it easy"	83%	4. Threat of unemployment	67%
5. Guaranteed earnings	78%	5. Fair distribution	67%
6. Social protection	74%	6. Unstable earnings	61%
7. Assignment to outside jobs	73%	7. Participation of ordinary workers in the management of production	57%

boss [*khoziain*] for themselves. And even though the relative share of owners should be less than that of wage laborers, in our view this represents a definite change in social consciousness. After all, until very recently the private sector was for many the focus of all ills and all conceivable evil.

The 1991 Taganrog study devoted considerable attention to comparisons of the state and nonstate sectors of the economy. In particular, the respondents ascribed certain characteristics to the two sectors. And while our respondents' knowledge of the state sector was certainly not based on hearsay, they judged the nonstate sector on the basis of their scant experience with it in the recent period. Moreover, certain conclusions were obviously drawn according to the principle of "opposites": if something does not exist in the state sector, then perhaps it exists in the nonstate sector.

Thus, in the opinion of participants in the study, the state sector is characterized by guaranteed but low earnings and by work at a low level of intensity and accompanied by social protection and social benefits. The nonstate sector is distinguished by its high but unstable earnings, a system of distribution that is assessed as just. At the same time, respondents note the presence of competition and the threat of unemployment. We emphasize once again that 67 percent consider the distribution of wages outside the state sector to be fair, and 57 percent believe that ordinary workers here participate in the management of production [see Table 2].

We noted above that the inclination of respondents to impose stricter sanctions on candidates for dismissal lessens substantially as the intensity of labor increases. When workers opt for one or another solution to the redundant personnel problem, they project it on to their own immediate work career.

Approximately two-thirds of the respondents at the nonstate plant consider a significant reduction in the number of jobs at their enterprise highly probable or possible. One-half of them are convinced that this will affect them personally. More than half of the men and over three-fourths of the women polled would like to remain at the enterprise if their job were eliminated.

In addition to creating appropriate conditions and mechanisms for labor mobility at enterprises, considerable efforts will be required of the workers themselves. The economic reform and the consequences accompanying it not only lead to a simple reduction in the number employed but also create different types of demands on workers. We refer to skill level and a substantially higher degree of responsibility for the results of their labor, but perhaps, above all, to the increased potential for mobility, to the readiness to adapt to the rapidly changing conditions of modern production. In the age of radical reform and rapid changes, this type of mobility will be downward in nature for many and will inevitably entail certain sacrifices—frequently very painful and involving a break with the customary stereotypes in the labor sphere that are oriented toward stability, invariability, and guarantees.

Here it is important to emphasize that the entire system of material and moral rewards and the distribution of social benefits in the USSR was traditionally oriented toward the strengthening of the professional and skill status of the worker in the production sphere. Hence there exists the danger that the inculcated orientation toward stability and not mobility, the low degree of adaptability to imminent change, the lack of readiness and inability to sacrifice some components of social and professional status in the name of preserving (or strengthening) others may be a difficult obstacle to surmount on the road to radical reform.

Unfortunately, we do not as yet have sufficiently representative social information to make a detailed and reliable forecast of the possible reaction of different sociodemographic and socio-occupational groups to the mass dismissal or restructuring of industrial jobs. Understandably, such a problem is arising in our country for the first time. Our studies provide grounds for a certain restrained optimism because they suggest that workers' potential for mobility today is at the very least sufficient for taking the initial steps in the direction of the market.

Let us cite data on the cooperative enterprise we studied. In order to remain at the enterprise where they worked at the time of the poll, 30 percent of the males and 48 percent of the females questioned were ready to master a new occupation; 48 percent and 42 percent, respectively, agreed to work to upgrade their skill level; 66 percent and 46 percent, to master new equipment; and one-third agreed to work more intensively. Eleven percent and 26 percent acknowledged that a shorter workday or shorter workweek with a corresponding cut in pay would be acceptable to them. However, practically no one agreed to transfer to a lower-paying job. And what is particularly important is that 43 percent of the males and 37 percent of the females consider a high level of job performance to be the main condition for keeping their present job in the event of mass dismissals.

The same range of questions (but in a different formulation) was also discussed with participants in the Taganrog study in 1991. We note first of all that only 28 percent were certain that they would easily find a new job if their current job was terminated. Workers (33 percent compared to 19 percent of engineers) and males (42 percent compared to 15 percent of females) were more certain of this. About 40 percent believed that they would encounter serious difficulties in finding work or that they would be compelled to make sacrifices (worse working conditions or lower pay).

On the average, according to their answers, one-third of the respondents are prepared to accept worse conditions if they are terminated and have difficulty finding an equally good job. The differences between the responses of males and females are not very great and do not exceed 10–15 percentage points. Females are more willing (than males) to perform community work, to take low-skilled jobs in the service sphere, to accept lower-paying jobs. Workers and male engineers appear willing to shift to more strenuous or hazardous working conditions or to work a less convenient shift (night shifts, alternating days off). We also note that according to various polls, between one-half and two-thirds of workers of prepension age would agree to retire on pension without waiting for the formal pension age. This makes it possible to count on a more flexible employment policy for this age group.

It should be noted that of all the possible measures to "soften" dismissal and to make the employment system more flexible, the least support is enjoyed by those that are directly connected with pay cuts. The expansion of part-time employment is one of the most popular measures (in the developed industrial countries) promoting the flexibility of the labor market. In this case, the curtailment of working time entails a corresponding reduction of pay. Only 16 percent of the respondents in Taganrog supported this measure, and fewer than one-third considered it feasible to introduce additional unpaid leave.

A larger number supported the solution of the unemployment problem "at the expense of" pensioners. We noted above that even the "prepensioners" themselves are prepared to accept their lot as pensioners quite calmly. On the whole, 60 percent would approve the temporary lowering of the pension age in unemployment-ridden regions, and 70 percent would agree to restrict the employment of pensioners in branches particularly beset by declining employment.

General Social Orientation Toward Reform of the Employment Sphere: Typology and Differentiation

I attempted to show above that individual components are reciprocally correlated and have common ties with one another. It is therefore entirely natural to try to make the transition from partial indicators to an integrated indicator: the general social orientation toward reform of the employment sphere. This type of indicator can be derived with the aid of factor analysis procedures.

Questionnaires of workers at two Taganrog enterprises (an August 1991 poll) were used for this purpose. The results of the factor analysis are presented below. Factor analysis confirms the existence of a close relationship between different elements of workers' views of the employment sphere. The factor cited in Table 3 can be interpreted as a general indicator of attitudes toward change in the

Table 3

Factor of Attitudes Toward Changes in the Employment Sphere
(method of chief components, without rotation; first factor; $n = 300$)

Characteristics	Factor loads
—The usefulness of your enterprise's output ("+" no one needs our output)	−0.30
—What should be done with unprofitable enterprises? ("+" close them down immediately)	−0.42
—The existence of redundant jobs and positions ("+" there are no redundant jobs or positions)	+0.46
—What should be done with redundant workers? ("+" no kind of sanctions)	+0.48
—Will you be affected by the reduction? ("+" reduction expected)	+0.24
—Inevitability of mass unemployment with the transition to a market economy ("+" unemployment is inevitable)	−0.48
—Will it be difficult for you to find another job? ("+" I will find another job without difficulty)	−0.48
—Choice: territorial mobility or unemployment ("+" mobility)	−0.31
—Choice: stable earnings or my own business with risk ("+" stability)	+0.77
—Desire to engage in entrepreneurship ("+" existence of desire)	−0.73
% dispersion	23%

Note: The "+" and "−" signs are connected with the design of the scales of the respective questions in the questionnaire.

employment sphere. Respondents that are more market minded and more realistic in their assessment of the situation are concentrated at the positive pole of this factor's scale. The other pole of the scale reflects a negative orientation toward market reforms. Those who are less prepared for radical changes in the economy are concentrated at this pole. The following chain of correlations may be observed for the first group (which gravitates toward the positive pole): no one needs our enterprise's output—unprofitable enterprises should be closed down immediately—there are many redundant jobs and positions—redundant workers should be fired—a lack of personal fear of possible dismissal—understanding the inevitability of unemployment—the ability to adapt to changes in the labor market—potential mobility—orientation toward higher earnings and the values of entrepreneurship. This type of behavior and consciousness has a clearly defined social and demographic profile: young, educated, skilled, relatively highly paid males. Naturally, the opposite of the plus sign signifies a logical sequence that is similar in its meaning but in which all the constituent elements have an opposite content. The respondents are convinced that their enterprise as a whole and individual workers are doing a good job, that if there are redundant workers they are few in number, and that sanctions should not be invoked against them. On the other hand, they are extremely afraid of unemployment because they will be unable to find another job, while moving to another city or the opening of their own business are out of the question as far as they are concerned. As a rule, the adherents of this position are elderly, low-paid females with a low educational and skill level [see Table 3].

Summary

There is *progress in the understanding of unemployment* as a socioeconomic phenomenon in Russian society. It is perceived less as an abstract and absolute evil. An increasing number of people are beginning to view unemployment as an inevitable consequence of the reforms, which should and can be combated, but which at the same time forces every person to take a more responsible and serious approach to his work.

The considerable redundant employment that exists is becoming one of the principal factors in open unemployment. This overemployment is acknowledged by practically all workers. However, with the increase in the intensity of labor connected with economic reform, some sociodemographic and occupational-skill groups are approaching the threshold of their internal potential for adapting to the accelerating changes. In this situation there is the possibility that orientations will change and there is the danger that workers will impede further reforms that might threaten them personally in the future. This means that the social base of support for reforms among workers will diminish.

The workers' consciousness is tolerant toward those it considers "redundant." Workers are more inclined to tolerate them and essentially to give them part of their remuneration than to impose sanctions for poor work. This is a manifestation of egalitarian psychology and uncertainty about the stability of their own situation.

The prestige of the nonstate sector has begun to increase of late. Many workers at state enterprises today connect the fairness of distribution of labor earnings and the participation of rank-and-file workers in the management of production specifically with the nonstate sector. In discussing the problem of increasing the flexibility of hiring in connection with possible reductions in the size of the work force, many Russian workers are ready for sacrifices and adaptations in order to keep their jobs. However, the majority categorically reject the possibility of lower pay and the forms of flexible employment that lead to lower pay. At the same time, the proportion of workers who are psychologically ready for more flexible work schedules is sufficient to begin their introduction.

Notes

1. V. Zaslavskii, "Rossiia na puti k rynku: gosudarstvenno-zavisimye rabotniki i populizm," *Polis*, 1991, no. 5.

2. Ibid., p. 67.

3. Max Weber, *Izbrannye proizvedeniia* (Moscow, 1991), p. 82.

4. *Obshchestvennoe mnenie v tsifrakh*, 1990, no. 12 (19), p. 13.

5. Ibid., 1991, no. 8, pt. 1, p. 16.

6. A. Nesterenko and A. Lukovenko, "Vostochnaia Evropa: formirovanie rynochnoi politiki zaniatosti," *Voprosy ekonomiki*, 1991, no. 9, p. 76.

7. *Obshchestvennoe mnenie v tsifrakh*, 1991, no. 8, pt. 1.

8. *Moskovskie novosti*, 12 January 1992.

9. The orientation toward earnings was measured as the difference between desired earnings in rubles ("What level of average monthly earnings do you consider sufficient for yourself?") and average actual monthly earnings (also in rubles). The statistical probability of the reciprocal independence of this indicator and support for stiff sanctions is very small $(P \leq 0.005)$.

10. V. Kosmarskii, "Vysvobozhdenie rabotnikov: nereshennye problemy," *Khoziaistvo i pravo*, 1989, no. 10.

New Buyers and New Sellers in Russia's Labor Markets

Boris Rakitskii

An Important Preliminary Remark

It seems to me that Americans and Russians discussing the prospects for the development of labor relations would do well to take the three following circumstances into account.

First. Russians think they know what is behind the concepts "democracy," "labor market," "market," "unemployment," "social protection," etc. Alas, this knowledge as a rule is very superficial and outdated.

Second. Many Americans proceed from the premise that Russians want to learn the Western way of life, to adopt Western market techniques of economic management and apply them in Russia. These Americans sincerely believe that all they have to do is to explain clearly how to live and work in the American way and Russians will have the desire and ability to do so as well. Incidentally, the Yeltsin government views our problems in approximately the same way. In vain. No country in the world has ever been able and willing to live and manage its economy by copying the life and economy of another country. Neither culture as a whole nor social psychology allows people to be nonindependent in history.

Third. Americans and Russians are very sympathetic to one another. By preserving our own dignity and protecting the dignity of others, by trying to raise the level of mutual understanding, we shall benefit greatly, *inter alia*, in the scientific perception of the prospects for the development of labor relations.

The Initial (Totalitarian) State of Labor Relations in Russia

To know the initial state of labor relations is to know the reality of various prospects for their development. The inevitable inertia that slows down or blocks change is primarily rooted in the prevailing system of economic management and in all social life.

Labor relations in Russia (as in other parts of the Soviet empire) were for a long time based on antidemocratic principles. A person was not sufficiently free to choose an occupation, where to work, and where to live. There were prohibitions

The author is director of the Institute of Employment Problems, Russian Academy of Sciences.

and restrictions on occupations. It was practically impossible to assert and defend a working person's interest with respect to pay, working conditions, etc. An individual without rights had no possibility of joining together with others to protect his interests and formally proclaimed rights. The lone worker confronted the tyrannical system of the ruling caste (the *nomenklatura*). The degree of exploitation was (and still is) exceptionally high. The forms of exploitation were cruel and based on command-punitive principles. Such values as social protection and social justice acquired an extremely deformed, distorted form. An individual felt protected if he submitted to the tyranny absolutely. What was "offered," i.e., granted by the leadership, was considered just. Distinctions between the different castes (the party apparatus, the military-industrial complex, the generals, state security, ordinary workers, peasants, etc.) as well as egalitarianism in what was "offered" within each caste were simultaneously considered as just.

With the transition from antidemocratic to democratic procedures, the old order of labor relations has a noticeable and, what is more, a negative impact. First, it impedes the formation of partnership relations because working people are accustomed to behaving passively and obediently toward their employers. Second, the old order encourages dictatorial methods of managing labor, the infringement of rights and freedoms, and the ignoring of problems of social protection.

This is vividly illustrated by the beginning of the reform in Russia. The government promised very little in the way of social protection. In actual fact it launched an economic attack on the people and drove 100 percent of workers, employees, and peasants to the poverty level. The government organized a manyfold increase in prices (10–40-fold for most goods), did its utmost to prevent earnings from rising, and did not even keep its extremely modest promises to raise incomes. It snarls spitefully at critical remarks. And for all that, the population is as yet powerless to resist the robbery, to defend at least its previous (essentially beggarly) standard of living. The totalitarian nature of the initial labor relations has acted as a reserve of the government in its antipeople reforms and has stripped working people of the ability to resist.

The Labor Market

The labor market began emerging back in the totalitarian era with the formation of shadow (illegally acquired and illegally employed) capital. Naturally, the labor market also emerged as a form of illegal relations, as a shadow labor market. With the corruption of the ruling *nomenklatura* caste, illegal economic activity, including shadow labor-market relations, ceased to be risky and superprofits became stable. Part of the superprofits were channeled into increased earnings. The shadow labor market retained a high degree of exploitation and thereby showed that the totalitarian state was shamelessly squeezing a great deal out of working people.

The legalization of nonstate economic forms after 1986 (cooperatives, individual labor activity, and later, private capitalist enterprises with hired labor) helped to legalize the shadow labor market and expanded the sphere of labor-market relations that differed from the earlier nonmarket relations.

Here we must note a very important point that is a key to understanding the entire Russian situation. Formally, people were hired at state enterprises and joined collective farms. In actual fact, however, the labor relations were not market relations because labor power was not bought and sold and there were no subjects—buyer and seller—with equal rights. A totalitarian system distributes labor power in a centralized manner (either directly or by forming the structure of jobs), and *attaches* the worker to the enterprise. I fear that Americans will find it very difficult to understand the specific nature of these attachment relations. In extreme cases, this attachment takes the form of crude force (convict labor, stripping collective farmers of the right to leave a collective farm, etc.). But one should not think that all that needs to be done is to eliminate attachment and the worker will begin behaving like a free agent in the labor market. This does not apply to the majority of workers. The situation in recent months confirms this point.

In 1990–91 legislators and the governments of the USSR and Russia cleared the way for labor-market relations. In particular, employment laws were passed. Labor exchanges were established. The status of the unemployed was legislatively defined, and the procedure for retraining, for providing government assistance in job placement, as well as a democratic procedure for establishing the minimum wage were instituted. Previous laws guaranteeing employment rights have lost their legal force. Even though the norms of these laws were not observed in fact, they did have propaganda value. As practice shows, the new laws, just like the previous ones, are also not being implemented. On the whole, however, the labor-relations situation has shifted, has ceased to stagnate. Under these conditions, working people are finding—with some concern—that their declared labor rights that had just been guaranteed (under the old laws) are not guaranteed to the previous extent under the new laws. Instead of guarantees as a state obligation, a system of compensation and assistance is established and a system of guarantees is established only in part. Social protection (at least according to legal norms) is diminishing.

According to the logic of the transition from totalitarianism to democracy of the West European or American type, formal social protection may diminish (because the totalitarian state uses the norms of law only to conceal tyranny and in particular declares very high guarantees at a genuinely socialist level). But real social protection should increase in the process because the transition to a rule-of-law civil society is beginning and working people are acquiring rights that are protected by the state and society, i.e., it is becoming possible to oppose tyranny. But this is the case only according to the underlying logic of the process. In actuality, however, judicial and other protection of rights and freedoms in the labor sphere has not yet been put in place, and there are malfunctions on a major scale, while the previous stable situation (albeit based on the absence of rights and arbitrariness) is vanishing and is becoming unstable.

Labor-market relations are becoming legalized and are being diffused in modern Russia in a context in which the old, very stable economic and managerial structures are collapsing and new, initially extremely unstable structures are emerging. Psychologically the working masses perceive this as a dramatic increase in the instability of their own situation. This is most clearly felt by those who have been fired from their previous place of work in connection with the closing of a ministry, office, or enterprise, or in connection with a personnel cutback. They are forced to look for work immediately themselves or to apply to a labor exchange and feel that they are useless, redundant people. Their entire preceding life convinced them that their job was in fact guaranteed. It was extremely difficult to fire a person earlier, and everyone knew this.

But the advent of new labor relations is also felt by those who have a job and are not yet intending to change it. The general instability in society affects the situation of these workers as well. Everyone now has to keep track of the situation, to be concerned about the stability of the enterprise's economic position, about whether management intends to economize by cutting payroll costs, etc. In a word, the transition to market relations in the economy, which has increased the economic risk for every enterprise, is also introducing a real element of risk (indeterminacy, instability of the existing situation) into labor relations as well. This is probably the first real change that is connected with the advent of the labor market and that appeared before the labor market formed. The emergence of risk in existing labor relations in Russia has become a precursor of the future labor market. Such is the reality.

A developed labor market still lies far ahead. In modern Russia, the labor market begins with processes and problems that are blocked or compensated and in part actually resolved in a developed market economy. In addition to the already noted increased risk, we should note among such problems the threat of mass unemployment, the lack of social protection, the occasionally monopolistic position of the buyer and sometimes the seller in the labor market, the manipulation of the social consciousness and work behavior of the masses, etc.

The Present State of the Seller of Labor Power

Russian working people presently entering into relations of hire can be classified approximately as follows:

(a) According to their involvement (or readiness to become involved) in labor-market relations:

—feel deep aversion to labor-market relations;

—consider labor-market relations not only preferable, but also the only just relations;

—relate to the emerging labor market without prejudice, but with reasonable caution, as to any change in the customary order of things.

Youth and "misfits" [*neudachniki*] (those who did not adapt to the old relations) in our Russia are in particular placing great hopes on the labor market. Their expectations are exaggerated to a certain degree. Unfortunately, the quality of education, of specialized and general higher (especially university) education has declined appreciably in recent decades. Young people very often have to count on their youthful energy to make up for deficiencies in their knowledge. As for people deprived of a normal life by the old order of social and labor relations, instead of confronting the barrack harshness of relations, they will now have to face the harshness of the demands of the labor market and the need for a high level of self-organization. Not all of the "misfits" will be equal to the new demands.

The labor market encounters internal hostility among those working people who place moral and creative values above economic values. The low standard of living and the limited earning opportunities make it both easier and natural to prefer morality and creativity. The selfless and even sacrificial component in the attitude toward work gradually acquires a habitual character and in some people develops into a lifestyle, a conviction, a value orientation that becomes a part of their conscience. The encounter with the dirt and amorality characteristic of a period of initial capital accumulation (and Russia is presently going through just such a period) mobilizes specifically what is best in a person and his devotion to morality and creativity as eternal values. It remains for people to learn in the future that the labor market and the market economy in general are capable of creating much more favorable conditions for morality and creativity than totalitarianism. But for the time being, they are making judgments on the basis of facts drawn from real life.

The majority of working people are fearful of any changes. They relate to the emergence of the labor market guardedly. On the one hand, the pay is higher, but on the other, more is demanded. On the one hand, there are more rights, but on the other, there are many more obligations. On the one hand, it is possible to resist tyranny; on the other hand, one must be prepared to bear responsibility. And so forth.

(b) According to the ability to defend oneself in the labor market:
—those who have been out on strike;
—those who have not been out on strike.

For all its unexpectedness, this division reflects reality. There are no trade unions (in the West European or American sense) in Russia, except in the case of striking miners and the aircraft controllers and pilots who are threatening to strike. Only those who have gone out on strike have the capacity for unified action. Those who have already gone out on strike do not fear governments and management. They know how to formulate demands, to negotiate, and to monitor the execution of agreements (the government as a rule does not carry out very important points of the agreements).

But, up until now, a negligible minority in Russia has been out on strike. The seller of labor power is therefore usually a lone seller who does not know how to join with others to protect his interests. Most sellers are unprepared to enter into a three-sided negotiation process. Nor do they have reliable representatives capable of defending their interests in negotiations without betraying them.

Modern Entrepreneurs–Buyers of Labor Power

One is frequently struck by the new small-scale "fortune-seekers": cooperatives, private firms, partnerships, etc. But they are not the main buyers in Russia's labor markets. The main buyers are managers of large, presently state enterprises; they determine the atmosphere in the labor markets and will continue to do so for a long time to come.

Most directors are now bewildered. They are awaiting denationalization and privatization and major changes in the branch structure of the economy. There is the threat of enterprises being closed down in the course of conversion. There is the threat of the transformation of property to joint-stock enterprises and of the directors' loss of their former real authority in production (and this is considerable).

In December 1990 major elements of the economic *nomenklatura* assembled at an All-Union Meeting of Managers of USSR State Enterprises. An appeal to the highest legislative bodies and the president of the USSR was adopted. In it the managers presented a virtual ultimatum demanding that tighter restrictions be imposed on working people and that a moratorium on democratization processes be declared. In August 1991 these demands would comprise the program of the reactionary *coup d'état* (the program of the State Committee for the State of Emergency). In January 1992 the same directors assembled at a conference of industrialists and entrepreneurs. They now concluded that the actions of the Yeltsin government were entirely in conformity with their interests even though certain adjustments were desirable. The conclusion is obvious: the old economic hierarchy does not see any substantial difference between totalitarian power and bourgeois-dictatorial power. Both provide support for its authority in the economy. The alliance between Gorbachev and Yeltsin in April 1991 made it possible to launch an offensive against working people's rights and to secure advantageous positions for entrepreneurs in the labor market. Gorbachev immediately prohibited political strikes, and Yeltsin made trade-union activity at enterprises dependent on the discretion of management.

Most entrepreneurs are still managers of the old school. They are afraid to ignore the work collectives openly and endeavor to cover up their actions as supposedly being in the interest of and in line with the opinion of the work collective. They are even not averse to supporting demands that the ownership of state enterprises be transferred to the hands of the work collectives. They know perfectly well how to manipulate the work collective and how to be the *de facto* sovereign at an enterprise by using the collective as a democratic screen. For themselves, directors of the old system would like a certain percentage of the profits and some part of the shares when enterprises are privatized.

Young (new) directors, particularly if they are owners of large enterprises, are much more cynical and pragmatic and openly declare the irreconcilability of the interests of the employer and the hired worker. They perceive the weakness of the current labor and independent trade-union movement not as a temporary favorable situation but as a normal phenomenon. An interesting fact: the formation of the mechanism of tripartite partnership negotiations (trade unions, the government, employers) was impeded at the first stage of the reform because of the unwillingness of employers to sit down at the negotiating table. Some were unable to do what they had not done in the past, others did not want to lower themselves to conduct negotiations with workers and other working people.

Four circumstances are of great significance in the evolution of the employer-entrepreneur as an agent in the labor market:

—the desire to get rich quickly and at any price (a characteristic feature of the period of initial capital accumulation);

—the inability of most working people to work together to protect their lawful labor rights and freedoms;

—the Russian government's one-sided support for entrepreneurs and the government's reluctance to support working people;

—international capital's all-round support for initial capital accumulation processes and its frequently persistent recommendations on the type and direction of reforms.

This unique confluence of circumstances has produced a kind of euphoria among private entrepreneurs. The private owner in Russia today is glorified as the savior of the Fatherland. He is the most positive hero of the time. In the sixties young people dreamed of becoming cosmonauts, scientists, and builders; in the seventies—diplomats, party *apparatchiki*, KGB agents, or seafarers. The young people of today dream of becoming businessmen, stockbrokers, and corrupt deputies. "Get rich!" are words that resound throughout Russia, and this slogan appeals above all to youth who have grown up and lived in poverty. But how one gets rich, and the moral, ecological, and social constraints that should be observed in the process, are questions that are not raised today. They only irritate our new-wave entrepreneur. Competition among the new entrepreneurs spurs on the immorality race. Those who became rich long ago are legalizing and continuing to increase their power in society and in the economy and are encouraging support for the atmosphere of entrepreneurial euphoria. But they also see the inevitability of the disillusionment of the majority, the possibility that the masses will become dissatisfied with criminal methods of enrichment, and the possibility of "dekulakization." This is why the old and the new *nomenklatura* are evacuating their capital abroad, just in case. The solid foreign entrepreneur also refrains from investing in Russia because of the instability of the political situation. But there is no shortage of foreign operators who are not faring so well in their own country. They take risks in Russia and close their eyes to the uncivilized behavior, immorality, and criminality that make very high profits possible.

The Price of Labor Power

The initial situation was characterized by an extremely low customary standard of living. This was the result of decades of totalitarian exploitation of working people. It was the intent of the Gorbachev reforms to avoid a social explosion by preventing a decline in living standards. The scenario of "revolution under the direction of the party apparatus" presupposed the gradual conversion of the country to a market economy of the West German or Scandinavian type. In the process, the price of labor power would rise slowly but would remain appreciably lower than in Europe for a long time.

The failure of the "revolution of the party apparatus" opened the era of initial capital accumulation in post-totalitarian Russia, the era of robbery of the robbed. The real value of the population's income declined to one-sixth of its previous level in just one year (1991–92). The struggle for the so-called market wage will make it possible to win back from the government and the entrepreneur by the end of 1992 no more than 50–60 percent of the living standard that the urban worker and employee enjoyed in 1990. All city dwellers who work for hire are presently below the poverty line.

Preparations are under way for delivering a blow against the peasants' standard of living. The government needs land as a commodity. A mass attack on collective and state farms is beginning, not to liberate the peasants from the oppression of the *nomenklatura*, but to recreate millions of "individual farms." An individual farm here is understood to mean not a well-equipped peasant economic unit but a peasant with land that he is entitled to mortgage and sell.

Agrarian reform in Russia may result in millions of landless and unemployed peasants, especially in the densely populated southern national republics. At the congress of the Russian Peasants' Party in 1991, I heard the almost unanimous opinion that the individual farmer would be unable to feed the nation in the next few years. The individual farmer today is stable only where he derives some of his resources from a collective or state farm, just as a production cooperative in the city is stable only when it has an economic donor in the form of a state enterprise.

Russian president Boris Yeltsin assures us that the decline in working people's living standard is temporary and that the situation will stabilize by the autumn of 1992. It is unlikely that these promises will be kept. But even in the best, unlikely case, stabilization will be achieved by cutting the price of labor power at least in half. The laboring masses will hardly agree to such stabilization.

Miners, who have an independent trade union, are fighting successfully to keep the price of their labor power at the previous level. But their demands seem downright incredible. According to the draft of the general wage-rate agreement, the miner's average wage should be 17,000 rubles a month. This is 50 times the officially established minimum wage (342 rubles a month). In actuality, with the liberalization of prices, for the 17,000 rubles they demand the miners will at best maintain their previous level of consumption (which is very low when measured by the standards of the developed countries). The official minimum wage, however, does not make it possible to survive without losing one's health.

There will be a reaction in response to the economic attack on working people's living standards by the government and entrepreneurs. The strength and forms of this response have not yet been determined. Matters are thus far headed in the direction of the worst-case scenario: a blind explosion of dissatisfaction. The government is preparing to quell it by force.

The Job Market. Unemployment. Stabilization Factors

Outwardly the job market in Russia is still the same as it was: stable and favorable to the worker. But the foundations of this situation have been entirely destroyed, and hence the old order of things may collapse at any moment. The root change in the situation is the reduction in budgetary outlays on the military-industrial complex and the army. The situation is such that hyperinflation is prolonging job-market stability that is based on high employment in military production and the army.

The government proposed making deep military spending cuts already in early 1992, but it met with resistance. Consequently, there is a struggle in progress to postpone taking a realistic approach to Russia's economic situation. But this postponement can be for no more than a few months. After this, there will be mass unemployment (at least during the reorganization of the economic structure). At the beginning of 1992, Russia's employment services recorded 60,000 unemployed. Approximately 20 percent of them were receiving unemployment compensation. With military spending cuts, this figure may grow to several million (depending on the magnitude of the cuts).

The privatization of state enterprises may also give an additional impetus to the rise of unemployment. At present there is a stable tradition of distributing the burdens of the deteriorating situation uniformly. It is customary to cut wages, bonuses, and social support but not to dismiss part of the work force. The situation will inevitably be altered by the transition to private ownership. Firings will become a standard means of survival. If privatization is carried out rapidly, there will be mass unemployment.

The Russian working people have no experience combating unemployment and lockouts. The methods employed in the West cannot be applied in modern-day Russia: it has no organized labor movement or trade unions. Nor does it have political parties that reflect the interests of working people. The propensity for strikebreaking is great.

The following may become the basic factors in the stabilization of the incipient labor market and at the same time the principal factors of peaceful reform:

—the development of a democratic labor movement, especially independent, nonbranch trade unions, and the creation of truly workers' and truly peasants' parties;

—the Russian government's abandonment of one-sided support for entrepreneurship in favor of a more objective defense of the interests of all population strata and groups, i.e., the transition of the government from positions of bourgeois dictatorship to positions of bourgeois democracy.

Naturally, both of these stabilization factors will be the result not of wishes and propaganda but of energetic political action and counteraction. Russia is renewing itself. This is difficult, as it must be in history. Moreover, different versions of renewal are possible. The intensity of the struggle is specifically connected with the reality of different—occasionally qualitatively different— versions of the future.

The Struggle for Property Is a Struggle for Power in the Economy

Galina Rakitskaia

The defeat of the August 1991 offensive of the old *nomenklatura* would seem to have cleared the way for democratic reforms in Russia. But it would take another four months before the Russian leadership would undertake to carry out its program of economic transformations. Such sluggishness and indecisiveness are understandable. The government, basing itself on the powers of the president of Russia and with the consent of most members of parliament, chose a strategy that could not and did not receive broad support among the public. Even the new entrepreneurs and the directors of state enterprises, who were oriented toward vigorous economic activity, began to express dissatisfaction with a number of elements of the new program, particularly with the tax policy. However, an analysis of the normative acts that were adopted starting in November of last year and of the first practical steps undertaken by the Russian government confirms that its intention is to stimulate private enterprise at the cost of a decline in the standard of living and a curtailment of the working people's consumption. This is, in fact, how the essence of the new economic policy was characterized by President B.N. Yeltsin on 28 October 1991, when he called it a "reformist breakthrough."

The confirmation of "The Basic Provisions of the Program for Privatizing State and Municipal Enterprises in the Russian Federation for 1992" by the Presidential Edict of 29 December 1991 and the so-called price liberalization that started 2 January 1992 mark the beginning of a substantially new stage in the struggle for property and power in the economy, which has now been going on in Russia for five years. The leaders are arguing for the unpopular measures on grounds that they are inevitable in order to avert catastrophe and further boost the economy. In reality, however, they are channeling their efforts into ways to get out of the crisis using a variant that is advantageous to them but by no means the only possible one. These efforts are directed, first of all, toward concentrating major capital and material resources in the hands of a few private persons and, second, toward creating a numerous stratum of poor and very poor people who will be forced to become hired workers or be unemployed. Judging by all appearances,

The author is a Candidate of Economic Sciences and a senior research associate at the Institute of Economics, Russian Academy of Sciences.

the leadership of Russia thinks that these are the prerequisites for the transition to a market, for making Russia part of the modern Western world.

It would seem scientifically rigorous to define the new stage of social confrontation in Russia as an attempt by the authorities to facilitate and accelerate the process of primary accumulation of capital. Depriving the working people forcibly of the rights they formally had under the old constitution and the former laws and also depriving them of any real opportunities to do business on their own (the "fencing-in" of working people, to use historical analogies) are the natural elements of a policy of primary accumulation of capital. And this is the reason why it can in no way be equated with democratic reform.

* * *

Three circumstances are vital to an understanding of the strategy of the Russian leadership that is being implemented since the final disintegration of the USSR.

First. A total, manyfold and one-time, price increase. It is easy to demonstrate that this increase is called price liberalization without valid grounds. What took place, in fact, was a monetary reform that made current incomes and savings worthless and threw almost 100 percent of the working people below the poverty line. This virtually settled the matter of factually pushing the working people aside from the privatization process, of their participation in this process using their own resources. The government did not deem it necessary to protect the people's accustomed standard of living (extremely low though it might be), although it was announced many times that measures of social protection would be of a forestalling nature. With the beginning of so-called price liberalization, more and more people started to realize that the new "government of reforms" formed by the president was not inclined to take into account the interests of the working people and the demands for reforms emanating from the democratic workers' movement and the work collectives. Even the formula "Freedom for the strong, protection for the weak," which was vigorously inculcated in the public consciousness as being a rational state policy under present circumstances, was replaced through the actions of the government with the formula "Freedom and support for the strong."

Second. Leniency toward the speculative activity of the new brokerage exchanges, which operate essentially as fiscal institutions in favor of private individuals and constitute an important instrument for the formation of large amounts of capital.

And the third circumstance. The orientation of the program of forcible privatization toward the final, legal assignment of the property that was created by the labor of the people to the old and new nomenklatura, to the previous owners of shadow-economy capital, and to the new "businessmen" [*biznesmeny*]—speculators who have always managed to make themselves rich on unhealthy economic market conditions. In the basic provisions of the program for privatizing enterprises, the government has also included measures stimulating the massive participation of foreign capital in the privatization.

The plundering of state property that had been considered in the USSR as belonging to all the people took place actively both in 1990 and in 1991. To be sure, our *nomenklatura*—as embodied in ministries, boards of directors, CPSU committees, the bureaucratic apparatus of the trade unions, and so on—was the real owner even before. But under the slogans of destatization, privatization, and the transition to a market, over the past two years there has been an almost unconcealed parceling out of the common property of the *nomenklatura* among members of the ruling caste. Various mechanisms have come into being and are functioning to consign the common private property of the *nomenklatura* over to the private individual or group ownership of the functionaries of the old party–state and economic apparatus. To do this, in particular, the old ministerial structures were converted into new (but in name only) concerns [*kontserny*], associations [*assotsiatsii*], and joint-stock companies. This was done, as a rule, without the consent and without the knowledge of the work collectives. In the modified structures, the directors appropriated for themselves the authority of owners of the enterprises or of their representatives. The method also was used of directly transferring ownership rights to state enterprises to their managers on the basis of special lists that were drawn up in the ministries and announced in orders issued by the ministerial leadership.

The legitimacy of such methods of personalizing state property, and consequently power in the economy, was rationalized by reference to the USSR law adopted on 4 June 1990 "On Enterprises in the USSR." Given all the ambiguity of many of the provisions of this law, however, such a rationalization was the result of its tendentious interpretation. The law and the procedure for implementing it provided for delegating the rights of ownership of the property of state enterprises and the right to manage the enterprise to the Enterprise Council (Board). This new organ was supposed to be made up of representatives of the state and elected representatives of the work collective (as a rule, on principles of parity). The intent of the law was that the state was supposed to appoint members of the Enterprise Council and not its special owners. A similar free interpretation of the Union law on enterprises was also utilized to justify the usurpation of power in the economy and of state property by means of setting up various kinds of associations [*ob''edineniia*] of enterprises. The law did not give directors the right to make such decisions; it assigned these to the authority, again, of the Enterprise Council. There was no rush to set up these councils, however, while concerns, associations [*assotsiatsii*], joint-stock companies, so-called holding companies [*kholdingi*], etc., quickly multiplied behind the backs of the work collectives and without their participation.

One method of seizing property that has become widespread is the establishment of cooperatives, small businesses, and joint enterprises (together with foreign businessmen) in which the *nomenklatura* in effect has come to be the owner of state or party assets.

It needs to be emphasized once more that the Union laws did not constitute a sufficient juridical base for the transfer of enterprises to the lawful ownership of the management administration or for the buying up of enterprises by those who had accumulated the necessary funds for this by illegal or semilegal means. At the same time, the Union laws also gave very few rights to the work collectives. They infringed upon certain of the rights conferred upon them earlier (for example, by the USSR Law "On the State Enterprise [Association]" of 30 June 1987). For this reason, in the process of formulating the norms of Russian legislation, attacks on members of parliament basically came from, and served the interests of, three social forces:

—the *nomenklatura*, which realized the inevitability of change and desired cost-free privatization in its own favor;

—the owners of large amounts of capital, who desired the free sale of state property; and

—the work collectives and the workers' movement, which fought for the necessity of state guarantees of the rights of work collectives to own property, to participate in the management of enterprises, and to be self-managing.

The conservative position, which opposed any changes, did not play any serious role in the struggle among the social forces. The interests of the former ruling caste and the corrupt segments became transformed primarily into the task of exchanging their departing real power and stolen wealth for legal private property. This is apparently why the August rebellion of the most reactionary circles was doomed from the start. The rebirth of dictatorship in Russia remains a real danger even today. Moreover, methods of forcibly imposing the new forms of life are already under way. But the economic base of the dictatorship (the structure of economic relations) and its legal format can no longer be exactly the same as they were during the time of Stalin or before Gorbachev. There are no social forces that are sufficiently powerful, motivated, or capable of returning the country to the past. At the same time, the content of Russian laws has been substantially influenced by the interest of state bureaucrats in getting rich by using the methodologies inherited from the old party–state and economic apparatus—that is, by extorting money for dispensing favors and privileges and simply for performing their official duties. In the laws on enterprises and entrepreneurial activity and on privatization and in the program of privatization of 29 December 1991, there are a great many norms that needlessly farm final decisions out to state organs. It would be naïve to assume that this is the result of the incompetence of the authors of the laws and persons who advocated these norms. There is frequent proof in the press of the flourishing of corruption both in the legislative organs of Russia and in the central executive apparatus. It is reasonable to assume that the need to retain this possibility was a more important factor in the legislative assignment of quite broad powers to various state structures than was the necessity of ensuring permanent state control over the course of the reforms.

* * *

Reform, according to the scenario of the primary accumulation of capital, broadens the social base of the movement for the working people's right to power and property in the economy. The impetus was provided for this movement as early as 1986 by the Twenty-seventh CPSU Congress, in whose materials there was much discussion about expanding the working people's participation in management and (most important) the desirability of setting up elected councils of work collectives at enterprises.

The idea of the democratization of production has traveled a curious road since 1986—from the conception of socialist self-management of work collectives, to demands that enterprises be turned over free of charge to the collective–share-based ownership of the workers employed at them, and to the struggle for simply dividing up state property among the whole population through the use of privatization checks [cheki]. At present the Russian leadership seriously intends to use their sale at auction as the main method of privatizing enterprises. Under these conditions, many of those who previously advocated the idea of public property and collective self-management to the fullest extent are now going over to a position of rear-guard action: they are attempting to prove that the work collective has ownership rights to part of the enterprise's property and are trying to have this right recorded in the laws.

The mechanism of realizing the principle of the self-management of the work collective was first set forth, at least to some extent, in 1987 in the USSR Law "On the State Enterprise (Association)." In this law the principle was formulated in terms of participation by the whole collective in working out the most important decisions and monitoring their implementation, of the elective status of managers, and of one-man management in running the enterprise. The authority of the work collective was supposed to be exercised by the collective's general meeting (or by a representative conference) and by the Council of the Work Collective elected by them. The collective or the Council of the Work Collective (CWC) was given rights such as that of electing the manager of the enterprise; approving production-development plans and internal labor regulations; deciding matters having to do with improving the management of the enterprise and the system for remunerating labor, the use of economic incentive funds, the production-development fund, and a number of other rights.

The USSR Law "On Enterprises in the USSR" (of 4 June 1990) stripped the work collectives of state enterprises of those functions that the previous law had given them and introduced a new mechanism for managing the enterprise with the aid of a new institution—the Enterprise Council (Board). The work collective retained the ability to elect the Council of the Work Collective, but the law did not leave it any real functions or rights. Moreover, the enterprise manager is no longer elected by the work collective but is hired by the owner (the state) or by the Enterprise Council. The law of 4 June was an important victory for the *nomenklatura* that was restructuring itself on the road to privatization under conditions that preserved its power in the economy.

After the adoption of the Union law on enterprises, a campaign to disband the councils of work collectives began. Many of the councils, seeing no point to their existence, disbanded themselves. The ministries and departments concluded contracts with enterprise managers (directors) without the consent of the work collectives and without consulting with them about the terms of the contract.

In response to all these actions by the legislators and executive authorities, a new civic movement came into being in the country advocating the retention (reinstatement) of the previous mechanism and the expansion of the self-management of work collectives. The initiators and active participants in the movement were the representatives of the councils of work collectives. In December of 1990 their efforts resulted in the establishment of an interrepublic Union of Work Collectives, and regional unions were created, in particular in Leningrad and Moscow. The movement supported the genuine participation of the work collectives in the management of state enterprises; the collective's free choice of a new form of ownership in the course of economic reforms; and the transfer of enterprises to collective ownership by the workers on terms acceptable to the collective rather than by means of a plundering buyout. By the end of 1990 the movement had achieved a number of successes in Russia. The RSFSR Law "On Enterprises and Entrepreneurial Activity in the RSFSR" of 25 December 1990 reinstated the CWCs at enterprises and again conferred a number of genuine rights on the collective. For example, the Charter of an enterprise cannot be changed without the consent of the collective. The work collective alone can make decisions as to whether the enterprise should be leased and whether it should be bought out for the collective's ownership. Only in consultation with the collective can the owner of an enterprise (the state) decide the question of hiring a manager and the terms of the contract with him.

However, the activists of the movement celebrated their victory too soon. The law on privatization lay ahead. It was adopted on 3 July 1991. The unions of work collectives of Moscow and Leningrad and the interrepublic union tried for half a year to influence the content of the draft of this law through the Russian members of parliament. They even succeeded once in postponing its hearing so that a draft that did not take into account the demands of the movement would not pass. In the long run, however, the struggle in the corridors of power did not achieve very much. There was no mass support at that time for the position of the unions of work collectives. Their demands and the demands of the miners (who were the most highly organized part of the democratic workers' movement) were poorly coordinated. To be sure, as a result of the strikes in the spring of 1991, the miners did get the Russian president's promise to give economic independence to the mines and to turn the mines over to the management of the work collectives. However, the RSFSR Law "On the Privatization of State and Municipal Enterprises in the RSFSR" made very problematic any possibility that those who took advantage of the president's concessions would retain their new status.

* * *

To be sure, not all of the working people of Russia are striving to take part in management, to become the owners of enterprises, and to take on responsibility for the results of their business activity. Many would be content to labor under normal working conditions with good pay. There are many who believe that the basic task of the workers' movement and the trade unions is to get the state, enterprise management, and the new entrepreneurs to grant them more favorable terms for the sale of their labor—that is, to stand up for the interests of the working people as hired workers.

At the same time, an ideology that is oriented toward the struggle to eliminate the working people's real alienation from property and management in the economy remains firm in the social consciousness. Since the middle of 1991, moreover, this concept of the interests of the working people and the goals of the workers' movement has began to acquire more and more advocates and may constitute the basis of a mass movement. Such is the logic of the development of the situation that is taking shape as a reaction by the working people to the actions of Russia's leadership, which does not want to consider the specific nature of Russia and the real level of the working people's claims and does not wish to yield to demands that reforms be carried out without robbing the people.

The position of not agreeing to the working people's alienation from property and from power does not deny the necessity of making the transition to a market. What is being rejected is the kind of reform that will make just anybody the agent of market relations—except for the work collective. In fact, it is not just large private owners but also the self-managing work collectives that can function as normal agents of the market—this is the essence of the position that is opposed to the intentions of any *nomenklatura*-oriented privatization and the program of the present government of Russia.

Since the autumn of 1990, it is the unions of work collectives that, by advocating the idea of a self-managing sector in the economy, have essentially come out in favor of the democratic reform of property ownership.

* * *

A democratic reform of property ownership is a reform in which the work collectives themselves decide the question of changing the form of ownership, in which the collective has the right and the opportunity of choosing the new form. In order to make this a reality rather than something merely on paper, the first step ought to be to delegate all powers of ownership, except the right of selling a state enterprise, to the collective (if it so desires and without any buyout). In the language of the laws of Russia, this is called turning the enterprise (or the property of the enterprise) over to the full management authority of the work collective. Russian laws that were adopted in 1990 allow for this form of management.

Full management authority of the work collective means that the property is still owned by the state but that the representative of the state at the enterprise is the work collective rather than the director appointed by a ministry or other state organ. The work collective manages independently and freely. The collective and the CWC it has elected make the final decisions (within the framework of the laws) regarding all key questions of the organization of the enterprise and its management policies; they hire the manager (director) and conclude a contract with him that will reliably protect him against arbitrary action by state structures. Full management authority of the work collective is destatization. It is the kind of change that will eliminate *nomenklatura* property ownership and the command-punitive management of state enterprises. Any further change in the form of ownership or in the choice of its specific new form (collective–share-based, collective-indivisible, private with conversion into joint stock, or some other form) is the business of the collective itself, and it need not be hasty about it. It is first necessary to determine to what result some particular form might lead. The state, of course, is entitled to demand two important conditions from the collective and to stipulate them in a contract: (a) increasing the charter capital in accordance with the normative of accumulation set by the state; and (b) the right of the state to place its own orders, provided they are advantageous to the collective, or else (in case there are competitors) on terms that are no worse than those offered by competitors.

If the market compels it, the work collective itself can freely convert property into joint stock, attract foreign capital, or else, conversely, buy out the enterprise into collective ownership. The main thing is to avoid coercion in the course of reforming economic relations, not to farm the fate of the work collectives out to state bureaucrats, and to ensure that each collective can make a conscious choice about the new form of economic life that is most acceptable to it. This is what many people in Russia think today. This is the only way modern Russia can avoid the worsening and spread of social conflicts. The advocates of this variant of reforms are convinced that turning over the enterprises to the full management authority of the work collectives can, under conditions of the specific character of the state of the social consciousness, become the most effective factor in the economic resurgence of Russia.

The full management authority of work collectives, the replacement of forms of ownership on a voluntary basis, and privatization in favor of the work collectives without robbing them—these are the demands of the largest of the new nonpolitical organizations of working people. It is not just the unions of work collectives that are in favor of them, but also the Constituent Congress of the Independent Trade Union of Miners of Russia recently (at the end of 1991) spoke out for them. The same position was announced on 26 December at a conference of representatives of the flight personnel of civil aviation. The result of realizing this kind of model of reforming the economy would be the rise of a variety of new forms of property ownership and management. Let me note that the conception of democratic reform of ownership that has been sketched here is radically different from extremist demands (and these exist) that all enterprises be transferred immediately to the collective ownership of the workers exclusively and that, moreover, management mechanisms of the dictatorship-of-the-proletariat type be created.

* * *

Critics of *nomenklatura*-oriented privatization and the laws of Russia are proposing various plans for so-called democratic privatization. They propose distributing more than half the shares of an enterprise to its workers for a small (symbolic) sum and similar plans for dividing up all of the country's wealth. And, most important, they are proposing that the conversion to this allegedly "people's" capitalism be made quickly, without giving it thought, without letting the collectives have the right to choose for themselves.

Nomenklatura privatization constitutes direct, unconcealed robbery of the working people. But any forcible, imposed privatization that is based on dividing up property and the sale or giveaway of shares will result in a situation where the work collective falls apart and fails to act as a solid unit having shared interests and where the working people are again alienated from property and do not manage their own enterprises. Individual citizens holding a paltry number of shares will appear instead of a work collective. They will not have any real voice or weight in the shareholders' general meeting or on the board of the joint-stock company. And very soon, under conditions in our country, the working people will be forced to sell their shares. Both *nomenklatura* privatization and so-called democratic privatization are identical in terms of their results for the working people, for the work collectives. Most consistent with the interests of the working population is the procedure of changing forms of ownership by turning enterprises over to the full management authority of the collectives. It is most likely that this form will be stable and last for a long time: the collective will have the ownership function with full management authority, and it will not have to pay anything for this out of its own earnings. In addition, there will be much less risk of being deprived of work, less risk of having no social protection.

* * *

The Law on the Privatization of Enterprises and the Basic Provisions of the Privatization Program do not give collectives a chance to exert any substantial influence on the choice of the form of ownership. The government's program, which was approved by the president on 29 December, is of an obligatory nature; it contains obligatory indicators of privatization—precisely in the spirit of the previous era of administrative-command management. And the choice of the method of privatization is retained by the state organs. To be sure, a portion of the stock shares is to be turned over to the work collective free of charge, but these are so-called preferred stock, i.e., they do not give the workers a vote. Workers will have to purchase voting shares. The nominal value of the block that is to be sold to the workers of an enterprise at a reduced price is very low—not more than six times the minimum amount of monthly wages per worker and, moreover, not more than 10 percent of the amount of charter capital. Given the miserable level of working people's wages, they are naturally not going to be able to acquire additional shares at auctions or in the securities market.

The most cynical advocates of forced primary accumulation of capital speak frankly about the fact that giving out shares free of charge and dividing up state property are a good thing in that they lead to a rapid concentration of capital as a result of workers' selling off the stocks they have received. "The market will put everything in its place," say our "democrats," having in mind processes of exactly this sort.

* * *

In forecasting the course of the reform in Russia, we must keep in mind that the attempt to sell enterprises quickly may get bogged down because of the current lack of a sufficient number of real buyers within the country. This is why, evidently, the government's privatization program of 29 December calls for a number of measures to stimulate attracting foreign investors. However, it is difficult to count on these measures achieving their goal given the threat of an explosive social situation. Most likely our leaders will have to adjust the program. Certain signs that the leaders are taking a more sober view began to appear in mid-January. The president made obvious gestures in the form of the essentially free-of-charge transferal of several enterprises to the ownership of collectives, in the form of promising to turn over the controlling block of shares to the dock workers of St. Petersburg, etc. In January as well, the attempt—and not the first—was blocked to change the RSFSR Law "On Enterprises and Entrepreneurial Activity in the RSFSR" in such a way as to eliminate from it the results of previous concessions to collectives.

If the strategy of initial accumulation chosen by the Yeltsin–Gaidar "government of reforms" is retained, it is increasingly likely that the working people will assert their rights to property ownership and to power in the economy and in the state not only in resolutions at their congresses and meetings but also through more effective methods. Naturally, this kind of turning point will require a much more organized and more massive democratic workers' movement than at present.

The Old and the New Masters of Russia

From Power Relations to Proprietary Relations

Ovsei Shkaratan

The majority of journalists and scholars in looking at the tragic situation in Russia and the other states of the former USSR these days, view it as a product of socialism and Marxism. True, writers from Russia add the qualifiers "barracks," "feudal," etc., to the word "socialism." Writers from other states of the former USSR underscore that the Soviet system was a direct continuation of Russian imperialism and chauvinism. Some of our intellectuals write quite simply about socialism, which in their opinion has demonstrated that it is unworkable even in small doses (for example, in Great Britain under the Labour Party) and is the consequence of a theoretical utopia at variance with the normal course of life.

The upheavals of the past few years have caused turmoil in the collapsed Soviet empire. Its subjects have had to survive, to clarify their feelings, and to rethink the significance of the last few decades for the peoples of Western nations. Let us go back three years, to the end of 1988, to the elections of people's deputies of the USSR, the first relatively free elections. The everyday consciousness of the vast majority of people was filled with ideas of how to restructure the country into a good socialist state, how to improve the Communist Party, how to raise the quality of the economy while maintaining the dominant role of state property.

In the press, Soviet history was seen mainly as a history of socialism with distortions caused by Stalinism. And in the public consciousness, the dominant wish was to "return" to the origins of the Soviet system, i.e. to Leninist ideas and Leninist practice of the first years of peace, the days of the NEP. Lenin's name and times were still surrounded by a romantic haze of nostalgia for a lost justice.

Only three years have passed, a brief moment in the ordinary life of an ordinary country. The myths about Lenin and the noble and humane party of Leninists have fallen, faith in socialism of the Soviet variety has collapsed, and, finally, faith in socialism in general has been destroyed after August 1991.

The author is a vice-president of the Russian Sociological Association.

In the course of our society's intellectual quests, Andrei Sakharov and Aleksandr Solzhenitsyn—yesterday's social outcasts, the giants of Russia—by 1991 had become the principal teachers and interpreters of our past and its implications for the country's moral and social development. Alas, the ideas and feelings that Friedrich von Hayek, George Orwell, Aldous Huxley, Nikolai Berdiaev, Aleksandr Zinov'ev, and Vasilii Grossman brought to the world entered into people's consciousness with a generation's delay.

Russia was a Eurasian society for centuries, throughout its history and by dint of its geography—a society that sometimes drew closer to its European neighbors, and at other times moved in the direction of the Asiatic world in its overall way of life. On the eve of the October Revolution in 1917, it was the European line that was dominant. But at the same time, it should be noted that for most Russians private property had not yet become a tradition. The reforms of the great P.A. Stolypin did not succeed in transforming the members of the rural commune into independent farmers. The duality of the situation explains why bolshevism had to resort to destroying tens of millions of people to "build socialism," whereas in fact it was for the triumph of the Asiatic line of development. The bolshevik regime tried to destroy the national foundations for a European type of development of Russia, i.e., for the development of a democratic and proprietary society. But it did not wholly succeed in doing so.

On the one hand, seven postrevolutionary decades marked the triumph of a development that rested on "Asiatic" historical foundations, but on the other hand, under the influence of new production technologies and the vital activity that streamed in from the West and struck root on native soil, it was a tormented process of expanding and consolidating a base in European culture, a base for preparing for the market and civil society. The mutiny of 19 August, the putsch to restore war communism, which was at the same time a putsch for Asiatic despotism, was clearly the last terrible relapse into illness and the end of four centuries of struggle between the two tendencies in the development of the Eurasian territory that was Russia. In our opinion, a critical mass of human potential had accumulated among a great people so that it could now embark irreversibly upon a truly European or, in other words, a proprietary and democratic path.

The point of departure in our reflections is that the social order that formed in the USSR by the early 1930s and lasted until the August revolution of 1991 was a statocratic system. A statocratic system may be regarded as an independent socioeconomic formation in the dichotomy of "Western versus Eastern" civilization, as well as one of the political forms of modernization (industrialization) of countries in the non-European cultural framework. The following characteristics constitute the prime foundations of a statocratic society:

—the isolation of property ownership as a function of power, the domination of the "power-property" type of relations;

—the predominance of state property (about 90 percent in the USSR in 1990), a process of steady growth in state domination [ogosudarstvlenie];

—a state monopoly mode of production;

—the domination of centralized distribution;

—the dependence of the development of technology on external incentives (technological stagnation);

—the militarization of the economy;

—a hierarchical social structure, with various strata and estates, in which the positions of individuals and social groups are determined by their place in the structure of state power or—what is the same thing—by their degree of proximity to the sources of centralized distribution;

—social mobility as a selection, organized from above, of people who are the most obedient and loyal to the system;

—the absence of civil society, of a constitutional state, and, consequently, the presence of a system of servile submission, a partocracy;

—an imperial polyethnic type of national-state order, the fixation of ethnic affinity as status (defining it "by blood" and not by culture or self-awareness).[1]

Stalinism was the most barbaric and inhumane variant of statocratic relations. A comparison with the Nazi regime demonstrates how utterly merciless and bloodthirsty Stalinism was toward its own people, how cruel barracks-repressive forms of government were, as well as the lumpenization of the statocracy, and its isolation and segregation from world civilization.

The Stalinist regime necessarily embodied a miserable intellectual, moral, esthetic, and human standard. Proud people, with an independent character, who emerged to the surface during the revolutionary years of 1917 through 1920, dreamers, fierce and trustworthy heroes—they were not the ones who later formed the backbone of Stalinist officialdom. They were thoroughly ground to pieces by this regime, just as "specialist" intellectuals who believed in revolutionary virgin soil. What emerged to replace them was an apparatus stratum consisting of primitive, colorless, and ignorant little people, whose principal characteristic was conformity.

These were *déclassé* people, churned into a spiteful bunch, a new "class of managers." They knew nothing, had no abilities, but they "managed." These were not professionals, politicians, or intellectuals, but "cadres"—cadres not in the sense of the term used in the French tradition but in the Stalinist sense, a quasi-politicized grayness, blind servants of the system. The life and well-being of those who had knowledge and abilities depended on them. Until August 1991 they were the possessors of the Russian state, and indeed even today they have still not been pried away from their proprietary rights and privileges.

The core, the mainstay of this system of power in the statocratic society of the Soviet type, was the *nomenklatura* created by Stalin in 1923.[2] Appointment to high positions in the party, state, and economic apparatus on the basis of List No. 1 was made by the Politburo and the secretariat of the Communist Party Central Committee, while from List No. 2 it was made by the organizational and distributive department of the Central Committee. These lists were updated every year.

Officials at lower levels were confirmed by regional party committees. In 1932 the *nomenklatura* lists became a state secret.

From the very moment of its creation the *nomenklatura* in the USSR functioned as a hierarchical organizational structure. It comprised the heads of state organizations and their structural subdivisions, the leaders and the instructional apparatus of the party, the trade unions and other public organizations, the managers of state enterprises and collective farms, and the generals and senior officers of the army, the state security, and law enforcement bodies. It was characteristic that both progressive and conservative leaders could be found among the leaders at different ranks. However, this did not change their social position, and their special status, distinct from the rest of the people, remained stable. These were the ruling strata of society; it was they who formed the statocracy. Essentially the statocracy was not only a political but also a ruling economic stratum, which exercised practical control over all of state property. At the same time, all the other members of society were alienated from economic and political power.

The statocracy (or *nomenklatura*) reached its culminating point in the 1960s. Let us look at its concrete characteristics during the last stage of its life, i.e., from the 1960s through the 1980s. Let us begin with a graphic description from the pen of the outstanding sculptor Ernst Neizvestny:

> They can spit on and befoul the tendencies and discoveries most needed by the country, works of literature and art constituting the pride of the nation, with impunity.
> And they're as alike as can be, to a man. As soon as life demonstrates to them that they are wrong and that the people and the ideas they had all but badgered to death are correct, they will attend and give speeches at anniversaries and burials of the martyrs of culture and art.
> They take for their own the services and merits of those they have tormented, and they reward one another for the accomplishments of those they murdered.
> They adorn one another with the trinkets and regalia of titles and orders.
> They congratulate one another with awards. They get carried away with one another. They are inarticulate but they never stop talking. They are the only ones who speak, while others remain silent. They have radio and television, they have newspapers, and they have cinema. Everyone else has only one job: to run after them and thank them for not yet having taken away the air one breathes. They demand praise from everyone without exception. They are satisfied, and they are right in their satisfaction: when they say "life has become better, life has become happier, comrades," they are not lying. Where, when, and in what era have people with such qualities been able to obtain so much? And without having to pay for stupidity and boorishness, negligence and waste—or for the general disgrace of their own existence?
> History is not an innocent maiden; it has seen many scoundrels and sadists; but so many totally untalented victors have, I think, never existed before.[3]

The composition of deputies of the Supreme Soviet of the USSR, seventh (1966), ninth (1974), and eleventh (1984) convocations, was analyzed by A.

Shaikevich, with curious results. It seems from the brief biographical data of the deputies of these three convocations that between 1960 and 1984 the Supreme Soviet showed a positive correlation between advanced age, male sex, party membership, higher education, and membership in the *nomenklatura*.

Belonging to "rank-and-file working people" (i.e., those who manage no one), peasants, workers, teachers, and doctors is associated with the opposite attributes (youth, female, and not belonging to the party). A correlation of these polar attributes and groups was found for the Supreme Soviet of the USSR in all three convocations. These attributes form the skeleton of the vertical structure of the Supreme Soviet or the scale of power (the analysis suggested to the author an artistic metaphor for the structure of the Supreme Soviet of the USSR—something in the manner of a Rubens painting, "in which an elderly *nomenklatura* personage, heavily decorated with medals, would embrace a nonparty shepherd with non-Russian facial features."[4]

Now let us examine some statistical data bearing on the upper stratum of the Soviet statocracy.

The social origin of the upper-level *nomenklatura* in 1966, i.e., during the period of intensive development of electronic, nuclear, space, and other modern technologies in the world at large and in our own country, was characterized by a vast preponderance—67 percent—of people who were born in families of poor peasantry and unskilled workers, as well as in families of unskilled white-collar workers—17 percent; only 10 percent came from families of skilled workers, and only 7 percent from families of workers doing skilled mental work; 56 percent of the subjects were born in villages and 30 percent in small cities.[5]

The social selection that was characteristic of Stalinism always had a rigorously predetermined character; it was directed against the genuine intelligentsia because this system could only be built up from the social forces of marginal groups of the population. It is characteristic that in the period between 1965 and 1984, 65 percent of the Politburo came from the countryside, 17 percent from blue-collar workers, and 18 percent from the intelligentsia. But during this same period, personnel engaged in mental work constituted 30 percent of the total employed.

Technical (47 percent), military (15 percent), and agricultural (11 percent) specialists were dominant in the upper-level *nomenklatura* in 1966. This reflects the prevailing orientation toward giving priority to material production. Supplementary (second) education reinforces these priorities and above all the technical and military professions.

The dynamics of the professional and qualificational position of the subjects before they entered the *nomenklatura* demonstrates their high social mobility (in the age range from 19 to 32 years) directed toward managerial jobs in production, social, and state organizations. The group of persons who began their life careers working in agriculture showed the greatest mobility, with a pronounced tendency to enter the organs of social, Komsomol, party, and state organizations.

An analysis by age shows that those who entered into the top category of the *nomenklatura* in the 1960s (i.e., into the Politburo and the Central Committee secretariat) had begun their last job as precursor to a *nomenklatura* position at the age of 25; they finished their studies at the same age (on the average for the group), and these people entered the party on the average at the age of 25. This evidences a conscious choice of a *nomenklatura* career and an aspiration to power.

The upper *nomenklatura* of the 1960s–80s was formed in 1933–35 (entry into the party, etc.). Members of this group attained their first *nomenklatura* positions in 1939–40. Thus the period of formation of members of the top ruling elite during the Brezhnev period, as well as state personages, coincided with the period of the tyranny of the Stalinist state and mass repressions.

Let us examine the data on members of the Central Committee of the party for 1986, i.e., when *perestroika* was at its very beginnings and the regime had reached its peak. Among the 281 members of the CPSU Central Committee elected at the Twenty-seventh Party Congress, 91.5 percent were functionaries and managerial personnel of various kinds, and only 8.5 percent of the Central Committee members belonged to the ranks of skilled workers. Party leaders accounted for 36.7 percent of all Central Committee members (with members of the Politburo and Central Committee secretariat accounting for 8.9 percent). The secretaries of local party organizations were generally not represented in the Central Committee of the party.

Members of the central government accounted for 34.9 percent, leaders of Soviet and public organizations—9.6 percent, and top-level general military staff—8.2 percent. However, the Central Committee contained not one officer or general of lower rank. Only 10.7 percent of Central Committee members were working people in production, and of these 20 percent were managers of state enterprises.

Thus it is quite clear that, despite the simulation of democracy, which was expressed in the representation of *nomenklatura* workers and peasants in the Supreme Soviets and regional party committees, representatives of workers were not recruited to where true power was concentrated, even for outward displays of democracy. As a matter of fact, it was characteristic that even managers of large enterprises were also not part of the party elite. It is no accident that during the August 1991 events, they were not, as a rule, on the side of the conspirators.

It is interesting to see how membership in the CPSU Central Committee was combined with other prestige symbols of power, such as being a deputy in a Soviet parliament or possessing higher state awards and titles of Hero of the Soviet Union or Hero of Socialist Labor.

The correlation on the whole is quite high, since 76.8 percent of Central Committee members in 1986 were at the same time members of the Supreme Soviet, and 36.7 percent had the title Hero of Labor or Hero of the Soviet Union. The highest correlation between membership in the Central Committee and presence in the Supreme Soviet was found among the military elite—100 percent. The figure was 92.6 percent among representatives of Soviet and public organizations; 86.4 percent among members of party committees, including 96 percent among members of the Politburo and Central Committee secretariat; 79.6 percent for members of the government; and 20 percent for working people in production, including 12 percent among blue-collar workers. By way of contrast, we must point out that 75 percent of blue-collar worker members of the Central Committee and Parliament were Heroes of Labor, which tells us that they belonged to the labor aristocracy.

A total of 51.2 percent of members of the government had the title of Hero, while 44.4 percent of representatives of Soviet power and public organizations had this title. Of the Supreme Chiefs of Staff, 100 percent of whom were among the country's deputies, all had been awarded the title Hero of Labor or Hero of the Soviet Union. As for party leaders, the number of such persons with this award was substantially lower (on the whole—17.5 percent, and 36 percent among members of the Politburo and Central Committee secretariat). It should be noted that the first changes that Gorbachev initiated in the composition of the party elite are already in evidence here.

To sum up, one can conclude that, among those who combined all the symbols of a high-prestige position in society, leaders of the armed forces were in first place at the time of *perestroika*. It was not long before the consequences of this made themselves felt, for during the period of struggle for power between the democracy and the statocracy, five-star generals and marshals took the lead among those battling against democracy.

During the years of Gorbachev's *perestroika*, the *nomenklatura* stubbornly fought for power. They yielded their places to their younger compatriots without any special resistance, but they did not relinquish power itself from their collective possession. Thus in 1988–90, top people throughout the entire party and state ladder were replaced by their first deputies, who were much more rigid and cynical people.[6] And it was these recent "second figures" who led the struggle against the democratization of the country. Details of the latter in the last plenum in the history of the CPSU Central Committee in July 1991 are characteristic. The majority of the Central Committee members did not even pretend to be interested in such a trivial thing as the party program presented for discussion. They were interested in what was most important in the Stalinist system, namely, power over the still-mighty party apparatus. A speech by Andrei Grachev, a deputy head of one of the CPSU Central Committee's departments and a proponent of change, provoked an outburst of hatred from them. They screamed at him: "How can such a person be in the apparatus of the Central Committee!" Not the fact that he was a member of the Central Committee, but that he was allowed into the apparatus, the holy of holies, which existed to govern the country and its slaves, the caste of lifetime rulers—that is what this "inner party" had become.[7]

The disintegration of the USSR's *nomenklatura* took place in two stages, since it was a multilayered structure. On 15 October 1989, a declaration was made in *Pravda* that the "accounting and inspection *nomenklatura*" (a huge mass of it was outside the party and state apparatus) had ceased to exist, and on 23 August 1991, the higher-level state partocracy was stripped of the organizational basis of its power—the *nomenklatura* list.

The former *nomenklatura* is now for the most part in the process of vigorously transforming its possession of power, by virtue of which it had the right to appropriate state property, into the possession of private property. This process began in 1987–88. Thus, many of the first cooperatives were used for the privatization of party, Komsomol, and state property. Within a very brief period cooperatives were transformed into small enterprises whose proprietors were yesterday's secretaries of regional party committees and other representatives of the ruling elite. This process intensified with the creation of a system of commercial banks throughout the country. The Russian press, especially after August 1991, published quite a few documents confirming this concealed plundering of the nation under the guise of privatization of state property. The organizers of this process were secretaries of the CPSU Central Committee, in particular E. Ligachev and O. Shenin. In one of the documents, titled "On Some Urgent Measures for the Organization of the Party's Commercial and External Economic Activity," it is stated bluntly: "The ultimate objective obviously will be, in addition to the 'commercialization' of property at hand, systematically to create structures of an 'invisible' party economy, in which only a very narrow circle of persons determined by the general secretary of the CPSU Central Committee or his deputy . . . will be allowed to work."[8]

Managers in industry and "red landowners," i.e., chairmen of collective farms, etc., are actively carrying out their own *nomenklatura* privatization.

Life is not easy for energetic business people who are not enmeshed in the world of the former *nomenklatura* with its experience, connections, and accumulated capital. Nonetheless, not only wheeler-dealers in the shadow economy but also people from the ranks of scholars, scientists, engineers, etc., are appearing among the new rich, the possessors of considerable capital, predominantly finance capital. They include, for example, the largest stockbrokers of the country: Konstantin Borovoi, Doctor of Mathematics and president of the Russian Commodities Exchange; Marat Zolotdinov, formerly a brilliant civil engineer and today head of the Russian Securities Market; Oleg Kudinov, Candidate of Sciences and president of the Stock Exchange; Viktor Pavlov, Candidate of Sciences and the biggest shipowner, and dozens of other powerful financiers and entrepreneurs.

These groups in the new economic elite of the country have not been studied. V. Radaev and I have proposed to the government a research program entitled "Strategies of Development for Russian Business." The following questions were proposed for study: the social origins and professional biographies of representatives

of the new entrepreneurial strata; professional, economic, and political orientations; norms of behavior in business activities; lines of conduct in politics, etc.

In my view, this process of replacing a single elite that had ruled both in
politics and economics by the divided elites (economic, political, military, and
artistic) inherent in a proprietary and democratic society has already been largely
completed. A few words now on this emerging elite.

The government formed in early November 1991 by Boris Yeltsin, president
of Russia, is, in the last analysis, not a *nomenklatura* government. It was not bred
in the core of the apparatus. Most cabinet members are recent scientific staff
from the elite institutes of the Academy of Sciences and teachers in universities.
Izvestiia, one of the most authoritative Russian newspapers, published a list of
ministers and relevant biographical data on 22 November 1991. Twelve of the
twenty persons for whom the newspaper provided data had scientific degrees of
doctor or candidate of sciences and had already published in various areas of
science and technology; almost all were fluent in English. These people are
young and middle-aged (the vice-ministers were 46, 35, and 40 years old).

Almost all had completed prestigious Russian higher educational institutions,
most in Moscow. One can say bluntly that this is the most educated government
in the years of Soviet power. In addition, this government consists of people for
whom moving to the job of minister did not mean an increase in well-being,
since most of them were involved in the new economic structures.

A unique element of the new political elite are the president's representatives
in the regions and districts of the RSFSR, introduced by the Russian president's
decree no. 75 (22 August 1991), "Some Questions Concerning the Activity of Executive Bodies in the RSFSR." The president's representatives were confirmed in
November 1991 in all 6 districts and 49 regions of the RSFSR.

If one looks at the professional composition of the president's representatives,
the most common professions are engineers (21 representatives), followed by
teachers (6 persons), economists (5 persons), and physicists, doctors, and lawyers
(3, 3, and 3, respectively). About 70 percent are people's deputies and 90 percent
are members of the Union Parliament, 25 are in the Russian Parliament, and 2
were in the Union and Russian Parliament at the same time. The selection of the
new regional leaders of Russia is interesting. A rating scale for people's deputies
of the RSFSR, compiled on the basis of voting records during congresses of
people's deputies, is revealing. The rating varied from 100, the most pronounced
democratic position, to –100, an extreme conservative position.

Analysis shows that the majority of the president's representatives who were
parliamentary members belonged to the democratic wing (three had 100 points,
thirteen had 90 points, and eight had 80). But three of the representatives appointed later belong to the conservative camp. While the choice of persons with
a pronounced democratic orientation immediately after the putsch was dictated
in many respects by emotions, as a better awareness was acquired of the role that
these representatives play locally and of the qualities necessary for exercising

this role (competence, flexibility, and breadth of views, ability to understand one's opponent's point of view), it became necessary to take a different approach in putting together the new political elite. The principle of intellectual and personal devotion, tried and tested during the times of Stalinism, is increasingly being undermined. An indirect confirmation of this is the appointment of Iu.S. Iarovoi as representative in St. Petersburg; his rating never even reached the zero point at any single congress.[9]

Initial observations suggest that the composition of ruling groups is shifting toward persons from the intelligentsia in the large cities. After August 1991, dynamic and well-educated pragmatists, advocates of the market, for whom the values of liberalism are the only possible values, replaced the moralizers of the 1960s, who vacillate between ideals of social justice and equality on the one hand and the ideals of freedom and individualism on the other. The following fact is characteristic. On the eve of the appointment of a new government by the president of Russia, a large group of future ministers, including vice-premiers and their counselors, met with eminent representatives of Russian business.

However, what is interesting is that, starting in about October 1991, the press began with increasing frequency to report instances where democrats who had become ministers or were in other leading positions were emulating the lifestyle of the old *nomenklatura*. This was truly "the dead seizes the living." V. Vyzhutovich, one of the most interesting of the young journalists, noted that, just as in former times, politicians are again moving from one chair to another. Viktor Iaroshenko was minister of foreign economic relations and became chairman of the State Licensing Committee; Gennadii Fil'shin, who had been vice–prime minister, became vice-minister of foreign economic relations; Iurii Skokov had been the first deputy prime minister and became a state counselor on problems of federation and on security matters; Oleg Lobov had been a deputy prime minister and became a chairman of the Council of Experts under the Russian president.

"This is in a year and a half. If they were doing their job well, why the changes? If they were performing poorly, then why were they given other jobs? The cadre policy in the top echelons of the state continues to be made behind closed doors." The democratic elite, having become legitimate, inherited the offices, summer homes, garages, and government connections; they also inherited features of the lifestyle of the former communist *nomenklatura*.[10]

In the last years of existence of the USSR, the struggle between the defenders of the socialist choice and the advocates of a democratic renewal concealed a bitter battle between disciples of two different lines of development of the market and private property. These lines emerged after August 1991 in an open clash between individuals and groups who had totally discarded communist terminology.

The representatives of the former party *nomenklatura* and most of the management of the military-industrial complex are trying to create a market of monopolies, a market without free competition. They have already in effect privatized a good portion of state property, thereby sabotaging the application of existing laws.

Two forces serve as the main support for this former elite. First, managerial personnel from the agro-industrial complex, and not only directors of collective and state farms but also numerous officials of the central, regional, and internal collective-farm levels of administration. Altogether there are about two and a half million of them. These people have achieved practically their own control over the course of privatization in agriculture. It is under their pressure that workers on collective and state farms have received monopoly rights to a plot of land and other possessions. In actual practice today's "red landowners" are already appropriating the best pieces of land and will openly become large landowners.

Second, there are those in the huge distribution system (trade, supply, etc.). This was the mass stratum that supported the *nomenklatura*, a stratum of implementers and realizers of the planning and distributive function of the state. There were about ten million workers in this area of activity. Groups with different interests may be distinguished in this stratum. Top-level and middle-level officials in this system strive to retain the monopoly on distribution in their own hands, creating in place of the old forms of administration various associations and organizations that only imitate market structures.

The additional social army of these forces and their mass support are not so small. They make up many millions of functionally illiterate, unskilled, and semiskilled urban dwellers who have lost the peasant habits of those who live in the countryside. For them, the market and economic and civil liberties mean a loss of protectionism from those at the top, who had tossed them miserable pittances in exchange for their loyalty.

The other line is the line of struggle for a genuine market with competition, demonopolization, private ownership by enterprising people, numerous small firms, and venture capital. This line is not represented by an already formed elite, either political or economic—hence the organizational disorder of democracy insofar as it is not backed up by a mass of private owners such as is traditional in the West. An eclecticism of positions, the absence of mass parties, in other words, the absence of a stable institutional structure, is what is characteristic of the advocates of democratic entrepreneurship. The social underpinnings here are made up of educated people, skilled workers, and the mass intelligentsia. All these groups are certainly capable of forming the nucleus of an emergent middle class.

It is quite clear that the struggle for the second line of development urgently requires institutionalization of the democratic movement, its intellectual refinement, programmatic openness, and solid executive power. It is also clear that these forces also require the support and comradely assistance of the democratic and liberal circles of the West.

Yeltsin's government reflects the interests of those forces that have adopted positions of democratic privatization. However, powerful lobbies are operating in the administrative apparatus and in parliament, and they are actively supporting the interests of the *nomenklatura*-connected powerful bourgeoisie. A lobby of new entrepreneurs is also being formed. Actual politics, alas, is far removed from the hopes and dreams of humanists, far from the needs of those who will have to become the hired workers in one or another system of business enterprise.

Notes

1. See O.I. Shkaratan, "Pod sen'iu razvitogo etakratizma," *Radikal*, 1990, no. 1–2; O.I. Shkaratan and E.N. Gurenko, "Ot etakratizma k stanovleniiu grazhdanskogo obshchestva," *Rabochii klass i sovremennyi mir*, 1990, no. 3; V.V. Radaev and O.I. Shkaratan, "Vlast' i sobstvennost'," *Sotsiologicheskie issledovaniia*, 1991, no. 1.

2. See Mikhail Voslenskii, *Nomenklatura. Gospodsvuiushchii klass sovetskogo soiuza*, Moscow, 1991).

3. E. Neizvestny, "Lik–litso–lichina," *Znamia*, 1990, no. 12, p. 10.

4. See A. Shaikevich, "Portret v manere Rubensa (verkhovnyi sovet SSSR v epokhe zastoia)," *Obshchestvennye nauki i sovremennost'*, 1991, no. 2, pp. 105–18.

5. Here and below the calculations are by Iu. Figatner on the basis of biographies of members of the CPSU Central Committee published in *Bol'shaia sovetskaia entsiklopedia, Ezhegodnik BSE, Sovetskii entsiklopedicheskii slovar'*, etc.

6. See Andrei Nuikin, "Vtorye vykhodiat iz teni," *Ogonek*, 1990, no. 25, pp. 4–7.

7. See O. Latsis, "Chto zakonchilos'—znaem. A chto nachalos'?" *Izvestiia*, 31 December 1991.

8. See *Izvestiia*, 15 January 1992.

9. See B. Bogatov, "Kto ty—oko gosudarevo," *Nezavisimaia gazeta*, 6 November 1991.

10. Valerii Vyzhutovich, "Starye igry na Staroi ploshchadi," *Moskovskie novosti*, 1992, no. 1, pp. 6–7.

Changes in Social Policy
and Labor Legislation

The Gender Aspect

Natal'ia Rimashevskaia

The radical changes that are taking place in the country, and which have led to a total crisis both in the political and the economic and social spheres, have affected all segments and groups of the population—men and women, rich and poor, old people and children, and those engaged in physical and mental work.

It is common knowledge that it is the more vulnerable groups in a population that suffer most during periods of critical change, and in this sense it is women who bear the heaviest burden of the transition process. This applies to all spheres of life activity.

The exacerbation of problems in the sphere of labor activity is characterized by the following features:

(a) Under conditions of one of the highest levels of women's employment in social production, there is a substantial disparity in regional, sectoral, and occupational inclusion, verging on segregation of relatively leading [*avangardnye*] sectors and occupations (82 percent of workers in trade are women, 81 percent in health care, 72 percent in the cultural field; 1.9 million women are cleaning women, 1.37 million are salesclerks, 0.96 million are checkers, 0.82 million are garment workers, and 1.57 million are operators [*operatory*]);

(b) The danger is not merely that women are working in difficult conditions, on night shifts (4.5 million women), and in jobs that are monotonous and have little content; what is disquieting is that a large percentage of women want to stay in these jobs in order to receive certain benefits;

(c) Given an equal starting position of women and men at the "entryway" to production, women quickly give up their position, which is to say they:

—are less likely to upgrade their qualifications;

—are generally employed in "horizontal"-type jobs ("vertical segregation");

—occupy positions that frequently do not correspond to their education.

As a result, the structure of women's employment has the form of a pyramid: the higher the social status, the smaller the percentage of women.

(d) On the average, women's wages are two-thirds of those of men, regardless of

The author is the director of the Institute of Socioeconomic Problems of the Population, Russian Academy of Sciences.

what sector they work in (in machine building women's wages are 63 percent of men's; in metallurgy, 63 percent; in light industry, 70 percent; in transportation, 66 percent; in the sphere of science and culture, 64 percent; and in health care, 67 percent). This is not because women have lower qualifications; it is the result of the lower assessment of labor in the feminized sectors (among others), because, according to a certain kind of stereotypical thinking, a woman is considered the second worker in the family and can thus be paid less.

It is no accident that among low-paid workers, 85 percent are women, while among highly paid workers the figure is only 16 percent.

(e) A false stereotype has emerged concerning women's "superemancipation," which, in the opinion of those who propound it, is the cause of many of our current economic, social, demographic, and even political woes. The kernel of this stereotype is the division of the woman's and the man's role functions: she is the mother, he is the worker.

Two dangerous consequences have ensued from this. First, the barrier of social gender becomes apparent, in which, owing to the policy of protectionism, the woman is essentially placed in the position of a social invalid. Second, the transition to market relations is leading to the serious marginalization of the woman's labor power: the more protected she is as a mother, the more alienated she becomes in the sphere of employment and the more the choice of her life's paradigm comes to be gender determined. Women's labor power, "complicated" by social factors (including benefits), turns out to be noncompetitive in the labor market.

Three examples:

—among persons who have lost their jobs in the past two years, 60 percent are women;

—90 percent of the persons who were registered in Moscow's Labor Exchange in October of 1991 were women;

—when the administrative apparatus was cut back, more than 80 percent of those who lost their jobs were women.

The problems of women's unemployment and the feminization of poverty are no longer matters of theory but real facts of social life.

To complete the picture it should be pointed out that women participate very little in decision making. As of 1 January 1990, women made up only 5.6 percent of all managers. To this we should also add the "woman's inferiority complex" that has been nurtured in society.

At the same time it should be pointed out that there are a number of circumstances that serve to activate women, liberate them from all complexes, and demolish false stereotypes.

This applies, for example, to women's work behavior after a divorce, and especially when a one-parent [nepolnaia—incomplete] family comes into being. As a rule, divorce serves as an impetus to a woman's realization of a career in production. Women [heading] one-parent families are twice as likely as those from intact families to shift to new sectors of the economy, almost twice as likely to acquire a new, specialized education, and 2.5 times as likely to become managers of enterprises.

Any gender analysis involves not only the examination and study of the gender component of various social strategies that shape state policy as a whole (for example, the law on employment of the population, the structure of the budget, and so on) but also an analysis of those legislative acts that are clearly linked to the sphere of gender relations.

These acts include a number of articles in the Fundamentals of Legislation of the USSR and of the Union republics concerning labor, the RSFSR [Russian Soviet Federated Socialist Republic] Labor Code, and a number of special decrees passed by various state bodies (the USSR Council of Ministers, the USSR Supreme Soviet, the All-Union Central Council of Trade Unions, and others). Let us note, moreover, that in connection with the abrupt changes in the political situation in 1990–91, most of the bodies that adopted particular decrees either changed their names, ceased to exist, or turned their functions over to other bodies, generally on the republic level. In this connection, the implementation of these decrees— which, as a rule, were of an all-Union character—has now, under conditions of the political disintegration of the former USSR, come to be problematic. Nevertheless, in order to understand changing tendencies in the special legislation relating to this sphere, an analysis of the decrees that have been adopted can be of particular interest and can serve as a point of departure for the investigation of future transformations, this time at the level of the individual sovereign states.

Among the relevant decrees, two documents stand out: the USSR Supreme Soviet Decree of 10 April 1990 "On Urgent Measures to Improve the Position of Women and Protect Mothers and Children," and the USSR Council of Ministers Decree of 2 August 1990 "On Additional Measures to Provide Social Protection for Families with Children in Connection with the Transition to a Regulated Market Economy." These decisions have turned out to be the minimum possible portion of a formulated but unimplemented State Program that was adopted by the corresponding bodies to improve the position of women and protect the family, mothers, and children.

The first characteristic of these decrees is that they encompass aspects that are traditional in our legislation relating to the position of women: working conditions for women, measures relating to the birth of a child and caring for him in his first years of life, labor benefits for women who have family obligations, special measures to prevent poverty among families with chidren. Let us examine these measures from the standpoint of their consequences in terms of gender.

Women's Working Conditions

One of the traditional spheres of Soviet legislation is the regulation of women's labor. This includes issues such as the prohibition of night-shift work for women, prohibition against working under dangerous conditions, restrictions on lifting and carrying heavy loads, and additional benefits for working under conditions that do not comply with regulations and norms of labor protection (wage supplements, shorter work period, additional leave, early retirement, and so on).

This approach, which is oriented primarily toward either prohibitive measures or toward various compensatory payments and benefits, has demonstrated that its effectiveness is very low and perhaps even negative, inasmuch as it creates a powerful economic motivation, on the part of both the administration and working women, to retain jobs of this sort.

Starting in the 1930s, for example, the main state labor agencies, together with the trade unions, drew up and approved what were known as Lists of Jobs in which women were absolutely forbidden to work. However, there has always been a considerable number of women who continue to work in such jobs (at the present time there are about 8,000). In addition, more than four million women are working under conditions that do not comply with the regulations and norms of labor protection. Moreover, women are often compelled to be content with inadequate compensation, inasmuch as the administration charges a certain amount "for the risk." Forty-four percent of women in industry are doing heavy labor under harmful working conditions.

Obviously, new approaches are needed to create an effective mechanism to solve this problem, approaches that will motivate enterprises to liquidate harmful working conditions (since, of course, they are equally harmful to men) and will also motivate women to upgrade their skills, thereby gaining the opportunity to earn higher wages without impairment to their health.

How do the new decrees look in this light? Unfortunately, it has been decided once more to go through the very costly procedure of compiling a new list of jobs that are prohibited to women. Moreover, plans call for compiling a list of jobs for which women of childbearing age (and also adolescents) are recommended.

During the period of transition to market relations, when competition in the emerging labor market will become more intense, this decision, which appears to have been made in spite of its obvious ineffectiveness, may result in extremely negative consequences for the position of women in that market. The program for removing women from harmful conditions of production may end up, to a certain extent, becoming a program for removing them from production work altogether.

In addition, given the phenomenon of widespread sexist stereotypes in public consciousness, this list of types of work that are closed to women is hardly likely to be limited to specifically biologically conditioned criteria. In this connection, one particular scientific problem from the gender angle is the question of the essence of the biological and social determination of sex differences.

Labor Benefits for Women with Family Obligations

The general tendency is that on the legislative level women are receiving more and more benefits in labor activity, linked to the performance of family obligations. Frequently, however, these measures are of purely ideological significance, because there is no mechanism to implement them. Benefits of this sort include: the right to work part-time, to work on a flexible schedule, to have additional days off to take care of family matters, additional days of leave for working mothers, and so on. The criteria for awarding these benefits include having a certain number of children of the ages provided for by the law.

From the standpoint of gender analysis a benefit such as part-time work deserves particular attention. The very concept of part-time work, in the postsocialist context, has an interesting gender interpretation.

During the period of state socialism, one of the absolute norms, any violation of which entailed criminal liability, was full employment—that is, full-time work. In practice, naturally, this rule often turned out to be merely a formal proclamation, inasmuch as what was known as concealed unemployment existed in the workplace. Nevertheless, any formal departure from this rule was viewed as a deviation, an abnormality. This is why women's symbolic right to work part-time constituted a special gender-based structure of their labor, which made "women's labor" a field of particular, specific relations that were different from the norm and implied that women were a specific, "irrational" form of manpower. On the other hand, men's labor power was construed socially as the normal, "correct," rational form.

Such an interpretation can also be extended to other measures of labor legislation that are protectionist in regard to women, including the prohibition against working at night. But again, on the one hand, the prohibition is purely symbolic in character, inasmuch as there are more women than men working at night. On the other hand, the existing "exception" to the rule—if only on the level of ideology—produces and reproduces a type of gender relations in the sphere of labor in which the woman is accorded a special place that is "protected" by the state. Under conditions of the transition to the market, a benefit such as this also begins to take on a totally symbolic character, despite the fact that now the administration not only can but must, if the woman so desires, offer her the opportunity to work part-time (or on a flexible schedule). This is because the private enterprise always has the option to refuse to hire a woman whose labor is subject to strong social regulation, which is to say, whose work costs more. On the other hand, enterprises themselves, under conditions of genuine economic independence, are considerably more interested in making more effective use of their available work force—that is, to offer some of their workers the opportunity to work part-time.

Maternal (Parental) Leave

Maternal leave to take care of a child, constituting part of the leave time that continues after pregnancy and childbirth leave, was first introduced in our country in the mid-1950s. It can be asserted that this marked the beginning of the practice of legally designating parenthood as a function of the woman, while fatherhood was not accorded any corresponding legal status. In a legal sense this began to create a different structure of men's and women's opportunities in terms of the open (closed) character of the sphere of child care and upbringing.

In the 1960s, during the period of economic reform that was being carried out at the time, there was a tendency to extend maternal leave and strengthen its social guarantees (the payment of benefits). Certain demographers and economists began to advocate the introduction of payments, in the amount of the minimum wage, and the extension of maternal leave until the child reached school age— and, in the case of three or more children in a family, complete exemption of the mother from the obligation to work in social production, along with appropriate pay for household work and inclusion of the time devoted to child care in the woman's total work longevity (see B.Ts. Urlanis, A. Vermishev, and others). Because of economic considerations these proposals were never implemented, although in the 1970s and 1980s the tendency to extend maternal leave continued.

With the beginning of processes of *perestroika*, increased calls were heard for extending maternal leave and increasing payments for it as one possible strategy for reducing women's unemployment in connection with the impending mass dismissal of workers (see V.G. Kostakov).

It is important to see that the main point of this strategy is still the economic motive rather than the woman's interests, which emerge as instrumental, or practical.

In exactly the same way, it is only an instrumental role that is assigned to women's interests by demographers who advocate that the employment of women with children be cut back substantially, inasmuch as they are concerned by the declining birth rate that is characteristic of the population of the European part of the country and is attributable, as a rule, to women's professional employment (see A.I. Antonov, V.A. Borisov).

On the whole, this orientation toward reducing women's employment by providing longer maternal leave is also supported by the USSR Supreme Soviet decree of 10 April 1991. At present the total leave time is three years, of which a period of eighteen weeks is partially paid. It stipulates that at the end of the leave time the mother is to have the opportunity to return to her previous work place. Under conditions of present-day practice, unfortunately, when many enterprises are closing down or changing their status, this right frequently proves to be impossible to implement.

The procedure for leave pay has also changed: formerly, the leave was compensated by a fixed benefit, but now the total payment is equal to the amount of the minimum wage and changes depending on the level of inflation. For the first time, the right to receive assistance in the amount of 50 percent of the official minimum wage has been given to parents who do not have any work longevity. Under conditions of the market, this is an important change (to be sure, the regular announcement of the official level of the minimum wage has not yet become a firm practice).

The decree in question also contains another fundamentally important innovation (it is likely that a role was played in this by the recommendations of the authors of the Conception of the State Program to Improve the Position of Women and Protect Families, Mothers, and Children). Now this involves not maternal leave but parental leave, because it extends not just to the mother but also to the father as well as to a grandparent. It would seem, however, that again we are faced with a symbolic rather than a real achievement. Naturally, under conditions in which women's average wages are two-thirds of men's, it is hardly to be expected that men will make use of parental leave on an equal basis with women. Another inhibiting factor is the set of traditional gender stereotypes that foster a negative social attitude toward fathers who have an egalitarian orientation.

In our opinion, the introduction of parental leave should be supplemented by a whole strategy of positive actions. It would be useful, for example, to form a special independent body that would monitor the implementation of equal opportunities for men and women (on the model of the Swedish or Finnish ombudsman). It may be reasonable to establish a certain share of parental leave that would obligatorily be utilized by the father. The ombudsman would be obliged to examine any cases in which the administration denied a father his right to make use of parental leave.

At the same time, all these measures might prove to be ineffective in a time of mounting propaganda in favor of patriarchal stereotypes, which is a characteristic feature of postsocialist reality. Hence, it is important to support those mass media that are oriented toward the shaping of egalitarian gender relations.

Extending maternal (parental) leave under conditions of the development of market relations will bring about a situation in which enterprises will try to close down the child-care facilities on their books, in particular those for children under the age of three. In this way, women will once again find themselves in a position of having no choice. Whereas in the past they frequently had no choice but to work, now, conversely, sometimes the only possibility will be the household variant of caring for a small child.

In practice, therefore, prolonged maternal leave will limit the structure of women's opportunities and become a way of excluding the woman from the public sphere and isolating her in the private sphere.

In should be pointed out, in conclusion, that everybody loses in the resulting situation: society, because it is failing to make use of a vast human intellectual potential; and every woman, because she cannot find self-realization to the fullest extent as a person.

The way out is to be found through making the transition to a new ideology in the assessment of women's problems, one based on securing equal opportunities for women and men to find self-realization. Legislation should implement the kinds of social mechanisms and economic instruments that will assure neutrality of the factor of gender from the standpoint of the enterprise's economic interests.

Part 2

Postsocialist Marketization and Privatization: Western Views

What Direction for Labor-Market Institutions in Eastern and Central Europe?

Richard B. Freeman

The telephone rings. It is the new minister of labor of the former communist state of ———. "Professor, it's my first day in office and I'm at a loss. Prices are rising. Unemployment is growing by leaps and bounds. Output in the state sector dropped 20 percent. The finance minister says the budget hasn't a cent for workers. What can I do?"

The labor difficulties in the marketizing economies of Eastern Europe exceed those of competitive economies with stable labor institutions. Governments, ministers, laws, and countries change. Independent unions compete with successors to the old official unions to represent workers. The *nomenklatura* spin off profitable segments of state-owned enterprises. Managers with little knowledge of market economics struggle to run large state enterprises. Bankrupt state-owned firms seek government bailouts. Private firms develop their own employment relations. Westerners buy enterprises and introduce their nation's labor practices. Works councils pressure managers on wages and employment. Help!

When I told my colleague John Dunlop that I had agreed to analyze labor relations in the marketizing economies of Eastern Europe, he thought I was mad: "It's chaos, young man. Any sane person would wait until the dust has settled. Then maybe you will have something sensible to say." Mad or not, I here try to determine how labor relations and wage setting proceeded in Poland, Hungary, and Czechoslovakia during the initial phase of the transition to a market economy and to develop a framework for assessing how labor arrangements might affect that transition.

Section I reports surprising inertia in labor institutions despite new labor laws in all three countries. During the period under study, the successors to the old official unions remained in place at most work places; central authorities

This essay also appears in *The Transition in Eastern Europe*, ed. Olive Blanchard, forthcoming. © 1993 by the National Bureau of Economic Research. All rights reserved. Published here by arrangement with the University of Chicago Press.

The author is a professor of economics at Harvard University and program director of labor studies at the National Bureau of Economic Research.

regulated wage setting through taxes on wage increases and minimum wages; tripartite bodies discussed labor issues but did not bargain over wages or other outcomes. Section II tells a different story about wages and employment. It shows sizable reductions in employment in *state-run enterprises* that mark a sharp break with behavior under "reform socialism" (Kornai 1986; World Bank 1990a). It also reports increased private-sector employment, widening industrial wage structures in Hungary and Poland, increasing differentials between managers and other workers, falls in real wages, and increasing unemployment. Section III assesses the effect of labor institutions on worker tolerance of the costs of reforms, on the ability of workers who lose in transition to conduct mass protests, and on whether the institutions provide "voice" feedbacks that may improve programs.

I. What's Happening to Labor Relations?

The starting points for the marketizing countries are the labor-relations institutions of communist dictatorships. Communist labor-relations policies contributed greatly to the failure of their economies. They produced excess demand for labor, poor work effort, and distorted wage structures—all of which contributed to economic inefficiency. In addition, communist governments sought to restrict labor mobility and occupational choice and enrolled all workers in official communist unions that were "transmission belts" for authorities rather than the voice of workers.

On the demand side, state enterprises hired labor to meet output norms subject to centrally determined "soft" budget constraints. In extreme form, demand for labor evinced "a tendency to grow without limits" (Kornai 1982, 27–28). Job vacancies were immense and responded perversely to economic changes. In Poland in the mid-1980s, for instance, vacancies rose as output fell (Freeman 1987)—presumably because enterprises cared little about labor costs in their desire to meet output goals. Lehmann and Schaffer (1992) report sizable gaps, indicative of this "noneconomic behavior," between estimated marginal productivity and wages in Polish enterprises in 1983–88 and find no evidence that firms expanded employment to close the gaps. Shortages of inputs and consumer goods also impaired labor-market efficiency. Material shortages made it rational to hoard labor so that workers would be available when materials arrived. Shortages of consumer goods made nonmonetary remuneration, such as housing allotments or health care provided by the enterprise, critical in compensation, devaluing wages as a price and limiting the scope of labor and product markets. In 1988 as much as 80 percent of cars produced for the domestic market in Poland were supplied by allotment rather than sales (World Bank 1990a, 44). The individuals who received the allotments made roughly four-years' pay at the free-market resale value of the car (ibid., 45), while the producers had no price incentive to produce more cars. On the supply side, the state made open unemployment illegal (in 1985, 7,000 people in Hungary served a prison sentence for idleness), tolerated poor performance by the employed, forbade those with entrepreneurial skills from establishing firms beyond a minimal size, and often sought to limit labor mobility, though with little apparent success.[1] With low pay and a guaranteed job, workers often "put in time" in the state sector while devoting themselves to second-economy jobs, using state materials or properties for their personal economic activities. Hungary's "work partnerships" meant that many would do little during the normal workday but work hard for shares of profits during after-hours production.

State wage and price setting compounded inefficiency. Low wages made labor "cheap," contributing to excess demand. Piece-rate systems were often "demoralized": in the mid-1980s in Poland workers overfulfilled norms by 48–74 percent (Freeman 1987). Many enterprises paid workers largely with *add-ons* that made base rates a small component of pay and created significant divergencies between wages and labor costs. In 1986 Polish coal miners received just one-quarter of their monthly remuneration through base pay. *Wage differentials* between nonmanual and manual workers were excessively narrow. In 1980 the relative earnings of nonmanual to manual workers were 1.05 in Poland and 1.13 in Hungary, compared to 1.44 in four Western European countries (in 1978) (Redor 1986, 5). Differentials by industry were also narrow by world standards, save for favored heavy industries such as mining (Sziraczki 1990, Table 6). At the same time, bureaucratic distribution of the right to purchase shortage goods produced a rationing system with great inequality.

Finally, the state *suppressed independent trade unions*, forcing workers into official "transmission-belt" unions whose purpose was to carry out orders from the center. Unions owned considerable property (the facilities of the Hungarian union Balatonfured shocked ILO visitors in 1984) and allocated subsidized vacations, pensions, and the like. The party often placed its worst hacks in union jobs. Excess demand for labor and material shortages may have given local work groups "everyday power" to bargain with management (Kollo 1988) and allowed individuals to shift jobs despite legal sanctions, but overall the system made the most debilitating form of exit—half-hearted work effort—the main way of expressing discontent and ruled out productive "voice" methods of challenging work-place or national economic decisions.

In the 1970s and 1980s nearly all communist states attempted to reform this system, decentralizing some decisions and freeing some prices. However, in Eastern and Central Europe these efforts failed (Kornai 1986; World Bank 1987, 1990; Sziraczki 1990), just as did the longer-standing Yugoslav experiment with market-oriented workers-management (Estrin 1991). Some reforms may have been misguided. Others were half-hearted. Poland freed many prices in the mid-1980s but failed to curb the power of branch ministries; and it enacted a works-council law that nominally accorded great power to workers at the plant level but suppressed *Solidarność*. And so on. The ultimate cause of the failure of the reforms was not, however, their specifics but rather continued *nomenklatura* control of key decisions. When I visited Polish plants in 1986, managers shrugged at questions about the new reforms; they still relied on ministries to guide decisions, obtain supplies, and so on. Hungary's 1980s effort to engage labor in the productive process through enterprise councils failed to attract ordinary workers: 70 percent of participants in the councils were members of the communist party. In Czechoslovakia, "by far the biggest obstacle for undertaking fundamental reform . . . was the almost total lack of interest of the labor force . . . alienated from the political leadership . . . [while] enterprise management, which had learned to manipulate the existing system to its own advantage, formed a powerful coalition of resistance" (World Bank 1990b, 40). Not until the democratic revolutions of the late 1980s was it possible to replace political domination of the economy with markets. With formal state controls lifted and the informal *nomenklatura* controls greatly weakened, management had to listen to a new drummer—the economic marketplace.

How far have Poland, Hungary, and Czechoslovakia moved from the communist labor-relations system by 1991–92? Which aspects of the communist system have been replaced by more market-based practices, and which aspects persist, possibly slowing economic reforms?

Labor Laws

At the outset of the transition period, all three countries changed the rules governing labor in ways that brought them in line with Western practices (see Exhibit 1, pp. 116–17 below). They eliminated restrictions on labor supply, allowed freedom of association, accorded collective bargaining wide nominal scope in determining wages and rules of work (but in fact used taxes on increases beyond centrally determined rates to restrict wages in state-owned enterprises), gave workers rights to strike, replaced the guarantee (requirement) of work with unemployment insurance benefits, and introduced personal income taxes. In Czechoslovakia the law on employment requires that employers inform trade unions and local employment offices about job vacancies and intended dismissals but gives employers full rights to hire and fire. In Poland the obligation to list vacancies with state offices was abolished, then reinstated as unemployment rose. Each country devoted limited resources to active labor-market policies.

Despite the general similarity of the new market-oriented labor legislation, there are differences in the laws that foretell different labor-relations systems in the future. Czechoslovak law forbids lower-level bodies from bargaining for wages in excess of those agreed upon at a higher level, ruling out negotiated wage drift, and allows the Ministry of Labor to extend contracts to enterprises not covered in bargaining. These provisions set the stage for genuine centralized bargaining. The 1982 Polish works-councils law gave considerable power to workers at the enterprise level, including the right to hire and fire managers, creating something akin to genuine worker-managed firms (Schaffer 1991). This has affected privatization (Federowicz and Levitas 1992), with the state forced to "buy off" the works councils by giving them seats on boards of directors and discounted shares as part of privatization. The Hungarian communist regime gave unions veto rights over activities that contravene legal regulations or "offend socialist morality" (a power invoked in some 100–200 cases from 1980 to 1987 [Hethy 1991, 65]), which has the potential of augmenting union power in the future along German works-councils lines, but which has had little effect on practices during the transition.

Rates of Unionization

While union-reported membership figures in the marketizing economies are undoubtedly exaggerations due to rivalry between old and new unions,[2] and while there are always problems of interpreting membership data in different countries, the available information supports two observations.

First, that union densities have fallen from the artificially high levels under communism. This is to be expected, since communist unions were more akin to government agencies than workers' organizations. Indeed, one could view densities under the communist dictatorships as zero (save for *Solidarność*) and read the recent statistics as the growth of true unionism. The union-based figures in Exhibit 2 (see p. 118 below) suggest densities that have plummeted to perhaps 35–50 percent in some of the countries as late 1991. Membership is almost exclusively in state-owned enterprises, their immediate successor enterprises, or among pensioners. For Hungary, household data from the International Social Survey Programme survey show a unionization rate on the order of 40–50 percent (Blanchflower and Freeman 1992, 56–79), suggesting a greater fall in membership than indicated in the union-based numbers. For Poland, Federowicz and Levitas (1992, 32) estimate that "in a typical firm 20–35 percent of workers joined Solidarity and 20–35 percent remained in OPZZ [Ogólnopolskie Porozumienie Związków Zawodowych—All-Polish Trade Unions Agreement]," which suggests that, excluding pensioners, *Solidarność* may have a membership that is similar to OPZZ.

The second and more surprising observation is the continued viability of the "successor unions" to the old official unions. Despite their checkered past, these unions remain the largest worker organizations. In Exhibit 2 I have categorized the trade-union structure in the countries into three groups. The first is a "takeover pattern," in which the old unions were taken over by new leaders, as in Czechoslovakia, or where union members were absorbed into Western unions, as in East Germany. IG Metall initially intended to merge with the East German metalworkers' union but found that its East German pair was in fact a subordinate organization to the central communist federation with little real presence at work places. Instead, IG Metall enrolled 900,000 East German metalworkers (MacShane

1992). My second category is one of "dual union structures," where the successor unions compete with sizable free union confederations. It is found in Poland, Bulgaria, Albania, and Slovenia. My third grouping is one of multiple unionism, in which democratization has brought with it not only new free independent unions but also break-aways from the old official confederation. Hungary and Romania are the prime examples, though Russia may also fall into this case as successors to the old unions fragment.

Why, given freedom of association and the existence of new independent alternatives, have workers not "tossed out the scoundrels" or switched en masse to the newly formed democratic unions? Why have successor unions remained part of the new economic reality?

Three factors appear to account for the persistence of the successor unions: the resources of incumbency, the weakness of new unions, and the ambivalence of the new governments toward reforming labor relations.

With respect to *incumbency*, the successor unions own substantial property—vacation and holiday facilities, buildings, newspapers, and so on—amassed under the communist dictatorship and in many cases continue to manage social-fund expenditures in enterprises. They have experienced representatives in work places and large full-time staffs to communicate and organize activities. In Hungary the successor unions often maintain close ties with management (managers were members of the union until 1990), which discourages the formation of rivals. The monthly *LIGA News*, put out by the new independent union movement, reports cases of firings for new union activity in every edition. In Poland, the local leadership of OPZZ is in many cases made up of management.

The continued control by successor unions of assets obtained by taxing all workers is a major bone of contention. In Poland, OPZZ used financial chicanery to minimize the possibility that resources seized during martial law from *Solidarność* will be returned to that organization. In Hungary, the state enacted laws in July 1991 to prevent MSzOSz [Magyar Szallszervezetek Országas Szovetszge] from dispersing union assets in ways that would allow the old communist bureaucracy to maintain control of them. The 1992 meeting of independent unions in Gdansk made the redistribution of the trade-union property and assets of the former communist unions one of its three main declarations.

Incumbency advantages notwithstanding, had successor unions remained transmission belts of the state, their credibility among workers would have been zilch and they would probably have collapsed. But save in Czechoslovakia and East Germany, the official unions distanced themselves from the state in the closing days of communist rule, if not earlier, as their leadership and the communist party recognized that some autonomy was necessary for their operation. In Poland, OPZZ took a relatively independent stance after martial law, and many Poles came to view it as a genuine union rather than part of communist repression. The *Solidarność* leadership has very negative views of its rival, but at lower levels OPZZ and *Solidarność* unionists often cooperate on works councils or in other labor activity (Dabrowski, Federowicz, and Levitas 1992). In Hungary the old official unions protected workers at some work places and represented their interests in various forums (Noti 1987). "On several occasions branch unions were able to achieve far higher wage increases than originally planned by the government" (Kollo 1988, 27), often with the support of ministers whose incentive was to meet target outputs rather than to fight wage increases. In Russia the official union declared itself independent of the communist state in 1989 and led protests against the price increases of Yeltsin's reforms. As of this writing, it exists in the form of a federation of "independent" Russian unions.

There is often a sharp division between the position of local unions and the successor union central federation. Reformers may run some locals, while the central union bureaucracy is dominated by traditional communist types; or, as in Bulgaria, reformers may control the central federation, while older-style officials remain ensconced in lower-level union positions. Opportunistic or amoral the leaders of the old unions may be, but if they can run effective unions in the new environment, their organizations are likely to remain significant players on the labor scene.

On the other side, the *new unions* have weaknesses that limit their growth. Except for *Solidarność*, they are fledgling organizations with little financial resources and tiny professional staffs. The Democratic League of Independent Trade Unions [LIGA], for instance, was formed in January 1990 with 14 affiliates and 30,000 members. In the fall of 1991 it had just eight full-time staffers. Most of the new unions were initiated by medical, scientific, or artistic personnel (LIGA was founded by sociologists) and are dominated by intellectuals who may have difficulty relating to blue-collar workers. This contrasts with Germany after World War II, where experienced union leaders from the pretotalitarian period emerged to lead organizations that were successor to those banned under the Nazis. *Solidarność*, which has a longer organizational history, has a different problem: to transform itself from a national social movement with a regional structure (whose former head is president of the country) to a genuine trade union. Still, these unions often have considerable prestige in their countries and an influence that exceeds membership. In Russia, experts view their influence as being similar to that of the nominally much larger successor unions (Gordon 1992b).

The most serious problem the new unions face is developing an agenda and message to attract workers in a period of massive economic restructuring. *Solidarność* and LIGA are liberal promarket organizations that forthrightly recognize the costs of transition. Despite the potential for increasing union power, LIGA opposed eliminating taxes on wage increases in Hungary for fear it would create inflationary wage pressures (*LIGA News* 1991, no. 2); *Solidarność*, by contrast, has opposed Poland's taxes on wage increases (*Solidarność News* 1991, June). The link of *Solidarność* to the Wałęsa government has meant that some workers feel they may be better represented by OPZZ, which has the option for demagoguery. Honesty about a depressing economic reality during transition is not a rallying cry for attracting workers to proreform unions.

Finally, governments have been slow to challenge the legitimacy of the old official unions. As of this writing, only Hungary has tried to reduce the successor unions' advantage of incumbency and to level the playing field for new unions. In July 1991 it passed legislation that required workers to sign a written declaration permitting dues check-off, which had been automatically deducted and sent to the old official unions under legislation the communists introduced in 1988 to buttress those organizations. Given a choice between no union and a union that could affect their lives at work places, many workers chose to support MSzOSz, giving them a legitimacy they had lacked. A second law enacted in July 1991 set up an October 1992 election to divide the assets of all unions in proportion to their support among workers. The independent unions did reasonably well in this election.

Why have the new governments not tried to disestablish the traditional unions? One reason is to avoid state interference in union activity that would be mindful of communist interventions. Another is that the governments' first concern is macrostabilization and privatization. Labor relations is a back-burner issue, which governments would prefer to avoid for fear of precipitating a mare's nest of union rivalry and instability. Finally, some officials may prefer dealing with old unions with a history of subservience to the state and questionable legitimacy than with new representative bodies that could aggressively oppose stabilization programs. Some undoubtedly hope unions will wither away. Given the need to enlist worker support for reforms and the potential contribution of unions to marketization, this is a short-sighted and risky strategy (see Section III).

Wage-setting Institutions and Tripartite Organizations

Whereas marketizing economies have moved rapidly to market pricing of goods, they have maintained control of wages in the state-owned sector by levying high taxes on wage increases above a given level and by imposing minimum-wage laws. In both areas their policies mimic those of their communist predecessor regimes. Reform communist governments typically taxed changes in wage funds (= employment × wage) to discourage enterprises from raising wages. The policy innovation of the new regimes is to tax changes in average wages above a norm rate of increase dependent on expected inflation. The rules for taxing wage increases and for allowing catch ups when inflation exceeds expectations differ across the countries, as summarized in Exhibit 3A (p. 119 below). In Hungary, enterprises with rapid increases in value added are allowed greater increases in wages before being taxed; in Czechoslovakia the Ministry of Labor claims that taxes will be applied to wage funds (Riveros 1991, 11). Hungary and Czechoslovakia exclude from the taxes small state-owned enterprises, and all three countries exclude foreign-owned or private firms. Since large state enterprises employ the bulk of the work force, the taxation of wage increases in the state sector should determine the economy-wide level of increases from which private enterprises can be expected to deviate only moderately.[3]

The taxes on wage increases have not, however, controlled wage inflation. In Poland wage increases fell short of the norms in the first half of 1990 and rose to make up the deficit by the end of the year, when hundreds of enterprises paid the *popiwek* tax for increasing wages faster than the norm. In 1991, average wages exceeded the wage norm by a considerable margin (Schaffer 1992, 24), making the *popiwek* a major contributor to state budget revenue. In Hungary, the norm rate of increase in wages for 1990 was 14 percent (positing an inflation rate of 18 percent), whereas wages rose by 24 percent with an inflation rate of 29 percent. In Czechoslovakia wages increased by less than the permitted rate in the first quarter of 1991 (Nesporova 1991, 18). The fact that wage increases did not follow the tax-based norms does not, of course, mean that the policy was ineffective but does show that factors beyond the tax-based policy also affect wages.[4] In Poland the limited increases in the first half of 1990 are ascribed to fears that wage increases might cause bankruptcies and loss of jobs, while the ensuing wage increases in the latter half of the year are attributed to pre-election weakening of government budget constraints.[5] Schaffer (1992) links the slackening of wage pressures in Poland in 1991 to the collapse of enterprise profits and the sharp drop in output (to which I would add rising unemployment) rather than to the *popiwek* per se.

What might happen if the taxes were eliminated and market and collective-bargaining forces allowed free sway in wage determination in state enterprises? High unemployment in all three countries, continued central-government influence on enterprise behavior, and harder budget constraints than in the past suggest that wage inflation will be moderate even without taxes on wage increases. In January 1992 Hungary eliminated the tax on wage increases, providing a good test of this argument. With works councils having great power at many plants, Poland presumably would risk the most wage inflation by removing its tax, though the danger of job loss, uncertainty about future employment opportunities, and limited profits should still deter excessive wage increases. In 1992 it, too, began to consider the elimination of the tax on wage increases. My assessment is that elimination will not produce massive wage-push inflation. If workers think that wage restraint will give their enterprise a possible future in a market economy, they should be relatively moderate in their wage demands, given poor outside economic opportunities. Only in enterprises where workers see no future will they be tempted to engage in end-game bargaining by putting all available funds into wages.

All three countries buttress the lower part of the wage distribution through minimum-wage legislation. As can be seen in panel B of Exhibit 3, the minimum is sufficiently high in Czechoslovakia and Hungary to have some "bite" on employment but is quite modest relative to average wages in Poland. The minimum in Czechoslovakia is indexed to rise with inflation greater than 5 percent (Riveros 1991, 12), but this appears not to have been implemented (Nesporova 1991, 18). The 1991 increase in the minimum raised the wages of 22 percent of the Hungarian work force (Lado, Szalai, and Sziraczki 1991, 23).

Hungary and Czechoslovakia have established tripartite consultative organizations consisting of union confederations, employer federations, and the government to discuss wage and related labor issues (Exhibit 3C), including the level of the minimum wage and taxation of wage increases. Such forums existed toward the end of the communist era, when official unions met regularly with the government and the management of the state-owned enterprises. In Hungary, the new National Conciliation Council brings together representatives of seven union confederations (including the successors to the old official unions), employer groups, and government officials. In Czechoslovakia, labor is represented on the tripartite forum by the leadership of the successor unions. As state-owned enterprises dominate the employers' federations and decision-making power resides with the government, the forums should not be confused with West European "social-partners" negotiations. Some observers, including members of the forums, dismiss them as pro forma. In Czechoslovakia the unions argued for higher minimum wages at tripartite meetings, but the government refused their demands. The 1991 General Agreement set measures to regulate the growth of wages, inflation adjustments, and the minimum desired by the government. In Hungary employers and unions pushed successfully for elimination of the tax on excess wage increases earlier than the government desired. The Conciliation Council also played a role in ending the taxi-drivers' strike in 1990. The animus between *Solidarność* and OPZZ has kept Poland from using such tripartite bodies to any extent, though the unions lobby in the Sejm in defense of their interests. "Parliament is the only place where NSZZ *Solidarność* can effectively defend workers interests as long as the state remains the main employer" (*Solidarność News* 1991, no. 166 [September]). Many of the other marketizing economies have also instituted tripartite forums for discussing labor-market issues. Without federations of private employers and the unionization of private employers, however, these forums are best viewed as places for public-sector workers' unions to negotiate with the state.

II. What's Happening in the Labor Market?

Measuring labor outcomes in the marketizing economies is difficult. Employment and wage statistics refer largely to the state-owned sector. Information is sparse on sizable growing shadow economies. Unemployment figures refer to people who apply for benefits rather than to respondents to a labor-force survey. Price indices do not reflect shortages or quality of goods. This said, the available data suggest substantial changes in economic behavior in the transition:

(1) State-owned firms have reduced employment, largely through attrition and reduced hiring. Traditional job vacancies have disappeared, replaced by joblessness that can bankrupt incipient unemployment benefit systems.

(2) Real earnings and living standards have fallen; and the wage structure has widened in Hungary and Poland but not in Czechoslovakia. Still, opinion poll

data show that the costs of transition had not seriously taxed the population as of late 1991.

Employment and Vacancies

Employment in the socialist sector (corrected where possible for changes in form of employment as some enterprises became private) fell sharply in the initial phase of transition in all three countries. In Poland, socialized-sector employment fell by 15 percent from the first quarter of 1988 to the first quarter of 1991. In Czechoslovakia, employment dropped by 2.5 percent between 1989 and 1990, with the decline accelerating toward the end of the year (fourth quarter 1990 employment was 5 percent less than fourth quarter employment a year earlier) (Nesporova 1991, 5). In Hungary employment fell by 23 percent from the first quarter of 1989 to the first quarter of 1991. By contrast, in each country private-sector employment rose. In Poland, the share of the private sector in nonagricultural employment increased from 16 percent to 21 percent between 1989 and 1990 (Berg and Sachs 1992, Table 14); in Hungary it grew from 5 percent in 1983 to 11 percent in January 1990 (Lado, Szalai, and Sziraczki 1991, 11); in Czechoslovakia, it rose from 3 percent in 1990 to perhaps 7 percent in 1991 (Nesporova 1991, 6). As in the West, most of the fall in employment was accomplished through attrition. In Hungary "enterprise managers systematically targeted elderly employees and working pensioners" (Lado, Szalai, and Sziraczki 1991, 9). In Poland, just 16 percent of the registered unemployed were involved in group layoffs (10 percent or more of the work force, or at least 100 persons, is laid off) in 1990. Information on hiring and separation rates in the state-owned sector in Poland shows that the drop in hiring was more important than rising separations in the reduction in employment of full-time employees (see table below, in thousands):

	1986	1987	1988	1989	1990	Change, 1987–90
Hirings	2,375	2,255	1,960	1,908	1,453	–36%
Separations	2,377	2,361	2,178	2,417	2,594	10%

Because the official data classify as separations retail-trade workers who shifted from cooperative to private employment when their enterprises privatized, the role of separations is in fact exaggerated in the data. Adjusting for the change in classifications suggests that there were 2,195,000 separations in 1990, a 7 percent decline since 1987, making the fall in hirings the sole cause of the 1987–90 reduction in employment.[6]

Consistent with this picture of changed state-enterprise behavior, the vacancies that had characterized communist economies plummeted while previously "nonexistent" unemployment rose. In Poland in 1986 there were over a quarter million vacancies; in 1991, there were just 40,000–50,000. In Hungary there were over 75,000 vacancies in the second quarter of 1986; in early 1991, 13,000. The ratio of unemployment to vacancies rose almost exponentially. By mid-1991, the ratio of unemployment to vacancies was nearly six to one on Czechoslovakia, eleven to one in Hungary, and thirty-three to one in Poland.

Relative Wages

Given the narrow wage distributions under communism, marketization should widen wage structures. There is evidence of widening in state-owned manufacturing in Poland and Hungary but not in Czechoslovakia (Exhibit 4, p. 120 below) and evidence of rising skill differentials along various dimensions in Hungary.

In Poland the widening of the interindustry wage structure roughly coincided with the change in regime at the end of the 1980s and was accompanied by a rising dispersion of wages across firms related to profitability. In 1989 wages were essentially unrelated to enterprise profitability, whereas in 1990 wages were higher in the more profitable enterprises (Schaffer 1991, 43). While competitive theory suggests that profitability and wages should be uncorrelated in a well-functioning market, in fact profitability and wages go together in many Western countries, such as the United States.

In Hungary, the interindustry coefficient of variation rose from 0.106 in 1981 to 0.162 in 1987, then jumped to 0.227 in 1990. The ratio of nonmanual to manual earnings rose from 1978 to 1987 by 13 percentage points; the earnings of small-scale private-sector producers went from 20 percent above national income per capita in 1982 to 55 percent above in 1987 (ILO 1990, Table 30); and income from work in the private sector rose from 6.5 percent of net income in 1980 to 14 percent in 1990 (Lado, Szalai, and Sziraczki 1991, 60). There is also evidence of sizable increases in the pay of managers relative to other workers in state-owned firms: between 1986 and 1990 the ratio of managers' pay to physical workers' pay jumped from 1.9 to 3.0 in the food industry, from 1.6 to 2.4 in textiles, and from 2.3 to 2.7 in engineering (Vanyai and Viszt 1992, Table 6). In addition, earnings were higher in small than in large companies[7] (ibid., 64) and in private than in state-owned companies (Lado, Szalai, and Sziraczki 1991, 64–65). From 1989 to 1991 over two-thirds of managers, professionals, and skilled workers had increases in real earnings compared to one-half of less-skilled workers (Ferge 1991b, 12). The ratio of earnings between the top and bottom decile in Hungary jumped from 5.0 to 6.0 largely "because the rich are getting significantly richer" (ibid., 11). The college–high school differential in Hungary in 1986 was 1.53 compared to 1.29 in Czechoslovakia (1988) and 1.16 in Poland (1988).

In Czechoslovakia, the data show no rise in wage differentials by industry, but public opinion seems quite favorable toward increased inequality. A 1990 opinion poll reports that a majority said "definitely yes" to the question whether differences in wages should be higher, while 42 percent said it is right that really competent people should have lots of money, be it even millions (Stem Survey Organization, December 1990).

Unemployment

The contraction of the state-owned sector is an important step toward a market economy based on private ownership. If workers displaced from state jobs and new entrants to the job market quickly found employment in the growing private sector, we would proclaim the transition a roaring success. Data on private-sector employment and on unemployment show that this has not been the case. The private sector has not grown enough to absorb all the jobless, with resultant sizable rates of reported unemployment by 1991 and forecasts of even larger rates. By the end of 1991 unemployment approached 12 percent in Poland and 7 percent in Czechoslovakia and Hungary (Boeri and Keese 1992, Chart 3). As unemployment refers to persons who apply for benefits, however, there is ambiguity about the magnitude and cost of joblessness. Some of the unemployed hold jobs in the shadow economy or are secondary earners in families where others are employed. Others are located in one-factory areas with little opportunity for irregular jobs. The experience of West European countries, such as Spain in the 1980s, makes it clear that rates of unemployment have very different implications for society depending on who is jobless, the social benefits paid for unemployment, and the ability of families to provide a private safety net, especially for the young. Through 1991 many East Europeans believed that quite a few of the unemployed were working or not suffering greatly. In the fall of 1991 a Polish opinion survey asked, "If government spending must be reduced, which should be cut first?" and found that 40 percent were for reducing unemployment benefits, compared to 28 percent for reducing defense, 6 percent for reducing pensions, and 1 percent for reducing health spending (*Gazeta Wyborcza*, 29 October 1991, cited in Malinowski 1991).[8] Polls in Czechoslovakia support the proposition that "unnecessary jobs should be reduced, even at the price of unemployment."[9] The vast majority of Poles surveyed viewed unemployment as too high, but 29 percent regarded it as a normal part of the market; 38 percent said it should be fought but not at any cost, compared to 29 percent who viewed it as impermissible. In Hungary, where one-third or so of work occurs in the shadow economy (Lado, Szalai, Sziraczki 1991, 18), a key issue is whether the unemployed obtain work there or whether they lose shadow-economy opportunities that are associated with regular jobs because their regular job puts them into contact with potential shadow-economy employers or clients.

Real Earnings and Living Standards

Measures of real earnings based on official wage and price statistics in the marketizing economies are likely to overstate income losses during the transition. Price indices fail to adjust for the shortages of goods under communism, the queuing for goods that reached shops, and the poor quality of goods. Wage figures fail to take into account earnings from the second or shadow economy. In Hungary three-quarters of families had additional income from the second economy, and upwards of one-third of working time was allotted to jobs in that sector. According to Lado, Szalai, and Sziraczki (1991, 6), "the capacity of the second economy turned out to be sufficient to preserve previous standards of living even amid the worsening conditions of the 1980s." In Poland measured real wages in the final days of the communist regime rose sharply, contrary to actual changes in living standards. During transition, GNP may have been as much as 10–15 percent higher upon inclusion of second-economy output. Still, no one would argue that the transition was "smooth sailing" on the income front. Ferge (1991b) reports that the proportion of Hungarians regarding themselves as poor or having difficulty managing their household budget rose markedly between 1987 and 1990. Berg and Sachs (1992) estimate that consumption in Poland fell by 7 percent during the initial phase of transition. Projections suggest continued economic troubles for some time in all three countries, which raises the question as to what form of labor-relations system might serve them best during the costly transition.[10]

III. Designing a Labor-Relations System for Transition

In a fully developed capitalist economy, a labor-relations system has three functions: to determine wages and working conditions through market forces or collective bargaining; to give workers a "voice" in the internal decision making of enterprises; and to provide a countervailing force to capital interests in the political system. The tasks for labor relations during transition from a communist to a market-driven economy are more complex and difficult. Labor institutions must remove the legacies of communist labor relations described in Section I (narrow wage distributions, reliance on the enterprise for commodities, low productivity and effort, politically chosen management, and moribund trade unions) and help create capitalist markets.[11] At the same time, those institutions must induce workers to accept the short-term costs of transition and guarantee that they share in future benefits. Trade unions also should protect members against management or government policies that may place excessive burdens on workers during transition.

The ability of labor institutions, particularly unions, to promote market reforms and convince workers to accept transitional costs while protecting them from the excesses of incipient capitalism and dying state firms will have a profound effect on the success of transition programs. In this section, a general framework for analyzing how different labor arrangements might best carry out these important functions is developed. The analysis is broad rather than specific, as economics does not have a sufficiently compelling theory or empirical knowledge to answer questions about the institutional design of advanced capitalist economies, much less of economies in transition.[12] To keep from being overly abstract, the model for commenting on labor-relations developments described in Sections I and II is used.

Costs of Transition and Worker Attitudes

Let us consider an economy that moves from a command system with a compressed wage distribution to a market-driven system with greater wage inequality. For the sake of simplicity, let us assume that prior to transition all workers earn a numeraire 0 and are employed by the state. A minority benefit immediately from the change in regimes (entrepreneurs, employees in private enterprises, the highly skilled). These "winners" obtain $W > 0$ after the reforms. The majority (losers) lose L through falling real wages or unemployment. Let us think of them as state employees, workers in heavy industry, the unskilled. Eventually they will benefit from the change in regimes by moving into the winning group, but in the initial phase of transition their living standards fall. If p is the probability that a worker moves from the losing to the winning group at every time period and winning is an absorbing Markov state, the expected value of a worker's wage income during the first year of the reform is

(1) $pW - (1 - p) L$

Similarly, the value of a worker's wage income in the second year is

(2) $(p + p (1 - p)) W - L (1 - p)^2$,

where $p (1 - p)$ is the proportion of first-period losers who moved to the winning group in the second period and $(1 - p)^2$ is the proportion who remain in the losing group.

The expected value of a worker's income in year t is

(3) $(p \Sigma (1 - p)^i) W - L (1 - p)^t = W - (W + L) (1 - p)^t$.

As t grows, an increasing proportion of workers are in the winning group, so that the workers' annual (nondiscounted) expected income approaches W.

The continuous time analogue of this expression from year 0 to t is

(3') $W - (W + L) (\exp - pt)$.

Since transition is costly, (3) is negative in early periods: at $t = 0$, expression (3) is $-L$. As time proceeds, however, more people become winners and the gain approaches W. With interest rate r, the present value of the regime change is

(4) $W = \int (\exp - rt) - (W + L) \int (\exp - rt - pt) = (pW - rL) / r (r + p)$,

which must be positive for the change in regimes to be worthwhile. Here infinite life is assumed solely for convenience, and different values of r are used to allow for the effects of differing years of work on (4). The assumption that all workers end in the winning group with wage W is also for convenience; allowing for differences in productivity among workers will not affect the argument.

Present value formula (4) provides a useful framework for considering the benefits and costs of the new economic program. Since older workers have relatively few years to reap the benefits of the change, r is high for them. They will benefit less from reforms and thus be more opposed to the change than younger workers. This is, I believe, in accord with the observation that younger workers are more favorably inclined to market reforms in Eastern Europe than older workers. More interesting, W and L enter (4) in such a way that even workers who initially lose from the transition may prefer more to lesser inequality of earnings ($W - L$). Losers will prefer a program that raises W by one unit to one that reduces the loss L by one unit whenever $p > r$. Why? Because they foresee high chances of becoming a winner and benefiting more from high W than from lower L. This is a variant of Hirschman's (1973) "tunnel effect," according to which people left behind in the early phase of a growth spurt tolerate their falling relative position if they believe increases for others are a signal that growth will spill over to them. The analogy is with drivers in a stalled lane in a tunnel who are happy when another lane moves because they think this means their lane will soon move also.

Most important, the model generates a distinct time pattern of changing support for reforms in a *fixed* population. Initially, everyone supports the transition because it has positive expected value. In period one, there are p winners and $1 - p$ losers. The winners are happy with the program, but the expected benefits to losers fall due to the reduced years for reaping benefits. In period two there are $p + p(1 - p)$ winners, and $(1 - p)2$ losers, whose benefits fall further. At some period T, the present value becomes negative for losers, who turn against the new regime, potentially producing massive opposition. Since p percent of the losers gain from the reforms in T (and succeeding years), however, overall support in the population bottoms out and rises thereafter. The result is a U-shaped "support curve," in which support falls (given some heterogeneity, the fall will be gradual) as winners and losers sort themselves out during transition, then rises as the benefits of the market economy reach the entire population (see Exhibit 5, p. 121 below). The key period for the transition is at the bottom point of the support curve. If 50+ percent turn against the program then, a democratic government might back away from a valid transition program—though if it were to "stay the course," support would rise.

The analysis is more complex when we allow for a population that changes, as new cohorts enter and older cohorts leave the work force. By assumption, new entrants expect to gain from reforms and thus add additional supporters of reforms to the group. As all the new entrants will be for reform while some older retiring workers will be against reform, there will be an upward tilt to the support curve. Thus, there are two forces at work affecting the aggregate proportion supporting reforms: the U-shaped curve of support for existing workers, and the upward tilt due to the influx of new workers. If the vast majority of workers are in the group experiencing the U-shaped decline, the aggregate relation will still evince a U shape. But if the groups are more evenly balanced, there may be no U shape in the aggregate.[13]

It is unlikely, however, that the costs of transition fall evenly on all cohorts. As pensioners seem to be major losers in marketizing economies, it is possible that even workers in the winning group may, upon leaving the work force, oppose continued or further reforms if they see them as endangering payment of social security or pensions. If, moreover, costs of transition are concentrated among the young, as also may be the case, their attitudes toward reforms may not be accurately captured by the simple assumption that they uniformly favor reforms. All of which implies that additional information and analysis is needed to lay out the situations in which the U-shaped pattern that follows simply for a single cohort is also found in the aggregate.

Updating Expectations

The danger that a population will erroneously reject reforms during the transition process grows when we consider the way people may form expectations about their chances of benefiting from reforms. Assume a population consisting of two groups: those with a high probability of being in the winning group (p_h), for whom the expected return from the program is positive, and a smaller group with a low probability (p_l), for whom the return is negative. Initially, each group knows that the population is so divided, and each has the proper expectation of its chance of gaining in the reforms.[14] But individuals revise their expectations on the basis of their personal experience. Then, as time proceeds losers from the high p group may mistake bad luck for being a low-p person and erroneously choose to oppose the program. They will form erroneous expectations by updating their experiences. For instance, they might have the correct expectation of success of, say, $p = 0.25$ in period 1 but revise this expectation down to, say, 0.20 in period 2, to 0.16 in period 3, and then erroneously oppose the program.[15] This can readily produce a U-shaped support curve, as in Exhibit 5, as support falls among high-p losers. The problem is that whenever losers weigh their *own* experiences more heavily than those of others with their same characteristics, they will understate their p and undervalue the program.

Finally, there is yet another way in which a population that forms expectations of gaining from reforms in a highly plausible and reasonable way can erroneously reject a beneficial reform program during a transitional period. Assume a world with a continuous distribution of unknown p's. Again, initially individuals have correct priors about their chances of advancing, but they update their expectations in each period on the basis of the proportion of the population that moves into the winning group (as opposed to their personal experience). Note that in this case, more high-p than low-p people will move into the winning group in the first period, so that the losing group will consist disproportionately of people with lower p's. High-p losers will erroneously reduce their expectations of gaining from reforms over time as they adjust their p's toward the (falling) average. The result is once again an "erroneous" increase in the proportion of people opposing reforms among those who have not yet made the transition into the winning group.

These considerations highlight the importance of convincing losers in a transition to a market economy that in fact they will ultimately gain from reforms. In a world with different types of labor, it is important that losers see persons like themselves benefiting from transition: blue-collar workers will expect gains only if they see blue-collar workers with whom they identify gaining, and so on. This suggests that workers in the private (winning) sector as well as in the public (losing) sector should be in the same union organization. Unions limited to losing groups in the public sector, as in the marketizing economies, can endanger reforms. For a similar reason, profitable enterprises should be encouraged by policy or forced by collective bargaining to share economic rents with workers during transition to a greater extent than they might otherwise do. Why? So that there will be clear examples of workers who benefit from the gains. This point has been recognized by promarket unionists, who have noted that "the union which wants to be actively involved in market-oriented reforms is facing a tough challenge. Persuading union members to adopt a different optical perspective—from wage demand to concerns about efficient production and market competition—will by no means be easy if the advantages of such a shift do not show up in the example of the most advanced enterprises" (*Solidarność News* 1991, 3).

The U-shaped curve of support has a further implication for the timing of government safety-net programs. It suggests that expenditures be concentrated in periods when support bottoms out rather than being spread over time (or, which may be worse, declining over time as the fiscal costs of interventions become clearer, as appears to be the case in Eastern Europe). With respect to specific interventions, even "bribes" or subsidies that keep alive unprofitable enterprises may be justifiable *if* they buy additional time for painful reforms or are easier to earmark for the crucial period when support is near its minimum level than other forms of social expenditures. Taxing winners and paying off losers is an obvious intervention to preserve support, but in East European marketizing economies many winners are in small private firms, in some cases in the shadow economy, which makes taxing them difficult.

Collective Action

Labor institutions can also affect the success of a transition program through the potential for collective action and social upheaval. Consider what might happen in a marketizing economy when support for reforms falls sharply along the U-shape curve of Exhibit 5. Many people have lost faith because they have been losers. Specific groups of workers—miners, workers in heavy industry—may see an opportunity for demanding substantial "gains" or special treatment for their sector, which will seriously impair the transition strategy. If the government continues on course, the danger to reforms is the "hot spring" or "angry autumn" of mass protests, strikes, etc., about which many in marketizing economies worry, or the coups that have plagued Latin America. Such collective action can become a self-fulfilling prophecy of failure: if people had greater tolerance for the costs of transition, the program would work, but if losers are sufficiently aggrieved to protest, the program may fail. Alternatively, the government may decide to back away from its reform program. The danger that collective actions based on short-term costs could overturn or destroy a reform program argues for labor arrangements that make broad collective action difficult in the transition period and thus for policies that restrict union activity or powers in ways that would be undesirable in a fully functioning capitalist system.

A fragmented or divided union movement, of the type found in most marketizing economies, offers one institutional model for reducing the threat of collective action. In Poland, if OPZZ organizes protests against a transition program, *Solidarność* may sit on its hands, and vice versus. Or both unions may accept the logic of certain reforms, while informal groups of workers do not. But lacking wide support, the informal groups will be unable to force changes in policy. Unions with a legacy of communist leadership, like MSzOSz in Hungary, may be able to organize protests, but many citizens will distrust their activities. And so on. But fragmentation based in part on the persistence of successor unions is not without its problems. The leadership of successor unions could manipulate discontent in ways inimical to the reform program. A labor system that encourages enterprise-level unionism or democratically elected works councils and discourages wider union groupings might be a more desirable way to reduce the risk of mass collective action.

Finally, there are examples of suppression of free trade unions—Korea, Singapore, Taiwan, Franco's Spain, Pinochet's Chile—accompanied by economic growth to make a strategy of suppression attractive to some with limited commitment to democratic rights. If a 1960s–1970s Korean-style authoritarian labor-relations system and dictatorship could guarantee 6–8 percent annual growth of real wages to Eastern Europe for two decades, many in the marketizing economies would readily sign on. But comparisons of the economic success of dictatorships (which invariably suppress unions) and democratic regimes in developing countries show that suppression is neither sufficient nor necessary for successful stabilization or economic growth. (World Bank 1991, ch. 7). And who wants General X or Colonel Z running the show if they cannot guarantee growth? East European tolerance for such regimes after the failure of communist dictatorships may be quite low.

Collective Voice and Labor Input into Transition

If reforming governments had reliable blueprints for the transition and acted solely in the "public interest," one could support a labor-relations system based on weak institutions for the transition period. However, no one—not even economic experts—knows for certain the correct road to a market economy, and no government, however well-intentioned, is immune to the aggrandizement of some groups at the expense of the rest of society. Even the best-constructed stabilization and transition programs can, and do, go wrong. Inflation costs may be higher than expected; unemployment and output losses may be bigger; workers, pensioners, or children may suffer more than anticipated. The greater the uncertainty about the blueprint and the more removed officials and experts are from the lives of the citizenry, the greater is the need for labor institutions to provide feedback about the real effects of programs and to pressure politicians to change the cost or benefit structure of those programs. The most efficacious labor-relations system for carrying out this voice–pressure function would be an all-encompassing union confederation with the resources to assess and criticize transition programs and the incentive to internalize distortionary costs in favor of a broad national economic perspective. On the information side, such a union body would provide a sorely needed reality check for government programs and technocrats and politicians attuned to the world financial community. Had Poland's advocates of rapid privatization developed plans with greater attention to work-council power at local work places, the pace of privatization might have been much faster (Federowicz and Levitas 1992). A strong union movement would also provide workers who lose during transition with an institutional mechanism for carving out a share of gains in the future through "tripartite pacts" or centralized wage-setting arrangements. The inefficiency losses due to union monopoly power stressed by economists may be of second-order importance if that power promises labor a share of the future and thus "buys" support during the critical transition. Explicit profit sharing or distribution of stock to workers in firms undergoing privatization or of national bonds can also offer losers options to benefit from the future gains of reforms.

Centralized labor-relations systems are not, however, easy to institute or maintain, as the decentralization of bargaining in Sweden shows. The labor movement must be strong and unified. It must have the credibility to vouch for reform programs to workers and the strength to win gains or transfers for losing members, particularly those who may suffer for long periods of time. Czechoslovakia and Hungary have tripartite councils designed in part to centralize labor relations, but the union movements in both countries would have to be much stronger and, in the case of Hungary, less divided for a genuine social pact to emerge. The division between OPZZ and *Solidarność* makes it unlikely that Poland could develop along these lines. Finally, note that a strong centralized labor organization would have the potential for massive collective action, which contravenes the desire to minimize the chances of such action against a valid transition program.

Conclusion

The preceding analysis has described the evolution of labor-relations institutions and outcomes during the initial phase of marketization in Poland, Hungary, and Czechoslovakia and has developed a model of changing support for reforms during the transition to a market economy. The examination of institutions and outcomes has revealed surprising stability in labor institutions in the first stage of transition to a market economy but dramatic changes in labor outcomes. Successor unions to the official trade unions remained on the union scene. Central governments taxed wage increases so enterprises would not give increases that matched or exceeded inflation, enacted minimum-wage legislation, and instituted tripartite forums to seek consensus on labor issues—as they had done under reform communism. By contrast, labor-market outcomes changed greatly. State-owned enterprises reduced employment even without privatization, producing sizable joblessness and eliminating massive vacancies. The dispersion of wages increased substantially in Hungary and Poland, though not in Czechoslovakia.

The model of changing support for reforms predicts a U-shaped curve of support for a successful reform program, with support falling among those who fail to advance rapidly in the new economic environment. It has shown that such a pattern is likely under a range of "reasonable" assumptions about the gains from reforms and individual expectations of those gains. Given this pattern, three criteria for assessing labor arrangements in marketizing economies were examined: whether they increase workers' tolerance for the costs of transition; whether they are conducive to organizing mass protests by those who suffer from transition; and whether they provide information flows to governments about program failures and pressure governments about potentially valuable changes in the direction of programs through worker "voice."

While a system of tripartite agreements that create a social consensus during transition has the greatest appeal for dealing with the problems of transition, my examination of the development of labor-relations institutions in the marketizing economies suggests a very different outcome: weak and fragmented unionism, concentrated in the public sector, and little or no unionism in the growing private sector, save in large joint ventures. This will minimize the probability of mass protests but is unlikely to increase tolerance for the costs of transition (so other government policies may be needed to keep enough popular support) and is unlikely to provide the optimal information flow or voice to the political system that might lead to more realistic and successful marketizing strategies.

Exhibit 1

Changes in Labor Laws in Transition

Hungary

April 1989 Right to Strike Guaranteed:
Extensive conciliation and mediation: seven-day conciliation period; allow two-hour warning strike; "if identity of employer cannot be determined, Council of Ministers shall appoint representative; no coercive measures to terminate employment"; workers participating in lawful strike shall be entitled to all rights, save for wages or benefits; cannot strike if court has jurisdiction over issue or during agreement safety or security of essential importance.

ACT II of 1989 on Right of Association
"Questions regarding employment shall be regulated by collective agreements," but set up for SzOT (Szallszervezetek Orszá́gas Tanácsa).

Employment Act (IV) of 1991
Establishes principles for collective bargaining; unemployment insurance from Solidarity Fund; active manpower policies to be determined by tripartite bodies.

1991 Acts on Financing
11 July—On the Check-off System: workers to give written declaration to check off dues to union;
12 July—On Trade-Union Property and Equality of Opportunity in Workers' Organizing: requires unions to account for assets, with total to be distributed among unions by four union groups (LIGA, Workers' Councils, MSzOSz, and one other) in proportion to support in election.

Poland

Law on Unionization
April 1989 very similar to October 1982 law, which had been passed as compromise between government and *Solidarność*.

Employment Law of March 1991
Provisions on dismissals, retraining, severance pay after four years of service; nominally gives unemployment benefits of 70 percent of pay for first three months of eligibility, 50 percent for next six months, and 40 percent thereafter, but in fact limited to one-third of forecasted average pay (minimum wage).

Trade Union Act of 23 May 1991
No discrimination against union members; provision for multiple unionism (ten people); right to be heard by Sejm; responsible for health and safety laws; cannot divide income among members; role in social and housing funds; employer must provide information on wage and employment issues; premises and equipment for union activity; released time; compulsory mediation before strike fourteen days after dispute; can choose to go to social arbitration committee of court; chap. 4 of Article 17.4—"When taking the strike decision, the union should ensure that demands are proportional to the losses connected with the strike"; majority vote if 50 percent vote; five days advance; two-hour warning strike; participation is voluntary; employees retain rights during strike.

Czechoslovakia

Strike Law/Act No. 83, December 1990 — Amended labor code—Act on Association of Citizens abolished all restrictions on freedom of association; establishes unions, which must notify Ministry of Interior; illegal to give wages above those agreed upon by higher level—sect. 4.2.c outlaws wage drift.

Collective Bargaining Act 1990 December, No. 2 of February 1991 — Ministry of Labor and Welfare can extend contracts; Section 7; one-year disputes—mediator required with shared costs, then arbitrator; 50 percent of labor force (not just those who vote) needed for strike; three-day notice; essential services; no coercion; viewed as authorized leave of absence; mentions lockout.

Employment Act of 4 December 1990, effective as of February 1991 — Right to employment; employment services; 60 percent unemployment benefits for job seeker drops to 50 percent of net monthly income on basis of past job for those who work one year. One-year maximum; three-month advance notice on layoffs.

Source: ILO, "Translations of Labor Laws. Ministry of Labor and Social Policy of Poland," 1992, no. 1 (January).

Exhibit 2

Trade Unions in the Eastern Bloc
(density or membership in parenthesis)

Takeover of Old Official Unions

East Germany	Subsumed into West German DGB; many workers join IG Metall and other DGB unions.
Czechoslovakia (70 percent density)	CS KOS formed in March 1991 as strike committees replace union; one-third of old officials reelected, but complete change at top; receive all property but "cannot find its place in new market economy" (5,000,000); Confederation of Cultural Workers—intellectuals (300,000).

Dual Union Structure

Poland (35 percent)	OPZZ (4,500,000, including pensioners)—successor to communists; opportunistic alliance with Communist Party; branch structure; strong among professionals (associations); still controls all union properties; *Solidarność* (2,000,000)—favors market reform; related to government; elected to Sejm; regional structure with rivalries; Some unaligned unions—miners, and local strike groups.
Bulgaria (45 percent)	Confederation of Independent Bulgarian Trade Unions (Association) (1,800,000)—reformed traditional unions; *Podkrepa* (250,000)—favors market reform; for big bang; *Edinstvo*—early 1991 (250,000)

Multiple Unionism

Hungary (60 percent) (September 1991)	MSzOSz—old official union, SzOT, declared independence 1988; dissolved 1990 (2,000,000); Breakaways from SzOT: Association for Intellectuals (90,000); Solidarity Association (150,000); Autonomous (350,000); Forum (750,000); Independent unions: LIGA—major opposition, aligned with Free Democrats, based on intellectuals (250,000); Workers' Council—aligned with LIGA (45,000).
Romania (65 percent)	CNSLR (National Confederation of Free Trade Unions)—successor to communists (2,500,000); Breakways from old communists: *Aliate* (1,000,000), *Cartel-Alpha* (1,300,000), *Neafiliate* (1,100,000), *Hercules* (300,000), *Conosenerz* (100,000); Independent unions: *FRAȚIA*—drivers, oil, teachers, scientists (500,000).
Russia (100 percent?)	Independent unions: Miners Union, Air Traffic Controllers, Pilots Federation, *SOTsPROF*—largely intellectuals' unions, Confederation of Labor—social and political movement, Strike Committees; Successor unions: GCTU (successors to old communist unions)—1989 declares independence; Russian branch becomes Federation of Independent Unions of Russia (*FNPR*); United Front of Workers—conservative union groups; Unions of Workers in Moscow.

Source: Hungary, *HUG* 14 September 1991, p. 6; Reti 1991; Jones 1992; Gordon 1992a

Exhibit 3

Wage-Taxes and Minimum and Average Wages

A. Tax-based Incomes Policies

Poland	"*Popiwek*" tax based on wage bill in 1990, then on wages per worker. Penal tax of 500 percent of wage increase beyond norm, where the norm is based on expected change in inflation of retail prices with a modest indexation coefficient. The difference between expected and actual inflation is used to adjust the norm increase in later months. When enterprises give increases below the norm in a given period, moreover, they can give larger increases without being taxed in the future. Private firms are excluded from the tax.
Hungary	In 1990, 18 percent increase in wages were tax free, a tax of 43 percent is applied to wage increases between 18 percent and 28 percent; wage increases above 28 percent lead to a tax on the entire increment, producing a very steep rising price of wage increases just beyond 38 percent, which then falls as the increases continue, since the big extra tax is the addition of the tax on the increment. There are exceptions for companies whose value added grows at twice the growth of the wage fund; small companies with a wage bill less than 20 million forints; joint ventures where foreigners own 20 percent or 5 million forints of the capital.
Czechoslovakia	On 1 January 1990 enterprises were given freedom to set wages, but taxes on increases according to following schedule: no tax for increases 3 percent above the agreed norm; tax of 2 crowns per crown for increases 3–5 percent above the norm; and tax of 7.5 crowns for increases more than 5 percent above the norm. At roughly average wages this implies that wage increases 3–5 percent higher than the norm plus the 3 percent allowable extra increase will cost the firm twice the increase while increases over 5 percent above the norm (plus the 3 percent allowable extra increase) will cost 7.5 times the increase.[a] Does not cover firms with less than 25 workers or private-sector firms.

B. Minimum-Wage Regulations

Poland	Minimum wage (zlotys)	642,000
	Average wage	1,800,000
	Ratio	0.36
Hungary	Minimum wage (forints)	7,000
	Average wage	11,000
	Ratio	0.64
	Percent at minimum	0.22
Czechoslovakia	Minimum wages (crowns)	2,000
	Average wages	3,300
	Ratio	0.60
	Percent at minimum	0.20

[a]3,000;

3,300—allowed 10%—cost 300;

3,390—allowed 3%—cost 90;

3,540—allowed 3–5%—cost 300;

3,690—allowed 5%—cost 1,125, so essentially confiscatory.

Exhibit 3 (cont.)

C. Tripartite Forums

Hungary

1980s—Communist union and state–party bargain behind closed doors; also establish Labor and Wages Council referred to in 1984 ILO report;

1988—Open bargaining with SzOT–management with National Council for the Reconciliation of Interests;

1990—New government with set of unions under National Conciliation Council —"organ of competence to address issues" (Hethy 1991, 37); solved taxi-drivers strike push for local-level wage settlements; ending tax on wage increases.

Czechoslovakia

1989—State sets up Council of Economic and Social Consensus;

October 1990—Council for Economic and Social Agreement to reach general agreements on wages above minimum in law January 1991; twenty employers' confederations deal with government through Coordinating Council of Employers; council has members from unions, government, employers; to recommend labor-market policy and resolve disagreements;

January 1991 agreement on wage increase far below inflation; sets minimum wages.

Bulgaria

April 1990—National Council for Coordination of Interests;

January 1991—Signed agreement.

Poland

1989—Establishes Confederation of Polish Employers; employer organization dominated by public-sector employers; Polish Employers' Confederation—500,000 private enterprises supposedly are members, but they employ just 10 percent of the work force; limited tripartite because state agency is one of two parties and because Solidarność and OPZZ are not friendly.

Source: Malinowski 1991; Góra et al. 1991; Nesporova 1991.

Exhibit 4

Coefficients of Variation in the Interindustry Wage Structure: Manufacturing in the Socialized Sector, 1981–1990

	1981	1984	1987	1988	1989	1990
Hungary	10.6	14.2	16.2	20.5	21.6	22.7
Poland	12.0	11.4	11.7	11.0	16.0	
Poland, B					21.8	25.1
Czechoslovakia	12.0	12.3	12.2	11.9	11.4	

Source: All data based on 27 industries given in ILO *Yearbook of Labour Statistics*, except for Poland, B, where the data cover 23 industries from *Rocznik Statystyczny*. Hungarian wage figures prior to 1988 are gross earnings before income-tax deductions, whereas those after 1988 are net of income-tax payments. Industries are three-digit SIC codes.

Exhibit 5. **Changes in the Proportion of Support for Reforms**

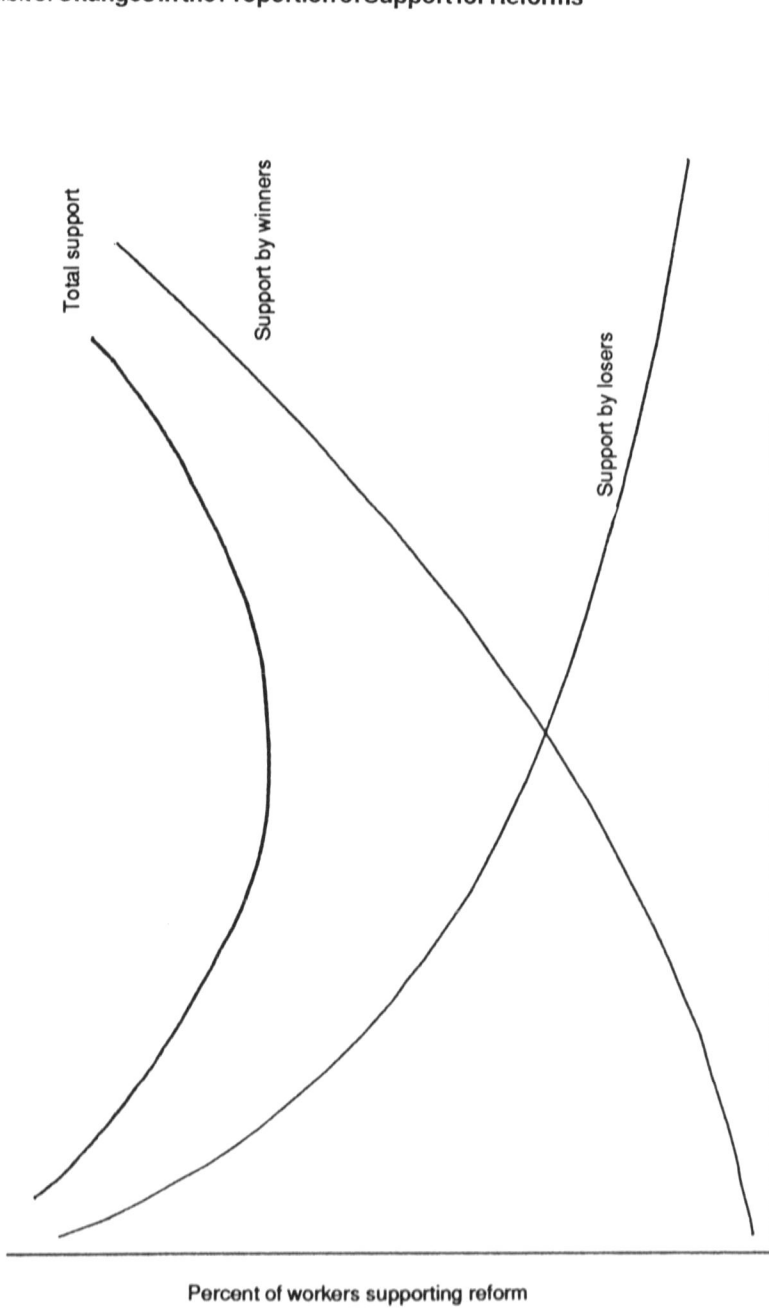

Total support

Support by winners

Support by losers

Percent of workers supporting reform

Notes

The observations that served as a basis for this study are derived from discussions with trade union and government officials and researchers in the various countries. In addition, I benefited from the research assistance of Peter Orszag and discussions with Mark Schaffer, Hartmut Lehmann, and Saul Estrin of the LSE Centre for Economic Performance; and from written comments by David Laibson of MIT.

1. In some communist countries, state restrictions on labor supply were more severe: the USSR required permits to live in cities; China allocated school leavers to work sites.

2. They include pensioners, need not refer to dues-paying members in a given time period, and may include many inactive members.

3. At General Electric's Tungsram operation in Budapest, in the fall of 1991 wages were just 13 percent above those in the overall economy. The economy-wide minimum was 7,000 forints; the minimum at Tungsram was 7,900; pay averaged 14,000 forints in the economy and 15,800 at Tungsram.

4. Without a clear counterfactual, it is not easy to tell the effect of an incomes policy on wage setting. A spike in wage increases at the point where the tax "kicks in" may reflect its use as a norm for wage setting rather than the effect of the tax per se, perhaps causing enterprises that would have given smaller increases to give the norm increase. Increases greater than the norm may still be less than they would otherwise have been.

5. Calvo and Coricelli (1992, 47) argue that wages increased because firms realized that all enterprises were facing similar financial problems and thus that "policy makers should try to devise ways to make the wage targets stick other than through sustained tight credit policy."

6. The adjusted figures remove the increase in private-sector retail-trade employment from reported separations. These data were provided by Mark Schaffer from the *Polish Statistical Yearbook*.

7. This is contrary to the results in virtually all other countries and may reflect the noneconomic size of the large state enterprises.

8. The responses are not due to the particular wording of the question. Asked which form of spending should be increased, 3 percent said unemployment benefits, 3 percent said defense, 17 percent said health, and 21 percent said pensions.

9. These polls are for June and December 1991, as reported by the Institute of Sociology of the Czech Academy of Sciences. The sociologist Siklova (1991, 2) warned that "people [have] the feeling that the state and old civil servants are responsible for a citizen's having or not having a job . . . , [whereas] unemployment is first of all evidence of their own incapacity."

10. Why the transition has been so costly in terms of falling output is an interesting question that goes beyond the scope of this study.

11. The Russian miners' union has stated: "We need to struggle for real businessmen to appear in our economy. And then, or rather simultaneously, to fight with these businessmen for real wages and worthy labor conditions" (cited in Gordon 1992a, 4). This parallels statements by *Solidarność* and LIGA.

12. Assessing the future of labor relations in marketizing economies would be much easier if there were a single recognized "best" set of labor institutions associated with market economies. But advanced OECD countries exhibit a wide spectrum of labor arrangements, which produce differing macroeconomic outcomes over time, but all of which are basically "workable."

13. This can be seen in a three-period overlapping-generations model, in which the three cohorts are indexed by i, where $i = 1$ is the oldest cohort, $i = 2$ is the next oldest, and so on. The probability of getting into the winning group is 0.3 in each period, so that

every cohort has a U-shaped support curve, with each new cohort supporting the program at rates of 100 percent, 30 percent, 51 percent over time. That is, new cohorts will express 100 percent support in period 1 since the present value of expected gains is positive; 30 percent support in period 2; and 51 percent support in period 3. But in period 1 there are two older cohorts. One possible assumption about them is that they have the same expectations as the youngest cohort. Then, the following table shows the pattern of support over time:

	Cohort 1	Cohort 2	Cohort 3	Cohort 4	Cohort 5
Period 1	0.30	0.30	1.00		
Period 2		0.51	0.30	1.00	
Period 3			0.51	0.30	1.00
Period 4				0.51	0.30
Period 5					0.51

If the cohorts are of equal size, 53 percent of the total population will support the program in period 1, 60 percent in period 2, and 60 percent thereafter. Only if cohort 3 makes up the largest share of the population will the aggregate support curve be U shaped.

14. An alternative model would be to assume that people do not know whether they are in the high or low probability group but have an accurate idea of the distribution of types. As losers from the high probability group update their probability of winning on the basis of their experience, they will become increasingly confident that they are in the low probability group. David Laibson (1992) has examined this model in a comment on this paper and shows that it, too, can give a U-shaped support curve.

15. This follows if the individual updates his prior probability by the simple relation that $p_t = 1 / (4 + t)$, where t is the number of periods in which he has failed to move into the winning group.

Bibliography

Berg, A., and Sachs, J. 1992. "Structural Adjustment and International Trade in Eastern Europe: The Case of Poland." *Economic Policy*, vol. 14 (April).

Blanchflower, D., and Freeman, R. 1992. "Unionism in the United States and Other Advanced OECD Countries." In *Labour Market Institutions and the Future Role of Unions*, ed. M. Bognanno and M. Kleiner. Cambridge MA: Blackwell.

Boeri, T., and Keese, M. 1992. "Labour Markets and the Transition in Central and Eastern Europe." Paris: OECD, Winter. Mimeographed manuscript.

Calvo, G., and Coricello, F. 1992. "Stagflationary Effects of Stabilization Programs in Reforming Socialist Countries: Enterprise-Side and Household-Side Factors." *Bank Economic Review*, January.

Daborowksi, J.; Federowicz, M.; and Levitas, A. 1992. "Polish State Enterprises and the Properties of Performance: Stabilization, Marketization, Privatization." May. Mimeographed manuscript.

Estrin, S. 1991. "Yugoslavia: The Case of Self-Managing Market Socialism." *Journal of Economic Perspectives*, Fall, pp. 187–94.

Federowicz, M., and Levitas, A. 1992. "Works Councils in Poland." Draft paper for NBER Conference on Works Councils, May.

Ferge, Z. 1991a. "Unemployment in Hungary." Mimeographed manuscript, Budapest.

———. 1991b. "Marginalization, Poverty, and Social Institutions." Presented as Paper No. 4 at the Round Table on Social Institutions for Economic Reform in Central and Eastern Europe, organized by the International Institute for Labor Studies, Geneva, and the Research Institute for Labour, Budapest, Balatonfüred, 29 September–October.

Freeman, R. 1987. "If It Doesn't Work, Fix It . . . If You Can: Reforming the Labor Market in Socialist Poland." Report to the World Bank, January.

———. 1989. "The Changing Status of Unionism Around the World." In *Organized Labor at the Crossroads*, ed. Wei-Chiao Huang. Michigan: Upjohn Institute for Employment Research.

Góra, M.; Kotowska, I.; Panek, T.; and Podgórski, J. 1991. "Labour Market, Industrial Relations, and Social Policy: A Report on Poland." ILO OECD-CCEET Conference on Labour Market and Social Policy Implications of Structural Change in Central and Eastern Europe, Paris, September.

Gordon, L. 1992a. "The Labor Movement in Days of Difficult Reforms: To Suppress or to Support?" Mimeographed manuscript.

———. 1992b. "The Independent Workers' Movement in the USSR (An Analysis of the Experience of 1989, 1991)." Mimeographed manuscript.

Hartl, Jan. 1991. "Economic Expectations and Attitudes of the Czechoslovak Population." Paper presented at the Conference of the Paul Lazarsfeld Society, Vienna, February, pp. 12–23.

Hethy, L. 1991. "Social Institutions for Economic Reform: The Industrial Relations Institutions." Paper delivered at Social Institutions for Economic Reform in Central and Eastern Europe, Blatonfüred, Hungary.

Hethy, L., and Csuhaj, I. 1990. *Labour Relations in Hungary*. Budapest: Institute of Labour Research.

Hirschman, A. 1973. "The Changing Tolerance for Economic Inequality." *Quarterly Journal of Economics* 87 (November).

International Institute of Labour Studies. 1991. Country Profiles, East and Central Europe; Country Profile, Hungary.

International Labor Organization. 1984. *The Trade Union Situation and Industrial Relations in Hungary*. Geneva.

———. 1990. Committee on Employment. "Wages, Labour Costs, and Their Impact on Adjustment, Employment, and Growth." November.

———. 1990–92. Labour Law Documents: Hungary, Right to Strike, pp. 41–43; Poland, Trade Unions, pp. 101–105.

———. 1991. Poland. The Trade Union Act of 23 May; The Act of 23 May, Respecting Employers' Organizations; The Act of 23 May, Respecting Settlement of Collective Disputes.

———. 1991–92. Labour Law Documents: Czechoslovakia, Collective Bargaining Act, 1–12, Employment Act, 13–24.

International Labour Review. 1991–92. "Labour Market Transitions in Eastern Europe and the USSR," vol. 130, no. 2.

Iovcheva, S. 1991. "Unemployment—New Phenomenon in the Bulgarian Labour Market." Paper delivered at 3rd EALE Conference, September.

Jones, D. 1991–92. "The Bulgarian Labor Market in Transition." In *International Labour Review* 1991–92.

———. 1992. "The Transformation of Labor Unions in Eastern Europe: The Case of Bulgaria." *Industrial and Labor Relations Review* 45, no. 3 (April), pp. 452–70.

Kabos, E., and Zsilak, A., eds. 1977. *Studies on the History of the Hungarian Trade Union Movement*. Budapest: Akademiai Kiado.

Kollo, J. 1988. "Without a Golden Age—Eastern Europe." Paper presented at Harvard University, mimeographed manuscript.

Kornai, J. 1982. *Growth, Shortage, and Efficiency*. Oxford: Basil Blackwell.

———. 1986. "The Hungarian Reform Process: Visions, Hopes and Reality." *Journal of Economic Literature* 24, pp. 1687–1737.

Lado, M.; Szalai, J.; and Sziraczki, G. 1991. "Recent Labour Market and Social Developments in Hungary." ILO OECD-CCEET Conference on Labour Market and Social Policy Implications of Structural Change in Central and Eastern Europe, Paris, September.

Laibson, David. 1992. "Comments on East European Paper." Mimeographed manuscript, 8 July.

Lehmann, H., and Schaffer, M. 1992. "Productivity, Employment, and Labour Demand in Polish Industry in the 1980s: Some Preliminary Results from Enterprise-level Data." Centre for Economic Performance Working Paper 91, January revision.

LIGA News. 1991. Budapest, vols. 1–8.

MacShane, Denis. 1992. "Workers and Their Unions in Eastern Europe—May 1991." In *Labour/Le Travail* 29, Spring, pp. 211–20.

Malinowski, T. 1991. "Unemployment, Family Policy, and Social Assistance." Paper prepared for the conference Social Costs of the Political and Economic Transformation of the CSFR, Hungary and Poland, Vienna.

Nesporova, A. 1991. "Recent Labour Market and Social Policy Developments in the Czech and Slovak Republic." ILO OECD-CCEET Conference on Labour Market and Social Policy Implications of Structural Change in Central and Eastern Europe, Paris, September.

Noti, S. 1987. "The Shifting Position of Hungarian Trade Unions Amidst Social and Economic Reforms." *Soviet Studies*, January, pp. 63–87.

Polish Statistical Yearbook (Rocznik Statystyczny).

Przeworski, A. 1991. *Democracy and the Market.* Cambridge: Cambridge University Press.

Redor, D. 1986. "Differentiation des Rémunérations et incitation au travail: Une comparaison international." Paper presented at the International Workshop on Wages and Payment Systems and Their Socioeconomic Environment, Siófok, 12–17 September.

Reti, Tamas. 1991. "East European Trade Unions and Labour Representation." Mimeographed manuscript, Budapest, May.

Riveros, L. 1991. "Wages and Employment Policies in Czechoslovakia." World Bank Policy Research and External Affairs Working Papers no. 730, July.

Schaffer, M. 1991. "A Note on the Polish State-owned Enterprise Sector in 1990." Centre for Economic Performance Discussion Paper no. 36.

———. 1992. "Poland." Centre for Economic Performance Working Paper no. 183, January.

Scott, Andrew. 1991. "Hungary: A Summary of Recent Events and Reforms." Centre for Economic Performance, London School of Economics paper series, 17 October.

Siklova, J. 1991. "Unemployment: The Czech Way." *Literary Newspaper*, 29 August.

Simpson, W. 1991. "Tripartite Structures in Central and Eastern Europe and the USSR, Freedom of Association and the Role of the State in Industrial Relations." ILO mimeographed manuscript, July.

Solidarność News. 1991. Coordinating Office of NSZZ *Solidarność*, Belgium.

Stem Survey Organization, Prague. Monthly publications, various years.

Sziraczki, G. 1990. "Economic Adjustment, Pay Structure, and the Problem of Incentives in Eastern European Labor Markets." Labour Market Analysis and Employment Planning Working Paper no. 46, December.

Vanyai, J., and Viszt, E. 1992. "Human Resources and Structural Change in the Hungarian Industry." Research Institute of Industrial Economics, Hungarian Academy of Sciences, Budapest, mimeographed manuscript.

World Bank. 1987. *Poland: Reform, Adjustment, and Growth.*

———. 1990a. *Poland: Economic Management for a New Era.* World Bank Study.

———. 1990b. *Czechoslovakia: Transition to a Market Economy.*

———. 1991. *The Challenge of Development.* World Development Report.

Democratic Self-management

An Alternative Approach to Economic Transformation in the Former Soviet Union

Thomas E. Weisskopf

As the successor nations of the Soviet Union proceed with the transformation of their administrative-command systems into market-based economies, increasing attention is being focused on the restructuring of enterprises. It is often presumed that only capitalist firms characterized by individual private ownership and top-down management control can operate effectively in a market environment. Yet there are many possible forms of enterprise ownership and control in a market economy, ranging from conventional capitalist firms to public enterprises to producer cooperatives, with a wide variety of ownership and management structures.

In recent decades, scholars in the fields of economics, business administration, and industrial relations have analyzed enterprise organizational forms in which workers play a prominent role as owners and/or participants in the process of management.[1] This literature points to potential advantages as well as disadvantages of worker self-management and sheds much light on the conditions under which it can be successful. Worker self-management was put into practice most extensively in the Yugoslav market-socialist economy; this experience helped to illuminate (largely by negative example) the conditions necessary for worker-managed enterprises to succeed. Many examples of worker-managed enterprises can also be found in Western market-capitalist economies, and some of these—e.g., the Mondragon cooperatives of Northern Spain—suggest that under appropriate circumstances such enterprises can be more democratic and more egalitarian, and at least as efficient and dynamic, as conventional capitalist firms.

Under Communist Party rule in the Soviet Union, workers in practice had very little opportunity to play any role in enterprise management. In the context of the current transition to a market economy, however, authentic forms of worker participation in management may be able to develop. Indeed, the concept of self-management seems likely to have considerable appeal as a way to make the transition from a centralized administrative-command system, ostensibly devoted to the welfare of all citizens, to a decentralized market system in which people will have much more responsibility for their own economic well-being.

This paper explores the concept of democratic self-management and its potential

The author is a professor of economics at the University of Michigan.

promise as a basis for economic transformation in the former Soviet Union. The term "democratic" is used in order to stress the philosophical foundation of the idea of self-management and to emphasize the point that it encompasses all working members of an enterprise—including managers and technicians as well as white-collar and blue-collar workers. Section I defines the general concept of democratic self-management, and Section II discusses the major arguments that have been advanced to support it. Section III presents a criticism of democratic self-management and identifies a number of potential problems requiring serious consideration; Section IV proposes ways in which to address these problems. Finally, the concluding Section V argues that a suitably organized system of democratically self-managed enterprises does indeed offer a very promising basis for the construction of an efficient and equitable market economy in the nations of the former Soviet Union.

I. The Meaning of Democratic Self-management

The concept of democratic self-management has been advanced as a potentially desirable alternative to the conventional structure of management in both private and public enterprises. In a conventional private enterprise, management is responsible solely to the owners of the capital assets of the firm. These owners—whether they are shareholders in the firm's equity or direct owners of the firm's assets—hold voting rights and hence exercise control over management in proportion to the size of their ownership share. In a conventional public enterprise, management is responsible to the government agency under whose authority the enterprise is operating. In neither case do those who actually work in the enterprise have any formal right to participate in enterprise management—except insofar as they happen to share in the ownership of a private enterprise.

The organization of conventional firms is thus clearly at odds with the basic principles of democratic governance, according to which those who govern should be accountable to those whom they govern. The exclusion of enterprise workers from any say in management has led many people over the years to explore various forms and mechanisms for workers to influence enterprise management. Some have favored the formation of strong trade unions, which can represent worker interests in bargaining with managers responsible to enterprise owners, as the best way of providing workers with some say over the conditions under which they work. Others have argued that trade unions are not enough and that the structure of authority within the enterprise must be modified so as to provide for some kind of worker participation in the management process itself.

Mechanisms for worker participation in enterprise management include (in the order of the degree of influence accorded to workers): (1) schemes to involve employees in discussions with managers about issues connected with enterprise decision making; (2) procedures whereby employees can elect representatives to sit with representatives of capital owners on enterprise governing boards; (3)

employee stock-option plans (ESOPs), under which arrangements are made for employees to acquire substantial amounts of enterprise equity through which they may be able to influence enterprise management as shareholders; and (4) full-fledged producer cooperatives, in which the capital assets of an enterprise are fully and collectively owned by its worker-members.[2] Only the last of these forms of worker participation is consistent with democratic governance.

What characterizes democratic self-management of enterprises is one very simple principle: control over enterprise decision making is formally vested in all the working members of the enterprise on a one-person–one-vote basis. The working members include managers, technicians, and supervisors as well as white-collar and blue-collar workers.[3] Democratic control over decision making may be exercised directly in an assembly of all enterprise members or indirectly via the election of an enterprise governing board; management is accountable either to the assembly or to the elected governing board.

This definition of democratic self-management leaves open many important questions about enterprise organization. In particular, it does not specify how enterprise capital assets are to be acquired or how enterprise revenues are to be distributed. These are crucial issues, which will be discussed further below; at present it will suffice to note that democratic self-management allows for any pattern of capital acquisition and any pattern of revenue distribution that is agreed to by the working members of the enterprise through democratic procedures of voting and representation.

II. The Case for Democratic Self-management

Advocates of democratic self-management stress its ability to promote a variety of social goals as well as to contribute to economic efficiency. With respect to social goals, self-management is seen as an important expression of *humanity*: what distinguishes us as human beings is our ability consciously to shape our own life experience, and self-management at the work place brings an important arena under the conscious control of those who participate in it. Self-management also contributes to the social goal of *democracy* by extending democratic institutions and mechanisms from the political arena to the work place. Furthermore, self-management fosters *community* among the members of a democratic enterprise—by bringing workers, managers, and all enterprise members as equals into a common organizational association. Finally, advocates of self-management point to its contribution to *equality* in the distribution of income and wealth— both because it discourages large wage and salary differentials among the members of particular enterprises and because it prevents individuals, groups, or agencies from acquiring control over massive business empires.

From the perspective of the new nations of the former Soviet Union, struggling to build viable economic institutions in an environment of economic disorder and decay, the achievement of such social goals may well seem much less important than the promotion of economic efficiency and growth. Thus the case for democratic self-management will ultimately depend most crucially on its ability to contribute to economic revitalization in the context of the inevitable transition from an administrative-command system to a market economy. Advocates of democratic self-management can indeed point to a number of important ways in which it can improve the economic performance of enterprises.

One of the principal virtues of self-management is its potential for stimulating *enhanced individual worker effort and productivity*. Efficiency gains may arise from greater positive motivation and consequently better work on the part of individual workers, or they may arise from reduced costs of maintaining negative sanctions against shirking and poor work—for example, reduced supervisional expenses due to greater mutual monitoring by workers. Such gains may arise simply because democratic structures of self-management—as compared with traditional hierarchical structures—create in workers a stronger commitment to the welfare of the enterprise as a whole. Such gains may also be stimulated by the sharing of workers in enterprise residual income, so that their material reward varies to some degree with enterprise performance.[4] Some degree of worker sharing of residual claimancy can of course be organized in conventional externally controlled firms—via profit sharing and similar bonus schemes—but there are good grounds for believing that the associated efficiency gains can best be realized when residual sharing is an element of a larger institutional environment characterized by democratic self-management and a reasonable degree of overall income-distribution equality.[5]

A related efficiency gain due to democratic self-management arises from *greater cooperation among enterprise members* in an atmosphere of greater mutual loyalty and trust. Many operating problems faced by enterprises take the form of prisoners' dilemmas involving managers and workers, in which each side would opt for a second-best solution if it could not trust the other side to cooperate, but both sides could reach a first-best solution if they could trust one another to cooperate.[6] Democratic self-management creates an environment in which it becomes easier to reach cooperative solutions to such enterprise coordination problems, thereby contributing to greater rationality in the organization of work at the enterprise level and helping to avoid costly labor–management conflicts.

Democratic self-management also promises significant efficiency gains insofar as it promotes *greater competition* in product markets and *less concentration* of economic power than conventional forms of enterprise ownership and control. An economic system characterized predominantly by democratically self-managed enterprises favors the development of small and medium-sized firms and precludes the emergence of highly concentrated and powerful business conglomerates. The resultant dispersion of economic power restrains the development of monopolistic power in product markets, thereby allowing product market competition to enforce good firm performance. The dispersion of economic power also reduces opportunities for collusion among powerful business interests and government officials, thereby reducing the overall efficiency losses associated with the pursuit of individual gain at the expense of the general public.

One final efficiency advantage associated with democratic self-management is its potential for *greater internalization of externalities* at the local community level and, to some extent, at the society-wide level as well. Because the members of a democratically self-managed enterprise are much more likely to be living in the community in which the enterprise is located than the private or public owners of a corresponding externally controlled firm, democratically self-managed enterprises are much more likely to take into account the impact of enterprise activity on community welfare in making decisions about enterprise operation—for example, by curbing pollution of local air and water.[7] A related advantage of a democratically self-managed enterprise stems from the fact that the claim to the residual income of the enterprise is spread widely and thinly among many voting enterprise members rather than being concentrated heavily among a small group of controlling shareholders or public officials. This means that the income gains from generating "public bads"—e.g., pollution and other such negative externalities—are less likely to offset the welfare losses from the public bad itself from the point of view of the individuals with control rights over the enterprise, and enterprise decisions are consequently less likely to generate public bads.[8]

III. Potential Problems of Democratic Self-management

The arguments presented in the preceding section in favor of democratic self-management do not, of course, tell the whole story. Critics of self-management have pointed to numerous potential problems that they believe outweigh its potential advantages.[9] While most of the criticism has been directed at the efficiency characteristics of a system of democratic self-management, some concerns have also been raised about the ability of such a system to meet important social goals. This section will review the major arguments advanced in both lines of criticism and will seek to determine to what extent these arguments pose a serious challenge to a system of democratic self-management. The following section will consider ways in which to structure democratic self-management so that it can overcome the most serious problems cited by its critics.

A. Economic-Efficiency Goals

Perhaps the most common criticism of self-management schemes in which workers gain substantial decision-making power is that they will use this power in *pursuit of short-term worker interests* rather than promoting the long-term interests of the enterprise. This line of criticism takes various specific forms. First, it is argued that workers will be unwilling to lay off fellow workers, favoring employment security over organizational "rationalization" or labor-saving technological change, and that they will be reluctant to expand employment, preferring to increase wages in response to increased demand. It is also argued that self-managed enterprises will have "weak pay discipline" as compared to owner-controlled enterprises: workers will push for pay increases at the expense of profits. And it is argued that workers will favor the use of enterprise net revenues for individual or collective worker consumption rather than for new enterprise capital formation; or that workers may even want to strip the enterprise of its capital base in order to support greater current consumption. This is the so-called "horizon problem," attributed to the fact that workers receive benefits from enterprise performance only during the time period in which they are actually working at the enterprise.

If democratically self-managed enterprises operate in an environment in which there is effective product market competition and in which there are "hard budget constraints" (i.e., enterprises cannot expect to be bailed out whenever they sustain losses), then the force of the above arguments is limited, because enterprises would be required to maintain their profitability simply in order to survive. However, within the remaining degree of freedom for enterprise management, it remains true that self-managed enterprises would have a tendency to maintain more stable employment and to allocate less revenue to capital formation than comparable externally controlled firms. A bias in favor of employment stability is not necessarily undesirable, for there are hidden external costs of employment variability (e.g., the costs of unemployment compensation and of labor mobility), which are thereby in effect internalized in enterprise decision making. The possible bias against capital formation, however, is a potentially serious matter.

A second major criticism of democratic self-management is that there will be *inadequate incentives for good managerial performance*. On the one hand, democratic enterprise managers lack the discipline imposed by conventional stock markets in the form of the threat of a hostile takeover, when low or falling share prices suggest to potential new shareholders that better management could render the firm more profitable. On the other hand, democratic enterprise managers are accountable not to any small and well-focused ownership group but to a large and diffuse group of enterprise members.

There is an enormous literature on the effectiveness of conventional stock markets in eliciting good management performance via the threat of hostile takeover. It is fair to say, at the very least, that there is no consensus on this issue; indeed, strong arguments have been advanced to suggest that alternative mechanisms relying more on "voice" and less on "exit" are considerably more effective in eliciting good management performance.[10]

As far as the absence of a small, well-focused ownership group is concerned, it should first be noted that this is also the case with conventional capitalist firms in the common event that their equity shares are dispersed among a large number of external shareholders. But it is also often the case that effective control of a capitalist enterprise is in the hands of just a few large shareholders, and such firms are indeed characterized by well-focused ownership with very large stakes in the successful management of the firm. Whether democratically self-managed enterprises can generate a similar degree of concern on the part of their stake holders in successful management is an important question.

Third, critics of democratic self-management argue that it will confront an *inadequate supply of capital*—and, in particular, an inadequate inflow of foreign capital. Under a system of democratic self-management, suppliers of capital cannot buy equity shares that automatically confer corresponding control rights in the enterprises to which they supply capital. By precluding a common instrument of capital finance, the principles of self-management arguably limit the ability of enterprises to raise capital funds.

The salience of this concern is diminished by the fact that much of the capital supplied to conventional capitalist corporations is supplied by people (or institutions) who do not acquire any effective control over the corporation. Not only can democratically self-managed enterprises use their retained earnings for capital formation, but they can lease assets and borrow from financial intermediaries in order to purchase capital assets outright. However, the fact that democratically self-managed enterprises cannot issue equity shares with voting rights does still appear to cut such enterprises off from a potentially important source of capital, and it seems especially likely to discourage potentially valuable foreign investment; here again there is need to address a potential problem with democratic self-management.

Finally, it is charged that under democratic self-management there will be *insufficient entrepreneurship and innovation*. On the one hand, workers are likely to have much of their personal and financial assets effectively tied up in the enterprise in which they are working; they will therefore be reluctant to take the kinds of risks that are associated with successful entrepreneurship and innovation. On the other hand, the rewards to successful risk taking would be spread widely among members of a democratic enterprise; so it is arguable that the absence of high individual payoffs would discourage even people otherwise prepared to undertake risky ventures.

The risk-aversion problem is a potentially serious one, but the individual payoff problem should not be a major cause for concern. Most research and development is carried out in large research divisions of large firms, where individual researchers face constraints and potential rewards very similar to what they could expect in a democratically self-managed enterprise. As far as cases of individual ideas and inventions are concerned, a system of democratic self-management need not and should not rule out space for independent individual and small-group private enterprise—allowing thus for substantial individual rewards within the context of a small business. Only when and if such activities begin to turn into substantial business firms would they have to become democratically self-managed enterprises (in much the same way as entrepreneurs in capitalist economies often find themselves selling out to a bigger private corporation after their initial success).

B. Social Goals

The most serious potential failure of democratically self-managed enterprises with respect to the achievement of social goals is the likelihood of *substantial inequalities in the distribution of income and wealth*. While it can be claimed on behalf of democratic self-management that it would reduce intra-enterprise inequalities and that it would inhibit the development of large business empires, there are several reasons for concern about its overall impact on the distribution of income and wealth. First of all, if workers in existing state or private enterprises gain substantial claims to the capital assets of their own enterprises in the process of transition to a system of self-management, then great inequities would arise both between workers and nonworkers and between workers in successful enterprises and workers in unsuccessful ones. Second, even if the transition could be handled in a fair and equitable manner, a system of democratically self-managed enterprises is likely to give rise to growing inter-enterprise differentials of income and wealth; workers in the more successful enterprises would find themselves increasingly better off than their counterparts in less successful or failing enterprises.

The potential for inequality of income and wealth in a democratically self-managed system is surely much less than in a capitalist system. Yet because greater material equality is both an important social goal and an important element in some of the efficiency advantages associated with democratic self-management, concerns about the development of inegalitarian tendencies in a system of democratically self-managed enterprises must be taken very seriously.

A second problematic social consequence of democratic self-management is the likely *concentration of worker assets into undiversified portfolios*. Not only would the returns to a worker's firm-specific skills and knowledge be tied up with the performance of her/his enterprise, but it is also likely that a substantial amount of workers' financial wealth—in the form of retirement benefits, if not claims on enterprise capital—would be dependent on the performance of the enterprise. This would expose individual worker-members of self-managed enterprises to greater risk than they would be exposed to as wage earners in conventional firms (assuming that their wealth were diversified through private capital markets or protected by public trusts). Even if democratic enterprise decision making leaned in a risk-averse direction, workers' long-term economic security might be threatened. Like the efficiency problem of risk aversion in enterprise decision making, the social problem of inadequate worker asset diversification must be confronted by proponents of a system of democratic self-management.[11]

IV. Toward a Desirable System of Democratic Self-management

The preceding section identified a series of potential problems that must be addressed in any effort to construct a successful system of democratic self-management. The evocation of such problems has often been used by critics of self-management to dismiss altogether its feasibility or desirability. There are, however, readily available ways in which to overcome the problems raised and thereby to fashion a system of democratic self-management that can benefit from its promise while suffering minimally from its problems.

How can *sufficient reinvestment of enterprise revenues* be assured? The problem only arises to the extent that enterprise members do not share in the benefits from reinvestment—for example, if the future income stream generated by the reinvestment of enterprise revenues is channeled to people other than those whose foregone consumption opportunities made the reinvestment possible. For example, if enterprise members can benefit from reinvestment only to the extent that it increases their future earnings while they are still at work in the enterprise, then the return on their investment is limited—especially if they are close to retirement age (hence the "horizon problem").

The solution to this problem is clearly to find a mechanism whereby enterprise members can receive a return on their share of reinvested earnings that does not hinge on the length of their subsequent employment at the enterprise and that is comparable to the return that they could expect from investing the same amount of money elsewhere. This could be accomplished by setting up a system of "internal equity" within the enterprise, with each member holding an equity capital stake that is augmented by the amount of income the member foregoes whenever the enterprise reinvests net revenue that could otherwise have been distributed to members.[12] Under such a plan, members would receive current capital income from their capital stake in the form of periodic (fixed) interest or (variable) dividend payments, and upon retirement they would cash in the value of their principal; the amount of the current income and/or the value of the principal would depend on the overall performance of the firm. This kind of plan enables enterprise members to share fully in the fruits of enterprise reinvestment, but, of course, it exposes them to the risk of uncertain enterprise performance. This risk problem will be returned to below.

How can *good management performance* be assured in the absence of a well-focused group to whom managers are responsible? Under democratic self-management, managers are responsible to all the members of an enterprise, no one (or few) of whom will have the means or the incentive to make sure that managers are doing their job well. To keep managers on their toes, there must be a good source of information about the long-run vitality of the enterprise, and there must be strong motivation for managers to maintain that vitality. There are many possible indicators of current enterprise performance, but it is arguable that reasonably reliable information about the long-run vitality of an enterprise requires a process in which potentially well informed outside observers have the means and the incentive to do a good job of evaluation. This is indeed one of the functions of a stock market in enterprise shares; what is needed in a system of democratic self-management is a way of taking advantage of the information-conveying function of stock markets while preserving self-management and minimizing the tendency of such markets to concentrate wealth and power.

This can be accomplished by creating a market in enterprise equity shares in which equity holders gain the right to receive capital income from their share holdings but not any corresponding right to vote for enterprise governing boards. The value of enterprise equity shares would still rise and fall in such a market according to assessments of long-term enterprise vitality by potentially well-informed and interested outsiders, but insiders would maintain democratic control of enterprise management. To assure that managers are highly motivated to perform well, their employment contracts should gear their earnings to the value of enterprise shares as well as to other indicators of enterprise performance that are deemed important by enterprise members.

Yet will an *adequate supply of external capital* be forthcoming if potential investors cannot acquire external equity shares with voting rights? Democratically self-managed enterprises can, of course, borrow funds from financial intermediaries and reinvest their own earnings, and they can issue nonvoting equity shares. But there are still likely to be some potential external investors who are ready to supply capital only if they retain some control over the enterprise whose performance will affect the return on their investment—and this is especially likely to be the case with foreign investors. While democratic self-management principles exclude automatic acquisition of enterprise control rights in proportion to the amount of equity shares acquired by an external investor, these principles need not preclude negotiation between enterprise management (democratically accountable to enterprise members) and potential external investors over the terms on which they are willing to acquire nonvoting equity shares. If capital from an external investor were critical to the future viability of an enterprise because alternative sources of sufficient capital were simply not available, then enterprise members and their managers might well find it worthwhile to grant to the critical investor certain control rights *de facto* that such an investor could acquire *de jure* in a capitalist economy. The key point is that under democratic self-management any such control rights are for enterprise members to grant rather than for capital suppliers to assume.

How will it be possible for members of democratically self-managed firms to attain a *sufficiently diversified portfolio of assets*? The concentration of one's assets in one's own enterprise can have desirable incentive effects on work motivation since it increases the stake of members in the performance of their enterprise; but by the same token it exposes members to risks that will be only partially alleviated by (potentially inefficient) risk aversion in enterprise decision making.

The only way to deal with this dilemma would appear to be via compromise—by limiting the degree of worker asset concentration so as to reduce risk while maintaining some worker stake in enterprise performance through the sharing of equity in the enterprise. This is precisely what is achieved by combining the systems of internal equity for enterprise members and external equity for outside capital suppliers proposed above. In this way members of any given enterprise can choose to divide the risk (and the return on equity shares) between insiders and outsiders in whatever proportions seem most appropriate. In democratically self-managed enterprises that combine internal and external equity in this way, both enterprise finance and workers' portfolios can be much better diversified than is possible in pure producer cooperatives in which all enterprise equity is collectively owned by its members.

Finally, how can a system of democratically self-managed enterprises assure *the maintenance of a reasonably equitable distribution of income and wealth*? Here attention needs to be focused both on the initial process of transition to democratic self-management and on the subsequent operation of a system of self-managed enterprises.

Proposals for a transition to self-management from a command-administrative economic system like that of the former Soviet Union call for a shift in authority over state enterprises from government agencies and officials to the working members of those enterprises. If this shift of authority is accompanied by a corresponding shift of ownership claims on the productive assets of the enterprises, however, it will generate enormous inequalities between enterprise members and nonmembers and among members of different enterprises. To achieve distributional equity in such a transition, there must be a process whereby claims on existing enterprise assets are shared equally among all members of the relevant population, even as decision-making authority in each particular enterprise is allocated only to the members of that enterprise.

A good way in which to achieve this objective is to distribute to every adult citizen an equal amount of shares in a large number of mutual funds, each of which initially holds external (nonvoting) equity claims to an equal proportion of the productive assets of every democratically self-managed enterprise.[13] Shares in mutual funds would entitle their owners to a corresponding proportion of the net revenues of the funds (themselves organized as democratically self-managed enterprises or small private businesses); these shares could be traded in a mutual-fund share market. There would thus be a two-tiered stock-market system—a market in mutual-fund shares and a market in enterprise shares; consistent with the principles of democratic self-management, shares would in neither case confer voting rights.[14]

Stock markets are, of course, notorious for generating inequalities; even the initially equal distribution of mutual-fund shares proposed here could and would quickly lead to great inequalities if the purchase and sale of shares were unrestricted, as many people would liquidate their share holdings for cash, and a few lucky and/or astute people would accumulate large and valuable portfolios. In order to assure that the distribution of wealth remains reasonably equitable, the stock market in mutual-fund shares may be isolated by barring the exchange of such shares for anything but other mutual-fund shares, and participation in the enterprise equity market may be restricted to the mutual funds themselves and to foreign investors. In other words, citizens could neither increase their mutual-fund share holdings by purchasing more shares with cash or other assets nor liquidate their portfolios for cash or other assets; and citizens could not operate directly in the market for enterprise shares. These restrictions assure that every citizen would continue to hold some claim to the economy's capital income (and could assure her/himself the average claim by maintaining a completely balanced portfolio), while allowing individual citizens to seek to increase the value of their claims (and risk decreasing their value) through trades of shares in different mutual funds.

Thus, what is being proposed is that democratically self-managed enterprises be embedded in a larger economic environment that would assure a reasonable degree of equity in the distribution of income and wealth. The two-tiered restricted stock-market system is designed to complement democratic self-management at the enterprise level in such a way as to meet simultaneously a series of important objectives: (1) to generate useful information about enterprise performance; (2) to expand the range of mechanisms whereby enterprises can raise capital funds for investment; (3) to offer individuals a substantial amount of freedom of choice with respect to the allocation of their wealth; and (4) to prevent the accumulation of concentrated capital holdings by individual citizens.

V. The Advantages of Democratic Self-management in the Context of the Former Soviet Union

The system of democratic self-management described above has much to recommend it in any type of society. There are good reasons to believe, however, that it may be particularly appropriate for societies seeking to make the transition from command-administrative to market economies. A number of conditions prevailing in many of the states of the former Soviet Union appear to render especially attractive the possibility of a route to a market economy based on democratically self-managed enterprises.

Consideration of this possibility must first confront the currently widespread skepticism on the part of many economists and policy makers in the East about any form of worker self-management. This skepticism has much to do with a negative evaluation of the experience of self-management socialism in Yugoslavia as well as with an association of the idea of worker self-management with discredited forms of socialism. Comparison of the type of democratic self-management that is being proposed here with the forms of worker self-management actually practiced in Yugoslavia should serve immediately to dispel this source of concern.[15]

First, worker self-management in Yugoslavia was institutionalized within a political context that remained bureaucratic and authoritarian; workers' effective control was seriously limited by the continuing power of the League of Communists (the Communist Party) and the state agencies it controlled. Second, even though centralized economic planning was relaxed, a soft budget constraint remained endemic; the Yugoslav government provided financial support for otherwise failing enterprises and tended to allocate investment capital with little regard to enterprise economic performance or to the scarcity value of capital. Many of the self-managed firms operated in rather monopolistic environments, and opportunities for entry and exit of firms were limited. Finally, property rights in the capital assets of worker self-managed enterprises remained very ill-defined; these assets officially belonged to the state, but in practice this meant that nobody had any strong ownership rights in them.

The positive case for the relevance of democratic self-management in the former Soviet Union is based on several features of the postcommunist context. Among these the most important may be considered to be (1) the weakness of the environment for capitalism, (2) the strength of workers and their organizations, and (3) the popular desire for fairness, stability, and security.

A. The Environment for Capitalism

Those who favor a purely capitalist approach to a market economy are clearly and understandably reacting to the obvious failures of bureaucratic administrative-command socialism in the East and the comparative success of capitalism in the West. Yet conditions in the former Soviet Union are in many ways very unpropitious for the development of a dynamic form of capitalism.

Seventy-five years of communist rule did not succeed in eliminating the entrepreneurial instincts of Russians, Ukrainians, and other nationalities, but it obviously placed great restraints on their development. Especially in the period since Mikhail Gorbachev launched his program of *perestroika*, there has been an impressive resurgence of small-scale enterprise in many parts of the former Soviet Union, and throughout the communist era there were opportunities—often illegal or semilegal—for the development of entrepreneurial skills and even large-scale accumulations of wealth. Yet there was no capitalist-style finance and virtually no significant capitalist-style operation of medium- and large-scale enterprises. As a result, there is simply no social or economic force that could be identified as a domestic capitalist class with the experience and the instincts to operate a successful capitalist economy.

Furthermore, there is an enormous lack of institutional infrastructure needed for the efficient operation of labor and capital markets within a context of capitalist property rights—e.g., opportunities for labor mobility, information about investment opportunities, effective government regulation. The needed institutional infrastructure developed very slowly and over a long period of time in the countries where capitalism has been most successful in stimulating economic growth. Those people who have the wealth to acquire productive assets today are almost exclusively formerly privileged state officials (the "*nomenklatura*"), people who have acquired their capital via rather shady means (the "mafiosi"), or foreigners. Rapid introduction of private property forms into the chaos created by the demise of administrative-command economies threatens not to replace but simply to change the form of the monopolization, corruption, and inefficiency that plagued the Soviet Union for so long.

B. The Role of Workers

In the transition to a market economy, it surely makes sense to take advantage of any elements in the old system that are potentially conducive to successful operation within a new decentralized competitive market context. One important legacy of administrative-command socialism is a highly educated—if poorly motivated—work force. The skills and the detailed knowledge about production processes embodied in the managers, engineers, technicians, and operatives of the old state enterprises seem most likely to be harnessed by a system in which management remains more accountable to the members of the enterprise community themselves than to external financiers. Involving workers in important ways in decision making at the enterprise level can not only provide the economic benefits of greater worker motivation and productivity but also make an important contribution to the strengthening of democratic institutions.

Furthermore, an approach that builds on worker self-management rather than rejecting it also provides the opportunity to recognize the growth of workers' political and economic power at the work place during the late reform stages of many of the command-administrative systems. If working-class organizations can be enlisted in a cooperative social endeavor to change the economic system rather than antagonized in a process that strips them of all their power and influence, both the economic and the political obstacles to the transition can be greatly reduced. To some extent, worker democratic control rights may actually substitute for higher real wages, conferring greater legitimacy on policies for economic and social changes that in other ways will lead to difficult times for workers. Far from leading to wage indiscipline, worker control in the declining sectors of transitional economies can lead to greater acceptance of real wage decreases as an alternative to higher unemployment.

C. The Need for Fairness

In spite of the failure of the administrative-command systems to live up to communist promises of equality, there remains among many people in the former Soviet Union a certain belief, if not in egalitarianism *per se*, then at least in the proposition that a small minority should not benefit out of all proportion to the vast majority. Perhaps even more important, the success of the erstwhile communist regimes in assuring economic stability and security—albeit at a modest level of material welfare—has generated expectations among the people for continuing stability and security. However successful it may be in stimulating economic growth, capitalism—especially in the early stages of its development—systematically generates inequality, instability, and insecurity.

An alternative system based on democratic self-management along the lines suggested here can assure a much more egalitarian distribution of claims to capital income as well as greater stability and security in the process of transition to a market economy. Even though the capital income generated by state enterprises under administrative-command socialism was in fact distributed rather unevenly, the idea that the general population built the nation's capital stock and deserves to share in its fruits remains a compelling one. The proposal presented here for mutual funds in which all citizens are guaranteed shares appears especially salient in the context of the "spontaneous" or "wild" privatizations of public assets that have all too often become an element of the capitalist route to the market in the former Soviet Union. Surely the best way to generate popular support and a political constituency for market reforms and the whole privatization process is to spread the benefits of ownership widely and broadly throughout the population (rather than narrowly to the *nomenklatura*, mafiosi, and foreigners).

The process of transition to a market economy—no matter what precise form it takes—will surely require economic sacrifices on the part of many people; it is simply impossible to engineer a sequence of steps from the present disorder to a new system in which everybody gains. But people are likely to be much more willing to endure such sacrifices if the gains and/or losses during the transition are seen as reasonably equitably distributed. The fact that a more equitable transition is more conducive to maintaining popular support means that it also offers more hope for keeping up the momentum for change within a context of political democracy. A route to the market based on democratic self-management may therefore offer the best hope for a transition to democratic market societies in the former Soviet Union.

Notes

1. Among the major contributions to this vast literature are Jaroslav Vanek, *The Labor-Managed Economy* (Ithaca, NY: Cornell University Press, 1977); Derek Jones and Jan Svejnar, eds., *Participatory and Self-Managed Firms: Evaluating Economic Performance* (Lexington, MA: Lexington Books, 1982); John Bonin and Louis Putterman, *Economics of Cooperation and the Labor-Managed Economy* (New York: Harwood Academic Publishers, 1987); and David Ellerman, *The Democratic Worker-Owned Firm* (New York: Unwin Hyman, 1990).

2. There are, of course, a variety of possible forms of producer cooperatives, which vary according to such questions as whether all the workers are voting members of the cooperative, how cooperative revenues are distributed, etc.

3. There may be a probation period before new workers become full voting members of the enterprise community, but this is a minor qualification of the general rule.

4. Of course, the greater the number of workers who share the residual, the less impact

variations in enterprise performance have on any individual worker; but a given amount of additional income is likely to mean much more to a worker than to a more highly paid manager or financier.

5. There is a substantial literature on the productivity gains associated with various forms of worker participation. For a representative sample, see the contributions to *Paying for Productivity*, ed. Alan Blinder (Washington, DC: The Brookings Institution, 1990). David Levine and Laura Tyson ("Participation, Productivity and the Firm's Environment," in *Paying for Productivity*, ed. Blinder) make a strong case that the economic benefits of worker participation are positively related to the extent of their involvement in management as well as the larger institutional environment.

6. For an analysis of enterprise coordination problems as prisoners' dilemmas, see Samuel Bowles, "Productivity-Enhancing Redistributions," in *Savings, Investment and Finance: A Progressive Strategy for Sustainable Economic Growth*, ed. Gerald Epstein and Herbert Gintis (forthcoming, 1993).

7. While this does not show up in higher recorded profits for the enterprise (precisely because the relevant effects are not internalized in company accounts), it nonetheless represents an efficiency gain from a larger society-wide perspective.

8. This argument about "public bads" was initially formulated and has been extensively analyzed by John Roemer; see John Roemer, "Would Economic Democracy Decrease the Amount of Public Bads?" Department of Economics Working Paper No. 376, University of California, Davis, 1991.

9. For examples of criticism of self-management, see Janos Kornai, *The Socialist System* (Princeton, NJ: Princeton University Press, 1992), chap. 20, and many of the works surveyed in Bonin and Putterman, *Economics of Cooperation*.

10. See, for example, Pranab Bardhan and John Roemer, "Market Socialism: A Case for Rejuvenation," *Journal of Economic Perspectives*, vol. 6, no. 3 (Summer 1992), and Ajit Singh, "The Stock Market and Economic Development: Should Developing Countries Encourage Stock Markets," unpublished paper, University of Cambridge, UK, October 1991.

11. A third potential social problem generated by a system of democratically self-managed enterprises is self-interested syndicalist behavior on the part of individual enterprises. Although democratic self-management can help to internalize some externalities at the level of the local community (by virtue of the fact that workers are likely to be community residents) and at the level of the larger society (because the benefits of public bads are spread thinly among enterprise members), it will not internalize all the externalities that arise above the enterprise level. For example, individual democratic enterprises competing with one another will have incentives to cut costs at the expense of other enterprises or consumers. Such problems, however, are at least as salient in the case of conventional autonomous private or public enterprises. Solving these problems requires in all cases enlightened national government policies—e.g., taxes, subsidies, and regulations—designed to align the economic behavior of individual economic entities with general society-wide interests.

12. This proposed system of internal equity is similar to the kind of "internal capital accounts" recommended by David Ellerman and put into practice in Mondragon, which also provides a capital stake to workers in proportion to the earnings they forego when the enterprise reinvests rather than distributes net revenue to collective consumption or individual wages and salaries; the proposal offered here differs, however, in allowing for dividends—varying with firm performance—as well as fixed interest returns on the accumulated capital stakes. See Ellerman, *The Democratic Worker-Owned Firm*.

13. The mutual-fund shares of deceased citizens would revert to a pool from which shares would be distributed to other citizens coming of age; newly adult citizens would be

assured of receiving shares of equivalent value to the average society-wide claim at the time they come of age.

14. The two-tiered stock-market system that is being proposed here was inspired by a similar plan for a "coupon economy" advanced originally by John Roemer (see John Roemer, "Can There Be Socialism After Communism?" in *Market Socialism: The Current Debate*, ed. Pranab Bardhan and John Roemer (Oxford: Oxford University Press, forthcoming, 1993); but the proposal offered here differs from Roemer's in a number of key respects.

15. Limited forms of worker self-management were also introduced in Poland, Hungary, and even the Soviet Union as part of efforts to decentralize cumbersome administrative-command systems in their latter years; but only the Yugoslav case will be discussed here since it is by far the most important instance of worker self-management on a national scale. This very brief evaluation of worker self-management in Yugoslavia is based on a vast literature on this subject; for representative examples, see Saul Estrin, *Self-Management: Economic Theory and Yugoslav Practice* (Cambridge: Cambridge University Press, 1983); and Harold Lydall, *Yugoslav Socialism* (Oxford: Oxford University Press, 1984).

The Problem of "Egalitarianism"

Continuity and Change
in Soviet Attitudes

Murray Yanowitch

In the final years of the old Soviet Union, the country's economic literature was characterized by the widespread questioning of what had earlier been traditional Soviet views on a wide range of issues. The most familiar and "sacred" elements of Soviet ideology bearing on such issues and concepts as central planning, state ownership of property, the approach of a communist society, the normalcy of subsidized prices, the nature of modern capitalism, and so forth, were all challenged and increasingly repudiated. Indeed, the "socialist idea" itself was subject to the same process. But in the midst of the abandonment of many old orthodoxies, one could also observe certain continuities between traditional and reformist views. For example, the intensity of the denunciations of "egalitarianism" (*uravnilovka*) in some of the economic literature in 1989–91 seemed to echo similar attacks that initially appeared in Soviet publications some six decades earlier, following Stalin's condemnation of this alleged danger. Of all the themes introduced into Soviet public discourse (in both its journalistic and more "academic" forms) during the period of the prewar five-year plans, why should the rhetoric of anti-egalitarianism continue to be reproduced frequently in the midst of democratizing political and economic reforms? The differences between the intellectual and economic environments of the early thirties on the one hand and the late eighties and early nineties on the other are so striking that the occasional continuities that may be observed here appear all the more interesting.

The prolonged and recurrent nature of the anti-egalitarian theme in the Soviet literature does not mean, of course, that the arguments invoked in its support have remained unchanged throughout. Although the essential message of both the earlier and more recent versions of anti-egalitarianism is obviously the same—i.e., the baleful economic consequences of inadequate income differentials— the particular way the message has been defended and elaborated has varied considerably. Some of the similarities and differences between the older and newer versions of this durable phenomenon will be examined below.

The author is a professor emeritus of economics at Hofstra University.

Earlier Versions of Soviet Anti-Egalitarianism

Stalin's indictment of "left" egalitarianism in 1931 focused on the alleged failure of prevailing wage scales to incorporate sufficient skill differentials and to provide adequate monetary rewards for workers engaged in "heavy" as distinct from "light" labor. "In a number of establishments, the wage rates are established in such a manner that the difference almost disappears between qualified labor and unqualified labor, between heavy labor and light labor." The consequence, according to Stalin, was that the unskilled often lacked the incentive to acquire needed skills, while the high turnover rates of skilled workers reflected their need to move from plant to plant until they finally found one that properly valued their rare skills. Who or what was responsible for this state of affairs? The time had not yet arrived when all such problems and policy mistakes would be attributed to the nefarious activities of "enemies" of the regime. Indeed, Stalin's explanation seemed to focus on the failure of state and union officials responsible for wage fixing (and prematurely guided by egalitarian sentiments) to heed the policy implications of the Marxist classics:

> Marx and Lenin say that the difference between qualified and unqualified work will exist even under socialism, even after the destruction of classes, that only under communism must this difference disappear, that in view of this wages even under socialism must be paid according to work done, and not according to need. But our egalitarians among the managers and trade unionists do not agree with this and suppose that this difference already has disappeared in our Soviet system. Who is right—Marx and Lenin or the egalitarians?[1]

Stalin's remarks obviously signalled a policy of increasing occupational and interindustry wage differentials. The next two decades also witnessed a distinct escalation in the rhetoric of anti-egalitarianism. No longer did egalitarianism imply only a comparatively innocent misreading of the requirements of socialist economic development; the term took on much more ominous political overtones. Perhaps the peak of these escalating attacks was reached in the early 1950s, as reflected in the following remarks in a volume on socialist labor published at that time:

> The socialist principle of distribution according to work was affirmed in the course of an irreconcilable struggle with petty-bourgeois egalitarianism. Trotskyists, Zinovievites, Bukharinites, and other enemies of the people attempted to implant petty-bourgeois egalitarianism into distribution and thereby to cause serious damage to our economy, to undermine the building of socialism in the USSR. The party crushed petty-bourgeois, reactionary egalitarianism in distribution, which was designed to disorganize production, and created the necessary conditions for strengthening and developing the socialist principle of distribution in accordance with work.[2]

The elements of economic logic that occasionally accompanied these ritualistic denunciations of egalitarianism came down to the following familiar propositions.

The current stage of economic development—in particular, the comparatively backward state of the "productive forces"—required that wage differentials be large enough to encourage workers to learn needed skills, to master new technology, and to improve their work performance. In other words, the guiding principle of wage structure must be "payment in accordance with the quantity and quality of work," a principle that was clearly incompatible with egalitarianism. The implementation of this principle under Soviet conditions obviously required that central authorities be responsible for establishing the appropriate occupational and interindustry differentials in basic wage rates.

Although the intensity of the attacks on egalitarianism diminished somewhat in the years following Stalin's death, the term continued to be used invariably in a negative context. Thus, even when Soviet wage policy—in the late 1950s and 1960s—was explicitly oriented toward reducing inequalities between the extremes of the wage distribution, the justifications offered for such a policy invariably stressed that the latter had no connection with egalitarianism. Whatever the real motivation behind the reductions in wage differentials during those years, they were officially justified on the grounds that prevailing differentials—at least in some cases—had come to exceed "differences in the level of complexity of the labor" of high- and low-paid groups of workers. In other words, there was no departure from the familiar socialist principle of distribution (in accordance with "the quantity and quality of work"). The notion that reduced wage inequality was desirable as "an end in itself" was explicitly condemned, and egalitarianism continued to be characterized as a "petty-bourgeois" phenomenon, as reflecting an attempt to "leap over" a necessary stage of economic development.[3] Of course, responsibility for determining the delicate balance between a legitimate narrowing of wage inequalities and one guided by egalitarian sentiments remained in customary hands.

There was a peculiar quality in the repeated denunciations of egalitarianism during those years. One would think that if egalitarian sentiments were a continuing and significant element in Soviet public consciousness rather than merely a historical relic or the consequence of the nefarious influence of domestic "enemies" of socialism, there must have been certain features of the current Soviet system that constantly generated such sentiments and operated to reinforce them. But there was nothing in the ongoing condemnations of egalitarianism to suggest what elements of the existing system helped account for this persistent phenomenon. However, the more recent literature points to a factor that could hardly be discussed openly in earlier years. In the words of a recent commentary, "under the banner of the struggle against egalitarianism," there emerged enormous differences in real incomes and in access to a wide range of goods and services, with the state and party elite occupying the most privileged position in the income structure. If current estimates of the real incomes of the top levels of the party and state bureaucracy can be taken at face value, they reached levels that were "100 to 150 times" those of the lowest income groups.[4] It would certainly be surprising if income inequalities of this magnitude and the privileges associated with them, which could hardly be kept completely secret, failed to generate egalitarian sentiments among sectors of the Soviet population, or at least the sense that there were strong elements of social injustice in the prevailing income structure. Such inequalities surely contributed more to egalitarian sentiments than the continued propagation of the Soviet version of socialist principles of distribution and the promise of a "socially homogeneous" society in the future when the development of the productive forces would permit "distribution in accordance with need."

Recent Versions of Anti-Egalitarianism

The early years of the Gorbachev political leadership—1985–86—witnessed a scattering of publications that appealed for a policy of "active redistribution" of income from the top downward, especially where the most well-to-do groups had access to what the critics characterized as "nonlabor incomes." The writings of the sociologist Vadim Z. Rogovin, who called for the "effective taxation of excessive incomes" and a "sizable" inheritance tax and characterized the prevailing ratio of approximately 3 : 1 for the decile coefficient of wage determination as "completely normal," offer the clearest illustration of what might be characterized as the egalitarian position in Soviet discussions of wage and income structure during the early years of *perestroika*.[5] By the end of the 1980s, however, the dominant position in these discussions was clearly occupied by those who argued in the long-standing tradition of anti-egalitarianism. But as noted earlier, there were new as well as familiar elements in this position during these years.

The new rhetoric no longer condemned "petty-bourgeois" or politically more ominous expressions of egalitarianism. But it did identify an erroneous mode of thinking on this issue as "infected with the bacilli of redistributive philosophy." Those who were not so "infected" surely realized that the plight of the poor was not the result of the existence of well-to-do groups in society but was often the consequence of the poor groups' employment in sectors of low economic "effectiveness." Moreover, to offset the poor economic performance of these sectors (typically the consequence of incompetent management) at the expense of workers' incomes in more efficient sectors (through redistributive taxation) would simply be "to chop off the branch on which we all sit." For the economist Gennadii Lisichkin, on whose writings we rely here, the idea of payment in accordance with work contribution remained the guide to an appropriate wage structure. But reflecting the markedly changed intellectual environment in discussions of economic issues in the late 1980s, Lisichkin insisted that the assessment of inequalities in work performance (in the "quality of labor") must be entrusted "not to the State Committee on Labor but to the market." More than enough harm had already been caused by decades of reliance on the "leveling" (*uravnitel'nyi*) version of socialism.[6]

The writings of the economist Gavriil Popov also exhibited particular sensitivity to the alleged dangers of egalitarian sentiments. What concerned Popov was that the emergence of a market economy and privatization of property—which he obviously welcomed—would inevitably mean relatively high incomes for groups commonly identified in Soviet public consciousness with the receipt of "nonlabor incomes," i.e., those functioning as "intermediaries," entrepreneurs, recipients of property income (those who derived income from "previous labor"). Did the Soviet public, wondered Popov, have a sufficiently high level of culture to understand that the increased wealth of such groups was the price that had to be paid in order "to increase the general level of well-being for all"? The dilemma, for Popov, was that the masses—whose support was essential if the existing system was to be reformed fundamentally—would have "to struggle so that one part of society would be able to earn ten times more than another." Would the masses agree to such a struggle? Unfortunately, indicated Popov, the outcome was not at all clear, given the egalitarian heritage of "administrative socialism."[7]

Whatever the differences between such appeals for the acceptance of increased income inequalities and the more primitive anti-egalitarian rhetoric of the 1930s–50s, there is also an essential similarity. In both cases the essential justification for increased income inequality in the present was that it would ensure increased economic well-being in the future. In the Stalin years and for some time thereafter, substantial skill differentials were justified on the grounds that they were necessary to accelerate the development of the "productive forces" and thereby to raise living standards and prepare the groundwork for "distribution in accordance with needs." More recently, as in the case of G. Popov, increased income differentials hold out the promise of creating "all the conditions for a normal life" and a higher "general level of well-being for all." But none of the literature concerned with undoing the damage of egalitarianism appears to have given much thought to a possibility suggested by the recent economic history of the former Soviet Union: the prolonged coexistence of increasing income inequality and declining living standards for the bulk of the population.

In some respects, however, the arguments invoked in the recent anti-egalitarian literature are quite distinct from those of the past. This is particularly apparent in those cases in which the Soviet (and post-Soviet) critics of egalitarianism appear to have assimilated the antistatist or neoconservative views commonly found in some of the Western writings of recent years. An article by Aleksandr Shchelkin published early in 1991 (in a journal still carrying the label *Kommunist* at the time) may serve as an illustration. Shchelkin appealed to his readers to heed the conclusion reached by "modern neoconservatives," namely, that "the egalitarian principle of 'equality of results' undermines a market economy and at the same time makes for an increase in the scale of state regulation."[8] What was relatively new in Shchelkin's discussion—new, that is, in the Soviet context—was his stress on the presumably negative impact of the state's taxing and redistributive activities on the freedom of consumer choice and the threat to individual liberty necessarily associated with any serious attempt to implement egalitarian policies. Shchelkin's formulation of these issues was strikingly similar to those that might be found in the Western literature of a particular ideological orientation:

> Why must we turn over to the state, in the form of a tax, what we will then receive through social programs, public consumption funds, etc.? Would it not be more just and efficient to return part of the taxes to taxpayers and propose that they buy their own services without an intermediary? Perhaps each of us individually knows the structure of his own needs better than the state and would allocate the money more economically and efficiently than anonymous bureaucratic agencies.[9]

Shchelkin noted that the attempt to escape from the "social guardianship" of the state had become a world-wide phenomenon (its earlier manifestations in the United States took the form of "taxpayers' revolts" and the emergence of Reaganomics). While some state support was surely justified to assure citizens a "subsistence minimum," the more wide-ranging forms of "social patronage" threatened to destroy the "self-supporting motivation" of ordinary citizens. Hence the turn to policies based primarily on "helping those who help themselves," policies that in Shchelkin's view were at least as just—if not more so—as policies that guaranteed benefits from "cradle to pension." The implications for Soviet policy (this was still 1991) seemed obvious.

But perhaps the most striking element—certainly unusual in the Soviet context—in Shchelkin's discussion was his association of egalitarianism with the loss of personal freedom. What was the connection? The more thorough the implementation of the principle of egalitarianism, "the stronger grows the controlling function of the state." An enormous hierarchical apparatus would be required to calculate the appropriate levels of income, consumption, and housing space for the population, then to incorporate these "norms" into assignments for particular economic sectors and ultimately into "directives for the whole of the national economy." A commitment to "universal equality" (Shchelkin did not make it clear just who, if anyone, was demanding this version of equality) would obviously require constant and intrusive checking on people's economic status. Those who sought to transcend the officially established limits of income differentials, or even "grumbled" excessively, in Shchelkin's view, would be subject to "repressive measures." Carried to an extreme, egalitarian policies would be accompanied by "direct despotism."[10]

Would it be unfair to suggest that in some respects this version of anti-egalitarian rhetoric functioned as the counterpart of the literature of the early 1950s that sought to link egalitarianism with "Trotskyists, Zinovievites, . . . and other enemies of the people"?

An additional illustration of the new directions taken by some of the recent anti-egalitarian literature should suffice. Criticisms, indeed denunciations, of the social-democratic movement and its economic policies had long been a staple item in the Soviet economic literature. But to the extent that such criticisms still appeared in the late 1980s, they were markedly different than in earlier decades. While in the distant past social-democracy had signified a betrayal of genuine (Marxist-Leninist) "socialism," the critiques of the late 1980s focused on the damage that excessive intervention in the market mechanism (implemented by governments led by social democrats) had allegedly inflicted on the economies of several West European countries earlier in the postwar period. The problem was that the social democrats, in the words of Boris Pinsker—a principal critic—assumed that their party and government "could allocate resources better than the market."[11] This was particularly apparent in their support for redistributive policies that shifted income from the more industrious and skilled groups to lower-income strata. "To the extent that incomes are leveled with the help of a system of redistribution, they weaken the incentives to intensive and innovative work." The redistributive policies of the welfare state not only inhibit the more capable but "demoralize and weaken the poor."[12] Pinsker's conclusions were based largely on his analysis of social-democratic policies in England, West Germany, and the Scandinavian countries, with no explicit references to their implications for domestic Soviet policy. The latter hardly seemed necessary, however, given the unambiguous nature of these conclusions.

Our objective here has not been to give a comprehensive review of the more recent Soviet literature in this area but to illustrate the highly selective manner in which the Western experience and Western writings have been invoked in the Soviet anti-egalitarian cause. It is, of course, perfectly natural—especially under circumstances of the current market transition—to draw on the experience and ideas of the developed capitalist countries in issues related to economic inequalities and their impact on work performance and the political sphere. But one looks in vain in Soviet (and post-Soviet) publications for any recognition that there is also a substantial Western literature that points to a positive association between egalitarian policies on the one hand and relatively high levels of economic performance and political democratization on the other. We refer here to the considerable Western critical literature on the "equality–efficiency trade-off" and to empirical studies that appear to support the position that "advanced capitalist countries with more equal distributions of income also display better economic performance, sustaining, for example, higher levels of investment and more rapid rates of productivity growth."[13] Similarly, it is not difficult to find Western political-science literature that points out that the "institutionalization of inequalities in wealth and income" tends to reinforce inequalities in political resources and thus to limit the democratic nature of political institutions.[14]

Our point is not that these views are "correct" and the Western neoconservative views cited in the Soviet anti-egalitarian literature are "incorrect." It is rather that the lessons to be learned from the West—from "normal, civilized" market economies—

tend to be identified with the latter views, while the former tend to be ignored. The situation here is somewhat analogous to what may be observed in recent Soviet (and post-Soviet) discussions of appropriate responses to the threat of unemployment (see our Introduction to this volume, co-authored with Bertram Silverman). The warnings of foreign "specialists" about the dangers of excessive unemployment benefits are more likely to be cited than those Western studies that point to the potentially positive effect of job security on productive performance.

There is a final, somewhat curious feature of the recent Soviet attacks on egalitarianism that is worth noting. They often tend to exaggerate the strength of the population's egalitarian sentiments. For example, writing at the beginning of 1991, Aleksandr Shchelkin refers to the common tendency to identify social justice with "full equality" and the continuing hold that the ideology of "equality of results" has on Soviet thinking.[15] Similarly, an article by the economist Efrem Maiminas published at the end of 1991 characterizes the typical Soviet citizen's conception of the ideal of equality as "equality of results," while for the average American this ideal is identified with "equality of opportunity."[16] This contrast is invoked by Maiminas as a perfectly obvious generalization not requiring any qualification or supporting empirical evidence.

But the late 1980s and early 1990s witnessed the emergence of empirical surveys of public attitudes on wage and income inequality that—at the very least—place these characterizations in doubt. Thus, a public-opinion survey conducted by the Soviet Union's principal polling organization in 1989 (the All-Union Center for the Study of Public Opinion (*VTsIOM*), headed by Tat'iana Zaslavskaia) found that almost two-fifths of the respondents accepted the view that without "large differences" in pay people would not be interested in performing "good work." A similar proportion opposed the establishment of any upper limits on people's incomes. In a somewhat later survey conducted by the same organization, Zaslavskaia found that approximately one-third of respondents adhered to an "egalitarian" conception of distributive justice. However, this did not mean that they favored an equal distribution of income but rather that income differentials should be "very limited, without great disparities." Perhaps most surprising, a 1990 study by a team of Soviet and U.S. scholars found that Soviet citizens "appear to be no more concerned with income inequality" than their U.S. counterparts, "and they appear to have the same or even stronger appreciation of the importance of incentives."[17] We do not suggest that this scattering of studies provides a definitive picture of Soviet attitudes toward income inequality, but it certainly does not lend support to some of the more extreme characterizations of a population "infected" with irrational egalitarian sentiments.

Why this tendency to exaggerate the prevalence of such sentiments? After six decades of almost continuous attacks aimed at the same target, the more extreme anti-egalitarian literature retained some of the features of an old-fashioned Soviet "campaign." That is, it relied on familiar rhetoric and tended to ignore evidence of more receptive or tolerant—although hardly enthusiastic—public attitudes toward market-determined income differentials. But even some commentators who may have been aware of the empirical findings cited above could hardly be certain that Soviet workers were prepared to accept as "just" or "equitable" the kind of income differentials that the market transition might eventually generate.

Moving Toward New Conceptions of "Social Justice"

It should come as no surprise that some of the recent literature on egalitarianism and related issues has sought to redefine the concept of social justice. We conclude with a brief review of some of these efforts. In some cases these attempts at redefinition seem to be essentially an extension of the anti-egalitarian theme. In other cases the concept of social justice has been linked to a wide range of institutional changes projected in the reformist literature. Perhaps of greatest interest are some of the difficulties that serious Russian scholars who favor the market transition have had in reconciling the concept of social justice with the functioning of a market system.

For Efrem Maiminas it seemed vital to break the habit of associating social justice "exclusively" with policies aimed at redistributing income and wealth in favor of the "poor and needy." Social justice would be served "first of all" by policies that gave support to and stimulated the growth of the "middle strata." The core elements of the policies required to accomplish this were summed up by Maiminas as "free enterprise and free labor." After all, noted Maiminas, in economically developed countries it was the "middle strata" who comprised the majority of citizens on whose tax payments and philanthropic contributions the poor depended. Moreover, a growing middle class would provide a strong base of public support for a market economy—the transition to which would surely provide increased scope for social justice.[18]

The writings of Larisa Piiasheva, an early and consistent advocate of market reforms, convey an essentially similar message. But Piiasheva formulated the issue in somewhat broader terms: "What is a socially just state?" Her answer consisted essentially in specifying the kinds of equalities such a state would seek to ensure and those it would reject. Above all, such a state (which would necessarily be based on "the rule of law") would implement the principle of the "equality of all citizens before the law." This would include—a partial listing follows—the equal right of all citizens to own property, to receive an education, to start a business, to choose a particular area of residence, to work in the private or state sector. Thus the conception of social justice and social equality that would guide such a state would be based on the principle of equality of rights and opportunities. But Piiasheva also made it clear that the conception of social justice she was defending was "incompatible with the ideal of equality understood as an equality in the division of material benefits," the kind of equality some sought to achieve by simply redistributing income from the rich to the poor. This was the kind of equality that stood in the way of the community's "affluence." The principle of distributive justice that a socially just state would seek to protect involved "distribution of incomes on a merit basis, that is, in accordance with the objective results of one's work and personal contribution." Policies that sought to achieve the leveling of incomes in the name of social justice would simply help break the connection between the monetary rewards for work and the "actual usefulness of that work for society."[19] It was clear from the general context of Piiasheva's discussion that the market mechanism would be the instrument that could be relied on to record the "objective results" and "actual usefulness" of different people's labor activity.

These are only some examples of the growing literature of the early 1990s that sought to associate the concept of social justice with promarket and antiegalitarian policies.[20] But not all participants in these discussions spoke in the same unambiguous voice. Thus Tat´iana Zaslavskaia, the sociologist whose writings in 1986–87 pointed to the distinctly inequitable nature of the Soviet distribution of real income, was among those who questioned the increasingly common identification of distributive justice with market-determined income differentials in the early 1990s.[21]

Zaslavskaia distinguished between social justice as a "normative" concept (which has been embedded in public consciousness "perhaps since the time of Christ or earlier," and which she obviously shared) and social justice as a socioeconomic concept (which derives its meaning from a specific environment and is obviously destined to vary with changing historical circumstances). Using the concept in the latter sense, Zaslavskaia made it clear that she continued to regard as just or equitable the familiar principle: "From each according to his abilities, to each according to his work." However, she noted, whatever the problems in applying this principle in earlier years, the current movement toward a market transition was accompanied by the emergence of fundamentally new types of work activity whose contribution to output could hardly be estimated by relying on familiar "quantitative and qualitative" criteria. Zaslavskaia then posed the issue explicitly in the context of what was becoming commonly referred to as entrepreneurial or "business" (*predprinimatel´skaia*) activity: "And thus the question arises, do business incomes that may exceed the wages of the most skilled labor by dozens of times conform to the principles of social justice?"

Zaslavskaia's response seemed almost consciously ambiguous, perhaps even self-contradictory. But it also served to highlight the dilemma of those intellectuals who were unambiguous supporters of market reforms and simultaneously less than enthusiastic about their consequences for relative incomes. There were two possible answers to the above question, noted Zaslavskaia. One was in the negative—such entrepreneurial incomes were unjust, and as such should be prohibited or restricted. But if this were to occur, "we would once again fall into the swamp of 'stagnation' from which we are painfully trying to extricate ourselves." An affirmative answer to the above question, i.e., that entrepreneurial incomes corresponded to the principle of distribution according to work, simply required that the concept of "work" be extended beyond the boundaries that seemed to apply in the socialist past. In effect, noted Zaslavskaia, an affirmative answer would imply that the market, "in its own way," was also just or equitable. This was certainly a "possible" approach. But was it really appropriate to proclaim the "formal equality of rights of the poor and the rich on the market"? Was it not clear that the justice imposed by the market could be "cruel and harsh"? To the degree that the market was "merciless toward the weak and the dispossessed," social justice was completely at odds with the market. But after all this, Zaslavskaia also reaffirmed that there was no single universally applicable conception of social justice (presumably using the term in its "socioeconomic" rather than "normative" sense) and that, therefore, a "compromise" was necessary.[22] It should be stressed that none of her characterizations of the possible relationship between social justice and the market was accompanied by any appeals for a retreat from the goal of a transition to a market economy.

In some respects Zaslavskaia's own views seemed to mirror the peculiar mix of contradictory sentiments revealed in public-opinion surveys during the initial stages of the market transition. Thus by 1991 almost one-half of the respondents in one such survey (48.6 percent) agreed that "large differences" in pay were necessary to elicit a sense of involvement in work. But no more than 20–25 percent shared what Zaslavskaia characterized as "market conceptions of justice" (the remainder identified social justice with the familiar principle of "from each . . . to each . . ." or with "egalitarian values," i.e., differentials should be "very limited").[23] Put somewhat differently, a substantial proportion of the population seemed to accept the need for a transition to a market economy, but the vast majority—apparently including Zaslavskaia—retained conceptions of social justice that seemed at odds with the requirements of a market transition. It would seem natural under such circumstances that some commentators would continue to point the finger of blame at the "egalitarian" sentiments instilled in the population by the socialist ideology of the past. But would there also be some who would consider the possibility that one of the difficulties in accepting the "market conception of justice" was the "normative" concept of justice that Zaslavskaia suggested had been an aspect of public consciousness "perhaps since the time of Christ or earlier" and that was impossible to abandon?

Finally, if we may conclude with a minimum dose of unsolicited advice: The urgency of improving workers' productive performance would suggest that the roots of the widespread sense of social injustice (reported by Zaslavskaia) be sought in the actual structure and increased magnitude of real income differentials generated by the market transition rather than in the "bacilli" of egalitarian sentiments.[24]

Notes

1. Abram Bergson, *The Structure of Soviet Wages* (Cambridge, MA: Harvard University Press, 1946), p. 178. Although we rely here and elsewhere on Bergson's translation of Stalin's remarks, we have taken the liberty of rendering his "equalitarians" as "egalitarians."

2. A. Liapin, *Trud pri sotsializme* (Moscow, 1951), pp. 60–61.

3. N.E. Rabkina and N.M. Rimashevskaia, *Osnovy differentsiatsii zarabotnoi platy i dokhodov naseleniia* (Moscow, 1972), pp. 20–23; V.F. Maier, *Zarabotnaia plata v period perekhoda k kommunizmu* (Moscow, 1963), p. 95; R.A. Batkaev and V.I. Markov, *Differentsiatsiia zarabotnoi platy v promyshlennosti SSSR* (Moscow, 1964), p. 6.

4. E. Manevich, "Wages Under Conditions of a Market Economy," *Voprosy ekonomiki*, 1991, no. 7, p. 137. Such inequalities, of course, were perfectly compatible with considerable "wage leveling" within occupational groups and comparatively low incomes for such skilled occupations as physicians (mainly women) relative to those of some skilled workers.

5. Murray Yanowitch, *Controversies in Soviet Social Thought* (Armonk, NY: M.E. Sharpe, 1991), pp. 90–93.

6. G. Lisichkin, "A Prosperous Worker—A Thriving State," *Izvestiia*, August 8, 1989.

7. G. Popov, "On the Benefit of Inequality," *Literaturnaia gazeta*, October 4, 1989.

8. A. Shchelkin, "Inequality with Which All Agree," *Kommunist*, 1991, no. 3, p. 40.

9. Ibid., p. 38.

10. Ibid.

11. B. Pinsker, "The Bureaucratic Chimera," *Znamia*, November 1989, p. 189.

12. Ibid, pp. 194, 199.

13. Samuel Bowles, David M. Gordon, and Thomas E. Weisskopf, *After the Waste Land* (Armonk, NY: M.E. Sharpe, 1990), p. 221. For an example of a critical approach to the notion of an "equality–efficiency trade-off," see Robert Kuttner, *The Economic Illusion* (Philadelphia: University of Pennsylvania Press, 1987). See also the papers in *International Journal of Sociology*, vol. 21, no. 3.

14. Robert A. Dahl, *Dilemmas of Pluralist Democracy* (New Haven: Yale University Press, 1982), p. 174.

15. Shchelkin, "Inequality with Which All Agree," pp. 37, 39.

16. E. Maiminas, "Can the Economy Be Just?" *Svobodnaia mysl'*, 1991, no. 16, p. 101.

17. The empirical findings summarized in this paragraph draw on the following sources: "Economic Reform in the Eyes of Public Opinion," *Rabochii klass i sovremennyi mir*, 1990, no. 3, pp. 43–44; T. Zaslavskaia, "Social Justice: Six Years Later," *Svobodnaia mysl'*, 1992, no. 1, p. 30; Robert J. Shiller, Maxim Boycko, and Vladimir Korobov, "Popular Attitudes Toward Free Markets: The Soviet Union and the United States," *The American Economic Review*, vol. 81, no. 3 (June 1991), p. 399.

18. Maiminas, "Can the Economy Be Just?" pp. 102–3.

19. However, Piiasheva also made it clear that a socially just state would not leave the poor, the sick, and the elderly "to the mercy of fate." See L. Piiasheva, "In Pursuit of the Blue Bird," *Oktiabr'*, 1990, no. 9, pp. 156–58; L. Piiasheva, *In Pursuit of Social Justice* (Moscow: Progress Publishers, 1991), pp. 252, 255–56.

20. For another illustration of this tendency, see Iu. Volkov, "The Market Economy and Ensuring Social Justice in the Sphere of Labor Relations," *Problems of Economic Transition*, vol. 35, no. 5 (September 1992), pp. 50–62.

21. See Murray Yanowitch, ed., *A Voice of Reform: Essays by Tat'iana I. Zaslavskaia* (Armonk, NY: M.E. Sharpe, 1989), esp. pp. xiv–xvii.

22. Zaslavskaia, "Social Justice: Six Years Later," pp. 29–30, 36.

23. Ibid., pp. 30–31.

24. For evidence of substantial increases in income inequality between 1990 and 1992—a period of declining living standards for the bulk of the Russian population—see G.I. Khanin, "The End of Illusions," *EKO*, 1992, no. 10, pp. 31–32. Khanin observes, "Obviously, the real incomes of the least well-off part of the population declined much more rapidly than those of the population as a whole."

Part 3

Labor Strategies in a Postindustrial Society

High-Performance Production Systems in a More Competitive, Knowledge-Intensive World Economy

Ray Marshall

Introduction

The economies of the United States and the former Soviet Union are involved in a transition from traditional economies, whose characteristics became firmly entrenched between the 1930s and the 1950s, to more competitive market-oriented global systems. There are some important similarities and differences between these transitions, but it seems fairly clear that to be successful in more competitive, knowledge-intensive economies, both the U.S. and the former Soviet economies must achieve some of the same outcomes.

A comparative study of these transitions and others going on in Europe and Asia provide some very important lessons for policy makers everywhere. One of the most important of these, often misread by free-market advocates in the United States, is that joint public/private governance mechanisms become more, not less, important in more global competitive systems. Those who believe that the collapse of communism and the success of market-oriented systems signal the triumph of laissez-faire capitalism misread the causes of the successful performance of economies in Asia and Europe. In all cases, success has resulted from consensus-based public/private strategies to take advantage of market forces, not from unbridled market forces alone.

There also seems to be emerging consensus on the prerequisites for stable, progressive industrial systems. These include pluralistic democracies, human rights, and market-oriented economies. These prerequisites form a comprehensive whole—they are not contradictory, as some observers argue. In other words, both a respect for human rights and democratic institutions are essential to progressive market systems; a "trade-off" among these prerequisites not only is not required but will cause industrial systems to be less stable and progressive.

A third lesson is the need for comprehensive economic policies that give higher priority to labor and human resource development policies than has been the case in the economy of either the United States or the former USSR. It is

The author is a professor of economics and public affairs at the University of Texas, Austin.

particularly important for policy makers to understand the significance of human resource development for high-performance economic systems.

This conclusion raises three basic questions: What is meant by a "high-performance" system? Why have such systems become more important for economic success in the 1990s and beyond? What is the role of labor relations in such systems? The remarks in this paper will attempt to answer these questions in the context of developments in the United States. However, the United States will be contrasted in some particulars with developments in Western Europe and Japan.

The following are the basic propositions developed in this paper.

(1) Traditional labor movements in the industrialized market-oriented democracies (IMODs) were reactions to the conditions of workers in national industrial systems. By the end of the 1930s, and certainly by the end of the 1940s, labor movements had become integral components of the economic systems in all of the IMODs. These labor movements were justified by the prevailing political and economic philosophies and policies of the time as essential both to speak for and to protect workers' interests and to provide workers with purchasing power to keep the mass-production system going.

This combination served the industrialized market-oriented democracies very well. They experienced what was probably the longest period of equitably shared prosperity in history, made possible mainly by the mass-production system, full employment or "Keynesian" economic policies, collective bargaining, and the social safety nets. In most of the IMODs, income distribution shifted from a pyramid with a few people at the top and most at the bottom to more of a diamond with larger proportions of income recipients in the middle.

The industrialized market-oriented democracies recognized the need for economic and social justice, or equity, which means that policies should be tilted toward those who need the most help. Equity was required to counteract the natural tendency for elitist management systems and market forces to produce inequality. Not even their staunchest defenders believe free markets alone are adequate to produce equity or facilitate the development of human resources.

(2) The traditional (i.e., mass production, Keynesian economics, and adversarial industrial relations) system's foundations have eroded since the 1960s, mainly because of *internationalization* and *technological changes*, which are closely interrelated. Internationalization increased economic interdependence among countries and greatly altered the rules of the game for countries, enterprises, and unions. The initial impact of these changes has been to undermine the conditions of workers, especially in the United States. Income distribution is now becoming more like an hour glass instead of a diamond, real wages are falling, union power has declined, and the social "safety nets" are being shredded.

These developments have caused some analysts to argue that *unions are obsolete*, along with the *national oligopolies* to which they were closely related. The new locus of power, according to this view, is in the "high-tech" companies, which are largely unorganized, and in multinational corporations (MNCs), which are beyond the reach of most national governments and labor unions. According to this view, these changes occurred because of the mobility of capital relative to labor and the fact that the effectiveness of unions' traditional basic operating procedures (taking labor out of competition) has been greatly reduced by intensified international competition.

The implication of this argument is that the "monopoly wage" that the unions in the industrialized democracies were able to extract will now be lost, and workers' wages and employment conditions must be set in a global economy, which implies lower wages for high-wage countries like the United States.

(3) What do the above-mentioned developments suggest?

This scenario *could* come about, but it is not predetermined. Indeed, it would be wrong to generalize from the U.S. experience because unions in other countries, especially in Scandinavia and Western Europe, have generally maintained or improved their density (i.e., proportion of the work force organized) since the 1960s, and even during the 1980s (see Figure 1). In fact, the Canadian labor movement has increased its density since the 1960s, despite being subjected to some of the same environmental conditions as U.S. unions. A different set of policies and choices could therefore:

—strengthen both *workers'* incomes and working conditions and *labor movements* and make it possible to achieve convergence by raising the wages of Third World workers rather than lowering them in the United States and other high-wage countries.

—However, this scenario requires very different policies, structures, and practices, especially from those currently being pursued in the United States, which have put downward pressure on wages, polarized incomes, and greatly weakened unions.

—We should note, moreover, that the nonunion high-tech companies are losing competitiveness along with the more highly unionized basic industries.

What are the forces that have produced these changes? What kinds of national policies are required? What do these changes imply for labor relations?

In order to answer these questions, we must understand the economic context within which traditional industrial-relations systems developed, the nature of the changes that have eroded the foundations of those traditional systems, and the kinds of adjustments that have been made by labor movements in Scandinavia and Western Europe, which have continued to grow despite being subjected to the same kinds of external economic conditions that have troubled American unions. The experiences of these more successful labor movements provide some lessons for the United States, the main focus of these remarks.

The Changing Economy

Traditional U.S. labor–management relations are deeply rooted in the economic policies and institutions that made the United States the world's strongest industrial economy during the first half of this century. In addition to its supportive

Figure 1. **Union Membership of Nonagricultural Workers as a Percentage of Nonagricultural Wage and Salary Employees: 1970 to 1986–87**

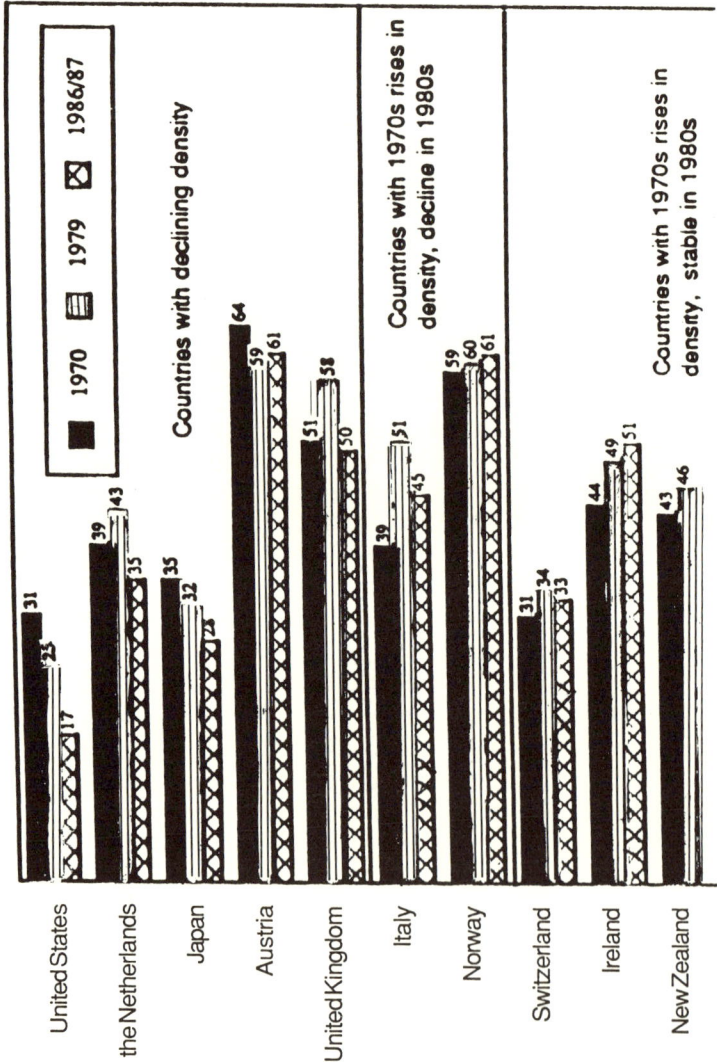

Source: David G. Blanchflower and Richard B. Freeman, "Going Different Ways: Unionism in the U.S. and Other Advanced OECD Countries," NBER Working Paper No. 3342, 1990, p. 42.

institutions and a steady flow of highly motivated immigrant and migrant workers, the most important factors in America's economic success were abundant natural resources, the mass-production system (which made it possible to achieve relatively rapid improvements in productivity and total output through economies of scale), and reinforcing shifts of resources from lower to higher productivity industries. American industry was, in addition, strengthened by a so-called "virtuous cycle," whereby improvements in productivity in basic industries reduced the costs of inputs to other industries.

The mass-production system organized work so that most thinking, planning, and decision making was done by managerial, professional, and technical elites. Line work was simplified so that it could be done by relatively unskilled workers. The assumption was that there was "one best way" to perform a task. It was management's responsibility to discover that one best method and impose it on the system through detailed regulations, enforced by supervisors, inspectors, and administrative staffs. It was assumed by "scientific" management experts like Frederick W. Taylor that workers would "soldier" or loaf unless they were closely supervised. Management, therefore, sought to gain control of the work by standardizing work processes and transferring ideas, skills, and knowledge to managers and machines.

Monotonous working conditions were made more bearable by wages that were much higher than those that could be earned on the farm or in the home countries of the immigrants who flocked to America's factories, mills, and mines during the early part of this century.

The system had major weaknesses, some of which were gradually worked out by the 1940s. A major problem for mass-production companies was to control markets and prices in order to guarantee profits to justify the large investments required for these systems. These firms therefore worked out oligopolistic arrangements to avoid price competition and adjusted to change mainly by varying output and employment while holding prices relatively constant.

There was, however, another problem. Once they stabilized the prices of their products, the mass-production companies experienced cyclical instability because production tended to outrun consumption at administered prices. The industrialized market-economy countries fixed this problem through so-called "Keynesian" monetary-fiscal policies, which manipulated government spending and interest rates to generate enough total demand to keep the system operating at relatively low levels of unemployment.

Another problem was to make the system more just or equitable in order to strengthen democratic institutions and social cohesion. As noted, the mass-production system and market forces produced inequalities, which were only partially offset by public policies. And the offset was less in the United States than in most other industrial democracies, which had stronger social safety nets and better-organized political and economic labor movements. Industrial relations and "welfare" or "income-maintenance" policies nevertheless reinforced

Keynesian macroeconomic and administered price policies. Unions, collective bargaining, unemployment compensation, and social security were all justified as ways to sustain purchasing power. Although they were brought into it reluctantly, oligopolistic companies could see the wisdom of providing purchasing power, especially when it became clear that unions and collective bargaining were not really going to challenge their control of the system—they were merely going to codify work practices and protect workers from some of the most arbitrary company policies. The unemployment compensation system also helped companies maintain their work forces by, in effect, supplementing wages during layoffs.

Unions and their supporters had the same aversion for competition in labor markets as the oligopolists did for competitive product markets. Early unions learned that competition forced many employers to depress wages and working conditions. Workers in all industrial market-oriented democracies, therefore, organized not only to extend democracy to the work place but also to remove labor from competition through collective bargaining and government regulations. Labor theorists, like the Webbs (1897), argued that removing labor from competition through collective bargaining and government regulations increased efficiency by preventing companies from depressing labor standards, thus forcing them to compete by becoming more efficient. The Webbs reasoned that employers who paid less than the living wage were being subsidized either by workers and their families or by society. Such subsidies thus generated inefficiencies and made it difficult for countries to develop their human resources.

Both the mass-production system and demand-management policies were justified by the American economy's remarkable performance in World War II. After the war, the combination of economies of scale, abundant natural resources, strong global demand, and a backlog of technology (much of it, including the computer, developed by the military) ushered in the longest period of equitably shared prosperity in U.S. history. Progressive government policies and collective bargaining counteracted the market's natural tendency to produce inequality. This whole system was reinforced by fixed exchange rates, international trade rules, and supportive financial institutions, all of which aided the expansion of America's mass-production system.

The System Erodes

Toward the end of the 1960s, the foundations of America's traditional economic system began to crumble. The main forces for change were technology and increased international competition, which combined to render much of the traditional mass-production system and its supporting institutions anachronistic. These changes also dramatically altered the conditions for economic viability. In a more competitive world dominated by knowledge-intensive technology, the keys to economic success become human resources and a more effective organization of production systems, not natural resources and traditional economies of scale. Indeed, as the work of Theodore Schultz, Robert Solow, and other economists demonstrated, the process of substituting knowledge and skills for physical resources had been the main source of improved productivity at least since the 1920s (Marshall and Tucker 1992; Carnevale 1983; Schultz 1981).

Technology not only contributed to the globalization of markets but also made the mass-production system and traditional economies of scale less viable in high-wage countries. Although the assembly line can be automated, that probably is not the most efficient use of the new technology. Computerized technology makes it possible to gain many of the advantages of economies of scale and scope through flexible manufacturing systems, which have enormous advantages in a more dynamic and competitive global economy. The new technology provides economies of scope as well as scale because the same technology can be used to produce different products.

Technology makes new organizations of production *possible*, but competition makes them *necessary* for those who wish to maintain and improve incomes. This is so because a more competitive internationalized information economy has very different requirements for national, enterprise, organizational, and personal success than was true of largely national goods-producing systems. One of the most important changes for public-policy purposes is that national governments have less control of their economies. It therefore is no longer possible for a single country to maintain high wages and full employment through traditional combinations of monetary-fiscal policies, administered wages and prices, and fixed exchange rates. In the 1970s and 1980s, internationalization weakened the linkages among domestic consumption, investment, and output that formed the basic structure of the traditional "Keynesian" demand-management system. The weakening of these Keynesian linkages became very clear when U.S. tax cuts in the early 1980s increased consumption but also greatly stimulated imports and therefore produced much smaller increases in domestic investment than had resulted from earlier tax cuts in less globalized markets.

It would be a mistake, however, to conclude, as some have, that this more internationalized environment requires less government involvement. In an internationalized economy, national government policies must be more selective as to both function and economic sectors, but they are at least as important to successful economic performance as they were in more national goods-producing systems. In fact, careful research by David Alan Aschauer (1988, 1989a, 1989b) has demonstrated in work at the Federal Reserve Bank of Chicago that a major cause of the decline in productivity growth in the United States since the 1960s has been the decline in *public investment* for infrastructure, not, as many conservatives believe, because of a decline in private investments. These matters will be explored at greater length after a discussion of how internationalization and technological change have altered the conditions for economic viability.

The Basic Choice: Low Wages or Higher Quality and Productivity

These altered economic conditions do not just change the *magnitude* of the requirements for economic success, they fundamentally alter the *necessary structures* and *policies*. This is so because economic success in the more competitive global information economy requires greater emphasis on some factors that were much less important in traditional mass-production systems. These new factors are quality, productivity, and flexibility.

Quality, best defined as meeting customers' needs, becomes more important for two reasons. First, as the mass-production system matured and personal incomes rose, consumers became less satisfied with standardized products. Second, the more competitive environment of the 1990s is largely consumer driven; the mass-production system was more producer driven, especially after governments and oligopolies "stabilized" prices. In the more competitive environments of the 1970s and 1980s, oligopolistic pricing became anachronistic; flexible prices became more important. Furthermore, the mass-production system depended heavily on controlling national markets; with internationalization, American companies have much less market control.

Productivity and flexibility are closely related to quality. The difference is that now productivity improvements are achieved through using *all factors of production* more efficiently, not, as in the mass-production system, mainly through economies of scale and compatible and reinforcing interindustry shifts. Indeed, in the 1970s and 1980s, interindustry shifts lowered productivity growth because they were, on balance, shifts from more productive manufacturing activities to less productive services.

Flexibility enhances productivity by facilitating the shift of resources from less to more productive outputs and improves quality through the ability to respond quickly to diverse and changing consumer needs. Moreover, flexibility in the use of workers and technology improves productivity by reducing the waste of labor and machine time. Indeed, it is probably the case that flexibility, which makes it possible to deliver a variety of automated goods in a timely manner, has at least as much to do with competitiveness (in the sense of competing on terms that make it possible to maintain and improve incomes) as lower costs.

Firms and economies can compete in more global knowledge-intensive markets either by lowering their wages or by becoming more productive. Since the early 1970s, American companies have been competing mainly through reducing domestic wages and by shifting productive facilities to low-wage countries. This is one of the reasons for the fact that real wages were lower in the United States in 1990 than they were in 1970, and why in 1989 American wages were about tenth among the major industrialized countries (Bureau of Labor Statistics 1990; Mishel and Frankel 1990). Not only does the low-wage option lead to lower and more unequal incomes, it also limits personal, enterprise, or national economic progress. With a cost-cutting strategy, the only way to improve incomes is to use more resources and work harder, which is clearly self-limiting. The high-productivity option, by contrast, puts people and enterprises on steep learning and earning curves, where the potential for improvement has no clearly defined limits (Marshall and Tucker 1992).

Worker Participation, Lean Management Systems, and Higher-Order Thinking Skills

The fundamental issue, of course, is how to arrange production in order to achieve quality, productivity, and flexibility. The answer appears to be to restructure production systems and to develop and use leading-edge technologies. Productivity is improved by work organizations that reduce waste of materials through better inventory control, promote the efficient use of labor, and develop more effective quality controls to prevent defects. High-performance systems have a high degree of employee involvement in what would have been considered "management" functions in mass-production systems. Indeed, in more productive and flexible systems, the distinctions between front-line "managers" and "workers" become blurred.

A number of features of high-performance production systems encourage worker participation and lean management structures. For one thing, these systems require workers to have more knowledge and skill. And skilled, educated workers are less tolerant of monotonous, routine work and authoritarian managerial controls. Second, quality, productivity, and flexibility are all enhanced when production decisions are made as close to the point of production as possible. Mass-production bureaucracies were designed to achieve quantity, managerial control, and stability, not flexibility, quality, or productivity in the use of all factors of production. Mass-production systems are based on managerial information monopolies and worker controls; high-performance systems require that workers be free to make decisions. To accomplish this, information must be shared, not monopolized, because in high-performance systems machines do more of the routine, direct work and front-line workers do more indirect work formerly done mainly by administrative staffs.

A high-performance system has a number of features that change the hierarchical management systems. First, since machines take over more of the direct work and front-line workers take over more of the indirect work, there is less need for inspectors, schedulers, and other indirect workers. Second, since workers manage more of their own work, individually or in teams, there is less need for managers. Thus, a major function of Tayloristic managers was to control the flow of information, a function that can be performed more effectively by computers and other information technology, which can provide everybody a common data base or "score." The role of managers, therefore, changes in a high-performance system from "bossing" or managing to supporting front-line workers, who assume more responsibility for quality, productivity, and flexibility.

One of the most important differences between high-performance and Tayloristic systems is in the attitudes between managers and workers. As noted, the Tayloristic attitude is that workers are naturally lazy and must be forced to work out of fear that they will lose their jobs or be reprimanded. The Taylor system assumed, in addition, that most frontline workers did not have to think and, indeed, were incapable of the kind of higher-order thinking done by supervisors educated in "scientific management." This Tayloristic attitude naturally created resentment and distrust of management by workers and their unions. High-performance managements, by contrast, establish trust and respect between workers and managers by assuming that most workers instinctively want to do a good job, which enhances their self-worth and gains them the respect of management and their fellow workers. These managers assume, in addition, that workers and effective work organization, not managers or technology, are the keys to high performance. They assume, further, that workers understand their jobs, are capable of higher-order thinking, and are motivated by positive reward systems, especially managers who value their work.

High-performance systems, therefore, require that workers have different kinds of thinking skills than was the case in Tayloristic systems. One of the most important skills required for indirect work is the ability to analyze the flood of data produced by information technology. Workers who can impose order on chaotic data can use information to add value to products, improve productivity and quality, solve problems, and improve technology.

Indirect work also is more likely to be group work, requiring more communication and interpersonal skills. These skills are necessary because productivity, quality, and flexibility require close coordination between what were formerly more discrete components of the production process (e.g., research and development, design, production, inspection, distribution, sales, services). These functions were more linear in the mass-production system but are more interactive in dynamic, consumer-oriented production systems.

Another very important skill for high-performance systems is the ability to learn. Learning is not only more important than in mass-production systems but also very different. The simplification of tasks and the standardization of technology and productivity in the mass-production system limits the amount of learning needed or achieved. More learning is required in a dynamic, technology-intensive work place, and more of that learning must be through the manipulation of abstract symbols. For line workers, mass-production systems stressed learning almost entirely by observation and doing.

Learning in more productive work places is also likely to be more communal and cooperative. The mass-production system's adversarial relationships impede the sharing of information among workers, managers, and suppliers. A high-performance system, by contrast, encourages the sharing of information and cooperative efforts to achieve common objectives. A high-performance system creates a community of interests among all of those involved in the system—

managers, front-line workers and suppliers, and other components of the networks high-performance organizations establish to enhance their competitiveness. The mass-production system created adversarial relations designed to keep costs down. There clearly is much more learning in a community-of-interest network than in an adversarial system. Communal learning, in addition, becomes more important as a means of building the consensus needed to improve the performance of more highly integrated production processes. High-performance workers are required not only to be self-managers but also to perform a greater array of tasks and adapt more readily to change. This requires a reduction of the mass-production system's detailed job classifications and work rules. Well-educated, well-trained, highly motivated workers are likely to be much more flexible and productive, especially in supportive systems that stress equity and internal cohesion. Indeed, humans are likely to be the most flexible components in a high-performance system.

Other features of high-performance work places require greater worker participation. One is the need for constant improvements in technology—or what the Japanese call "giving wisdom to the machine." Technology is best defined as how things are done. The most important fact about technology is not the physical capital itself but the ideas, skills, and knowledge embodied in machines and structures. Technology becomes standardized when the rate at which ideas, skills, and knowledge can be transferred to a machine or structure becomes very small. Standardized technology, therefore, requires fewer ideas and less skill and knowledge than leading-edge technology. High-performance organizations emphasize developing and using leading-edge technologies because standardized technologies are highly mobile and therefore are likely to be moved to places where they can be employed mainly by low-paid workers. Some American companies have responded to competitive pressures by attempting to combine high technology and low skills through automation. This combination has proved to be little, if at all, more productive than standardized technology and low-skilled workers. The most productive systems, therefore, have workers with higher-order thinking skills who can develop and use leading-edge technology. And the shorter life cycle of products and technologies in a more dynamic and competitive global economy provides important advantages to continuing innovation and creativity.

The need to pay more attention to quality control and productivity is another reason high-performance systems work better with more worker involvement. In cases where direct contact with customers is required, flexible, highly skilled employees can provide better customer service than is true of highly specialized mass-production workers, who can only provide their narrow specialized service. In manufacturing systems, moreover, even the most sophisticated machines are idiosyncratic and therefore require the close attention of skilled workers to adapt them to particular situations. With the smaller production runs permitted by information technology and required by more competitive and dynamic markets, workers must control production and be able to override machines; the mass-production system usually made it impossible for people to override machines. The mass-production system's long production runs made it possible to amortize start-up defects over those long runs. Systems with short production runs cannot afford many start-up defects. They must therefore have workers who override the machines if the latter start producing defects. Quality-driven systems must also provide for more self-inspection by workers, and this must often be on the basis of visible observation to *prevent* defects rather than by inspections to *detect* them at the end of the production process. Quality control is facilitated by just-in-time inventory and other mechanisms that make defects more visible or detectable early in production processes. Productivity and quality are enhanced by early detection; otherwise, those defective components become invisible when they enter the product, and they are discovered as the products malfunction when used by customers.

Incentive Systems

The explicit or implicit incentives in any system are basic determinants of its outcomes. This is so because organizations ordinarily get the outcomes they reward.

High-performance organizations ordinarily stress positive incentive systems. Mass-production incentives tend to be negative—fear of discharge or punishment; they also tend to be more individualistic and implicit. Mass-production incentives are sometimes even perverse in that they actually impede improvements in productivity. Process and time-based mass-production compensation systems, for example, are often unrelated to productivity or quality and may even be counterproductive, as when workers fear they will lose their jobs if productivity improves or when "incentives," especially for managers, bear no relationship to objective performance or equity and therefore create disunity within the work group. Sometimes, moreover, expressed incentives are to improve productivity, whereas the operative implicit incentives stress stability and control or some component of the production process (e.g., reducing shipping costs or the cost of supplies), which often has negative effects on the whole system. Consensus-based bonus compensation systems can motivate workers as well as improve internal cohesion. It is, for example, easier not to pay a bonus for reasons everybody understands than it is to cut wages. High-performance incentives, by contrast, are more likely to be communal, positive, explicit, based on measurable outcomes, and directly related to the enterprise's stated objectives.

We should note that positive incentives enhance flexibility as well as productivity and quality. Group incentives and job security encourage flexibility by simultaneously overcoming the resistance to the development and use of broader skills and providing employers greater incentives to invest in those skills. Similarly, bonus compensation systems can simultaneously provide greater incentives for workers to improve productivity and quality and create a more flexible compensation system. Participative systems, therefore, in themselves create positive incentives.

It would be hard to overemphasize the importance of internal unity and positive incentives for high-performance, knowledge-intensive work places. This is so in part because all parties must be willing to go "all out" to achieve common objectives. In traditional mass-production systems, workers are justifiably afraid to go "all out" to improve productivity for fear they will lose their jobs. This is the reason job security is one of the most important incentives a high-performance company can have. Similarly, the fragmentation of work within mass-production systems gives workers little incentive to control quality—quality is somebody else's responsibility. A high-performance system, by contrast, makes quality control everybody's responsibility. Positive incentives are required, in addition, because the effective use of information technology tends to give workers greater discretion (Zuboff 1988). It is difficult to *compel* workers to think or even to tell whether or not they are doing it. It is also very hard to compel workers to go all out to improve quality and productivity.

It should also be stressed that high-performance incentive systems must be based on a high level of consensus and trust. Indeed, traditional American managers have so much trouble understanding this concept that they actually are surprised when workers refuse to accept unilaterally imposed "incentives" that will improve the workers' earnings and the firm's economic viability. It is, moreover, difficult to transform adversarial relations into cooperative ones. The most successful transformations in the United States ordinarily have required demonstrable threats to jobs and company survival.

Thus, we may summarize the characteristics of high-performance organizations as follows:

(1) They are quality driven and therefore establish closer and more cooperative relations with customers and suppliers. Mass-production systems are producer driven and play suppliers off against each other through price competition.

(2) They have lean management structures that promote horizontal cooperation and participative management styles that establish mutual trust and respect between managers and workers and decentralize decisions to the work place. This contrasts with the hierarchical, segmented mass-production approach to management.

(3) They stress internal and external flexibility in order to adjust quickly to changing technology and markets. The mass-production system seeks stability through rules, regulations, and contractual relationships. High-performance organizations achieve stability through quality, productivity, and flexibility.

(4) The most successful enterprises give high priority to positive incentive systems to relate rewards to desired outcomes. Such incentive systems are important because the efficient use of leading-edge technology gives workers considerable discretion. Mass-production systems stress negative (punishment and

layoffs) or even perverse incentives, which make it more difficult to achieve desired outcomes, as when workers believe improving productivity will cost them their jobs. Mass-production hierarchical arrangements, fragmented work, and adversarial relations discourage the kind of cooperation required for high levels of quality and productivity. Positive incentives used by high-performance organizations include bonus compensation systems; internal cohesion, fairness, and equity; job security; and the ability to participate in decision making.

(5) High-performance organizations develop and use leading-edge technology through constant improvement on the job and by adapting advanced technologies produced elsewhere. They understand that standardized technologies imply competing mainly according to wages.

(6) These enterprises give heavy attention to education and training of all workers. The mass-production system stresses education and training mainly for managerial and technical elites. The most successful organizations know that higher-order thinking skills are required for high performance and the development and use of leading-edge technologies.

7. One of the most controversial aspects of high-performance production systems is the role of labor organizations. As noted in the following section, the view of this author is that the right of workers to organize and bargain collectively is an important requirement for a high-performance system. It is not a coincidence that companies in other industrialized countries that are taking market shares from American companies usually have strong worker organizations, both through works councils and other shop-floor organizations and trade unions.

Evidence

It has been argued above that greater worker participation will improve productivity, quality, and flexibility. Unfortunately, the evidence for this proposition is difficult to establish because worker-participation processes in the United States are relatively new, have different meanings, are qualitatively different from place to place, and never occur in isolation from other factors.

There is, however, growing evidence that worker participation and work reorganization are important factors in improving productivity and economic competitiveness (Dertouzes, Lester, and Solow 1989). This should not be surprising, of course, since labor accounts for at least 70 percent of total costs. Small improvements in labor productivity can have much greater impact on total productivity than larger increases in physical capital. A recent Brookings study edited by Alan Blinder acknowledged the positive contribution of worker participation, though Blinder considers such productivity improvements to be "transitory," albeit potentially "impressive" (Blinder 1989–90, 1990). Blinder, like most economists, believes that the "best way to raise productivity growth, and perhaps the only way to do so permanently, is to speed up the pace of technological innovation" (Blinder 1989–90, 33). The trouble with this view, of course, is the implied assumption that technological innovation is external to the production process and not an integral part of it. This view also fails to recognize that high-performance production systems with positive incentives, skilled workers, and a high degree of worker involvement have the capacity for *continuous improvements* in productivity and technology. The Brookings studies nevertheless show that incentive compensation systems raise wages about 11 percent an hour more than for other workers, and they do this without reducing fringes or hourly wages (ibid., 37). Blinder concludes that "worker participation apparently does help make alternative compensation plans . . . work better—and also has beneficial effects of its own. This theme was totally unexpected when I organized the conference [that led to these studies]" (ibid., 38).

David Lewin and others at Columbia University studied the relationships between the financial performance of 500 publicly traded companies and the degree of employee involvement. Analysis of the data for 1987 concluded that

> the mere presence of an employee involvement process was not significantly related to positive improvements in any of the financial indicators. However, the further a firm moved up the employee-involvement index [measuring degrees of employee involvement] and the more employees were involved in decision-making, the greater the magnitude of financial performance. What appears to be critical is the scope or comprehensiveness of employee involvement and participation programs.
>
> High employee involvement is associated with better financial performance, particularly on the return on investment and return on asset measures. (Economic Policy Council 1990, 16)

There is, in addition, abundant case-study evidence of the relationship between worker participation and improved quality and productivity. Perhaps the most clear-cut and compelling evidence is from the New United Motor Manufacturing Co., Inc. (NUMMI), a joint venture between Toyota and General Motors in Fremont, California. This was a plant that GM closed in 1982 because its managers could not make it competitive. Toyota reopened the plant as NUMMI in 1984 with a new management system but with mostly the same UAW members and essentially the same equipment, which was much less automated than in GM's most-modern plants. One of the most important changes NUMMI made was to guarantee the workers a high level of job security. Other changes included a reduction in job classes from about 100 to four; the elimination of such management perks as private dining rooms, parking lots, private offices, and separate dress codes; and the establishment of work teams of five to ten people who set their own work standards, lay out the work area, determine the work-load distribution, and assign workers to specific tasks.

NUMMI's key managerial concept is a commitment to high quality standards by workers and managers. Quality control is built into the production process. NUMMI uses a modified just-in-time inventory system to reduce costs and improve quality by immediately identifying faulty parts. The company also imposes very high quality standards for suppliers but works closely with those companies to solve quality problems. The inspection function is largely decentralized to line workers.

From a production standpoint there can be little doubt that NUMMI, which makes Toyota Corollas and the GEO Prism (Chevrolet Novas were discontinued in 1989, and the plant will start producing light trucks in 1991), has been a success. Productivity at the plant is 50 percent higher than at the former GM plant, and in 1989 NUMMI ranked first among all GM plants in the United States. A 1988 MIT study reported that productivity was about 40 percent higher than traditional GM plants and about equal to that of Toyota's Japanese plants (Krafcik 1989). *Consumer Reports* judged NUMMI's Chevrolet Nova to be the highest quality of any American-built car. As a result of these successes, there has been strong interest in NUMMI among American managers. GM uses the plant as a managerial training center, and other companies have hired NUMMI managers.

Toyota's main objectives at NUMMI were to establish an American production and marketing center and to ascertain whether or not that company's management system could be successfully used with American workers and unions. There is no doubt that Toyota succeeded in demonstrating that this could be done. Toyota has improved on the NUMMI experience with its Camry, produced in its newer plant in Georgetown, Kentucky. In 1990, the Corolla was still ranked as one of the highest quality American-built cars by J.D. Powers & Associates (it ranked ninth and the Camry third); Toyota's Cressida was ranked first. What makes the Corolla and Camry performance so impressive is the fact that almost all other cars ranked were luxury vehicles, whereas they are lower-priced subcompacts (White 1990).

General Motors' main objective was to learn more about the Japanese production system. GM managers had relied more heavily than Toyota or Ford on automating to improve productivity and competitiveness. NUMMI taught GM that the workers were not the problem, and it learned from many other experiences that machine technology alone was not the answer. The NUMMI experience has helped GM to produce even better results in Shreveport, Louisiana, than at NUMMI and has caused that company to rethink its Saturn strategy.

Saturn was originally designed to leapfrog the competitive advantage enjoyed by Japanese auto companies. The NUMMI experience caused GM not only to change the kind of car it planned to make in its Saturn plant but also to give much greater attention to worker participation and work organization. In many ways the Saturn agreement improves on NUMMI's. Saturn uses the team concept, but the union participates at every level in the management system, not just on the shop floor as at NUMMI. As at NUMMI, job classifications have been greatly reduced to one for production workers and three to five for skilled workers. Like NUMMI, Saturn dispenses with management perks but goes further: all workers are on salary equal to 80 percent of average UAW wages in other U.S.

auto plants. The other 20 percent varies according to such factors as productivity, profits, and quality. Saturn, unlike NUMMI, assigns relief workers to each work team, and the work is more self-paced than at NUMMI. Moreover, the team leaders at Saturn are elected by members of their work units or through an election designed by the UAW; at NUMMI they are determined by management.

Saturn also follows NUMMI's lead in giving workers job security by providing for no layoffs for 80 percent of workers except for severe economic conditions or unforeseen catastrophic events.

Critics argue that NUMMI has subjected workers to "management by stress" by speeding up the production line and by eliminating easy jobs and slack time. Some workers also have been very critical of NUMMI's very strict absentee policies. Other critics argue that some NUMMI managers have regressed to their former authoritarian ways and criticize the "team" concept for weakening union solidarity (Parker and Slaughter 1989).

Despite these criticisms, the UAW and the overwhelming majority of the plant's workers strongly support NUMMI's participatory processes. As the Saturn agreement demonstrates, however, NUMMI's system can be improved upon.

Indeed, it may be said that the management systems in Sweden and Germany are much better than those in Japan. This is so because the former systems are more pervasive and give workers control at every level. The Japanese system actually only applies to 15–20 percent of workers; the Swedish and German systems are more universal.

The evidence strongly supports the conclusion that restructured production systems emphasizing worker participation can greatly improve productivity and quality as well as the quality of work life. As noted, in a more competitive global economy, firms can compete either by reducing wages or by improving productivity and quality through worker reorganization and improving work-force skills. There is also strong evidence, however, that *genuine* worker participation is much less pervasive in the United States than in Japan or Western Europe. How do we account for this? Several hypotheses might be advanced:

(1) The mass-production system was both more successful and more entrenched in the United States, so unions and management are more reluctant to abandon the adversarial and authoritarian systems that it produced than are their Japanese or European counterparts.

(2) Most American employers are not convinced that participatory systems are more effective than traditional mass-production systems and authoritarian management procedures. There appears to be enough uncertainty about these new approaches that most American managers apparently believe the risks outweigh the potential benefits.

(3) Government policies in the United States encourage companies to follow low-wage strategies. The United States, for example, has been extremely reluctant to restrain managerial decision making either by requiring the kind of worker-participation processes that exist in almost all other major industrial

countries or by strengthening the workers' right to organize and bargain collectively, which has been greatly diluted since the 1940s and 1950s. U.S. polices have also been reluctant to interfere with the "employment-at-will" doctrine, which made it easy for American companies to shift the cost of change to workers and communities through layoffs and plant closings. Indeed, U.S. tax and tariff policies actually encourage American companies to shift employment to low-wage countries. Unlike other advanced industrial countries, the United States has not adopted a high-wage, full-employment strategy. We have, for example, encouraged the perpetuation of industries that are viable only through low wages; most other industrialized countries actively discourage such industries through high minimum or negotiated wages and other restrictions.

Perhaps the most serious limitation of American policy has been our failure to have a human resource development strategy to produce the skilled workers needed for high-performance work systems. Our mass-production schools were designed to produce literate students for a more natural resource-oriented goods-producing economy but do not teach the thinking and learning skills required for a more global and competitive knowledge-intensive world. The mass-production educational system had two main tracks—one for the college-bound elites, and another for all other workers. The American system still reflects this orientation; we have no standards that all students must meet, and we do more than any other country for the college educated but almost nothing for the other 75 percent of our work force. All of our major economic competitors have policies to provide strong basic education and work training for those skills that do not require four years of college. American secondary-school graduates, by contrast, consistently score near the bottom on international math and science assessments—even below many developing countries. And we have almost no postsecondary skill training programs for most non–college-bound youths. A recent report, for example, found that in mathematics only 2–3 percent of American high-school students match the median test score of their Japanese counterparts (Marshall and Tucker 1992, 66). Without higher-order thinking skills, dropouts—and even most high-school graduates—are increasingly condemned to lives of low wages and joblessness. Our principal competitors see to it that all young people acquire basic thinking skills by the time they are 15 or 16 years old (Commission on the Skills of the American Workforce [henceforth CSAW] 1990). These basic academic skills provide the foundation for further education, professional and technical job training, or work. These countries also have a variety of technical training and education programs for those who do not elect to go on to technical college immediately. However, higher education remains an option even for those who elect technical training or work options after completing their basic education.

The provision of high-quality basic education followed by apprenticeship or other technical training reinforces a high-wage strategy in two ways. First, highly skilled workers are not content with low-skill work. Second, workers with higher-order thinking skills are equipped to handle high-performance work organizations.

How Do All of These Developments Affect
Traditional Industrial-Relations Systems?

Globalization has strengthened employers relative to unions in several important ways. As noted, unions received considerable public support during the 1930s as being necessary not only to protect workers from arbitrary treatment in Tayloristic management systems but also to reinforce Keynesian economic policies. In advanced democratic countries, most people continue to recognize the need for unions to protect and promote workers' interests in the polity and society as well as in the work place. But they increasingly question the economic value of collective bargaining. This is due in large measure to the reduced efficacy of Keynesian policies, which created the perception that unions are no longer needed because their functions in maintaining purchasing power and stabilizing wages and prices are no longer as critical as they were in the 1930s. For the main problems confronting more-competitive global economies—the control of inflation and competitiveness—unions and collective bargaining are often seen as negatives. Similarly, many employers who valued the stabilizing functions of collective bargaining see less need to cooperate with unions since traditional collective-bargaining processes are less effective in taking labor out of competition. On the other hand, internationalization gives employers greater market, resource, and production options, thereby strengthening companies relative to unions. The reduced public support for unions, together with the pro-employer biases in American laws and policies, have enabled employers to intensify and expand their anti-union activities.

Unions have also suffered because their appeal has been mainly to skilled manual and mass-production workers and less to workers in the rapidly growing service and technical occupations. Most industrial unions have been more adept at administering contracts under largely adversarial relationships than at establishing cooperative relationships and improving productivity, flexibility, and quality. Exceptions include unions in the highly competitive garment and clothing industries, which always had to give greater attention to productivity in order to sustain a wage advantage over the nonunion competitors. Another exception is in areas like construction, where unique customer needs made mass production difficult, thus requiring more highly skilled workers and labor-management cooperation to meet customers' needs.

Some people interpret the relative decline of union strength in the United States to mean that unions are, like their related oligopolistic mass-production and regulated industries, anachronistic. As noted, this author reads it otherwise. The fact that the relative strength of American unions has declined much more than their counterparts in other countries (especially Canada, where union strength has increased since the 1960s) suggests that their problems are due to unique factors in the United States, not to the obsolescence of trade unions *per se*. In fact, a case can be made that unions continue to have a vital role, though their methods, like those of mass-production companies, must be adapted to a more competitive global economy. Genuine worker participation in high-performance enterprises, for example, is unlikely unless the workers have independent sources of power to represent their interests. Indeed, unions are an integral part of high-performance companies in Sweden, Germany, and even Japan. Independent sources of power are essential in more national high-performance economies for three major reasons. First, workers are not likely to be willing to go "all out" unless they are able to protect themselves from the adverse consequences of doing so. Second, it is very difficult to have effective participatory, cooperative arrangements between parties with greatly unequal power. This is so because the stronger party ultimately will be inclined to exert unilateral control, thus destroying cooperation and internal unity and causing the weaker party to seek countervailing power. This happened, for instance, during the 1920s and 1930s, when management's unilateral actions encouraged workers to form or seek independent unions. Finally, more cooperative relationships between labor and management do not mean an end to adversarial relationships. Indeed, adversarial relationships between managers and workers are both functional and inevitable. What is required, of course, is to prevent conflict from becoming "functionless," to use a German term: this means conflict that makes all parties worse off. There is no necessary conflict between cooperating to make the pie bigger and bargaining to split it. However, both processes—cooperating and bargaining—require that workers have an independent source of power to represent their interests.

This is not to argue that effective nonunion systems are impossible, but it does imply that they are hard to maintain in the long run. It is especially difficult for these systems to work where management's main motives are to avoid unions or to reduce labor costs. There can be little question that the workers' ability to organize freely and bargain collectively has been an important check on arbitrary and discriminatory actions by companies or unions. It is also this author's belief that the right of self-organization has been sufficiently diluted in the United States that it no longer provides adequate safeguards to nonunion workers.

As has been argued at length elsewhere (Marshall 1987), under modern conditions labor organizations are at least as essential for the economy, society, and polity as they were in mass-production systems. However, the methods used to protect workers must change to reflect a very different economy. For one thing, unions must play a more active role in strengthening high-performance production systems. They can do this by strengthening such non–collective-bargaining participatory processes as labor–management safety and health committees and joint programs to improve productivity. Unions could also encourage or force companies to develop global strategies that compel companies to take longer time perspectives, develop leading-edge technologies, and adopt more positive incentive systems. Unions should continue to challenge elitist management per-quisites and unfair compensation systems that not only create disunity but also have little or nothing to do with individual or company performance.

It is particularly important for unions to challenge management practices that maintain short-run profits but that are contrary to the best interests of workers, communities, and the country. Examples include company policies to compete by reducing wages and employment rather than improving productivity. Other countries promote high-performance management practices through collective bargaining or regulations that require consultation with workers' representatives or justifications to public bodies before plants can be closed, wages cut, or workers laid off.

Finally, unions should continue to champion public policies designed to make the United States a high-wage, equitable, full-employment economy. This will require, above all, developing more-democratic institutions, effective public schools, school-to-work transition processes, and on-the-job learning systems for line workers. Worker learning systems are at least as necessary to high-performance systems as managerial training, which now consumes an inordinate share of corporate education and training resources. The joint programs in the construc-tion, automobile, and communications industries are good beginnings, but they are only a fraction of what they should be. According to the American Society for Training and Development, 15,000 firms, less than one-half of 1 percent of all companies, account for over 90 percent of all work-place training in the United States. In addition, the Commission on the Skills of the American Work-force (CSAW 1990) found that American companies were far behind their principal Asian and European competitors in both training and organizing for high perfor-mance.

What is required, of course, is for unions and their supporters to develop the modern intellectual equivalent of Keynesian economics to show that unions are good for the economy as well as for the polity and society. Although unions must modernize their policies, methods, and structures to make them more responsive to their members' needs, stronger public support requires a rationale that over-comes organized labor's reputation as narrow special interests and demonstrates that unions are essential economic institutions whose activities strengthen the entire economy.

Role of Labor Movements

Public policies can help create the context within which labor movements operate, but labor movements themselves must develop the strategies, policies, and struc-tures to strengthen their ability to protect and promote workers' interests. Labor movements can do this by being major active forces for just, democratic, full-employment, high-wage economies. Labor movements in different countries have varying degrees of power to influence national policies. While it is always possible to argue that particular national labor movements have not made the right strategic choices, it is impossible, as a practical matter, to determine how much the outcomes for a particular labor movement are due to context and how much to strategic choice. Critics of U.S. unions, for example, argue that they should have become more "political" and been less wedded to collective bargaining. However, this argument is usually advanced by people who do not seem to understand either the political activities of American unions or the political structures workers face in the American context. It is highly unlikely, for example, given the political structures of the United States, that American unions could ever establish the kind of independent political labor movements that their counterparts have developed in parliamentary systems. The structure of American government makes it very difficult for third parties to get started, gives inordinate power to nonmetropolitan areas with low union densities, and makes it possible for willful minorities to block legislation.

It is nevertheless instructive to speculate about what those labor movements that have maintained and improved their strength since the 1960s have been able to do relative to those, such as the American, that have not. My reading of the international comparison leads to the following list of factors for high-performance labor movements, most notably those in Scandinavia, which have maintained and improved their economic and political strength in the same international economic environment that has produced large losses for some unions, especially those in the United States (see Figure 1, pp. 162–63).

(1) Successful labor organizations have adopted clear goals and objectives as well as strategies simultaneously to achieve those objectives and to gain greater support from nonlabor groups.

Strong labor movements continue to advocate full-employment policies, but they also want full employment at high and rising wages. And they advocate policies to prevent wages and incomes from polarizing as much as they have in the United States.

These labor movements realize the extent to which international competition has changed the ability to take labor out of competition and maintain full employment by traditional means. This means developing policies that permit companies to compete in international markets while maintaining full employment and equity. Labor movements have developed different strategies, but generally they recognize the need to limit wage increases to changes in productivity, plus or minus the difference between changes in domestic and international policies.

All of these labor movements, in addition, recognize the need for *equity*, but they are also concerned with the creation of wealth, not just its distribution. The policies that flow from these objectives include measures to *stimulate national investment* in job- and wealth-creating activities. Sources of investment funds include private and collective pension funds, lower real interest rates, and measures to promote the development and use of leading-edge technology.

Successful labor movements give particularly high priority to public policies and collective bargaining to strengthen the education and training for all people, but especially for workers. They also have adopted high-wage strategies to force companies to become more productive as well as adjustment policies to shift labor and other resources from low-wage to high-wage sectors.

Labor movements have always supported such human resource development activities as universal education, health-care, and family-support policies. Indeed, it would not be surprising to find a strong correlation between union density and the degree of support for human resource development activities. There can be little doubt that in an age of multinational corporations, investing in people is the best way to strengthen a country's economy.

(2) High-performance labor movements also have global strategies that are designed to support high-wage, full-employment, equity policies. Unlike groups with ideological commitments to "free markets," labor movements owe their existence to a healthy appreciation of the *limitations* as well as the *strength* of markets. They understand that markets must operate within the framework of *rules*, especially those that protect basic labor standards. Such standards promote human resource development and force companies to compete by becoming more *efficient*, not by *reducing basic labor standards*. In a global economy, however, labor standards must now be part of *international trade rules*.

Trade-linked labor standards could, in addition, provide global purchasing power by giving Third World workers a means to participate in the economic growth of their countries. It should be emphasized, however, that international labor standards do not imply an international minimum wage—wage differentials are too great for that to be practical. There is, however, a difference between having low wages because of a low level of economic development and suppressing wages to attract capital; the latter would violate international labor standards, the former would not. Labor standards would also allow workers to organize and bargain collectively and protect them from hazardous work places, forced labor, child labor, and discrimination because of such factors as race, ethnic origin, or union membership (Marshall 1990).

Labor movements also have a vested interest in seeing equitable solutions to the Third World debt problem, which acts as a strong depressant on world growth, and the establishment of international financial institutions to promote an expanding world economy and avoid a recurrence of financial threats such as that posed by the Third World debt during the 1980s. A real world bank could bring discipline to international financial markets by acting as a lender of last resort, by restructuring loans, and by recycling funds to promote growth.

High-performance labor organizations are pro-active, not merely reactive. They adopt goals and set agendas; they do not simply respond to agendas set by others. These labor movements are particularly aggressive in asserting workers' interests in international negotiations, events, policies, and institutions that affect workers.

International Cooperation

One of the greatest problems facing labor movements is thus to gain enough power to see to it that workers' interests are protected in international transactions and institutions. The logical development, as John R. Commons taught us, would be for labor organizations to coincide with the market—otherwise wages and working conditions can be undermined by shifting resources to areas not covered by labor standards. However, the disparities between countries and workers are too great to permit a true international labor movement, which will give international companies important advantages in whipsawing unions.

There are, however, things that unions can do, including using their economic and political leverage over multinational corporations (MNCs) in their "home" countries, promoting stronger codes of conduct for MNCs in international organizations, strengthening international cooperation through international organizations, especially at the trade secretariat, and cooperating to see to it that workers' interests are represented in international negotiations of all kinds. Workers' interests are now not very well represented in such organizations as the GATT, the International Monetary Fund, the World Bank, or the so-called "summit" economic conferences by industrialized countries. Most of the economic experts at these meetings, especially those from the United States, consider high wages, labor standards, full employment, and equity to be negatives.

Strengthening Labor Movements Within Countries

Labor movements will have very little ability to represent workers' interests in a global economy unless they operate from strong national bases. Some of what is required to strengthen labor movements is fairly obvious, such as organizing, developing internal democracy, and being responsive to workers' concerns. There are, however, a number of factors that all strong labor movements seem to have in common. These include:

(1) Broad public support, because labor movements have articulated a rationale that goes beyond narrow "special-interest" concerns such as higher wages and better working conditions. Democratic countries generally accepted the idea that free and democratic labor movements are essential to democracy, but unions have not always been considered in the national economic interest. Unions gained support after the 1930s because they were considered to be essential to help stabilize economies and increase purchasing power, in keeping with prevailing Keynesian policies. The successful labor movements of the 1980s have articulated high-wage strategies. These strategies emphasize equity, growth, full employment, the essential role of worker involvement in high-performance enterprises, and the importance of human resource development for national welfare. These labor movements have stressed economic growth as well as the equitable distribution of income.

(2) Successful labor movements have therefore been able to develop and implement coordinated goals that attract broad support. Because these labor movements have been led by skilled, well-informed leaders who were able to convince other groups of the importance of their role, they have been able to participate in a fairly sophisticated manner in tripartite (labor, management, government) processes.

(3) High-performance labor movements have strong local work-place entities as well as strong national economic and political organizations. Labor movements that are only organized around one of these dimensions (work-place, national, political, or economic) have not been as strong as those that emphasize all of them.

(4) The strongest labor movements develop mechanisms for interactive communications with their members. These labor movements, therefore, have extensive educational and research services, both to help members advance job skills as well as for general education and the strengthening of labor leaders' ability to participate effectively in national organizations and political processes.

Conclusions

The goals, policies, and objectives of labor movements in the democratic industrial countries are rooted mainly in national, mass-production economies. This was particularly true for unions in the United States, where the mass-production system was larger and more deeply entrenched than elsewhere. Political and economic conditions in the United States have made it more difficult for unions to survive, grow, and adapt. It has particularly been more difficult for unions to establish independent political movements, which is a major difference between unions in the United States and those in other countries. However, unions have also faced much greater opposition from employers.

A major factor in the strength of the U.S. unions has been public opinion, which was more favorable during the 1930s and 1940s than during the 1970s and 1980s. At least part of this popularity was due to the belief that unions were good for the economy because they helped maintain purchasing power, in keeping with the prevailing Keynesian policies. However, these policies became anachronistic in a more competitive internationalized information world, which also makes the oligopolistic mass-production system less effective. This leads some people to believe that unions also have become obsolete. It has been argued here that this is a false conclusion: high-performance organizations require much greater worker involvement, which, in turn, is most effective if workers have an independent source of power to represent their interests.

A major problem in the United States is the fact that unions have been so weakened since the 1960s that workers do not, in fact, have effective options to organize in the face of much stronger employer opposition. Part of the reason for intensified employer opposition is the erosion of the mass-production Keynesian safety-net system, which provided mutual accommodations for employers before the 1970s, when the eroding effects of technology and more-competitive global markets became more apparent. These changes greatly strengthened international companies relative to unions and made it possible for almost all American companies to respond to change with cost cutting rather than quality- and productivity-improving strategies. In addition to weaker unions, American companies are not restrained in their wage-cutting strategies by public policies that create constraints and offer incentives for companies to become high-performance organizations. One of the most serious defects in the U.S. policy mix is poor public schools and the absence of the kind of high-quality comprehensive worker training systems that exist in every other major democratic industrial country.

Stronger labor movements are clearly in the national interest. The United States should therefore modernize its labor-relations laws to make it easier for workers to organize and bargain collectively and more difficult for employers to thwart those rights by legal and illegal means.

However, unions and their supporters must strengthen their internal processes and gain greater public support if more favorable public policies are to be adopted. In achieving these objectives, unions and their supporters can learn from the experience of those labor movements that have continued to prosper despite a hostile international economic and political environment. These successful labor movements have adopted broad, popular goals for public policies to establish high wages, full employment, and economic justice. These strategies constitute the modern intellectual equivalent of Keynesian economics, which complemented and strengthened the equity, industrial-relations, and labor-market rationales for unions and collective bargaining. They have, in addition, developed strategies to promote international, national, and enterprise policies and institutions to achieve these objectives. These strategies require strengthening unity among workers within and between countries and promoting national policies to improve productivity, quality, flexibility, and equity. Those who believe in free, democratic, prosperous, just societies have a strong stake in how well unions and their supporters achieve these objectives.

References

Aschauer, David Alan. 1988. "Rx for Productivity: Build Infrastructure." *Chicago Fed Letter*, September.
_____. 1989a. "Is Public Expenditure Productive?" *Journal of Monetary Economics* 23, 177–200.
_____. 1989b. "Public Investment and Productivity Growth in Seven Countries." *Economic Perspective*, Federal Reserve Bank of Chicago, September–October, 17–25.
Blinder, Alan, ed. 1989–90. "Pay, Participation, and Productivity." *The Brookings Review* (Winter), 33–38.
_____. 1990. *Paying for Productivity: A Look at the Evidence.* Washington, DC: Brookings Institution.

186 RAY MARSHALL

Bureau of Labor Statistics. 1990. Unpublished data, May.

Carnevale, Anthony. 1983. *Human Capital: A High-Yield Corporate Investment*. Washington, DC: American Society for Training and Development.

Commission on the Skills of the American Workforce. 1990. *America's Choice: High Skills or Low Wages?* Rochester, NY: Center on Education and the Economy.

Dertouzes, Michael L.; Lester, Richard K.; and Solow, Robert M. 1989. *Made in America*. Cambridge, MA: MIT Press.

Economic Policy Council of the United Nations Association. 1990. *The Common Interests of Employees and Employers in the 1990s*. New York: Economic Policy Council.

Krafcik, John. 1989. "Triumph of the Lear Production System." *Sloan Management Review* (Fall), 41–52.

Marshall, Ray. 1987. *Unheard Voices*. New York: Basic Books.

_____. 1990. "Trade-Linked Labor Standards." In *International Trade: The Changing Role of the United States*, ed. Frank Macchiarola. New York: Academy of Political Science, 67–78.

Marshall, Ray, and Tucker, Marc. 1992. *Thinking for a Living: Education and the Wealth of Nations*. New York: Basic Books.

Mishel, Larry, and Frankel, David. 1990. *The State of Working America*. Washington, DC: Economic Policy Institute.

Parker, Mike, and Slaughter, Jane. 1989. *Choosing Sides: Unions and the Team Concept*. Boston: South End Press.

Schultz, Theodore. 1981. *Investing in People: The Economics of Population Quality*. Berkeley: The University of California Press.

Webb, Sidney, and Webb, Beatrice. 1897. *Industrial Democracy*. London: Longman Green & Company.

White, Joseph B. 1990. "Car Makers Gear Up to Turn Good Marks in Quality Poll to Competitive Advantage." *Wall Street Journal* (3 July), B–1.

Zuboff, Shoshona. 1988. *In the Age of the Smart Machines*. New York, Basic Books.

Trade Unions and Collective Bargaining

Suggestions for Emerging Democracies in Eastern Europe and the Former Soviet Union

Harry C. Katz, Sarosh Kuruvilla, and Lowell Turner

I. Introduction

This paper provides lessons for industrial relations reform efforts in the new nations emerging from the former Soviet Union and Eastern Bloc. Our purpose is to identify the basic industrial-relations practices that enable the advanced industrial countries to compete in world markets. The paper does not provide a detailed descriptive account of the existing industrial-relations institutions in the formerly communist countries, nor does it assess the likely short-run consequences of the economic restructuring under way across the new nations. Rather, our focus is on the experiences in the advanced economies and the lessons those experiences contain regarding successful industrial-relations practice.

II. Two Key Assumptions

Two key assumptions guide our approach: one concerns the likely course of economic development in the new democracies, and the other involves the recent changes in industrial relations that are occurring in the advanced industrialized countries.

A. The Need to Come Up to World Standards Quickly in Economic and Industrial-Relations Practice

The reason we draw lessons from the advanced industrialized economies is that we believe the new democracies in the former Soviet Union and Eastern Bloc will have to come up to world standards rapidly in order to sustain significant economic growth. The experiences of Third World countries in recent years shows that import-substitution development strategies that were associated with

A longer version of this paper prepared with funding provided by the World Bank will appear in *Impediments to Competitive Labor Markets: An Overview of Policy and Research Issues*, The World Bank, PHREE, forthcoming.

The authors are, respectively, a professor of industrial relations and assistant professors of industrial relations at the School of Industrial and Labor Relations, Cornell University.

the protection of domestic producers have not led to rapid development. Rather, the more rapid developers have been those countries (such as Korea, Taiwan, and Singapore) that have entered export markets quickly and forcibly. In the rapid developers, given the heightened demands of world competition for quality and production flexibility, export success has required adoption of state-of-the-art production techniques. Perhaps most important is the lesson learned from recent rapid developers—that modern and competitive production requires modern industrial-relations practices. Countries that have had the former and lagged in the development of the latter (such as Korea) have confronted substantial social pressures and instability.

The need for rapid modernization of production and industrial-relations capacity is highlighted by recent developments in the auto industries in the new democracies. One illustration is the Eisenbach assembly plant located in what used to be East Germany. The plant is now owned by General Motors (as part of its Opel subsidiary) and is currently being retooled (Ingrassia and Aeppel 1992). Although the new Eisenbach plant is just in the start-up phase, it is already clear that General Motors is determined to use just-in-time inventories and other practices associated with "lean production." A critical part of these production techniques is team-based work organization and decentralized decision structures. It remains to be seen how well the new plant performs and how the work force reacts. Yet the important point is that this plant is being designed so as to meet modern automobile production and industrial-relations standards. The pressure for this approach comes from the fact that General Motors expects to export a significant share of the plant's output and from the fact that even the Eisenbach cars that will be sold in the former East Germany will confront intense competition from cars produced by other state-of-the-art competitors.

A similar message comes from the Volga Auto Works in Tolgiatti, Russia (Uchitelle 1992). This plant has two sections: the side that produces cars for sale in Russia uses extremely old and inefficient machinery, while the part of the plant that produces cars for export uses modern technologies, including a large number of robots. Again, production oriented toward exports requires leapfrogging up to world standards. It is unclear if the "old" half of the Volga works will be able to survive as the Russian market is opened up to more competition. What is clear is that this plant, like so many other parts of Russian industry, must find a way to compete directly in world markets. Old technologies and old industrial relations will not suffice in the face of market pressures.

B. The Change Under Way in Industrial-Relations Practice in the Advanced Economies

A second key assumption of this paper is that there is enormous change under way in industrial relations in the advanced economies. While thirty years ago it was commonplace among social scientists to assume that in the long run other countries would converge on variants of the "most advanced" U.S. model of collective bargaining and industrial relations, this assumption has been swept aside by history. The rise and success of very different models in countries such as Japan and Germany has demonstrated both a cross-national diversity of stable industrial-relations patterns and new lessons regarding what does and does not work.

The important starting point is a recognition of the impact of changing world markets and new technologies in driving industrial restructuring and industrial-relations transformation. Above all, perhaps, the rapid growth of Japanese economic strength, rooted in part in a successful system of enterprise unionism and shop-floor teamwork, has put pressure on firms in other countries to reorganize production and work and to seek some kind of "new industrial relations." Within Europe, not only the coming of Japanese competition but closer to home the relative success of German industry and industrial relations, along with the more recent "relaunching" of European economic integration, has pressured British, French, Italian, and Spanish (among other) firms to reorganize. Everywhere, intensified world market competition has called into question established relationships and ways of doing things and called forth managerial imperatives to raise productivity and product quality, achieve new flexibility, and cut costs.

At the same time—and closely related—the past fifteen years have witnessed a rapid spread of new microelectronic technologies in the work place. "New production concepts," often based on the new technology, aim to make more flexible use of labor, both in the products produced and in the process. As managers demand more responsibility from (and sometimes even give "semi-autonomy" to) individual workers and groups of workers, traditional labor–management relationships are called into question.

In some cases, employers have gone on the offensive against union influence that is perceived to defend rigidities in the work place and stand in the way of necessary work reorganization. In other cases, employers have sought a new collaborative relationship with entrenched unions; and sometimes the second strategy has followed the first. Unions, for their part, have in some cases fought against the changes and defended the traditional ways on which their power is based. But in other cases, unions have demonstrated a willingness to cooperate in new ways, both to save jobs and to promote the human-side benefits of more flexible work organization. And in some cases, unions have played a pro-active reformist role, pushing management toward new forms of organization, such as group work. In addition, the state, through public policy, has often played an important role (through regulation, deregulation, or other policy changes) in promoting industrial-relations reform.

In this period of uncertainty, trial and error, and change, there is also a great deal of cross-national, interfirm, and interunion communication and exchange. The opportunity to learn and combine lessons from various versions of successful (if not "best") practices is one of the benefits of intense contemporary processes of economic globalization.

Nowhere is this need greater than among the emerging and unstable democracies of Eastern Europe and the former Soviet Union. We would like to emphasize at the outset, however, that it is not possible to transplant another model, either discrete elements or the model in its entirety. In every case, it is necessary to build on existing practices and institutions, or institutional remnants. How the lessons presented in this paper can be adapted for specific use in specific national settings is a matter for careful case-by-case study and experimentation.

III. Basic Principles of Law and Institutions

Modern industrial relations requires that workers be afforded the basic right to form unions, and those unions should be granted the right to bargain collectively with employers and to strike if a negotiated settlement is not reached.

A. Why the Right to Strike and Collective Bargaining Are Necessary

The social advantages gained from the provision of these rights are revealed in the experiences of the industrialized democratic countries. The advantages include the fact that workers are entitled to a say in the determination of their employment and working conditions. Not only is such input justified on grounds of rights, but in addition, contemporary experience shows that to compete in world markets requires the active participation and commitment of the work force in order to meet quality and product performance standards.

There are also clear virtues derived from industrial-relations systems that give the parties involved in the production process direct involvement in the determination of work conditions and employment terms. Employers and workers and their representatives know their own problems best and can be remarkably adept at devising practical solutions to problems or conflicts. Interference by outside parties in the resolution of problems often leads to apparent solutions that prove unworkable or impractical in the long run.

Furthermore, third-party interference eliminates the constructive learning the parties receive in problem resolution and identification as they work through their own problems. Even if a third party could impose a solution that solves a problem in the short term, this process prevents the parties from developing the capacity to solve their own problems. Thus, a clear advantage to collective bargaining is that it avoids a cycle of dependence on third-party interference.

Experience in the industrialized democratic countries also shows that unions, the right to strike, and collective bargaining are more likely to produce outcomes that are acceptable to workers and employers as compared to solutions that are imposed by governments or other third parties. Not only are employers and workers more likely to develop solutions that meet their own needs, these parties are also more likely to feel a commitment to making such solutions work. Imposed employment terms, in contrast, are often resented and resisted, in part because the parties that must live with these terms had little say in their development. Thus the process through which employment terms are set is often as important as the actual terms themselves. Collective bargaining has the advantage of being a process that is "owned" by the parties involved.

Since collective bargaining is a healthy process, it should be applied widely. This suggests that the right to strike should be granted in nearly all cases. There may arise some instances where an alternative to the right to strike is necessary, yet experience demonstrates that the use of strike alternatives should be limited.

In the bargaining process, a very constructive role can be played by independent mediation entities in a modern industrial-relations system. The proper role of mediation is to facilitate communication between labor and management and to provide advice. For mediation to serve such a function, there must be a sufficiently large cadre of well-trained mediators who understand practical labor-relations issues. Countries that have recently experienced the spread of democratic political institutions especially need to devote resources toward the training of such mediators.

There is also an extremely healthy role to be played by grievance procedures or labor courts that solve the problems that arise during the terms of contractual agreements. Research shows that grievance procedures can provide employee voice and thereby lower employee turnover as well as assist in the identification of problems and informal resolution of conflicts (Freeman and Medoff 1984). Successful grievance procedures are designed by the parties that directly use them and not by the government or other third parties. At the same time, as is the case with mediation, the successful operation of grievance arbitration requires the existence of arbitrators who are experienced and well versed in specific practical industrial problems. The government can play a role in furthering the development of a cadre of such arbitrators or assist in the creation of third-party bodies, such as the American Arbitration Association, that can facilitate the grievance arbitration process.

In Europe, government-administered labor courts that resolve individual complaints are common. Labor courts, like grievance arbitration, can effectively settle problems, provide practical resolution of them, and avoid larger social conflicts. It is possible for an industrial-relations system to contain both grievance arbitration and labor courts, yet most national industrial-relations systems emphasize one or the other. An advantage to labor courts is that they cover all employees, unorganized as well as organized. Furthermore, labor courts tend to give employees more direct control over the processing of their complaints. Grievance procedures, on the other hand, give more influence to the unions involved. In a grievance system it is the union and not the employee that owns the grievance, and the union thereby is empowered to decide whether or not to press a complaint to arbitration.

There are some clear strengths of grievance procedures. They tend to be very responsive to the preferences of the parties, as they can be tailored to their desires and to the requirements in particular occupations or industries. Furthermore, the parties have more direct control over the design and operation of a grievance procedure and thereby gain a strong commitment to the outcomes of the grievance system. Yet grievance procedures have at times become cumbersome and fraught with delays. In the end, there are trade-offs involved in the design of complaint-resolution procedures and choices in their design. Our view is that a modern industrial-relations system should have either a grievance or a labor-court system or some combination of the two.

B. Proper Union Roles

The earlier discussion highlighted the pressing nature of current international competitive conditions. There is clearly much for employers and unions to focus on concerning how the work place can produce employment terms that are socially acceptable and products that are competitively successful. This does not imply that there is no role for unions to play as political actors or participants in political debate. It does suggest, however, that the representation of worker interests often requires unions to focus their attention on employment and work-place issues.

It is also clear that society benefits from the presence of politically independent unions that are free from domination and government control. Such domination eliminates the democratic representation of worker wants and constructive employer–union interchange. The drawbacks of state domination of unions are many, including a violation of workers' rights. Furthermore, state-dominated unions or state-controlled industrial-relations systems tend to generate periodic explosive conflict.

As representation and bargaining entities, unions should not serve functions that are properly the domain of government social-service institutions. For example, there are proper social-service needs in the areas of social pensions (e.g., social security) and vocational education that should be regulated and financed by national governments and/or regional governments. Unions are not only poor providers of such services, they can also become diverted away from the areas where they can make more substantial private and social contributions by pursuing social welfare provision activities. We do not intend to convey that there is no useful role to be played by unions in the provision of any social services. In some countries (e.g., Sweden), unions, for example, play a constructive role in the administration of unemployment benefits. And in many countries unions are effectively involved in vocational-education programs.

Unions should also not become the vehicle for the direct provision of consumer goods, such as housing or food distribution, as they did in the former Soviet Union. Not only are unions relatively inefficient as a distribution and pricing system, consumer-goods provision through the union or work place also unfairly and inefficiently ties workers to specific firms. Workers are unable to engage in necessary labor-market mobility if their housing, for example, is provided through the union or firm. The harmful effects of this sort of union role have been revealed in the rigidities apparent in the former Soviet states as they have struggled to create a more free-flowing labor market and to move individuals into a private market economy.

These concerns do not mean that unions should be blocked from addressing specific worker health or educational issues. Union-administered health and welfare funds have played constructive roles in many countries. The point is that social programs should be administered by governments and private programs should have narrower bounds and a narrower focus. In addition, as discussed above, consumer goods should be priced and allocated through markets and not through unions or other work-place institutions.

C. Work-Place Representation

There are great advantages to an industrial-relations framework that includes parallel representation at the work place through institutions such as works councils. In the most successful examples (Germany, the Netherlands, Denmark), basic pay and work standards are set in collective bargaining at an industry level (for an entire industry or group of industries, either regionally or nationally). Plant and firm-level works councils, composed of elected blue- and white-collar representatives, enforce the collective-bargaining agreements and, in addition, engage in ongoing discussion and negotiation of plant-specific issues. Works councils typically have formal rights, backed up by national legislation, to extensive information regarding company plans as well as to consultation and in some cases (usually personnel issues) to veto rights in management decision making.

In Germany, the works councils have integrated employee representatives into management decision making and provided a flexible instrument for restructuring and adaptation. Although works councils have imposed some external rigidity on firms (it is more difficult to hire and especially to fire), this has been more than compensated for by added internal flexibility (Streeck 1984a). Because they are able to negotiate relative employment security for the work force, works councils are more willing to accept internal flexibility of deployment (Katz and Sabel 1985). Works councils also push firms to increase in-house training and the hiring of apprentices; because firms are less able to hire and fire from outside, they have a strong incentive to pursue internal labor-market strategies and to move into high value-added product markets.

Although management decision making can be slowed in the legally established, consensus-building process, managers have important allies in the works councils to smooth implementation once decisions are reached. Works councils at large plants often take on comanagement functions, relieving management of important personnel responsibilities.

Works councils bargain for pay upgrades and bonuses, often on the basis of firm performance. They negotiate the terms of rationalization and the introduction of new technology, protecting employee interests as well as providing useful employee input into production and work reorganization (Turner 1991). Works councils provide a voice for white-collar employees, who are traditionally underrepresented in industrial-relations systems; and the councils provide some representation for employees even where unions are weak or absent.

Where works councils function well, they contribute to a virtuous circle that includes employee voice, especially on issues of immediate interest such as personnel and organization, comprehensive representation, labor–management cooperation (since the works council identifies with the interests of the firm), high trust based on joint efforts, flexibility in labor deployment, and high productivity and high product quality (Streeck 1984a). These plant-level institutions of codetermination make it possible for works councils, unions (often working through the works councils), and managers to build successful "productivity coalitions." It is important to emphasize, however, that the virtuous circle is possible not just in isolated cases (as in the United States and Britain) but throughout the economy only because works councils are established and defined in national legislation.

The parallel representation afforded by works councils is also buttressed, and made more successful, by arrangements at the strategic level. The latter include both collective bargaining between industrial unions and employer associations and union–works council participation (also mandated by law in Germany) on company supervisory boards. Other features of the German system help to make the works councils successful, including the presence of strong unions and employment security.

Although works councils are not a part of Japanese industrial relations, enterprise unions at large firms fulfill some of the same functions. These include comanagement, facilitating labor–management cooperation, building productivity coalitions, receiving extensive information regarding company plans, consultation, and giving a voice to white-collar concerns. Enterprise unions are also integrated to some extent into management decision making through firm-level bodies, such as joint labor–management committees. But as in the U.S. case, this form of plant-level representation has no legal backing in formal participation rights and is weak or nonexistent for the majority of work places that are nonunion.

Below we examine in detail some of the basic requirements of any industrial-relations system. We build upon our earlier discussion of the basic principles that should be followed in industrial relations.

IV. Wage-Setting and Bargaining Structures

Two related issues that are of central importance in industrial relations in any country are the structure of wage setting and bargaining (the latter is referred to as bargaining structure). Normally, there is a close connection between these matters, since wages are set as part of the normal bargaining that occurs between employers and unions.

A. Bargaining Structure

A critical choice in the process of collective bargaining is the degree to which the bargaining structure is centralized. The most decentralized case is where wages and other terms in the labor contract are set in a contract that covers only the workers in a single plant (or a subset of the work force in a plant). The most extreme case of centralized bargaining (and wage setting) occurs during incomes policies when a government imposes pay standards that apply to all workers in the economy. Where there is no government-sanctioned incomes policy, the most common "centralized" bargaining structure occurs when a large employer association negotiates with a union (or federation of unions) and sets wages and other employment terms for all the unionized employees in all the firms that are members of this employer association.

B. The Disadvantages of Fragmented Bargaining Structures

The challenge in emerging democracies is to develop wage-setting and bargaining structures that meet the parties' needs and the pressures of international competitive forces. For instance, highly fragmented bargaining units should be avoided. A number of problems have appeared in industrialized countries in situations where bargaining units were too fragmented and numerous. In Britain, for example, craft bargaining is said to be an impediment to integrative problem solving and the effective introduction of technological change (Ulman 1968). A large number of bargaining units also contributes to inflationary pressures through the promotion of wage imitation and leapfrogging across jurisdictions (Flanagan, Soskice, and Ulman 1983).

C. The Virtues of Coordinated Bargaining

One potential solution to the problem of bargaining-unit fragmentation is to conduct wage bargaining at the level of industrial sectors. In Germany, for example, bargaining occurs within sixteen major industrial sectors. The German structure has the advantage of inducing unions to consider broad worker economic interests. So, for example, because unions in Germany often include workers from a variety of companies and industries, there has been less trade protectionist sentiment within German unions since these unions often include members whose livelihood depends on the export success of their employers. In this way, particular firm or industry interests become muted in the bargaining process (Streeck 1984a). The coordination across work groups provided in the

German bargaining structure meshes with other aspects of German industrial relations to produce what has been called a "coordinated market economy" (Soskice 1990).

Another successful alternative bargaining structure is enterprise bargaining of the sort that occurs in Japan. The advantage of enterprise bargaining is that it is very responsive to the economic conditions facing particular firms. The potential problem of inflationary leapfrogging across enterprise unions is dampened in the Japanese system through the simultaneous occurrence of wage bargaining, which occurs in the "Spring Offensive" each year. In the annual offensive, the various enterprise unions communicate extensively with one another and often discuss their wage demands with their respective union federations. In this process, wage demands are coordinated and take account of macroeconomic circumstances. Japanese enterprise wage bargaining also has the advantage of often including a sizable share of pay increases in the form of annual bonuses that are influenced by the economic performance of the firm. The advantage of linking pay directly to economic performance through this and other alternative techniques is discussed more extensively below.

D. The Virtues of Annual Pay Agreements

Both German and Japanese wage bargaining have revealed relatively little inflationary tendencies. This appears to follow, in part, from the fact that in both countries most wage bargaining occurs on an annual basis, namely, the wage terms of labor contracts extend for only one year. In addition, in these countries there are various processes that provide coordination across wage bargains. These coordinating mechanisms seem to be especially critical in avoiding inflationary pressures (Soskice 1990).

In contrast, multiyear labor contracts in the United States (and some other countries) reduce the influence of contemporary macroeconomic factors on wage negotiations. In this way, multiyear contracts contribute to wage rigidity, a particularly worrisome problem during economic downturns (Wachter 1976). A countervailing advantage to multiyear contracts comes from the fact that they limit the possibility of the costly strikes that might ensue in more frequent bargaining, in effect, by reducing the costs and risks of bargaining. Yet the inflationary tendencies inherent in multiyear contracts appear to outweigh this virtue.

E. The Occupational Scope of Bargaining Structure

Another important aspect of bargaining structure concerns which employees are included in unions and other representation structures. In Japanese enterprise bargaining, white-collar employees of the firm below the executive rank are included as members of the union. In Germany, white-collar employees often press their interest through their participation in the codetermination processes, which provide these employees with the right to proportional representation in the works councils and in the election of supervisory board members. The provision of representation rights to white-collar employees is another aspect of bargaining structure worthy of attention. Both the German and the Japanese methods of providing white-collar employees with representation rights are commendable. An important industrial-relations task confronting developing countries is to avoid representation structures that only include "blue-collar" employees.

F. Recent Movement to More Decentralized Bargaining Structures in Advanced Industrialized Countries

In recent years in very many industrialized countries there has been movement toward more decentralized pay-setting and bargaining structures (Katz 1992). In the United States this involves the breakdown of multicompany bargaining (or the erosion of the extent of such bargaining) in the trucking, steel, and coal industries. In Sweden, in 1992 employers refused to engage in the traditional centralized bargaining. In Australia, the traditional heavy centralization in wage setting (the national "award" system) has been weakening even during a period when the government and the unions have engaged in a social contract. In some countries, such as Germany and Belgium, formal wage-setting structures have not broken down and become more decentralized. Nevertheless, in nearly all countries there has been a shift toward bargaining-structure decentralization through the elevation in the importance of, and an increase in the variation of, the outcomes of plant-level bargaining. Greater variation appears particularly in the work rules and work practices agreed to by union and company officials at the plant level.

There are many reasons for the recent decentralization of bargaining and wage-setting structures. The pressures of heightened international competition, increased volatility and uncertainty regarding economic trends, and the increased flexibility required in the face of more fragmented product markets have all contributed to bargaining-structure decentralization. Labor and management have turned to more decentralized bargaining as a way to develop contract terms that respond to their needs and economic pressures. More decentralized bargaining also fits well with the shift toward the new industrial-relations practices, such as the team systems discussed later in this paper.

V. Work-Place Issues

The relative success of Japanese and German industry over the past two decades has brought home the virtues of employee and union participation at various levels of management decision making. As changing world markets and new information technologies have increased the need for functional flexibility in the work place, production requirements can no longer be met only by armies of semiskilled workers following orders.

A. Recent Restructuring in Industrial Relations

In some countries, recent changes amount to a fundamental transformation in industrial relations. Aspects of this transformation have appeared in virtually all countries.

There are many dimensions to this transformation, including a shift in the focus of industrial-relations activity away from the "collective-bargaining" to the "strategic" and "work-place" levels (Kochan, Katz, and McKersie 1986). In contrast to the traditional arms-length and formal nature of collective bargaining, the "new industrial-relations system" involves more continuous and informal relations between workers and managers (Windolf 1989). The new system often includes contingent compensation, team systems of work organization, employment security programs, and enhanced worker and union participation in decision making.

B. Contingent Compensation

Contingent compensation links pay directly to firm or worker performance. The virtue of more contingent compensation comes from the fact that it provides responsiveness in wages to current economic circumstances. As Weitzman argues, if pay responds quickly to economic conditions, economic systems are able to lessen the need for large quantity adjustments in employment and output and thereby become less prone to stagflation and related macroeconomic problems (Weitzman 1984). As discussed earlier, the presence of annual pay agreements rather than multiyear pay agreements adds a significant degree of responsiveness. Yet it appears that economies benefit further from the presence of direct linkages between pay and measures of firm and/or worker performance.

The use of annual bonuses that provide one-third of total wage earnings in Japan provides a virtuous high degree of pay responsiveness to economic conditions. It should be noted that for these bonuses to provide a macroeconomic stabilization function, they must vary with firm performance, which does occur in Japan (Hashimoto 1979). Other systems would be well served to develop the mechanisms providing pay responsiveness that fit within their own industrial-relations systems.

In many countries there has been recent movement toward the use of pay procedures that provide such a contingent linkage. In some cases this has been introduced through profit sharing or stock ownership (Kochan, Katz, and McKersie 1986, 134). On the shop floor, more contingent pay has spread through the introduction of gainsharing programs that tie worker pay to work area or plant performance and through pay-for-knowledge that provides pay increases as the employee proves competence in a wider variety of jobs. (In the past, a worker's wage was often set strictly on the basis of the job classification or job tasks.)

C. Team Systems

A second important innovation of many new work systems is the shift to various forms of shop-floor and office teamwork (Windolf 1989). Traditional assembly-line organization based on isolated work stations, it turns out, contains built-in limitations on worker participation and flexibility. Traditional "fragmented" job assignments limit worker contributions to production improvements, commitment to product quality, and capacity for flexible deployment in the work place. Japanese team organization, by contrast, including cross-training, job rotation, integration of tasks, and regular team meetings, has demonstrated a dramatic potential for productivity and product-quality gains.

In response, many employers in manufacturing industries in the United States, Great Britain, and elsewhere have moved to introduce team forms of organization, with varying degrees of success. The exact form of team systems varies across firms, industries, and countries (Kochan, Katz, and McKersie 1986; Turner 1991). Team members often take on some inspection, material-handling, repair, and housekeeping tasks. In the more advanced teams, workers assume responsibility for some production-control and planning tasks, and hourly (in some cases unionized) team leaders perform job responsibilities formerly under the control of supervisors.

At the same time, unions in Germany, especially IG Metal, have been promoting "group work," both for its production improvements and as a more humanistic form of organization (Turner 1991, 111–17). The German version places an emphasis on broad work assignments, broadened responsibility and autonomy for the groups, as well as enhanced skills training and broad upgrading of group members.

Team or group systems are thus most likely to work well in countries such as Japan and Germany that already have strong institutional underpinnings for training and for worker–union participation. In other countries, it is necessary to establish such underpinnings to promote cooperation, participation, and training along with the introduction of more flexible team or group forms of organization. The necessary underpinnings can range from joint labor–management committees at the plant level to national legislation to promote training and to establish some nationally appropriate version of works councils.

D. Participation

A third essential element of innovative work systems and "new industrial relations" consists of mechanisms for employee and union participation. The elaboration of team systems brings with it wider roles for hourly workers as they become involved in production-control tasks. Team systems and the administration of new employment security are also often associated with a broadening of worker and union involvement in strategic business decisions. In part this strategic involvement arises as a consequence of the major corporate reorganizations that confront the work force. After watching plants close and work outsourced, workers and unions have sought avenues to affect the decisions that weigh so heavily on their future.

Strategic participation by workers and unions also expands by the very nature of the bargain being drafted in the new industrial-relations system. Workers and unions are often initially hesitant to adopt more contingent pay, teams, and other more-flexible work rules. They fear both the potentially lower and more volatile pay associated with contingent compensation and the potential increase in work pace and loss in protections associated with the modification of work practices. In response, labor has asked for greater shop-floor and strategic involvement in decisions along with employment-security provisions as both a form of compensation and a form of insurance for the protection of employee and union rights. In some plants in the United States, union officers serve on "administrative" committees that direct plant operations. GM's Saturn plant represents an extreme case. At Saturn, the president of the UAW local is a member of the executive management committee. This committee decides matters that include picking vendors to supply parts.

Participation can be structured in a number of different ways, including works councils established by law, informally established cooperation through enterprise unions, joint labor–management committees established through collective bargaining, and quality circles and suggestion programs in union and nonunion work places.

It is important to note that where unions are present, they need to be fully aboard and supportive of the introduction of new work organization. Management strategies that divide the local union to force teamwork on a reluctant work force are unlikely to work (Turner 1991). Institutional arrangements that ensure union participation, at least at some level, can facilitate the labor–management cooperation necessary for the high-trust, innovative modern work place.

While successful in Germany and Japan, the patchy track record in the United States, Great Britain, and France suggests that participation requires either legal backing or substantial protections and encouragement throughout the firm. Workers and unions need institutions with clear rules and protections to allow them to participate in firm decision-making processes, and management needs thorough-going reform from the top of the organization to the bottom to instill commitment for employee participation. Both sides need training in participatory processes and trust building to set successful participation in motion.

The role of middle management is especially important in this regard. It is here that employee participation is most often perceived as threatening to established prerogatives, and it is at this level that participation often fails or is sabotaged. Yet middle managers have a crucial role to play in participatory processes and can find their influence within the organization enhanced rather than diminished. They therefore need extra training in the management of participation, along with special encouragement, protections, and clarity about their own (often quite new) roles.

Participation is most likely to succeed and to be more than temporary if it occurs and is reinforced at all three levels of labor–management interaction in the firm: at the strategic level, in negotiation and agreement between top management and union leadership; at the functional level, in collective-bargaining agreements and contract enforcement; and at the work-place level, in team or group organization and other meaningful participation programs that have the full support of the organization and its management. National labor policy can play an especially important role in encouraging the spread of participation, through efforts ranging from education, to specific incentives, to enabling or even mandating legislation.

E. Employment Security

The generation of employment commitment to company goals requires that employees face the prospect of continued employment with their firms. This is particularly important in light of the spread of team systems and the development of more firm-specific skills. In the presence of these skills, employees become less attractive to the external labor market (Osterman 1988). If employees do not then receive more security from the firm, they may well be reluctant to acquire more-extensive skills and training or to participate in the sort of shop-floor decision making that is so crucial to the maintenance of competitive and high-quality products.

Employment security can come in a variety of forms. In Germany, there has been a longstanding and successful requirement that if firms seek to reduce the size of their work force, they must first negotiate social plans with their works council. These social plans then outline the compensation received by redundant workers, establish guidelines concerning which workers are to be laid off, and create other adjustment strategies. As a result, the German system has also shown relatively less use of layoffs as an adjustment strategy in the face of output declines. The "internal flexibility" provided in the German system through broad jobs and flexible work rules has created the possibility of more internal adjustments rather than recourse to extensive external adjustments through layoffs (Sengenberger and Kohler 1987).

In Japan, there is heavy use of the "lifetime employment principle." A relatively high percentage of employees spend long careers, often their whole career, with one firm (Cole 1979). The key is that employees are broadly trained and work rules are relatively flexible. This makes it possible for firms to make internal adjustments to respond to reductions in product demand. These internal adjustments include moving workers across parts of the enterprise, or in some cases even "loaning" workers to other firms. (This occurred during the mid-1970s at Mazda when their rotary car did not sell well. Some workers were sent into repair shops or out as sales staff while others were "loaned" to other firms in growing industries.)

The use of internal movements is, of course, not without its limits. In Japan, lifetime employment is afforded to "permanent" employees but is not provided to "temporary" employees and is more common in large firms. In the German system as well, the use of foreign workers (particularly in the 1960s and 1970s) on limited-term employment contracts also helped facilitate the less-frequent layoff of native German workers (Streeck 1984a).

In a number of countries in recent years, there have been a variety of new employment-security programs ranging from explicit employment guarantees to retraining and income support. The negotiation of such programs typically is linked to the introduction of more flexible work rules and other work practices associated with team systems.

There appears to be a direct link between participation, employment security, and work-force flexibility within the firm. To the extent that workers participate in decision-making processes, they become more flexible in what they are able and willing to do in production processes. And to the extent that they have employment security, employees are often willing to go along with even the most radical shop-floor innovations.

The United States, Great Britain, and France, among other countries, have weak participatory traditions, with industrial-relations systems that do little to encourage either participation or internal flexibility. Historically, managers act ("no one tells me how to run my business"), unions react (and often fight rearguard actions against innovation), and workers are supposed to do what they are told (but often sabotage innovation in more or less subtle ways). In these countries, a major challenge is to reform industrial-relations practices so that new participation and flexibility are possible in line with the demands of contemporary world markets. In the face of entrenched institutions and practices, however, such reform is quite difficult (see the Milkman paper in this volume). Reform is under way in all three countries, but the pace is halting, and the failures are many.

The crucial dilemma facing firms, unions, and policy makers outside Japan and Germany is not how to import foreign models but how to adapt and reform established institutions and practices to achieve the necessary participation and flexibility. Our point is that labor and management should try to find mechanisms that fit within their respective system to make use of internal flexibility as an alternative to external employment adjustments. At the same time, it is unreasonable to believe that all external employment adjustments can or should be avoided. The elimination of the possibility of layoffs can produce enormous inefficiencies and rigidities (and it has done so in some countries).

Firm-level employment-security practices can assist employees in making economic transitions and provide internal mobility. At the same time, governments should play a role in providing interfirm and career mobility, particularly during periods of slack economic growth and in regions or industries that confront abrupt employment declines. In Sweden, for example, there is a long history of successful "active labor-market policies," which have provided such assistance and mobility to workers (Meidner and Anderson 1973).

VI. Training and Work-Force Skill and Career Development

New work-place systems in the 1990s and beyond, based on such attributes as shop-floor and office teamwork discussed above, employee participation, and career development in internal labor markets, cannot succeed without broadly skilled workers capable of continual learning.

A. The Need for Greater Investment in Training

While traditional mass production may have required armies of semiskilled workers engaged in repetitive tasks, backed up by the few skilled workers necessary to repair and maintain machinery, modern production requires versatile, flexible employees who can perform various tasks and who can "participate" and contribute to production practices in a pro-active way.

The economic environment has put a premium on industry's ability to use batch rather than traditional mass-production techniques and to shift more rapidly across the types of products produced. This has generated new demands on industry's training procedures. (Evidence that the level and quality of training exerts a sizable independent impact on productivity is provided in MacDuffie and Kochan [1991]). More flexible manufacturing processes often entail the introduction of sophisticated electronically directed machinery (such as programmable machine tools) and automated storage and retrieval systems. These systems can be most effectively operated by a work force well informed about fairly advanced mathematics and statistics. The use of team systems fits into this network of new production techniques as the organizational vehicle through which workers take on the responsibilities of monitoring and often directing quality-control and production processes.

The training needs generated by these production and control systems go beyond traditional requirements. Not only must the work force have quantitative analytic skills, they must be skilled in the use of computers and other electronic technologies. Furthermore, since team systems are often associated with the new work practices, the work force needs communication and group skills to facilitate the operation and coordination of team tasks. Factory studies show increasing percentages of skilled workers, many of them newly cross-trained (in additional skills), accompanied by declining percentages of the traditional semiskilled workers (see, for example, Milkman and Pullman 1991). Even the latter require new training in organizational skills (for teamwork, participation, job rotation) and/or more substantive skills development for the monitoring of expensive micro-electronic-run machinery (Kern and Schumann 1984).

The problem for firms and governments is how to build up the necessary pool of skilled workers, how to build up the abilities and flexibility of the less skilled, and how to develop reliable structures and incentives for continual training and retraining. In this section, we consider the need for union involvement and the virtues of "productivity coalitions," the successful German apprenticeship system, successful Japanese internal labor markets, and the need for social and educational policies that are linked to and reinforce modern skill requirements and industrial relations.

B. The Advantages of Union Involvement in Training Design and Implementation

Union involvement in the promotion and operation of training programs can be a valuable asset in successful upskilling programs. At the firm level, such involvement can encourage cooperative labor–management relations and form part and parcel of the building of a "productivity coalition" (Streeck 1984b) that includes management, union, and work force. Local unions and/or works councils are often well placed to help run training programs in a way that appears fair and wins the trust of the work force. In addition, such local representative bodies may be well placed to know about missing skills and training requirements as well as the capacities and potential of individual employees. Works councils at large firms in Germany make an important contribution in this regard; enterprise unions in Japan to some extent play a parallel role.

In contrast to earlier efforts focused on management education, the new training programs often focus on occupational and "blue-collar" employees. As a consequence it now makes more sense for these training programs to be managed jointly by unions and management.

C. The German Training System

The German case also illustrates the constructive role that unions can play in the running of a successful national system of vocational education—as part of a productivity coalition at the macrolevel. Established and supported by comprehensive national legislation and funded both by government and employers, Germany's vocational education system offers three-year apprenticeships across a broad range of occupations: blue and white collar, manufacturing and service, from bakers to machinists to telecommunications technicians to hair stylists to preschool teachers to equipment programmers. At the national, regional, and local levels, the vocational education system is tripartite: employers, unions, and government all play an active role in establishing and updating occupational groupings and ensuring that training programs keep up with employer and work-force needs.

Because unions are broadly integrated into vocational education, they are committed to promoting a highly skilled work force. This commitment extends from the national and regional levels, where unions help set recruitment targets based on projected skill needs, to the plant and firm levels, where works councils press management to hire more apprentices. The British/American image of craft unions that restrict entry to the skilled trades (to maintain status and pay levels for the already skilled) is contradicted by the German picture of unions that actively promote widespread skills training. This is due in part to the industrial union structure of representation; equally important is the top-to-bottom integration of unions into the running of the vocational education system.

For individual workers, this system appears to work well. Fully two-thirds of the German work force has either completed an apprenticeship or graduated from a vocational school, and a large majority of these latter complete apprenticeships.

Employers have strong incentives to participate in apprenticeship hiring. The in-school training that apprentices receive is government funded; and apprentice wages, paid by employers, are low. The employer thus provides on-the-job training and in return gets inexpensive and often energetic and flexible young labor. In addition, the employer gets a multiyear period in which to work with and observe the young employee as a potential permanent, skilled hire. For employers as a group (and firms participate in the tripartite governing bodies through employer associations), the national system of apprentice training and vocational education assures a steady flow of skills on the labor market.

In auto plants, for example, there is often a surplus of skills. Semiskilled positions are in many cases occupied by workers who have completed apprenticeships but were unable to (or chose not to) find a position in their trade. These workers have proven ripe for further on-the-job training and added job responsibilities beyond what a traditional semiskilled position would require. Union demands in the German auto industry for shop-floor "group work" are based in part on the desire to offer new training and autonomy to these floating but essentially skilled workers. And the ability of German employers to develop and offer intermediate positions, such as "equipment monitors" for robots and other microelectronic-run machinery, is also based on the high skills base of the work force.

The nationwide tripartite comprehensive system of vocational education has often been cited as a major factor accounting for Germany's industrial success. A highly skilled labor force is clearly a central component of the virtuous circle that has pushed German firms upmarket into "diversified quality production" (Sorge and Streeck 1988).

D. Extensive Japanese On-the-Job Training

In contrast to the German system, the Japanese rely relatively little on formal apprentices and yet accomplish extensive training inside firms. The Japanese production system includes jobs that are relatively broadly defined, and workers are often rotated across jobs throughout their careers. These production techniques are facilitated by the extensive amounts of on-the-job training received by workers. In addition, skill acquisition and work-place flexibility are assisted by the high levels and quality of education provided in the Japanese primary and secondary schools. The provision of extensive on-the-job training in Japan is linked to other features of the Japanese industrial-relations system. The long tenure of workers in firms provides strong incentives to both workers and firms for investments in training by guaranteeing returns on training investments. In addition, the heavy reliance on seniority-based promotion makes job rotation easy and thereby facilitates training across tasks (Cole 1979).

First-line supervisors in Japan commonly plan workers' training and career progression carefully. Some of this planning and heavy first-line supervisor involvement takes place as part of the merit pay and performance appraisal that covers "blue-collar" workers in Japanese firms (Koike 1988). Thus extensive investments in training do not occur accidentally but rather are linked closely to other practices common to Japanese firms.

VII. Conclusions

History has shown that there are certain key moments of transition in industrial-relations systems, after which they get set and are hard to modify. Often these key moments are a result of legislative changes (e.g., the establishment of the National Labor Relations Act and the emergence of public-sector unions after the burgeoning of public-sector legislation in the United States). Other factors are also important in facilitating industrial-relations system change, such as important historical or economic junctures (e.g., the postwar reconstruction in Germany and Japan were significant moments of industrial-relations transition).

The recent movements toward democracy and markets in Eastern Europe and the former Soviet Union present an opportunity for major transitions in industrial relations. A key question is whether these countries will take advantage of this opportunity.

Another important issue is the need to recognize that various industrial-relations policies and procedures fit together and reinforce one another (i.e., the systematic nature of industrial relations). For example, changes in pay systems have implications for work organization. Work organization, meanwhile, has strong implications for employee participation and skill development. For the newly emerging democracies it is not just a question of choosing elements of industrial-relations policy from the experience of the leading industrial countries and making incremental adjustments but rather of striving for the reconstruction of entire systems so that various new policies will fit together.

It is not suggested here that the emerging democracies adopt an industrial-relations system from any of the industrialized countries in its entirety, since systems must reflect the unique institutional background, politics, and history of each country. Most importantly, we emphasize the necessity of coordinating and integrating industrial-relations policy with other economic, social, educational, and legal policies. The emerging democracies must develop their own unique institutional mechanisms to achieve these goals.

While it is clear that many often far-reaching changes are necessary in industrial-relations practices, the process through which change occurs is also important. The process of change has to be managed so as to provide for the active participation of the parties. Participation can help to achieve the necessary popular acceptance of changes. Experience has consistently shown that the top-down introduction of change in industrial relations (whether it is policy at the national level or systems at the company level) fails without popular acceptance of the need for change and participation in the change effort.

References

Cole, Robert E. 1979. *Work, Mobility and Participation.* Berkeley and Los Angeles: University of California Press.

Flanagan, Robert J.; Soskice, David W.; and Ulman, Lloyd. 1983. *Unionism, Economic Stabilization, and Income Policies: European Experience.* Washington, DC: The Brookings Institution.

Freeman, Richard B., and Medoff, James L. 1984. *What Do Unions Do?* New York: Basic Books, pp. 94–110.

Hashimoto, Masanori. 1979. "Bonus Payments, On-the-Job Training, and Lifetime Employment in Japan." *Journal of Political Economy* 87 (October), pp. 1086–1104.

Ingrassia, Paul, and Aeppel, Timothy. 1992. "Worried by Japanese Thriving GM Europe Vows to Get Leaner." *Wall Street Journal,* 27 July, pp. A–1 and A–6.

Katz, Harry C. 1992. "The Decentralization of Collective Bargaining: A Comparative Review and Analysis." Unpublished manuscript, NYSSILR, Cornell University, July.

Katz, Harry C., and Sabel, Charles F. 1985. "Industrial Relations and Industrial Adjustment in the Car Industry." *Industrial Relations* 24 (Fall), pp. 295–315.

Kern, Horst, and Shumann, Michael. 1984. *Das Fende der Arbeitsteilung?* Munich: C.H. Beck.

Kochan, Thomas A.; Katz, Harry C.; and McKersie, Robert B. 1986. *The Transformation of American Industrial Relations.* New York: Basic Books.

Koike, Kazuo. 1988. *Understanding Industrial Relations in Modern Japan.* London: Macmillan Press.

MacDuffie, John Paul, and Kochan, Thomas A. 1991. "Does the U.S. Underinvest in Human Resources? Determinants of Training in the World Auto Industry." Unpublished manuscript, Wharton School, University of Pennsylvania.

Meidner, Rudolf, and Anderson, Rolf. 1973. "The Overall Impact of an Active Labor Market Policy in Sweden." In *Manpower Programs in the Policy Mix,* ed. Lloyd Ulman. Baltimore: John Hopkins University Press, pp. 117–58.

Milkman, Ruth, and Pullman, Cydney. 1991. "Technological Change in an Auto Assembly Plant." *Work and Occupations* 18 (May), pp. 123–47.

Osterman, Paul. 1988. *Employment Futures: Reorganization, Dislocation, and Public Policy.* New York and Oxford: Oxford University Press.

Sengenberger, Werner, and Kohler, Christoph. 1987. "Policies of Workforce Structure in the American and German Automobile Industry." In *Flexibility in Labour Markets,* ed. Roger Tarling. London: Academic Press.

Sorge, Arndt, and Streeck, Wolfgang. 1988. "Industrial Relations and Technical Change: The Case for an Extended Perspective." In *New Technology and Industrial Relations*, ed. R. Hyman and W. Streeck. Oxford: Basil Blackwell, pp. 19–47.

Soskice, David. 1990. "Reinterpreting Corporatism and Explaining Unemployment: Co-ordinated and Non-coordinated Market Economies." In *Labour Relations and Economic Performance*, ed. R. Brunetta and C. Dell'Aringa. London: Macmillan Press.

Streeck, Wolfgang. 1984a. *Industrial Relations in West Germany: A Case Study of the Car Industry*. New York: St. Martin's Press.

———. 1984b. "Neo-Corporatist Industrial Relations and the Economic Crisis in West Germany." In *Order and Conflict in Contemporary Capitalism*, ed. John H. Goldthorpe. Oxford: Oxford University Press, pp. 291–314.

Turner, Lowell. 1991. *Democracy at Work: Changing World Market and the Future of Unions*. Ithaca, NY: Cornell University Press.

Uchitelle, Louis. 1992. "Russian Auto Maker Follows a Survival Blueprint: Exports." *The New York Times*, 23 July, pp. A–1 and A–10.

Ulman, Lloyd. 1968. "Collective Bargaining and Industrial Efficiency." In *Britain's Economic Prosperity*, ed. Ronald E. Caves and Associates. Washington, DC: The Brookings Institution.

Wachter, Michael. 1976. "The Changing Cyclical Responsiveness of Wage Inflation." *Brookings Papers on Economic Activity*, vol. 1. Washington, DC: The Brookings Institution, pp. 115–59.

Weitzman, Martin L. 1984. *The Share Economy*. Cambridge, MA: Harvard University Press.

Windolf, Paul. 1989. "Productivity Coalitions and the Future of Corporatism." *Industrial Relations* 28 (Winter), pp. 1–20.

Restructuring Human Resource Management in the United States

George T. Milkovich

Introduction

Change is endemic to market-based economies and consequently to the employment relationships embedded in them. Hence, it is yesterday's news that the terms and conditions under which people work in the United States are changing. Historically, the pace of this change has varied. But the restructuring of capital assets eventually affects the relations between employees and employers. The changes currently under way in North America signal fundamental shifts in these relationships. Descriptions of these changes differ, much as the blind men described the elephant. Some claim the changes include shifts from adversarial to more cooperative union–management relations, from bureaucratically burdened employees working for hierarchical, control-oriented employers to empowered employees with greater role flexibility working for more egalitarian employers; from earnings based on time and job to earnings based on profits, gainsharing, and so on. Others describe the change differently. They see not cooperation but cooptation and union avoidance, increased risk sharing and cost shifting to employees rather than success sharing, and diminished employment security rather than empowerment. Which view of the new, emerging employment relationship is accurate? Experience suggests that both are—-cooperation, empowerment, flexibility, and success sharing are emerging hand in glove with declining union membership, risk and cost shifting to employees, and diminishing employment security.

Almost daily, the press describes employers' decisions to reduce their work force and restructure incentive and benefit payments in response to competitive pressures. Simultaneously, these same employers adopt programs aimed at achieving high commitment and high performance among their work teams. This paper examines some of these major changes and their implications from the perspective of human resource management (HRM). After examining these changes, a framework is offered for analyzing and interpreting them.

The author is a professor of human resource management at Cornell University.

Perspective Matters: From Welfare to Industrial Relations and Personnel Administration to Human Resource Management

As did other aspects of management, human resource management evolved as a response to pragmatic pressures and problems rather than to any logical imperative based on theory or ideology. The motives ascribed to these changes varied. At the beginning of the twentieth century, several employers started "welfare" departments with the express purpose of improving the "welfare" of employees. Case studies of these welfare departments in about 50 firms are reported in a U.S. Department of Labor study.[1] In 1910, for example, the Cleveland Tool Company opened cafeterias for employees to obtain "wholesome food at cost, built washrooms, improved ventilation and lighting, and funded education programs to improve immigrants' abilities in English speaking and reading." Such welfare programs by employers were labeled paternalism by some. Many believed the programs fostered employee dependence on employers and would eventually lead to an "industrial feudalism."

By the end of World War II, these welfare programs had evolved; most employers managed employment relations through two specialized departments: labor relations, which dealt with labor-union relations, and personnel administration, which dealt with nonunionized employees.[2] For the next several decades, personnel and labor-relations departments became increasingly specialized and served to design and administer the programs and procedures that made up the employment relationships. These consisted of collections of activities such as recruiting, hiring, training, wage and salary, union negotiation, grievance handling, contract administration, and so on. Each activity was designed to accomplish some objective or respond to some pressure or problem. In the last quarter of the twentieth century, the name of the function has changed again, this time to human resource management.[3] The premise underlying the human resource management view is that employees are resources or assets, and, if the rhetoric is to be believed, they are critical to achieving competitive advantage for their employers. This notion is deceptively simple. For an enterprise to succeed, the capability, energies, and trust of employees must be recognized and rewarded. The activities emphasized include organizing employees into work teams, empowering employees to assume added responsibility for managing the work, implementing profit and gainsharing, and emphasizing total quality of products and services as well as customer satisfaction. Fads and fashion to some, these changes in name signaled shifts in the nature of the employment relationship from the employers' perspective. Welfare departments perceived employees as dependents, labor relations shifted the view to dealing with employees as union members, personnel treated them as individuals, and human resources views them in terms of team members and resources.

Common to all four historical perspectives is the treatment of employees as part of the operating costs of an enterprise. These costs can be simply modeled as

a function of the number of employees, their average wages and benefits, and other programs, rules, and conditions designed to facilitate the employment relationship.

Hence, the four historical perspectives can be seen as approaches to controlling these expenses plus efforts to obtain increased value added from employees. Simply stated, welfare programs were a form of return to employees, either substituting for or adding to wages. These programs helped insure employers with a relatively stable, healthy work force. Labor-relations mechanisms, after employers accepted them, also helped insure employers a stable, experienced work force with approximately the same labor costs as their competitors. By negotiating similar terms and conditions for all firms within an industry, unions helped remove relative wages and benefits as a factor in competitive advantage. Contemporary human resource management approaches go beyond attempting to tailor various programs to fit the specific competitive pressures and opportunities facing an employer. Some of these approaches are examined later. The point is that in a very real sense these historical shifts in employers' approaches to employment relationships represent shifts in their approaches to controlling costs and improving the value added contributed by employees.

The historic transformation from the welfare approach to human resource management is in large part attributable to varying external changes. As noted earlier, the restructuring of capital assets and the increase in competitive pressure have a significant impact. Waves of immigrants in the early 1900s (and the late 1980s and 1990s), the passage of significant labor legislation in the 1930s and 1940s, the civil rights legislation, and pension and benefits regulations have all had their effects as well.[4] As if adapting to environmental jolts, employers have restructured their approaches to the employment relationship.

From a Personnel-Planning to a Strategic Perspective

What is known as strategic planning today evolved from personnel planning intended to provide answers to specific issues: How many employees should be employed and with what competencies? What is the break-even point between working overtime hours versus employing more people? Forecasting and planning models, developed in operations research, were applied to employment forecasting and planning.[5] However, little attention was devoted to reconciling these forecasts beyond identifying possible options (adding to staff, layoffs, promotions, training, work redesign, changing work rules, and the like). Little theoretical or practical knowledge was available to help inform choices among these alternatives. While personnel planning emphasized the interdependencies among the options to reconcile the forecasts, it suffered from being unable to help direct the choices. It was clear that redesigning work rules, retraining employees, and supporting the new behaviors with gainsharing were interrelated actions. What was not clear was whether one set of actions was in any way superior to another.

For example, was redesigning the work place and retraining employees a better option than replacing obsolete employees with more recently trained new workers at lower wage rates? Underlying models and research to help inform such choices were lacking.

More recently, a strategic perspective has evolved that focuses on the links between human resource (HR) policies and an enterprise's overall strategy. Here the issue becomes, How do HR policies help the enterprise compete? What are the competitive advantages or value added of HR policies? A strategic perspective retains the planning focus on the interrelatedness of HR policies. But it goes beyond to direct the choice among alternative policy options that best contribute to the organization's ability to compete. Planning for the succession or replacement of the leadership of the enterprise is also a critical aspect of a strategic plan. While the focus of HR practices is increasingly on treating employees as resources critical to the success of the enterprise, the evolution of scholarly theory and research to inform and support this perspective lags behind practice.

From Human Relations to Financial Performance and Customer and Employee Satisfaction

Two decades ago, the human-relations perspective of personnel held that employee morale and job satisfaction were the desirable features in employment relations.[6] Today, the employment relationship is focused on achieving financial performance, customer satisfaction, and employee satisfaction. Organization effectiveness is defined in terms of financial and market performance. Employee satisfaction is defined through surveys of employee attitudes toward their employers' HR policies and their feelings of fair treatment under various procedures. Customer satisfaction is variously measured in terms of on-time deliveries, quality, and surveys of customers.

This change to emphasize financial performance and customer and employee satisfaction is woven into the strategic perspective. For example, the emphasis on total quality, team work, cooperative union–management relations, empowerment, and gainsharing is based on the belief that these approaches will improve the organization's financial performance and improve customer and employee relations. This represents a shift in the mind set of decision makers. No longer is the employment relationship seen as an end in itself. Rather, the issue increasingly is becoming one of finding ways to change the relationship to improve competitive advantage.

From Labor Relations to Governance and Implicit Contracts

As noted earlier, from the 1940s to the 1970s the relationship between management and unions formed a core of industrial relations and employment relationships.[7] This relationship has been described as adversarial and lacking in trust, a zero-sum game. This premise is increasingly being called into question, due in large part to international competitive pressures that accelerated the decline of unionism in the United States. Only about one of every eight private-sector employees in the United States belongs to a labor organization. As has been widely documented, unions have not only been unsuccessful in organizing expanding sectors of the economy, they have also experienced sharp declines in membership in those industries where they enjoyed traditional strength. The 1980s and early 1990s bore witness to the major growth of nonunion business units in many companies.

Both conceptually and practically, the HRM orientation to employment relations focuses on work-force governance and employee relations rather than labor–management negotiations. Labor relations is no longer the primary mode of work-force participation in work-place governance. Collective bargaining is increasingly being perceived as merely one of several forums for employee empowerment.

Work-place governance exemplifies the transformation of the traditional notion of "web of rules" used by industrial-relations scholars to describe the procedures that regulate the employment relationship. Governance includes participative management, worker councils, peer dispute-resolution procedures, and quality-of-work-life programs. The traditional focus of labor relations in the United States on contract negotiations, administration, and dispute resolution has been supplanted. The notion of a contract between labor and management has evolved beyond legal attributes of a collectively bargained agreement to include implicit psychological, political, and social dimensions. The implicit contract involves reciprocal obligations and returns between employers and employees. Thus, for example, when several computer firms, such as Digital Equipment Company, Hewlett-Packard, and Compac, recently laid off employees, some felt an "implicit contract" of employment security had been violated. Consequently, these firms faced problems reestablishing or repairing their implicit social contract with their remaining employees.

Managers, unions, and employees are all becoming more aware of alternatives to collective bargaining. The dominant model of labor relations is shifting to models of implicit contracts involving political influence and participation in decision making.

From Training to Work-Force Preparedness and Continuous Learning

Increasingly, HRM regards training expenditures as strategic investments similar to investments in new plant and equipment. Continuous training is seen as vital to achieving competitiveness. This concern for training is expanding into concerns about work-force preparedness and continuous learning. The perspective is shifting from individual- and team-level training to encompass concerns about the quality of the entire U.S. system of education. While

Americans enjoy high levels of educational attainment, the Department of Education reports that 19 million adults cannot read well enough to cope with daily tasks at work. Many of these are recent immigrants unable to understand or speak English.[8] One has only to take a cab in New York City to hear the Russian language spoken or in Washington, DC, to hear Iranian accents. But the problem is not limited to new immigrants. For example, Blue Cross of Massachusetts discovered that 50 percent of its clerical workers tested for promotion read below high-school levels. At a General Motors Division, 22 percent of employees asked for training in reading simple words, signs, and labels; 32 percent needed help in understanding written directions, charts, and instructions. More and more training classes inside organizations are forced to cover basic math, reading, and computer literacy.

Many employers are trying to change this situation by getting directly involved in public education. Yet about 700,000 students are dropping out of high schools each year, and another 700,000 are graduating with only eighth-grade skills. At the same time, the skill requirements of U.S. employers appear to be escalating. For example, manufacturing workers may be assigned to teams or cells that require continuous learning and flexibility; each team member is expected to learn every job. Quality checking, statistical process control, resetting machines, work-force scheduling, and other tasks that were formerly the domain of supervisors are now common fare for all workers.

In brief, the orientation in training is shifting toward improving work-force preparedness and continuous learning beyond focusing only on specific, job-oriented skills.

From Wages and Employment to Total Labor Costs and Performance

Historically, determining wage levels and structures (e.g., differentials among jobs) and the level of employment and employment security were viewed as crucial objectives in HRM. As a result, managers focused on practices such as job evaluation, market wage surveys, and negotiations. Textbooks and articles in scholarly journals were concerned with the administrative aspects of wage determination and employment security (recruiting, hiring, promotions, bumping provisions, and layoffs) and analyzed alternative approaches to making these decisions.[9] Increasingly, the focus has shifted to understanding the effects of wages and employment security on total labor costs and their links with productivity or organizational effectiveness.

From this perspective, the objective is to manage total labor costs better. Simply conceived, three main factors influence total labor costs in U.S. firms: employment levels (both numbers of employees and hours worked), average compensation (wages, bonuses, etc.), and average benefit costs (health and life insurance, pensions, dependent care, etc.). The critical questions have become: What portion of wages and benefits should be fixed costs? Which should vary with financial performance? Who among the work force should have relatively stable employment security? Whose employment security should vary with financial performance and employer requirements?

Answers to these questions involve changing the implicit understanding, the reciprocal obligations and returns, between employees and employers. Reciprocal understandings about the nature of the risks involved in wages, benefits, and employability are being restructured. To illustrate, many employers are adopting different employment-security terms with different employees. Their approach is to segment the employees into core (i.e., employees critical to the business), contract (i.e., those on specific short-term projects, such as consultants, contract engineers, subcontractors, and strategic alliances), and contingent (i.e., part-time workers, those with indeterminate employment). Employment security has become increasingly variable and risky for a larger segment of the work force. Only core employees, those critical to the success of the organization, retain the more traditional employment-security relationship.

Similarly, the increased use of the "new pay," such as profit sharing and gain-sharing, has had the effect of increasing the variability and risk in employees' earnings.[10] The use of incentive pay plans has increased dramatically in the past decade. Most surveys of employer practices report that over 40 percent of employers are using some form of variable pay scheme. And greater portions of the work force are being covered by these plans.

From the employment-relations perspective, variable-pay incentives represent an explicit agreement or contract that clearly links the performance of the organization with specific payments to employees. Group incentive plans such as gainsharing and profit sharing can represent a form of success sharing with employees. And there is an increasing body of research that reports that under certain conditions incentive pay plans do improve performance. Evidence suggests that gainsharing can result in productivity improvements of between 15 and 20 percent. Some studies report sustained improvements up to three years. Other studies report that firms that paid more in bonus relative to base pay performed better. Specifically, increasing the ratio of bonus over base by 10 percent led to a 0.95 percent increase in return on assets. Further, those firms that had more employees eligible for long-term incentives (e.g., stock options) also performed better. Specifically, a 10-percent increase in eligibility yielded about a 0.17 percent improvement in return on assets.[11]

However, many gainsharing and profit-sharing plans also involve shifting risk to employees. There is uncertainty over whether bonuses will be achieved. Often couched in terms of empowering employees, these pay programs are by definition variable—they vary based on performance, however defined.

In sum, the change to a total cost and performance perspective has a profound effect on employment relationships. There is a change in the balance of the risks and returns in the relationship. More employees' earnings and employability are subjected to increased variability and uncertainty. The nature of the implicit understanding is changing, depending in large measure on whether employees are core, contract, or contingent workers.

From Individual Employee to Teams

Developed from the traditions of scientific management, industrial engineering, and psychology, the notion of tasks grouped into jobs and individuals matched to appropriate jobs provided the cornerstone of personnel and industrial-relations approaches. Job analysis was a core activity and formed the basis for selection, training, compensation—almost all personnel decisions. This model still tends to pervade much of the conceptualization of HR.

Concepts of groups and teams, along with more flexible concepts of work assignments, have emerged to contest the original job-individual model.[12] The concept of job is becoming less fixed and defined. Instead, work assignments are defined more by the skills of the employees than by rigid organizational specifications. In addition, teamwork and cooperation among employees rather than competition to come out ahead of co-workers is being emphasized. "Nobody sings solo" is the refrain heard across U.S. firms today. The team rather than the individual has emerged as the basic building block in the design of organizations.

Yet not all scholars are ready to reject the importance of the individual.[13] Solutions that concentrate on groups fail to take into account the underlying nature of the employment relationship in the United States. Teams are not hired, laid off, trained, and paid. Individuals are. People are employed individually, and their employment contracts, real or implicit, remain individual. Nor do groups face the issue of accountability; it remains an individual phenomenon.

From Mechanical Bureaucracies to Networks and Alliances

Advanced economies, including those of North America, the European Community, and the Pacific Rim, are witnessing a dramatic restructuring of the design of organizations.[14] Of the 500 largest U.S. companies in the 1950s, fewer than 250 exist today. Traditional hierarchical bureaucratic design, developed during the mid–twentieth century to take advantage of centralized planning, functional integration, and operating scale has given way to designs best described as networks and strategic alliances. Organizations in all sectors of the economy are being redesigned, with the possible exception of the public sector. Governmental agencies, educational institutions, and regulatory units seem to be the most resistant to these transformations.

Networks are based on the flow of resources, information, and raw materials required to meet customer needs. Rather than designs based on functions, such as manufacturing, research and development, marketing and sales, finance, and so on, networks focus on the processes and linkages required to produce products and services to satisfy customers. Specific networks seem to vary according to the products and services offered, the technologies employed, and the customer segments served.

Accompanying this development of network designs is the widespread use of strategic alliances among suppliers, producers, and customers as well as among former competitors. Further, competitors are forming joint ventures or equity-sharing arrangements, in which strategic assets such as technologies, capital, markets, and human resources are shared. It is no longer unusual to find employees of one enterprise located within the facilities of consumers, suppliers, and even competitors. The notion of boundaryless organizations, often used to describe these developments, focuses on insuring that the specifications and requirements of the suppliers, producers, and consumers are integrated.

These new organizational designs have profound implications for employment relationships. Reduced hierarchies, broadened work rules and accountabilities, eliminated work roles and procedures are examples of these effects. Corporate staffs and centrally controlled bureaucracies are reduced, entire layers of administration and managerial roles are removed from the hierarchy, and bureaucratic rules regulating terms and conditions of employment are reduced and modified.

In general, most U.S. enterprises—General Electric, AT&T, 3M, and even IBM—have shifted away from centralized, highly bureaucratic, controlled organizations to a more unique, individualized organizational design tailored to the consumer market segments, technologies employed, and capital markets in which they compete. General Electric, for example, has thirteen strategic business units operating throughout the world. They range from the entertainment unit (NBC) to financial services (Kidder Peabody) to the locomotive and aircraft engine manufacturers (GE Aerospace and GE Locomotive). Each unit competes in different product and service markets, using different technologies with different capital requirements. The employment relationships within each of these units are tailored to fit each unit's unique requirements to help each gain a competitive advantage.

In a generic sense, the HRM developments discussed in this paper are evidenced throughout GE business units (i.e., strategic orientation, customer-centered orientation, work-force preparedness, continuous learning, total costs and performance emphasis, and networks and strategic alliances). Nevertheless, the specific features of the employment relationships vary among these units. Many employees in both Kidder Peabody and GE Aerospace are on group-based incentive plans, but the earnings opportunities and risks each employee faces vary considerably. As with the rings of Saturn, the more understanding we gain of these employment relationships, the more diversity we observe.

From Integrated Uniform Employment Relations to Strategic Diversity

The basic premise underlying the HRM approach is that the terms and conditions in an employment relationship should be designed to be contingent upon or "fit" the external and institutional conditions confronting an organization. The better this "fit," the more likely it is that the organization will be successful.[15] Decision makers faced with diverse policy options must tailor them to fit the particular circumstances of each business unit. Consequently, the opportunities and risks inherent in these uniquely tailored employment relations will vary among organizations and even within organizations among different subunits.

Conclusions

In the United States, changes in the employment relationship are inseparable from the continuous restructuring endemic to the American economy and society. Change is inevitable; experimentation and renewal is continuous. Some of the changes in the employment relationships—such as from welfare to personnel and from industrial relations to human resource management—are gradual and evolutionary, while changes in specific employers are more abrupt and revolutionary.

How one views this change depends on what ideological lens one uses. Galbraith, for example, saw large corporations and the state acting in concert to utilize technology, public policy, and capital for planning and regulating economic, social, and political forces.[16] His "new industrial state" would create competitive advantages for a society. He advocated that organizations form large centralized planning units in which "the scale of operations of the largest should approximate those of government" (p. 87). "There is," he went on, "no natural presumption in favor of the market; given the growth of the industrial system, the presumption is, if anything, the reverse. And to rely on the market where planning is required is to invite a nasty mess" (p. 368).

Another view was expressed by Schumpeter, who coined the phrase "creative destruction" to depict the process that market-based economies go through to reconfigure assets to more productive uses.[17] While the term may be overly dramatic, it does convey the cauldron of change that includes bankruptcies, plant closings, massive job losses, as well as redesigned organizations, business alliances, flexibility, continuous learning, profit sharing, and risks and opportunities. The political and economic offspring of both these views offer similar prescriptions in this last decade of the century.

A generic pattern does emerge from the current restructuring of employment relationships in the United States. They (1) have become increasingly strategic; (2) have become more sensitive to costs, quality, performance, and customers; (3) offer greater earnings opportunities with less employment security and greater risk; and (4) require continuous learning and emphasize accountability and teamwork.

The HRM approach, in contrast to the welfare, personnel, and industrial-relations approaches, emphasizes treating employees as strategic resources and attempts to manage the strategic impact of the employment relationship. Within this strategic perspective, decision makers focus on tailoring the terms and conditions of employment to fit the unique circumstances of each organization. Consequently, while a generic pattern of change can be described, systematic study reveals considerable diversity in employment relations.

Finally, the HRM approach appears to have a dark side. With its principal emphasis on managing the employment relationship to achieve competitive advantage, the very nature of the socioeconomic contract among employees, employers, and governments has changed. Implicit understandings, reciprocal obligations, and returns among the stake holders have shifted. Reciprocal understandings about the nature of wages, benefits, employability, and the like are recast. It is my belief that the impact of this changing social contract on employees and their dependents has been virtually ignored. Without concern for social justice and fair treatment of employees, sustained competitive advantage may well be impossible to achieve.

Notes

1. Elizabeth Lewis Otey, *Employer's Welfare Work*, U.S. Bureau of Labor Statistics, No. 123 (Washington, DC, 1913).

2. Dale Yoder, *Personnel Principles and Policies* (Englewood Cliffs, NJ: Prentice-Hall, 1959); John T. Dunlop and Charles A. Myers, "The Industrial Relations Function in Management," *Personnel* (March 1955), pp.406–13.

3. Thomas A. Mahoney and John Deckop, "Evolution of Concept and Practice in Personnel Administration/Human Resource Management," *1986 Yearly Review of Management of the Journal of Management* 12, no. 1 (1986), pp. 223–41; Thomas Kochan, Harry Katz, and Robert McKersie, *The Transformation of American Industrial Relations* (New York: Basic Books, 1986).

4. *Human Resources Outlook 1992*, Resource Bulletin No. 241 (New York: Conference Board, 1989).

5. George T. Milkovich, Lee Dyer, and Thomas A. Mahoney, "HR Planning," in *Human Resources Management in the 1980s*, ed. S.J. Carroll and R.S. Schuler (Washington, DC: Bureau of National Affairs, 1983), chap. 2, pp. 1–28.

6. T. Kochan, H. Katz, and N. Mower, *Worker Participation and American Unions* (Kalamazoo, MI: W.E. Upjohn Institute, 1984); W.D. Scott, R.C. Clothier, and W.R. Spriegel, *Personnel Management* (New York: McGraw-Hill, 1961).

7. Dale Yoder, *Personnel Management and Industrial Relations*, 5th ed. (Englewood Cliffs, NJ: Prentice-Hall, 1962); John Fossum, *Labor Relations: Development Structure Process*, 3rd ed. (Plano, TX: Business Publications, 1985); Thomas A. Kochan, *Collective Bargaining and Industrial Relations* (Homewood, IL: Richard D. Irwin, 1980).

8. John Bishop, "Why High School Students Learn So Little and What Can Be Done About It," Cornell University Center for Advanced Human Resource Studies Working Paper No. 88–01, 1988.

9. George T. Milkovich and Jerry Newman, *Compensation*, 3rd ed. (Homewood, IL: Richard D. Irwin, 1990); A. Blinder, ed., *Paying for Productivity* (Washington, DC: The Brookings Institution, 1990).

10. George T. Milkovich and Alexandra K. Wigdor, eds., *Pay for Performance* (Washington, DC: National Academy Press, 1991).

11. Barry Gerhart and George Milkovich, "Employee Compensation: Research Practice," in *Handbook of Industrial and Organizational Psychology*, ed. M.D. Dunnette and L.M. Hough, 2nd ed. (Palo Alto, CA: Consulting Psychologist Press, 1992).

12. E.E. Lawler, *High Involvement Organizations* (San Francisco, CA: Jossey-Bass, 1991).

13. Elliot Jaques, "In Praise of Hierarchy," *Harvard Business Review*, January–February 1990, pp. 127–33.

14. David Nadler, Marc Gerstein, and Robert Shaw, *Organizational Architecture: Designs for Changing Organizations* (San Francisco, CA: Jossey-Bass, 1992).

15. R.E. Miles and C.C. Snow, *Organizational Strategy, Structure, and Processes* (New York: McGraw-Hill, 1978); C.C. Snow and R.E. Miles, "Organizational Strategy, Design and Human Resource Management," paper presented at National Academy of Management Meetings, Dallas, 1983; Lee Dyer and Gerald Holder, "A Strategic Perspective of Human Resource Management," in *Human Resource Management: Evolving Roles and Responsibilities*, ed. Lee Dyer and Gerald Holder (Washington, DC: Bureau of National Affairs, 1988), pp. 1:25–1:86; Cynthia A. Lengnick-Hall and Mark L. Lengnick-Hall, "Strategic Human Resources Management: A Review of the Literature and a Proposed Typology," *Academy of Management Review* 13, no. 1 (1988), pp. 454–70; Gloria de Bejar and George Milkovich, "Human Resource Strategy at the Business Level," paper presented at National Academy of Management Meetings, Chicago, August 1986; George Milkovich and John Boudreau, *Human Resource Management*, 6th ed. (Homewood, IL: Richard D. Irwin, 1991); C.W. Hofer and D. Schendel, *Strategy Formulation: Analytical Concepts* (St. Paul, MN: West Publishing, 1978).

16. John Kenneth Galbraith, *The New Industrial State* (Boston: Houghton Mifflin, 1967).

17. Joseph A. Schumpeter, *Capitalism, Socialism and Democracy*, 2nd ed. (New York: Harper, 1947).

The Impact of Foreign Investment on U.S. Industrial Relations

The Case of Japan

Ruth Milkman

The workers of the world are less united today than a century ago, when labor was international and capital national in orientation. Labor movements around the world now operate primarily on a national (or, in some cases, local) basis, even though capital has become increasingly internationalized. In recent years, as transportation and communication costs have dropped and barriers to international trade and investment have collapsed in nation after nation, capital's increased mobility has dramatically weakened organized labor in virtually every country.

The United States, which did so much to foster economic globalization, has become increasingly dependent on the reinvigorated economies of Western Europe and Japan. With relatively few barriers to foreign trade and even fewer to investment, the United States has been flooded with imports and with both direct and indirect foreign investment in the last two decades.[1] Once the world's largest creditor, it is now justly famous for its enormous trade and budget deficits; and foreign direct investment inside the United States now exceeds U.S. direct investment abroad.[2]

This paper explores a critical aspect of the changed position of the United States in the age of economic globalization: the growth of Japanese direct investment (JDI) and its impact on American workers and organized labor. Although still considerably smaller than direct investment from Western Europe, JDI in the United States has attracted disproportionate attention, both because of its high visibility, linked to persistent anti-Japanese racial prejudice, and because of its spectacular recent growth. From less than $5 billion in 1980, or 6 percent of worldwide direct investment in the United States, JDI skyrocketed to $83.5 billion (21 percent of the total) in 1990, the most recent year for which figures are available. Japan is now second only to Britain as a foreign direct investor in the United States; as recently as 1980 it ranked seventh among investing nations.[3] JDI is also of special interest because of its association—which, as we

An earlier version of this paper appeared in *Economic and Industrial Democracy* 13, no. 2 (May 1992). Reprinted by permission.

The author is an associate professor of sociology at the University of California, Los Angeles .

shall see, may be more imaginary than real—with "Japanese" management practices, such as quality circles and teamwork.

Against the background of an overview of the growth of JDI in the United States, this paper explores the implications of JDI for American workers and unions in the manufacturing sector. It shows that while a few high-profile Japanese-owned plants have cooperated with established American unions and have introduced a wide range of "Japanese" managerial practices, these cases are not representative of Japanese-owned plants in the United States. On the contrary, most Japanese firms that have established factories in the United States have resolutely opposed unionism and have adopted human resource practices that more closely resemble those of traditional nonunion American plants than those of their companies' plants in Japan. While no explicit conclusions are drawn about the implications of this chapter's findings for the former USSR, it is plausible to expect parallel outcomes there if large-scale foreign investment occurs in the future: such investment may do little to "modernize" or otherwise alter the organization of work or the industrial-relations system.

The Growth of JDI in the United States

Almost twenty years ago, Richard J. Barnet and Ronald E. Müller warned of the impending "Latin Americanization of the United States." As industrial production (much of it controlled by U.S.-based multinationals) moved to the Third World, they noted, the United States was increasingly faced with the classical dilemma of underdeveloped nations: it was becoming more and more dependent on exports of primary products to maintain its balance of payments while increasingly importing manufactured goods. Barnet and Müller also pointed to the growing polarization of income distribution and the expanding political power of corporations in the United States as symptoms of "Latin Americanization." In an especially prophetic chapter, they suggested that the accelerating international mobility of capital was undermining the power of organized labor in the United States, creating a new imperative for transnational forms of unionism.[4]

Barnet and Müller were primarily concerned with the consequences of outward investment. In the period since they wrote, however, international capital has increasingly flowed *into* the United States. "The tables have turned on foreign investment in America," the London *Economist* noted in 1988. "For decades it was American firms that bought foreign rivals and set up factories around the world. Now it is the foreigners writing the cheques."[5] The bulk of foreign direct investment in the United States still originates in Europe, but in the 1980s Japan emerged as an increasingly important source. In the 1970s, JDI in the United States was modest, totaling only $600 million in 1975 (compared to $18.6 billion from Europe that year). However, by 1981 JDI had multiplied more than tenfold, to $7.7 billion; that was also the first year in which JDI in the United States exceeded U.S. direct investment in Japan. During the 1980s, JDI expanded even more rapidly. While the magnitude of the increase is difficult to measure precisely due to the dramatic weakening of the dollar in relation to the yen during this period, by any standard JDI soared during the 1980s. By 1989 it stood at $83.5 billion according to U.S. Department of Commerce figures. That was more than four times the level of U.S. direct investment in Japan and over one-third the amount of direct investment in the United States from all the nations of Western Europe combined.[6]

The success of export-oriented industrialization in Japan in the 1960s and 1970s generated enormous amounts of capital, which made extensive direct investment abroad possible. As the largest market for Japanese products, the United States became an especially attractive site for JDI. The growing trade friction between the United States and Japan played a critical role here, for JDI was basically a preemptive strike against protectionism. When the United States attempted to alleviate its trade deficit by depressing the value of the dollar in the mid-1980s, the resulting cheapening of production costs further accelerated the growth of JDI. Labor conditions in the United States also made it attractive to foreign investors. By the late 1980s, wages were only slightly higher than in Japan, unionization rates had plummeted, and labor was more tractable than in other developed economies.

Nations with large internal markets have always been attractive sites for foreign direct investment, especially in the manufacturing sector. The United States, with the world's largest domestic market, was therefore a natural magnet for the Japanese capital that accumulated so rapidly in the 1970s and 1980s. This pattern was reinforced by the longstanding prestige of the United States as a market for Japanese goods, dating back to the immediate postwar period. By the 1970s and 1980s, Japanese manufactured goods were already being sold in vast quantities in the U.S. market, so that direct investment involved relatively low risks.

As early as 1975, the United States accounted for over a fifth of all JDI worldwide, according to Japanese government data.[7] The U.S. share has increased steadily ever since, even as JDI worldwide has skyrocketed. World JDI grew over 800 percent between 1980 and 1990, while JDI in the United States grew almost 1,500 percent in that period. The U.S. share of worldwide JDI expanded from 24 percent of world JDI in 1980 to 42 percent in 1990. The North American share of world JDI in manufacturing rose even more sharply, from 19 percent in 1980 to *49 percent in 1990*.[8] In fact, by 1990 Japan had invested $40.3 billion in North American manufacturing, twice the level of manufacturing JDI in all of Asia ($18.7 billion, excluding Japan itself) and over three times the level in Europe ($12.5 billion).[9]

As the United States–Japan trade deficit widened in the 1970s and 1980s, the specter of protectionism posed an increasingly serious problem, for which JDI quickly emerged as a solution. Much of the new JDI, especially in manufacturing, was essentially export substitution, whereby Japanese firms transferred to the United States the production of goods that were formerly made in Japan and exported to the United States. In contrast to the import substitution industry that developed in the Third World in earlier decades, here it was the investing country rather than the host that took the initiative in making the switch from exports to direct investment. While there was ongoing American concern about the trade deficit and continuing pressure to restrict imports, there was no significant opposition to the growth of JDI; on the contrary, it was widely embraced by policymaking elites as a welcome solution to the nation's trade problems. Organized labor, too, while critical of outward investment by U.S.-based multinationals because of the domestic job losses it usually produces, has generally welcomed inward investment. As Howard Samuel, president of the AFL–CIO's Industrial Union Department, recently stated: "We support foreign investment. It can be extremely useful in maintaining jobs and improving company prospects."[10]

In the mid-1980s, the Reagan administration deliberately depreciated the dollar, halving its value relative to the yen and other major currencies, hoping this would make imports more expensive and exports cheaper. As a strategy to resolve the trade problem, this policy was a dismal failure. Indeed, the dollar had already declined in value in relation to the Japanese yen and the German mark during the 1970s, yet the United States' historical trade surplus had been replaced by a trade deficit in that very decade. By the mid-1980s, many popular consumer products—such as videocassette recorders and other consumer electronics—were not even manufactured in the United States and thus continued to be imported regardless of price. Although the depreciation of the dollar did little to ameliorate the trade deficit, it did cut the cost of direct investment in the United States in half, as the yen–dollar ratio fell from 251 in 1984 to 124 in 1987.[11] This accelerated the growth of JDI and inward investment more generally. Foreign investors moved in rapidly in the late 1980s, acquiring existing firms, purchasing real estate, and setting up new operations—all at bargain prices.

Indeed, as *The New York Times* put it in a front-page story in the spring of 1991, "the United States, long derided as an industrial has-been, has become one of the world's low-cost manufacturers."[12] Labor compensation costs (wages and benefits) in the United States, although still high by world standards, declined dramatically (i.e., rose less rapidly) relative to other developed countries in the 1970s and 1980s. As the Table on pp. 226–27 shows, in the 1960s U.S. workers were better compensated than those in virtually all other nations, but by 1988 workers in West Germany, Belgium, the Netherlands, and Scandinavia had higher compensation rates than those in the United States.[13] As recently as 1980, compensation levels in Japan were only 57 percent of the U.S. level but rose to 95 percent of the U.S. level by 1988. Of course, this rise partly reflects the devaluation of the dollar, but the virtual disappearance of the wage gap is nonetheless a major spur to JDI.

Foreign firms find other aspects of the U.S. labor climate attractive as well. In their 1977 book *The New International Division of Labour*, Folker Fröbel and his colleagues identified several advantages the United States offered European investors that they lacked at home:

... skilled and often non–trade union organised workers, good sites for export-oriented production, indirect and direct government investment assistance, "political stability," and, in addition, the great importance of the U.S. domestic market. . . . U.S. companies have on average relocated their production to quite a considerable extent . . . to the new sites abroad. This has led to the creation of chronically high open and hidden unemployment and stagnating or falling real incomes for workers. The USA has therefore become a favourable location for technologically advanced production for West European countries. . . . Alongside changes in the value of the dollar, lower social benefits and more hours worked per worker per year also play their part. The pace of work is somewhat higher and working hours per year longer (fewer holidays and days off), and it is easier to dismiss workers. The existence of different degrees of union organisation is also influential in the choice of site. The low level of union organisation is offered as an incentive to foreign companies.[14]

Indeed, as the Table shows, hours worked per year in the United States are much more extensive than in most of Western Europe (where vacations and other leaves are customarily far longer) and are exceeded only in Japan itself.[15] Unemployment is low in the United States compared to Western Europe as well, but it is twice the Japanese level. The actual supply of labor for the manufacturing industry is even more ample than these figures suggest, due to surging immigration combined with the decline of domestic manufacturing.

Another major attraction of the United States, from the viewpoint of foreign investors, is the low, and rapidly declining, rate of union membership. For many decades, the United States had lower union density than most other developed nations, but in the 1970s and 1980s its already low unionization rate declined dramatically. The aggregate figures shown in the Table conceal an even steeper decline in private-sector unionization, which had fallen to 12 percent (for nonfarm wage and salary workers) by 1990. In manufacturing, the rate remains higher than for U.S. workers generally, with 21 percent unionized in 1990, but this is still a low figure by international standards.[16] The United States also compares favorably—from an investor's perspective—to many other countries in regard to time lost to work stoppages: of the countries shown in the Table, only West Germany and Japan lost fewer hours per worker.

The Impact of JDI on U.S. Workers: Promise and Reality

One reason for the lack of effective domestic opposition to increased foreign direct investment in the United States was the expectation that it would generate job growth. However, foreign-controlled jobs from all countries account for only 4.8 percent of all U.S. employment and 8.9 percent of employment in U.S. manufacturing. The number of U.S. residents who are directly employed by Japanese-owned companies remains surprisingly small—just over 500,000 people in 1989, the last year for which data are available. Firms based in the United

Wages, Hours, Unemployment, Work Stoppages, and Unionization Levels, Selected Countries, 1960–88

	Year	USA	Japan	France	FRG	UK	Italy	Sweden	Canada
Hourly compensation costs for production workers in manufacturing (in U.S. $)[a]	1960	2.66	0.26	0.82	0.85	0.84	0.63	1.20	2.13
	1970	4.18	0.99	1.72	2.33	1.49	1.76	2.93	3.46
	1980	9.84	5.61	8.94	12.33	7.43	8.00	12.51	8.37
	1988	13.90	13.14	12.99	18.07	10.56	12.87	16.85	13.58
Hours worked per worker per year in manufacturing	1960	1,940	2,509	1,957	2,079	2,127	2,046	1,970	1,881[b]
	1970	1,913	2,269	1,872	1,889	1,997	1,905	1,744	1,918
	1980	1,885	2,158	1,713	1,701	1,838	1,742	1,508	1,852
	1989	1,956	2,159	1,610	1,603	1,851	1,858	1,487	1,895
Civilian unemployment rate (%)	1960	5.5	1.7	1.5	1.1	2.2	3.7	1.7	6.5
	1970	4.9	1.2	2.5	0.5	3.1	3.2	1.5	5.7
	1980	7.1	2.0	6.4	2.9	7.0	4.4	2.0	7.5
	1988	5.5	2.5	10.5	7.1	8.3	7.9	1.6	7.8
Union membership as a percentage of all nonfarm wage and salary workers	1960	32	34	24	39	45	55–60	68	31
	1970	31	35	22	37	51	50–55	79	32
	1980	25	31	28	42	57	43	90	36
	1987	17	28	10–19[c]	43[d]	50[d]	38[e]	96[e]	36
Days lost to work stoppages per 1,000 nonfarm employees	1960	248	216	89	2	138	127	6	156
	1970	759	120	113	4	499	1,554	48	951
	1980	235	25	96	6[f]	529	1,002	1,173[f]	945
	1988	43	4	70	1[f]	169	174	201[f]	313

Sources: Hourly Compensation for 1980, 1988, Unemployment, and Work Stoppages: U.S. Department of Labor, Bureau of Labor Statistics, *Handbook of Labor Statistics,* Bulletin 2340 (August 1989), pp. 554, 572, 581. Hourly Compensation for 1960, 1970: U.S. Department of Labor, Bureau of Labor Statistics, *Handbook of Labor Statistics,* Bulletin 2271 (June 1985), p. 437. Hours worked for all countries and unionization except as noted below: unpublished data from the U.S. Department of Labor, Bureau of Labor Statistics, Office of Productivity and Technology, Division of Foreign Labor Statistics. Other unionization date from *The Economist,* 23 June 1990, p. 62 (for France, 1988 estimate); and for Italy in 1980 and 1985, computed from Guido Romagnoli, "Sindacalizzazione e rappresentanza," in *Le Relazioni Sindacali in Italia: Rapporto 1981,* ed. Guido Baglioni, Ettore Santi, and Corrado Squarzon (1982), p. 177; and Guido Romagnoli, "Sindacalizzazione e rappresentanza," in *Le Relazioni Sindacali in Italia: Rapporto 1985/86,* ed. Guido Baglioni, Rinaldo Milani, and Ettore Santi (1987), p. 181.

[a] Includes pay for time worked; for vacations, holidays, and leave; bonuses and special payments; and pay in kind, before payroll deductions. Also includes employer expenditures for legally required insurance programs and contractual and private benefit plans. For some countries, adjusted for payroll taxes and other factors that are regarded as labor costs.

[b] 1961 figure (1960 not available).

[c] 1988 estimate (1987 not available).

[d] 1986 figures (1987 not available).

[e] 1985 figure (1987 not available).

[f] 1987 figures (1988 not available).

Kingdom and in Canada both employ more people in this country than do firms based in Japan. Still, Japanese-based firms' employment is growing twice as rapidly as employment in foreign-based companies generally, and as JDI continues to grow, it will become a more significant part of the U.S. labor market.[17]

Another widespread expectation was that JDI would help the United States and its workers by establishing internationally competitive factories in the United States and by institutionalizing the human resource techniques and labor-relations policies that are widely presumed to have contributed to Japan's recent industrial success. In the popular imagination and in the management literature and media representations that feed it, Japanese management is associated with efficient, "lean" production and with a variety of mechanisms designed to foster worker participation in decision making. Raw materials and parts are delivered "just in time" for their use in the production process; workers meet in quality circles or similar small groups to discuss problems that were traditionally in the managerial domain; manual jobs are rotated among teams of workers to encourage a flexible, multiskilled work force; workers enjoy a high degree of job security, perhaps approximating "lifetime employment," and so forth.

Until recently, most commentators presumed that such "Japanese" management practices were culturally indigenous to Japan, or at least to Asia, and not readily transferable to the United States (or Europe). However, that claim cannot be sustained today in view of the striking success of the Japanese "transplants" in the auto industry. It is now indisputable that the Japanese model is compatible with a U.S. work force, and even with a unionized one. The best known example of this is the New United Motor Manufacturing Co., Inc. (NUMMI) plant in Fremont, California, a joint venture of General Motors and Toyota, which has achieved levels of productivity and quality superior to that of any other U.S. auto assembly plant and comparable to that of Toyota's plants in Japan.[18] NUMMI opened in 1984 at a plant GM had closed two years earlier, with a work force drawn from the ranks of former GM employees, who continue to be represented by the United Auto Workers' union (UAW).

Not only in its high productivity and quality but also from the viewpoint of workers themselves, NUMMI compares favorably to the traditional American system of work organization that characterized the plant when it was run by GM. NUMMI's blue-collar workers are centrally involved in improving the production process. Production workers are organized into flexible teams that rotate jobs and meet regularly to discuss how the efficiency of the operations they perform could be enhanced. The Japanese word *kaizen* (continuous improvement) is part of every team member's vocabulary. In sharp contrast to the many markers of status at GM, managers and workers at NUMMI wear the same clothes and share the same parking and cafeteria facilities. At NUMMI management is defined not as supervision but as leadership: each team has a "team leader," and at the next level up there are "group leaders" (roughly equivalent to foremen at GM). Although it does not offer "lifetime employment," NUMMI's contract with the UAW includes a pledge that no workers will be laid off without first cutting management pay and taking other cost-cutting measures. To date, despite periods of slow sales, there have been no layoffs.[19] The union has a dissident faction, but even this group prefers the team concept to the old GM system.

Although often touted as a model of labor–management cooperation in an age of intensified global competition, the NUMMI system has also been the object of serious debate. Its most prominent critics are Mike Parker and Jane Slaughter, who call the system "management by stress" and emphasize the fact that it greatly intensifies the pace of work. They warn that the "team concept" undermines unionism in the name of a dubious form of worker participation in management decisions. At NUMMI, they argue, workers "participate" in the intensification of their own exploitation, mobilizing their detailed knowledge of the labor process to help management speed up production and eliminate wasteful work practices. But even Parker and Slaughter acknowledge that workers themselves prefer the current setup to traditional "American" management. "Nobody says they want to return to the days when GM ran the plant," they note.[20]

Both critics and advocates of the team system often presume that NUMMI is representative of Japanese-owned plants in the United States. But a closer look reveals that this is generally not the case. Instead, most Japanese-owned manufacturing plants are resolutely opposed to unionism, and outside the auto industry most use American-style labor policies rather than replicating the "Japanese" model. The Japanese-owned plants I studied in California bear little resemblance to their parent companies' operations in Japan. Instead, they are like the Japanese-owned firms Harley Shaiken and Harry Browne studied in Mexico, where managers "seem to be satisfied with using traditional quality control and work organization methods to achieve internationally competitive quality and costs, passing over the techniques that are credited with bringing their parent companies stunning success in both categories." Few of the managers Shaiken and Browne interviewed at Japanese-owned plants in Mexico had ever heard of *kaizen*, and very few of these plants had anything resembling quality circles.[21] Similarly, Japanese-owned firms in Southeast Asia seldom use the participatory management practices for which their parent companies are known.[22]

Japanese-Owned Factories in California

I conducted detailed research on Japanese-owned factories in California, where almost one-fifth of the nation's Japanese-owned plants are located.[23] In 1989, under the auspices of the UCLA Institute of Industrial Relations, the sixty-six Japanese-owned manufacturing plants in the state with more than 100 workers were surveyed, obtaining a 76-percent response rate.[24] Following the survey, in the spring of 1990, plant visits and interviews with managers at twenty of these plants were arranged. All of these were in southern California, where almost three-fourths of the state's sixty-six plants are located. In the fall of 1990 five factories in Japan were visited, and managers there were interviewed.[25]

California, and especially southern California, attracts a disproportionate share of JDI for several reasons. Its long history as the main receiving station for Japanese exports to the United States is one important factor. In addition, like their domestic counterparts, many Japanese manufacturers find the state's ample supply of immigrant labor and the weakness of unionism highly attractive. "To many foreign firms, saving money on wage costs is far less important than control of the labor force," Norman Glickman and Douglas Woodward point out in their authoritative study of foreign investment in the United States. "Along with proximity to growing markets, numerous surveys show that an absence of unions and positive 'worker attitudes' consistently rank at the top of foreign firms' state and regional preferences."[26] Unionism is particularly weak in the California electronics industry, which accounts for over half (56 percent) of the state's Japanese-owned plants with more than 100 employees. Another 14 percent are in the metals and metal-products industry, 11 percent are in food products, with the rest in an assortment of other industries.[27]

The managers interviewed frequently cited labor considerations when asked why their plants were located in southern California. One American manager at a Japanese-owned electronics plant established in the mid-1970s, noting that "the Japanese are famous for location studies," recalled that in-depth research was done to select the site for the plant where he worked. "Cost was one concern," he said, "but other things were more important, especially the labor supply and a good working environment." Similarly, a manager employed by a large Japanese-owned electronics plant in San Diego, also built in the 1970s, said that in addition to its proximity to the Pacific Rim, San Diego was an attractive location for this firm because "the labor climate was good and availability of labor was ample." Another manager at a plastics plant located just east of Los Angeles attributed its site selection in the mid-1980s to low land and labor costs relative to other parts of southern California and to the perception that "the union situation seemed better here."

Just what is it about the labor situation in southern California that is so attractive to these firms? The evidence suggests that they are looking for tractable, nonunion labor that is available at low wages. Skill requirements are generally low, thanks to the routinized nature of most of the production processes carried out in these branch plants. Like many of their domestically owned counterparts, Japanese-owned factories in southern California rely heavily on the state's abundant supply of immigrant labor in recruiting production workers. Thus they combine foreign capital with foreign labor to produce goods "made in the U.S.A." The middle managers and clerical workers are typically the only native presence.

When asked what criteria they used in selecting workers for employment, the managers interviewed emphasized that they did not discriminate on the basis of race or ethnicity, and many cited the high proportion of "minorities" in their work force. Depending on the composition of the population in the vicinity of their particular location, these Japanese-owned plants employ Mexican,

Salvadoran, Vietnamese, Thai, Filipino, and/or other immigrant workers from Asia and Latin America. In one plant located near the U.S.-Mexican border, a manager claimed that some workers actually lived in Tijuana, Mexico, and walked across the border to come to work each day. Among the twenty plants visited, none had a production work force that was more than 50-percent native-born Caucasian. This upper limit was reported for only three plants; at the other seventeen at least two-thirds of the work force was comprised of immigrants, and in many cases the figure was 90 percent or more. African-Americans, on the other hand, were conspicuously underrepresented in the work force at most of these factories, and in many cases they were entirely absent.[28]

None of the twenty plants visited had specific educational requirements for their production workers. While some managers reported that they gave preference to applicants with a high-school diploma, almost all acknowledged that a substantial portion of their work force had less than a high-school education. While many said that they preferred workers with basic English language skills, this, too, was an ideal rarely realized in actual practice. When pressed to specify the criteria they used in hiring, managers reported that they look for workers with "stable job histories," "reliability," "commitment," "willingness to work," "a manufacturing mentality," and "people who are not looking to set the world on fire." Some admitted straightforwardly that "we have no special criteria." One manager laughed outright at the question. "With what we pay," he said, "if they wear shoes, we'll hire 'em." In fact the Japanese-owned plants surveyed paid wages significantly below the state average. In electronics, the Japanese plants averaged $7.19 an hour, compared to $11.18 statewide; for all manufacturing, the figures were $9.22 and $11.20, respectively.[29]

These Japanese-owned firms bear little resemblance to the Japanese management model. Few have quality circles or other forms of worker participation; flexible teams (as at NUMMI) are even more exceptional; and many managers chuckled when asked about "just-in-time" delivery and the like. Moreover, while their parent firms in Japan are normally unionized, almost all of the Japanese-owned firms in California are nonunion and are deeply committed to "union avoidance." Only one "Japanese" practice is widespread among these plants: most are devoted, in principle, to avoiding layoffs. However, even this is tempered by the fact that the plants typically have very high turnover rates, so that work-force reductions can often be accomplished without layoffs. In short, these plants conform to the human resource patterns of conventional American manufacturing, and especially nonunion manufacturing, rather than to the Japanese model.[30]

Quality Circles and Participation

A widely discussed feature of the Japanese model is its emphasis on worker participation, and especially the use of Quality Circles (QCs) or similar small group activities, to improve efficiency and to promote harmony between labor and management. The QC concept originated in the United States, but the practice became far more widely institutionalized in Japan, starting in the early 1960s. By 1984, 60 percent of all business establishments in Japan with over 100 employees had QCs or the equivalent, and the proportion rose to 84 percent for establishments with over 5,000 employees. Small group programs are especially pervasive in Japan's manufacturing sector. Regardless of sector, where such programs exist, typically more than 90 percent of employees participate.[31]

In the United States, QCs and similar small groups were institutionalized to a much lesser extent and later than in Japan—and largely in response to the success of Japanese industry. The best recent data on the use of QCs and small groups in the United States come from a 1987 survey of large firms in the United States conducted for the General Accounting Office (GAO). This survey found that 70 percent of the responding companies reported using either QCs or some other type of small group participation, but in most cases the programs included a relatively small portion of the work force. This survey found that, as in Japan, the use of QCs and other small groups is more common in manufacturing firms than in service-industry firms. At 32 percent of the manufacturing firms surveyed, 20 percent or more of employees participated in QCs, but only 13 percent of the manufacturing firms reported that more than 40 percent of their employees were in QCs. The figures were slightly higher for employee participation groups other than QCs: 37 percent of the manufacturing firms reported that 20 percent or more of their workers were in such groups, and at 17 percent of the manufacturing firms more than 40 percent of employees participated in them.[32]

My survey of Japanese-owned manufacturing firms in California with over 100 employees (with a median size of 275 employees) found that about 35 percent had QCs for at least some of their hourly workers.[33] Only two of the twenty plants visited had QCs, but seven others had some other type of small group participation for at least some of their blue-collar employees. These programs were typically quite limited, however. For example, in one plant a few department managers (but not others) hold occasional meetings with workers to discuss production problems and quality issues. At another plant, all blue-collar workers are required to attend quarterly meetings, for about an hour, where issues are identified for subsequent management attention. A third plant forms problem-solving project teams on an ad hoc basis; each such team includes two hourly workers but is made up mainly of engineers and managers. Another plant holds short (10–15 minute) morning meetings in each department to discuss problems from the previous day and plans for the day, with all meetings led by the supervisor.

I observed a QC meeting in progress at one plant at the time of a visit. Like most Japanese-owned plants in southern California, the work force here was made up almost entirely of immigrants. The plant cafeteria, where the QC meeting I attended took place, was decorated with some twenty flags—one for each of the countries represented in the work force. Although the national diversity of the work force was celebrated in the wall decorations, it presented serious problems in the QC meeting, since many workers had a limited command of English and no single language was shared by the entire group. The meeting I witnessed was facilitated by a woman manager who frequently prompted the workers who spoke, and there was almost no unsolicited participation in the discussion. Although QCs do exist at this plant, it is a far cry from the participatory model that strives to maximize the involvement of blue-collar workers in streamlining the production process.

While my sample size is too small to draw any definitive conclusions, the Japanese-owned manufacturing firms generally appear to resemble American-owned manufacturing firms more than their parent companies in Japan as far as the extent to which QCs and similar participatory small group programs are used. There is some employee involvement or participation in these firms, but the typical goal is to promote communication and harmonious relations between workers and management (often as part of a union-avoidance strategy) rather than to engage workers intellectually in the micromanagement of production, as in NUMMI's *kaizen* process.

The Team Concept and Labor Flexibility

Another characteristic feature of the Japanese management model, closely related to QC and small group participation, is the organization of workers into self-managed, flexible teams, sometimes labeled the "team concept." At NUMMI, for example, production workers are organized into teams of six to eight people, each with a team leader. Team members rotate jobs and make collective decisions about how to manage the parts of the production process for which they are responsible.[34] Even where team organization is absent, under the Japanese system workers are cross-trained to perform a variety of tasks, and job classifications are vague and few in number. This maximizes management's flexibility in deploying workers as needed and also reduces the boredom and monotony inherent in traditional manufacturing production jobs.

The team system is more characteristic of the Japanese auto transplants (both union and nonunion) than of Japanese-owned plants in other industries. In fact, most of the managers I interviewed were unfamiliar with the team concept as used at NUMMI. (Some had never even heard of NUMMI itself.) When asked if any production work in their plant was organized in teams, these managers frequently answered affirmatively at first, but further probing revealed that they were referring to a general emphasis on cooperation or the use of rhetoric about the importance of teamwork rather than flexible, self-managed work teams like those at NUMMI. One plant actually had "team leader" and "group leader" among its regular job titles, but these turned out to be ordinary lead workers and supervisors. Another plant had a program whose title included the word "team" and the manager I interviewed said that the plant eventually hoped to move toward the team concept, but it had not yet done so. Self-managing work teams are quite rare in U.S. manufacturing as a whole; according to the GAO survey, only 9 percent of large manufacturing firms have such teams for more than 20 percent of their work force, and none of those surveyed have them for more than 40 percent of their work force.[35] The Japanese-owned plants I visited conformed to this pattern; in fact, not one had work teams of the NUMMI type for their hourly workers.

Most of the plants I visited in Japan did not have a full-fledged team system either—it seems to be more common in the auto industry there as well as in the United States. But all but one of the Japanese plants did have some sort of job-rotation system. In contrast, only three plants among the twenty I visited in California had regular job rotation for production workers. In all three, managers reported that the intent was to offer relief from especially heavy or fatiguing jobs. In one case the plant had experienced high rates of repetitive motion injuries, according to a union organizer who had tried (unsuccessfully) to recruit its workers. In another plant, where assemblers rotate jobs every two hours, a manager reported that this system had been introduced some ten years ago in response to a union organizing drive, not as part of an effort to use Japanese management methods.

Closely related to flexibility is the question of job classifications. Whereas U.S. manufacturing, especially in unionized plants, traditionally involved relatively large numbers of job classifications with clear boundaries between them, the Japanese model is generally associated with a minimal number of broad classifications. Among the forty-nine plants that answered our survey question about this matter, the number of job classifications for production workers ranged from 2 to 120, with a median of 8 classifications. In interviews, however, several managers indicated that they hoped to merge classifications in the future. At NUMMI, there are only three classifications, and all the semiskilled production workers are in a single classification.

The team concept, job rotation, and cross-training function much more smoothly if wage rates are determined on a predictable basis. At NUMMI, where virtually all production workers earn the same pay (except team leaders, who get a small premium), cooperation among team members is never undercut by resentments over differential pay rates. The same is true under the *nenkō* wage-payment system that prevails at large manufacturing plants in Japan (but rarely at small firms in this dual economy), where wages are based mainly on age and seniority in the context of a lifetime employment system. Here, too, pay differences do not impede teamwork or flexibility since all workers are treated similarly over the course of their life cycle.[36] Even the Japanese auto transplants in the United States have not tried to emulate the *nenkō* wage system; instead they conform to the pattern set long ago by the unionized domestic auto firms, where wages are tied to job classifications and where pay differentials among production workers are minimal.

The Japanese-owned plants in southern California I visited are all owned by large firms in Japan, but their wage and promotion systems bear no resemblance to either the *nenkō* system or the domestic auto-industry pattern. Instead, at these plants starting pay rates are directly linked to job classifications, and within classifications individual wages are shaped by some combination of seniority and ability, with ability usually playing the dominant role. Most plants have substantial wage spread among their hourly work force, with the best-paid individuals typically earning two or three times as much as the worst paid. Except in the few unionized plants, each worker is evaluated biannually, and promotions and raises are awarded on this basis. In some plants, seniority influences wages, but in most, ability or "merit" is more important—at least officially.[37]

In the case of the low-wage, low-skill production workers who make up the bulk of the hourly work force at most of these plants, however, merit is defined in narrow terms: attendance (the most frequently mentioned item), punctuality, quality and quantity of work, and "attitude" are the usual criteria, not creativity or initiative. As one manager at a plastics plant put it, "We're not looking for the MBA type." An employee handbook summarized the typical notion of merit: "Your job has been awarded to you based upon your previous experience, education, training, ability, attendance, safety record, and attitude. Future job assignments and promotions will be made in the same manner." Many plants had instituted additional incentives for good attendance, tying it not only to raises and promotions but also to special rewards (cash bonuses, gifts, and/or public commendation) for perfect or near-perfect attendance or for not using sick days. Most plants also had progressive discipline systems to punish excessive absenteeism.

In short, both the absence of teams or regular job rotation in most of these plants and the highly individualized, merit-based wage systems used, like other aspects of their work organization, are generally typical of nonunion manufacturing firms in the United States, contrasting sharply with the practices of the parent companies in Japan.

No-Layoff Policies and Worker Attachment to the Firm

The one area in which many of the Japanese-owned plants in California do appear to conform to Japanese management practices involves employment security. The majority of these plants are committed to avoiding layoffs of hourly workers whenever possible, and many have *de facto* "no-layoff" policies that have yet to be violated. Among forty-nine plants that responded to a survey question on this issue, about two-thirds (64 percent) reported that they had had no layoffs over the previous five years. Similarly, among the twenty plants I visited, eleven had never laid off hourly workers, and a twelfth had not done so since 1974. The layoffs that did take place in the other eight plants usually affected small numbers of people and were often brief. It might be objected that many of these plants were opened or acquired since the 1981–82 recession and that these data predate the current economic slump. While the latter problem is real, it is noteworthy that six of the eleven firms that reported no layoffs in their entire history had opened or been acquired before 1980.

Some of the American managers interviewed stated that they would prefer to be able to lay workers off but that "the Japanese are against this." In one large metals plant, the manager reported disapprovingly, when parts of the plant are shut down due to lack of business, workers are not laid off but instead moved to other areas and are still paid for the highest job for which they are qualified. "The Japanese fear layoffs, which they think invite unionism." In another case, a manager in a health-care-products plant complained that the *de facto* no-layoff policy protected "bad workers." A third manager, at a Japanese-owned plastics plant that has never laid anyone off, reported with apparent amazement that when things are slow, people are put to work cleaning up the plant. He compared this to his previous experience in American industry, where "people would be laid off at the drop of a hat." Indeed, while some U.S.-owned firms do have no-layoff policies (especially in the nonunion sector), they have never been in the majority, and their numbers have dwindled recently under competitive pressures.[38]

One manager who had tried to establish a QC program at his plant indicated that the one layoff that workers there had experienced undermined the program to such a degree that the firm was now determined to avoid future layoffs of the regular work force, limiting any dismissals to temporary workers. Indeed, this is standard practice in Japan, where the permanent work force in large firms enjoys "lifetime employment" at the expense of temporary or part-time workers (often women) working directly for the firm or for its subcontractors. The no-layoff policies at Japanese-owned plants in this country are not fully equivalent to "lifetime employment," but both forms of employment security are often predicated on the existence of an expendable temporary work force. Many nonunion plants in the United States with no-layoff policies also rely on temporaries as a cushion. All the plants that reported no history of layoffs used temporary workers, as did most of the rest. One manager was explicit about the link between the no-layoff policy and the use of temporary workers. "We don't use the L-word here," he said. "Instead we used leased employees."

While their no-layoff policies set the Japanese-owned firms apart from their U.S.-owned counterparts, this is less true of the use of temporary workers. A recent survey of U.S. firms conducted by the Bureau of National Affairs (BNA) found that 74 percent of the manufacturing firms responding used agency temporaries, and 56 percent used "short-term hires." However, the BNA survey found that in most cases temporaries accounted for less than 1 percent of the regular work force and rarely more than 6 percent.[39] At the Japanese firms I visited, however, temporaries often comprised a more substantial proportion of hourly workers—as many as one-third in some cases, typically 5 percent or less.

The no-layoff policies of these firms rest on another cushion as well: high turnover, especially in the electronics plants and others where wages are relatively low. One electronics plant manager attributed the high turnover in entry-level jobs, which had climbed to 4.5 percent in the most recent *month* on record at the time of my visit, to the fact that "workers care about cents per hour and will leave for 50 cents more per hour down the street at K-Mart." (There is in fact a K-Mart warehouse next door to this plant.) While this was the highest turnover figure reported in my interviews, at about half the plants turnover was characterized as "high," with those managers who reported actual figures citing rates from 17 to 28 percent annually.[40] These rates compare to a national average for manufacturing of about 13 percent (although rates were slightly higher on the West Coast).[41]

In many plants, both firings and quits (the major components of turnover) were largely confined to the lowest-paying jobs; workers who rose into better-paid positions, in contrast, sometimes had turnover rates that were *lower* than management desired. "We would like to have more turnover in the assembly group," one manger of a food-products plant said, "because these are hustle-bustle jobs and it's hard for the older workers to keep up." Another manager in a large electronics plant that opened nearly twenty years ago was also concerned that turnover was not *higher*. "While many of our employees are young men who move on to other things after a few years, some of the people here have been around for a long time, and we're having some problems of motivation with them," he complained. A third manager suggested that the auto-accessories plant he worked for "would actually be happier to have a bit more turnover, to help keep the wage bill down." It appears that the high turnover rates characteristic of these plants are not entirely unwelcome. For some firms, they may even be the functional equivalent of layoffs, in that as business slows the work force can be reduced substantially by attrition.

The existence of *de facto* no-layoff policies at the majority of these plants (albeit mitigated by high turnover rates and made possible by extensive use of temporaries) and the infrequency with which layoffs occur at the rest are their most "Japanese" features. Even this is part of the human resources apparatus that has long been used in large domestic nonunion firms, after which California's Japanese-owned firms seem to model their policies.

Management Attitudes Toward Unionism

Only five of the sixty-six Japanese-owned plants in California with more than 100 workers are unionized, and all but one was effectively unionized prior to being bought by the Japanese. Several managers emphasized the link between their firms' human resource practices and their desire to operate on a nonunion basis. When asked if he was concerned about the prospect of unionization, one manager at an electronics plant replied, "Everything I do and breathe is designed to prevent a union from coming in here!" He added that if workers were unhappy enough to turn to a union, it would mean he had failed as a human resources manager. "I want to make unions superfluous," he said. This remark was echoed by many other managers. Several suggested that workers only turn to unions when management is abusive. "We treat our workers fairly," a metal-products plant manager said, "so they don't need a union to speak for them." Another manager at a steel plant expressed great concern about how his first-line supervisors treat workers and reported that he had even suspended some supervisors temporarily for "attitude adjustment." "If they're too hard [on workers]," he said, "we may be buying a union. We keep track of this very closely."

Several managers emphasized that their human resource policies were designed to forestall any interest in unionization. One electronics plant manager explained that union avoidance was a key reason for his efforts to promote frequent communications between workers and management. "This helps keep our finger on the pulse," he told us. "Without this you end up with an adversarial relationship, with unions fighting companies." Another manager at a metal-products plant attributed a union drive that took place there the year before our visit to "poor communications," adding that prior to the union election "we established better communications, and so the union lost." A manager at a plastics-products plant said that the participatory programs he was setting up were important "to avoid a union situation." Others noted the role of no-layoff policies in union avoidance. "The Japanese avoid unions by treating people right," one manager said regarding the no-layoff policy.

Virtually all the managers interviewed at the seventeen nonunion plants I visited spoke frankly about their desire to avoid unionization. None pretended to have a neutral stance toward organized labor, and several stated that keeping unions out was among their highest priorities. "I don't want a union here—ever!" one manager at an electronics plant exclaimed. A manager at a plastic-products plant told me that workers "realize that it's kind of anti-union around here," adding that "the company would probably move away if a union came in." At an electronics plant where there had been two separate unionization efforts, the manager told me that the Japanese are very fearful of American unions and that they would probably shut down the plant if it ever were unionized. "That's the first file folder in my desk drawer," he added, pulling out a red file folder labeled "Union Activities" to show me. He recalled that the two previous efforts to unionize there had been "nipped in the bud" thanks to his "anti-union campaign" in the plant. "Once it starts, we get all the supervisors together and tell them what they can and can't do. We tell the workers what to expect, what the union will do and what the consequences of unionization would be." At another electronics plant, among the largest in the state, a union campaign was underway at the time of my visit, and the firm had engaged three different labor consultants (one local, one national, and one in another city where the firm was setting up a new plant) to help them resist the effort.

At another electronics plant where a unionization drive had been defeated in a close election a few years before my visit, the company had hired a labor consultant to orchestrate such a campaign. "We spent a lot of money educating people," a manager there recalled. "The consultant told workers that it would be a mistake on their part to unionize, because they now have a voice in the plant and they would lose that." At this plant, even though the union was ultimately defeated, the Japanese company president felt personally responsible for the fact that unionization was even attempted. "He saw it as a sign of his own failure," the American manager recalled. "He carried it to such an extreme that he didn't even go back to Japan for the funeral when his mother died in the middle of the campaign."

I visited two steel plants that had been closed for a period prior to being acquired by the Japanese, both of which had been unionized before and had then made a "transition to a nonunion operation." Both plants rehired some hourly workers they had employed before the closures, but on a highly selective basis. "Many of the former workers were pro-union, and we don't hire them," a manager at one of these plants said. "Remember, we're trying to run it nonunion. We hire a lot of out-of-towners." At this plant, there had been a union drive right after the plant reopened, and "management brought out the big guns," he recalled. "We had a meeting with all the employees in a big room. It was staged so that at one point a worker asked if the managers would mind leaving, and then they passed around a petition which almost everyone signed, saying they didn't want a union."

These firms did not hesitate to express their anti-union views directly to their employees. One manager of a food-products plant told me that his firm wants to be "up front" about the issue. "We tell our workers, 'If you want a union, don't join us.' " Some firms published official statements to this effect in their employee handbooks. One such handbook included a section entitled "Company X—A Non-Union Company," which stated:

> At Company X, employees have chosen not to have a union. . . . In today's uncertain world, with all the pressures of our modern society, we want to keep Company X free from the artificially created tensions which could be brought on by an outside party, such as a union. We feel that a union would be of no advantage to any of us—*it could hurt the business which we all depend on for our bread and butter*. Furthermore, we have enthusiastically accepted our responsibility to provide you good working conditions, good wages, good benefits, fair treatment, and the personal respect which is rightfully yours. All this is part of your job with Company X and cannot be "purchased" by anyone having you pay union dues. We know that you want and are able to express your problems, suggestions and comments to us so that we can understand each other better. This can be done without having a union jammed between you and your supervisor. We want you to speak up for yourself—directly to us. We will do our best to listen and respond. [Emphasis added]

Another employee handbook's "Statement on Unions" was more menacing:

Company Y does not have a union, and you are not required to be a member of a union to work here. *Further, we will do all in our power legally to see that no employee ever has to pay union dues to work here.* Our employees seem to be satisfied with this arrangement. . . . Unions have not provided any of the wages and benefits we enjoy, and we do not expect them to help us improve upon these benefits in the future. . . . If any person attempts to pressure you into joining or signing a card in support of a union you should consider the matter carefully, and if there are any questions, feel free to go to your supervisor. . . . *Company Y will resist any efforts to bring a union into this plant by all legal means at our disposal.* [Emphasis added]

The fact that most of these plants have parent firms whose workers are represented by unions in Japan did not prevent them from resisting efforts to unionize their plants in the United States. One manager I interviewed at a food-products plant in Japan, a former union president himself, spoke at length about how good the union–management relationship was at the plant in Kawasaki that I visited. But he added that the firm had located one of its plants in North Carolina in part because, "honestly speaking, they have no big, strong labor unions there." I asked why, given how positively he characterized the union's role in Kawasaki, the firm was so eager to avoid unionization in the United States. "If we could find the same kind of labor union there, we would welcome it," he replied. "But in the United States, the unions tend to make trouble, they have a class struggle concept. It's very harmful." Other Japanese managers used a different logic to reconcile the contradiction between their acceptance of unionism at home and their resistance to it in the United States. At a unionized electronics plant in Japan, a manager told me that the union was a useful vehicle for communication between managers and workers. But in the same firm's California plant, "where there are American people working, with cultural values that we don't fully understand, we'd rather not have a union."

In the postwar period, and especially during the American occupation, Japanese unions were modeled directly after those in the United States. However, Japan's more radical unions were crushed in the 1950s, and the nation's labor movement developed its own distinctive character. Organized on an enterprise basis, Japanese unions today are generally viewed as less militant and as more management-oriented than their counterparts in the United States. While the differences are sometimes overstated, the Japanese managers who pointed out that unions in the United States are unlike those in Japan were correct.

These plants, then, do not conform to the "Japanese" human resource practices that characterize both NUMMI and other Japanese auto transplants in the United States as well as many large manufacturing facilities in Japan itself. The reasons for this are complex but include the fact that most of these plants perform highly routinized production tasks in their role as export-substitution branches of their parent firms, which continue to carry out the more complex phases of the production process in Japan. NUMMI shows that Japanese firms *could* replicate a high-trust, unionized model of industrial relations in their U.S. plants, incorporating many of the elements that brought them success at home. But it appears that most are bypassing that option and instead conforming to American management ideology and practice, choosing to avoid unions wherever possible and relying on the human resource practices developed by U.S.-owned nonunion firms rather than on those used by their parent firms' plants in Japan. Those who look to JDI as a source of improvement in the U.S. labor-relations system are likely to be deeply disappointed. And while the former USSR is starting from a very different position in the global economy, similar disappointments may await those who rely on foreign investment as a basis for amelioration in industrial organization and competitiveness there—even if foreign investment can be attracted to the region.

Notes

1. Direct investment involves foreign ownership of a controlling interest in a domestically based firm or in a parcel of real estate. In contrast, indirect or portfolio investment (not considered in detail here) involves foreign ownership of bank accounts, securities, or bonds of firms or governments.

2. The most recent figures available are for 1990, when the total value of U.S. direct investment abroad was reported at $422 billion, compared to $404 billion in foreign direct investment in the United States. See U.S. Department of Commerce, *Survey of Current Business*, August 1991.

3. U.S. Department of Commerce, *Survey of Current Business*, various issues.

4. Richard J. Barnet and Ronald E. Müller, *Global Reach: The Power of the Multinational Corporations* (New York: Simon and Schuster, 1974), especially chaps. 9 and 11.

5. "Love and Hate in America," *The Economist*, vol. 306 (19 March 1988), p. 74.

6. U.S. Department of Commerce, *Survey of Current Business*, various issues.

7. These data differ in some respects from those published by the U.S. Department of Commerce that are the basis of the previous discussion because of different reporting requirements and data-collection methods. The Japanese data are based on investment levels notified to and approved by the government (which are often higher than actual JDI), and they do not include disinvestment or reinvested earnings. Both countries count investments of more than 10 percent equity as FDI. See Masataka Fujita, "FDI Between Japan and the United States," *The Centre on Transnational Corporations Reporter* (United Nations), no. 29 (Spring 1990), p. 32. The U.S. data offer more detail about the composition of JDI inside the United States; however, only the Japanese data allow a comparison of patterns of JDI in the United States with JDI elsewhere in the world. The Japanese data cited in this paragraph are cumulative figures from fiscal year (FY) 1951 to the FY cited. Each FY runs from 1 April to 31 March; for example, FY 1988 is from 1 April 1988 to 31 March 1989.

8. This includes the United States and Canada; data are not published at this level of detail for the United States separately. However, for all years shown the bulk of JDI in North America was in the United States.

9. Institute of Fiscal and Monetary Policy, Ministry of Finance (Japan), *Monthly Finance Review*, no. 216 (June 1991), p. 22.

10. Quoted in John B. Judis, "Citizen Kawasaki: Race, Unions and the Japanese Employer in America," *The American Prospect*, no. 5 (Spring 1991), pp. 55–56.

11. United Nations, *Statistical Yearbook.*

12. Sylvia Nasar, "Boom in Manufactured Exports Provides Hope for U.S. Economy," *The New York Times*, 21 April 1991, p. 1.

13. U.S. Department of Labor, Bureau of Labor Statistics, *Handbook of Labor Statistics*, Bulletin 2340 (August 1989), p. 572.

14. Folker Fröbel, Jürgen Heinrichs, and Otto Kreye, *The New International Division of Labour: Structural Unemployment in Industrialised Countries and Industrialisation in Developing Countries*, trans. Pete Burgess from the 1977 German ed. (Cambridge: Cambridge University Press, 1980), pp. 251–52.

15. See Robert K. Landers, "America's Vacation Gap," *Editorial Research Reports 1*, no. 23 (17 June 1988), pp. 314–22.

16. The 1990 figure is from *Employment and Earnings* 38, no. 1 (January 1991), p. 229.

17. U.S. Department of Commerce, *Survey of Current Business*, July 1991, pp. 77, 85; Norman J. Glickman and Douglas P. Woodward, *The New Competitors: How Foreign Investors Are Changing the U.S. Economy* (New York: Basic Books, 1989), p. 34. All these data exclude employment by foreign-affiliated banks.

18. See James P. Womack, Daniel T. Jones, and Daniel Roos, *The Machine That Changed the World* (New York: Rawson Associates, 1990), p. 83.

19. There is now a large literature on NUMMI. A good overview comparing it to a GM plant that has unsuccessfully imitated the team system is Clair Brown and Michael Reich, "When Does Cooperation Work? A Look at NUMMI and Van Nuys," *California Management Review*, vol. 31 (Summer 1989), pp. 26–44.

20. See Mike Parker and Jane Slaughter, *Choosing Sides: Unions and the Team Concept* (Boston: South End Press, 1988). The quote is on p. 111. An analysis of the Ford–Mazda joint venture in Michigan from a similar point of view is Joseph J. Fucini and Suzy Fucini, *Working for the Japanese: Inside Mazda's American Auto Plant* (New York: Free Press, 1990).

21. See Harley Shaiken and Harry Browne, "Japanese Work Organization in Mexico," in *Manufacturing across Borders and Oceans: Japan, the United States, and Mexico*, ed. Gabriel Székely (San Diego: UCSD Center for U.S.-Mexican Studies, 1991), pp. 25–50.

22. See Magoroh Maruyama, "The Inverse Practice Principle in Multicultural Management," *The Academy of Management EXECUTIVE* 2, no. 1 (1988), pp. 67–68.

23. This figure includes only plants where Japanese companies held a majority ownership share. There were 245 such factories in California at the end of 1989, 18 percent of the national total. See "Japan's Expanding U.S. Manufacturing Presence: 1989 Update," *JEI Report*, no. 2A, 18 January 1991 (Washington, DC: Japan Economic Institute, 1991), p. 4.

24. Questionnaires were sent to the seventy-two Japanese-owned firms in the state listed as having more than 100 employees in the Japan Economic Institute's national listing of U.S. manufacturing affiliates of Japanese companies published in late 1988 (Japan Economic Institute, *Japan's Expanding U.S. Manufacturing Presence, 1987 Update*, Washington, DC, December 1988). Six of these firms were found to have been sold (and thus were no longer Japanese owned) or not to be engaged in manufacturing activity. Of the other sixty-six, twenty-six responded to the survey by mail, and responses were obtained from an additional twenty-four by telephone. Sixteen plants refused or failed to respond, for a total response rate of 76 percent.

25. No attempt was made to select a random sample for the factory visits in California or in Japan, but plants in a wide variety of industries, acquired and new, unionized and nonunion, were included. The fact that only one firm in California turned down a request for an interview suggests that the twenty cases are reasonably representative. The firms themselves designated the management interviewees, usually human resource managers.

The interviews lasted between 45 minutes and 3 hours; most were between 60 and 90 minutes. They were not tape-recorded; instead my research assistant and I took notes and wrote them up later the same day, together with our impressions from the factory tours that most visits included. No attempt at representativeness was made in the Japanese factory visits due to difficulties of access and time and language constraints, but I did attempt to visit plants in the same range of industries I had seen in California.

26. Glickman and Woodward, *The New Competitors*, p. 209.

27. Derived from data in Japan Economic Institute, *Japan's Expanding Presence*.

28. For a discussion of the tendency of Japanese-owned auto firms to avoid locating in areas where blacks make up a large proportion of the labor supply, see Robert E. Cole and Donald R. Deskins, Jr., "Racial Factors in Site Location and Employment Practices of Japanese Auto Firms in America," *California Management Review* 31, no. 1 (Fall 1988), pp. 9–22.

29. For Japanese-owned plants, these averages are weighted and are average wages for *employees* in the plants (not the average of each plant's average wage). The statewide data are for June 1989 and are computed from Economic Information Group, Labor Market Information Division, *California Labor Market Bulletin: Statistical Supplement* (Sacramento, June 1990), table 18.

30. Most conform to the pattern described in the classic account by Fred Foulkes, *Personnel Policies in Large Nonunion Companies* (Englewood Cliffs, NJ: Prentice-Hall, 1980). See also the discussion in Thomas A. Kochan, Harry C. Katz, and Robert B. McKersie, *The Transformation of American Industrial Relations* (New York: Basic Books, 1986), chap. 4.

31. Robert E. Cole, *Strategies for Learning: Small Group Activities in American, Japanese and Swedish Industry* (Berkeley, CA: University of California Press, 1989), p. 30; see also pp. 94–99 for a discussion of the origin of the QC concept in the United States and its spread to Japan.

32. The highlights of the GAO survey results are published in Edward E. Lawler III, Gerald E. Ledford, Jr., and Susan Albers Mohrman, *Employee Involvement in America: A Study of Contemporary Practice* (Houston, TX: American Productivity and Quality Center, 1989), pp. 26, 62. The response rate on this survey was 51 percent, with 476 responding firms. Data for manufacturing firms are not included in this publication but were kindly provided by the Center for Effective Organizations at the University of Southern California.

33. The questions were formulated differently; my survey did not ask about the proportion of employees involved in QCs; and the average firm size in the two samples is quite different. The firms surveyed by the GAO had a median size of 9,000 employees, compared to a median of 275 for the firms I surveyed. Although one can only speculate about the effects of these differences, they might cancel each other out. On the one hand, the larger average firm size in the GAO study should make the frequencies of QCs higher than they would be otherwise, since large firms are more likely to have QCs than small ones. On the other hand, the fact that some firms have QCs and other small groups for only a small portion of their employees may lead to an exaggeration of the frequency of QCs in the results of our survey of California's Japanese-owned large manufacturing firms. The GAO survey found that 70 percent of the manufacturing firms surveyed had QCs for 1 percent or more of their employees, and 75 percent had employee participation groups other than QCs for 1 percent or more of their employees. These levels are far higher than those found in my survey, which did not inquire about the proportion of employees involved in QCs but simply asked, "Are there quality circles for hourly workers?"

34. For details, see Brown and Reich, "When Does Cooperation Work"; Constance Holden, "New Toyota–GM Plant Is U.S. Model for Japanese Management," *Science* 233, no. 4761, pp. 273–77; and Parker and Slaughter, *Choosing Sides*.

35. Unpublished data supplied by the Center for Effective Organization at USC (see note 31).

36. See Robert E. Cole, *Japanese Blue Collar: The Changing Tradition* (Berkeley, CA: University of California Press, 1971), pp. 75–88, for a classic account.

37. See Foulkes, *Large Nonunion Companies*, chap. 9, for a discussion of the "mythical" aspect of the merit principle.

38. See Foulkes, *Large Nonunion Companies*, chap. 6, and "A Japanese Import That's Not Selling: Job Security Still Hasn't Gained Much Currency in the U.S.," *Business Week*, 26 February 1990, p. 86.

39. The response rate on the BNA survey was 55 percent. The figures on the proportion of regular employees made up by temporaries are for all respondents, not only for manufacturing. See Bureau of National Affairs, *The Changing Workplace: New Directions in Staffing and Scheduling* (Washington, DC: BNA, 1986), pp. 7–12.

40. This conflicts with the claim made many years ago by Johnson and Ouchi that Japanese plants in San Diego and elsewhere had lower than average turnover rates. See Richard Tanner Pascale and William G. Ouchi, "Made in America (under Japanese management)," *Harvard Business Review*, vol. 5 (September–October 1974), p. 63.

41. These figures are from a 1986 survey conducted by the Administrative Management Society. See Craig T. Norback, ed., *The Human Resources Yearbook, 1988 Edition* (Englewood Cliffs, NJ: Prentice-Hall, 1988), pp. 13.23–13.24.

The Enduring Labor Movement

A Job-Conscious Perspective

David Brody

The American labor movement has suffered a calamitous decline in recent years. The depth of its crisis is best captured in the numbers. In 1975, membership stood at an all-time high of 22 million. That translated into a union density in the nonagricultural sector of 28.9 percent, down only by 3.4 points from the peak of 32.3 percent in 1953. Today, union density stands at roughly 16 percent, a drop-off by nearly half in fifteen years. In absolute terms, membership is down by 4 million from the 1975 high mark. But for the surge in public-employee unionism since the 1960s, the labor movement would find itself in an even more parlous state. In the private sector, labor unions represent about 12 percent of the nonagricultural work force, perilously close to pre–New Deal levels.

Back in the recession of 1982—probably the darkest year for the labor movement since 1932—the business analyst Peter Drucker wrote a column entitled "Are Unions Becoming Irrelevant?" for *The Wall Street Journal* (22 September 1982). There was something very particular—and prescient—about how Drucker put the question: Are unions becoming irrelevant? It suggested some fundamental disjuncture: the industrial order had gone off in one direction, the labor movement in another and, in so doing, was in danger of becoming "irrelevant." Drucker's question has had a remarkable resonance: it defines a dominant strain of current thinking about the problems of American labor. And from that perspective there seems to have developed a broad consensus about the locus of that fatal disjuncture. It is on the shop floor. Thus Kochan, Katz, and McKersie write: "Over the course of the past half century union and nonunion systems traded positions as the innovative force in industrial relations. . . . An alternative human resources management system . . . gradually overtook collective bargaining and emerged as the pacesetter by emphasizing high employee involvement and commitment

This paper draws on three earlier essays by the author: "Labor's Crisis in Historical Perspective," in *The State of the Unions*, ed. George Strauss et al. (Madison, WI: Industrial Relations Research Association, 1991), pp. 277–311; "The Breakdown of Labor's Social Contract: Historical Reflections, Future Prospects," *Dissent* (Winter 1992), pp. 32–41; and "Workplace Contractualism in Comparative Perspective," in *Industrial Democracy in America: The Ambiguous Promise*, ed. Nelson Lichtenstein and Howell Harris (New York: Cambridge University Press, 1993), pp. 176–205.

The author is a professor of history at the University of California, Davis.

and flexibility in the utilization of individual employees."[1] Involvement, commitment, flexibility—these are the watchwords of the new industrial relations, and they are required, Ben Fischer tells us, "by very new forces in the patterns of ownership, management and market behavior, along with radical new technology. . . . The type of work being performed by workers is changing. The manner in which performance is sought contrasts drastically with yesterday's strategies."[2] The conclusion drawn by a distinguished panel of business and labor leaders for the Economic Policy Council (EPC) is that "a 'them and us' system of workplace relations [is] simply inadequate in today's social and economic environment. Finding the common interests of employees and employers, of unions and managers, and developing a process for overcoming the division between workers and managers, is the critical challenge that labor and capital must address in the decade ahead."[3] The foregoing quotations, which could be replicated many times over, fairly convey a broad consensus of what might be called "progressive" thinking (including inside the labor movement) about the obsolescence of the adversarial system of work-place relations.

What are the programmatic implications of the attack on the adversarial system? The way Peter Drucker initially defined the question—Are unions becoming irrelevant?—embodied the most important part of the answer: namely, it identified the unions as the problem. And if the gap between institution and environment was wide enough, then it would follow—as indeed Drucker says—that "the labor union will have to transform itself drastically." And those who have focused on the work place (as Drucker himself did not) draw the same conclusion. To adapt to the new industrial relations, says Ben Fischer, "will dictate a redefinition of what is a union."[4] Likewise, Morton Bahr, president of the Communications Workers and co-chair of the EPC panel, says, "Business and labor, the leaders as well as the institutions, must change the way we've been doing business with each other over the last forty to fifty years, if we are to regain our competitive edge."[5] So labor's crisis has brought the movement to a juncture where this question is seriously contemplated: Should institutional change of the scope needed to promote a shift from adversarial to cooperative work-place relations be undertaken?

That is a question of deep historical resonance. It goes to the issue of what has been enduring about the labor movement up to now. And, in more dynamic terms, it asks how the American movement made itself "relevant" to earlier industrial environments. How, so to speak, did it pass through comparable crises in the past?

To begin with, we have to take a long view of the subject. In *A Theory of the Labor Movement*, Selig Perlman coined the term "job-consciousness" to characterize the American movement. By Perlman's definition, job-conscious unionism was maximalist in two specific ways: first, in advancing the job interests of workers; and, second, in placing the union at the center of that effort. In this formulation, wages and hours mattered but so, at least equally, did work rules.

Indeed, it was over job rights that Perlman found the basis for specifying the distinction he was trying to make between German and Anglo-American unionism: the former concerned itself "only with wages, hours, and watchful scrutiny of the operations of the governmental bodies administering labor laws and social insurance . . . [but] utterly failed to put in any bid for the dozens and dozens of the job control rules achieved by American and English unions and designed to give the membership a right to the job, freedom from overwork and arbitrary discrimination, and the protection of their bargaining power."[6] The burden of Perlman's book was to argue that this was not an accidental or minor feature of American trade unionism but a fundamental characteristic that was historically rooted and central to its vitality.

Perlman was, of course, describing the trade unions of the early twentieth century, but the job-consciousness he attributed to the American movement remained a distinguishing feature into the recent era. In Western Europe, by contrast, unions characteristically left shop-floor issues to state-mandated works councils, with oversight and appeal functions lodged in labor courts or other public agencies. Elsewhere, as in Australia, work rules were informally regulated within the plant or, as in England (Perlman's Anglo-American category notwithstanding), through negotiation with autonomous shop-steward structures. In a sense, the current crisis over the adversarial system provides the ultimate validation of the continuing salience of Perlman's insight: work-place relations are a core union–management issue precisely because they are so intrusively a function of American trade unionism.[7]

The long historical view ought also, however, to make us relativists concerning the specifics of work-rule systems. There was probably a great divide stretching across the nineteenth century between artisan production, in which work rules were a form of self-regulation, and industrial production, in which work rules pressed up against managerial control. In that latter stage, there was an enormous variety of work-place systems. How various is evident in Sumner Slichter's great study of union–management relations as practiced just prior to the emergence of the particular system that dominates our own industrial world. Although *Union Policies and Industrial Management* was published in 1941, Slichter was concerned not with the emergent CIO unions but with the many kinds of workers—miners, machinists, railroaders, garment workers—long organized and experienced in collective bargaining. And we can see, in the case of miners, for example, an elaborate system of work-place regulation utterly different in the issues covered— how the coal was to be weighed, what maintenance work was compensable (i.e., not the deadwork that was the responsibility of the miner), the price for powder and blacksmithing, the fair distribution of coal cars—and in the forms of restitution—a complex system of fines—from those applying to factory workers.[8] Seniority, job classifications, and regulation of the work pace were matters notably absent from mine agreements—at least until the introduction of coal-loading machinery in the 1930s transformed the miner from a tonnage to a day worker and changed the labor process from unsupervised individual work to the team labor of specialized operators.

Yet, in the midst of a bewildering array of work-place arrangements, Slichter identified common underpinnings that he dignified with the term "industrial jurisprudence," by which he meant "a method of introducing civil rights into industry, that is, of requiring that management be conducted by rule rather than by arbitrary decision." American workers, Slichter wrote, "expect management to be conducted in accordance with rules . . . and to have an opportunity to appeal to the proper person."[9] Thus, to take the case of the tonnage miners described above: the specific job issues that concerned them became enforceable work rules; a formal grievance procedure began at the mine site and rose by steps to the district level, with noncompulsory arbitration as the final step; a pit committee to represent aggrieved miners; and all this incorporated into a collective-bargaining contract.

So here we have the context in which the adversarial system of our own time took shape. The locus was of course the advanced mass-production sector; the time, the 1930s. If past experience held, one would expect the process to yield a work-place system matching the particularities of the mass-production regime and understood to encompass what Slichter called industrial jurisprudence. Indeed, when the process was over, that was precisely how mass-production workers did perceive their work-place system. Consider the advice contained in a small booklet (dated January 1949) handed out by Local 7 of the United Auto Workers to new hires at the great Chrysler plant—now defunct—on Jefferson Avenue in Detroit: "If you think justice is not being done you . . . see your steward about it. . . . The grievance structure functions like a court of appeals—an agency to which the worker can appeal his case when he feels an injustice has been done him." The advice to new hires concludes, in italics, marvelously: "Remember! Your union is your best friend. It is that wonderful *defense lawyer*, at the point of production, that every worker needs and desires."[10]

* * *

Let us now try to describe the historical process by which that adversarial system took shape. The battle over the shop-floor rights of production workers stands at the very heart of the industrial-union history of the 1930s—not only as a stimulus setting that movement in motion but as the problematic at the core of the union-building process of the New Deal era. Industrial workers were not fighting for workers' control, the vogue this has enjoyed in recent labor scholarship notwithstanding. Too much had changed in the mass-production industries—the ministrations of Henry Ford and Frederick W. Taylor had gone too far—for workers to aspire to (perhaps even conceive of) regaining the kind of craft control and autonomous work that had earlier characterized American industry. What they did demand arose out of a sense of the rightness of things *as shaped by* the new bureaucratic, rationalized system of mass production within which they labored. Where tasks were minutely subdivided and precisely defined by job description, for example, there arose the characteristic set of demands for pay equity across the job-classification system. Time-and-motion study meant objective (that is, testable) standards for setting the pace of work so that, when workers complained of speedup, it was now less out of outrage that the foreman was a "pusher" than that the system itself was being violated or manipulated. And finally, the internal labor markets developed by corporate employers to counter high turnover implied uniform rules governing layoff, recall, even promotion.

We have to bear in mind that in this period industrial workers were overwhelmingly immigrants, the children of immigrants, or migrants from the South. In their experience, job opportunities came and went through family and kin networks.[11] It is a remarkable moment—rarely captured—when consciousness changes, when one set of values is replaced by another and ethnic workers begin to say: no, it's not right for one worker to be laid off while another keeps his or her job because of "pull." Gary Gerstle actually records such a moment among French-Canadian textile workers in Massachusetts.[12] But one does not have to capture the moment to know that, in the consciousness of workers, it happened. It is astonishing how consistent on this point are the oral histories by auto workers that I have read: nearly every one has a story of arbitrary or capricious layoff, of the "red apples" who received favored treatment (occasionally the informant himself!) intended to show how unfair the pre-union regime had been. And there is an entire mythology of favors granted to foremen—sexual in the case of women; bottles of whiskey, lawns mowed, houses painted, in the case of men—by workers desperate to keep their jobs after the Great Depression struck.

In a fundamental sense, employers could not dispute the legitimacy of these grievances, which, after all, arose from and were defined by the very industrial system they had created. This was true both in relation to the particular mechanisms—job classification, time-and-motion study, internal labor markets—and also more broadly in that the systematic labor management they espoused unquestionably required that workers be treated according to fixed, uniformly applied rules. The problem was that corporate managers did not carry through on their own logic: it was the *imperfection* of the system that brought it into crisis. There was too much resistance from foremen and first-line supervisors and, in the 1920s, too little counterpressure from an unorganized work force.[13] And, once depression struck, there were strong incentives to squeeze something extra out of workers through speedup and jimmied job classifications—as with arbitrary layoffs, complaints cited repeatedly by workers in their oral histories.

The coming of the New Deal, however, concentrated the mind of management wonderfully. The occasion was the passage of the National Industrial Recovery Act (1933) and, more specifically, the famous Section 7a of that act, which guaranteed workers the right to organize and engage in collective bargaining. Corporate employers across the board responded by setting up employee representation plans—company unions, so-called. This was a cynical maneuver, certainly, calculated to satisfy Section 7a while forestalling the independent unionization of workers. But employee representation—a works-council system—was not a new idea: it had been around for twenty years, espoused, experimented with, and legitimized by many progressive employers as a nonunion alternative for giving a voice to workers. And now, under pressure from angry workers, from the National Recovery Administration (NRA), and from the outside unions, the employee representation plans—toothless initially—began to evolve in some places into prototypes of the modern system of work-place representation—with a shop-steward structure, a formal grievance procedure, and some consensus on key work-place rights, in particular, covering the characteristic mass-production grievances already specified above: pay equity, speedup, and seniority. Where seniority came from as the impartial rule governing layoff and rehire is a particularly fascinating and revealing story, about which, unfortunately, the reader will have to be referred to another essay, where he or she will also find an account of the complex struggle that over the course of the NRA period brought into being the basic elements of modern work-place representation.[14] Suffice it to say, first, that corporate managers (if under some duress) accepted this system as legitimate and consonant with the mass-production regime they had created; and, second, that all this happened between 1933 and 1936 and *before* collective bargaining began.

Only at this point—beginning with the great Akron strikes by rubber workers in 1936 and the dramatic General Motors sit-down strike of early 1937—did the industrial unions force recognition from corporate employers and negotiate the first collective-bargaining agreements. "Negotiate" is actually not a very apt description for what happened, which was essentially that existing conditions—including the work-place system just described—were incorporated into the first contracts. General Motors was not kidding when it said (it was, of course, trying to put the best face on things) that it had not given anything away in the first contract it signed with the United Auto Workers in March 1937: not the committeemen designated to represent workers inside the plants, not the concept of a formal grievance procedure, and not the principle of seniority. But these were now contractual matters, agreed upon by two parties through collective bargaining (an adversarial proceeding) and enforceable as contractual rights, likewise an adversarial proceeding. This is where the specifically *adversarial* character of work-place representation enters the picture, although it should be recognized that, in its essential characteristics—that work-place rights would be specified, adjudicated through a formal grievance process, carried forward by designated representatives—this system already implied the adversarialism of any legal proceeding as understood in American jurisprudence.

Although they would have preferred it to have been otherwise, corporate employers accepted the absorption of this system (much of it their own handiwork) into their contractual relations with outside unions. There was this advantage: the unions, as parties to the contract, were obliged to enforce it on their members. In a time of raging wildcat strikes and shop-floor turmoil, this was no small advantage, and it quickly evolved into something of fundamental value—the union as disciplining agent on its members.

Remarkably, no faction, however militant (excepting perhaps a Trotskyite fringe), denied that unions had this responsibility and should honor it (although in fact they had a lot of trouble doing so initially). General Motors had ample opportunity to walk away from the union contract. The UAW was extremely weak—it lost the bulk of its members in the 1938 recession and virtually broke apart in factional confusion—and in any case, since it had not yet demonstrated its majority standing, it had no legal standing as a bargaining agent. There is no evidence that General Motors ever contemplated reversing history. It had accepted the fact that the adversarial system (so-called) was appropriate to its mass-production factory regime.

The story as described so far sounds like a private transaction among employers, unions, and workers. But there was a fourth party—the state. It was after all in these middle years of the New Deal that basic and enduring decisions were being made regarding a national collective-bargaining policy. The cornerstone was the National Labor Relations Act of 1935—the Wagner Act. As one reads that law in light of what has been said, one is struck by a remarkable omission: extraordinarily intrusive as it was in other ways, the Wagner Act was absolutely silent about how work-place relations should be structured. This is curious on two counts. Interventionist labor policy of comparable scope almost everywhere else— Australia's compulsory arbitration system comes to mind as the other exception—provided for some form of works-council system. Even more curious, it was not that such provision had never been contemplated in the shaping of American labor-relations policy. On the contrary, a works-council system was precisely what had been evolving—as the employee representation plans became increasingly subject to state regulation under NRA labor boards—up to the time the National Industrial Recovery Act was declared unconstitutional in May 1935. In fact, the furious debates over a national labor policy of the NRA period really turned on a systemic question: works councils (which is what employers, as an outgrowth of their employee representation plans, advocated), or collective bargaining (which the American Federation of Labor insisted on)? The Wagner Act represented a total—truly a stunning—victory for the unions. The objective of the law, stated in its first section, was to promote "actual liberty of contract" and to remedy the "inequality of bargaining power." Everything in the law itself— including the express guarantee of the right to strike—was calculated to foster independent employee organization and collective bargaining to a contract. It was not that the law did not contemplate some form of work-place representation but rather that it assumed that this would be the outcome of (the creature of) collective bargaining. So that, in a quite fundamental sense, it was the state itself that mandated the *adversarial* character of our system of work-place relations.

And not only that. Once the specifics of that system emerged—and, it needs remembering, those specifics were in place prior to the start of collective bargaining and had arisen out of the very same systemic struggle that had led to the Wagner Act—the state moved to legitimize the adversarial system. This happened because of a daunting legal issue raised by the new legislation. In the past, collective bargaining agreements had no—or only dubious—standing as enforceable contracts because trade unions themselves had no—or only dubious—standing as corporate entities.[15] The new legislation gave unions a definite legal standing insofar as, under the provisions of the law, they became certified bargaining agencies with whom employers were obliged to bargain. Any ambiguity on that score was definitively settled by the Taft–Hartley Act (1947): suits for violations of contracts arrived at under the provisions of the National Labor Relations Act were actionable and fell within the jurisdiction of the federal district courts. The trouble was that there was no federal law or precedent on which the courts could proceed. Rather than remedy that formidable oversight, the courts did a remarkable thing: they shifted the responsibility to the privately created grievance procedures of the collective-bargaining agreements. The key thing was that by this time—the 1950s—these almost invariably included binding arbitration as the final step. In the *Steelworkers Trilogy* (1960), the Supreme Court ruled that, insofar as arbitration covered disputes arising out of the contract, to that degree the finding of the arbitrator was binding and *legally enforceable* by the courts without review (save where it was "apparent" that an award did not arise from the terms of the agreement). In effect, this private arrangement of dispute settlement was elevated to quasi-legal status, and that carried with it powerful legitimating benefits for the larger system of work-place representation within which the grievance procedure rested. The collective-bargaining agreement, pronounced the Supreme Court, is "more than a contract." It is "an effort to erect a system of industrial self-government" and "calls into being a new common law—the common law of the particular industry or a particular shop."[16] What the Court of 1960 was describing, of course, is the embattled adversarial system of our own day.

* * *

Let us assume, for the sake of argument, that the mass-production regime to which that adversarial system was responsive is in fact coming to an end. Why should we believe that the succeeding regime will not in its turn set in motion a process that, like the one we have just surveyed, will end with a new adversarial system, a postmodern version, so to speak, of what Sumner Slichter half a century ago called industrial jurisprudence? The answer, at its most basic, would have to be that past experience no longer applies. Indeed, that is precisely what Ben Fischer does say about "the new face of much of industrial relations": it "is not a replay of history."

If that is true, then of course not much can be learned from labor's past. But we need to specify quite precisely the historical discontinuity that must transpire: namely, that the new industrial relations not give rise to a crisis over industrial justice.

Proponents do indeed make that assumption. New modes of flexible production and knowledge-based operation, they argue, require an abandonment of the Taylorist reliance on hierarchical control and a rationalized division of labor. The emerging post-Taylorist system of industrial relations is characterized by what Charles Heckscher calls "managerialism," whose aim it is "that *every* employee be a manager, involved in decisions and contributing intelligently to the goals of the corporation." To achieve these results, corporations have enlisted a sophisticated human resources science that Kochan, Katz, and McKersie assure us has mastered the mysteries of employee motivation. Under its guidance, a wide range of programs have taken shape—all-salaried compensation, profit sharing, work sharing, flexible work schedules, payment for knowledge, autonomous work teams, ingenious systems of communication and grievance handling. "At its best," concludes Heckscher, "the managerialist order offers genuine improvements in the situation of employees as well as in the effectiveness of the organization."[17]

If the managerialist order at its "best" becomes the norm, what are the prospects for the labor movement? The critical question is really not how successful the existing unions can be at transforming their relations with organized employers. Without penetrating the new dynamic sectors, as it did in mass production fifty years ago, the labor movement can look forward only to stagnation and decline. In these sectors, no amount of union enthusiasm for cooperative relations and employee involvement is likely to persuade employers that collective bargaining is preferable to a union-free environment. And if Heckscher's managerialist order lives up to its promise, what incentive would their employees have for joining a union?[18]

But there are contrary facts to consider. "Nonunion firms are subject to the same market and technological pressures as are union firms," concede Kochan, Katz, and McKersie. And, writing in the mid-1980s, they already could see that many of the nonunion growth firms of the 1960s and 1970s "are now facing the challenge of adapting their human resource management practices to maturing, more price-competitive markets." Under economic pressure, strategies that "valued low turnover and high commitment" might give way to "strategies that depend on low labor costs." What had seemed unassailable on its own terms—"the innovative force in industrial relations"—turns out to be hostage to the marketplace after all.[19]

And which were the vulnerable firms? In the mid-1980s, Kochan, Katz, and McKersie thought these included only smaller and midsized companies, especially those "most highly exposed to market pressures." Surely not the great exemplars of innovative human resource management like IBM. Indeed, IBM served as Kochan, Katz, and McKersie's model instance of corporate responsibility: in the hard times of the early 1980s, it was "achieving substantial manpower shifts without breaching its historic commitment to employment continuity."[20] Half a dozen years later, no one could speak with such confidence of IBM's intentions. At the end of 1991, performing poorly in a depressed computer market, the giant firm announced a sweeping corporate decentralization intended to gain for it the benefits of more robust competition: its major units would henceforth operate autonomously and be judged by their market performance and profitability. IBM had already undertaken a massive cost-cutting program eliminating 85,000 jobs between 1986 and 1992, 20 percent of its labor force. Thus far, the cuts had been achieved through attrition, voluntary buyouts, and early retirements. But, with IBM stock prices at a nine-year low, the company chairman told Wall Street analysts in December 1991 that he no longer ruled out layoffs. And life had become much tougher at Big Blue, with a new personnel evaluation policy that required failing grades for the bottom 10 percent. Wrote one former employee: IBM "has turned from a challenging and caring employer to one ruled by fear and intimidation."[21]

Other embattled members of the nonunion pantheon had long since given up the pretense of a no-layoff policy. Across the white-collar service sector, major employers hitherto sheltered from hard times—Citicorp in banking, Aetna in insurance, Sears in retailing, Xerox in information processing, and TRW, Inc., widely hailed as a model practitioner of the new industrial relations—were among the leading job cutters in the stagnant economy of the early 1990s. The structural problems that had afflicted manufacturing in the 1980s seemed now to be overtaking the service sector, which suffered from bloated payrolls, lagging productivity gains (a mere 0.7 percent annually), and, for many firms, heavy debt burdens incurred by the leveraged buyouts of the expansionary 1980s. Where earlier one white-collar job had been lost for every four blue-collar jobs, now in the early 1990s the gap was down to one for every two. White-collar unemployment stood at 4.2 percent in October 1991, and, by all accounts, desk jobs had become a prime target of corporate cost-cutting programs.[22]

Suddenly, instead of celebrations of the new industrial relations, there are lamentations over the corrosive effects of job insecurity on employee motivation. "It's very costly in terms of morale and trust that is lost," warns the human resources vice-president of the Intel Corporation. And, predictably, there is much talk about the need—to quote a bellwether commentary in the business section of *The New York Times*—for "Restoring Loyalty to the Workplace."[23]

Dissatisfaction among white-collar employees, however, seems to have been on the rise long before the current wave of layoffs. Consider what the Opinion Research Corporation (ORC) found in surveys among managers at about 200 companies over a thirty-year period from the 1950s to the early 1980s: those who rated their companies favorably in terms of fair application of policies and rules dropped from almost 80 percent to less than 40 percent; those who felt secure in their jobs declined from nearly 100 percent to 65 percent; and those who thought their company was a better place to work than when they had started comprised only a little more than 25 percent. Among clerical workers, ORC figures indicated an approval rating of company fairness down from 70 percent in the 1950s to 20 percent in 1979. The sharpest break occurred around 1975, just at the onset of intensifying market pressures on the American economy generally.[24] But it is not only the long-term erosion of the privileged status of white-collar employees that accounts for these rising levels of dissatisfaction. At least equally important is the other side of the equation: the sense of entitlement that employees today feel over their job rights.

Until quite recently, there was no such thing in law as "job rights." The basic common-law principle was "employment at will"—save for binding contracts to the contrary, employers enjoyed an unlimited prerogative to discipline and discharge workers for any or, indeed, for no reason. The Wagner Act had established the one major exception: employees could not be fired or punished for engaging in union activities. Then came Title VII of the Civil Rights Act of 1964, which prohibited job discrimination because of race, color, religion, national origin, or sex. Antidiscrimination protections expanded in later years to cover age, physical disability, and, in a variety of state laws, sexual orientation, political affiliation, marital status, and pregnancy. The right not to be discriminated against has in fact achieved an ironic universality as a result of the intensifying assault on affirmative action: "reverse discrimination," validated by conservative court decisions and by the new Civil Rights Act of 1991, stirs the rights consciousness of even the most unreconstructed of white males. A second form of job entitlement derives from the surge of regulatory laws covering occupational safety and health, pollution control, and other business activities. These laws specifically protect whistle-blowing employees from punishment by employers.

Finally, the "at-will" doctrine has come under siege at a more fundamental level. Since the mid 1970s, a number of state courts have begun to assert in their decisions the principle of "wrongful discharge," limiting the rights of employers where there is evidence of an "implied contract"—in which employees have been given reason to believe that they would not be discharged arbitrarily or without cause—or where dismissal is deemed to be inconsistent with "public policy," variably defined by the courts to include not only statutory expressions of public policy but extending more broadly to basic rights such as freedom of conscience and personal privacy and freedom from sexual harassment.

The cumulative effect of these remarkable legal developments, writes Charles Heckscher, "has been to greatly weaken the fabric of the legal veil of managerial prerogative," and, correlatively, to strengthen the expectations of employees to be treated fairly. Heckscher, indeed, sees signs of an emergent movement among white-collar employees, still inchoate and divided among many interest groups but acting "on a single premise: that corporations, while they may have property rights, have no right to abuse their employees."[25]

"This is quite different from the premise that fueled industrial unionism," Heckscher adds. His error here is fundamental, masking as it does a vital continuity between past and present. Recall the moment at which industrial unionism crystallized during the 1930s. There had been a prior period of struggle, driven, as now, by a deepening sense of industrial injustice among factory workers. That its roots may have been somewhat different from those animating the incipient movement that Heckscher describes seems not especially germane, so long as we are not prepared to say that injustice is less potent a conception for industrial workers than for semiprofessional white-collar employees and less potent if it arises from the factory regime than from a sense of legal entitlement (although, with the adoption of Section 7a, there developed in the minds of industrial workers as well a strong sense of legal entitlement). During the battles over employee representation of the NRA period, the terms of a just work-place system took shape and gained the broad assent of all parties (including, in large measure, management). Empowered by the Wagner Act, the industrial unions then seized that system, gave it contractual form, and, in short, made themselves the institutional embodiment of the job interests of the mass-production workers.

In this achievement resides the essential historical continuity on which I am insisting: that what made trade unionism compelling to American workers in the past—and is likely to do so in the future—was its job-conscious capacity to link itself to their aspirations for industrial justice. The labor movement cannot itself define those aspirations, nor very much influence the processes that give rise to them. This was true for the industrial workers of the 1930s and true likewise of the incipient movement for employee rights to which Heckscher calls our attention. Should that movement reach crisis proportions, however, the stage would be set, so to speak, for the next CIO.[26]

American industrial relations has arrived at an odd juncture. How can we be moving at once toward a cooperative labor-management system and also toward a deepening crisis over employee rights? The explanation would seem to be that basic structural forces are in contradiction: postindustrial technology demands involvement and commitment from employees, but the competitive market and corporate restructuring now deny to all but the most sheltered firms the means for assuring the job security and predictable treatment on which employee commitment depends. How that contradiction is resolved remains to be seen, but on its resolution probably rides the future of the American labor movement. Insofar as the outcome favors managerialism, to that extent labor's prospects are surely foreclosed. It was because the contrary happened in the 1930s—because welfare capitalism failed under the stress of the Great Depression—that the occasion was provided for the rise of the industrial unions.

Embattled as it is, the labor movement hears on all sides today calls for an end to "adversarialism." Insofar as this means responsiveness to the logic of a post-Taylorist system of production, the advise is sound and altogether consistent with historical experience. It bears repeating that, after all, the "adversarial" work-rules system now so roundly condemned was adopted not in opposition to but directly in conformity with the logic of the mass-production regime. But retreating from "them and us" as a basic orientation is a different matter. The labor movement will not prevail by trying to persuade nonunion employers. It is their employees that have to be persuaded, and, if and when that time comes, what will persuade them will be the only kind of appeal that has worked with American workers since the days of Samuel Gompers: namely, the identification of the union with their demand for industrial justice. The source of that appeal is the abiding job-consciousness of American trade unionism. In this sense, labor's past is deeply and irrevocably implicated in whatever future it has.

Notes

1. Thomas Kochan, Harry Katz, and Robert McKersie, *The Transformation of American Industrial Relations* (New York, 1986), pp. 226–27.

2. Ben Fischer, speech, 14 August 1989, reprinted in *Daily Labor Report* (19 September 1989), p. D–1.

3. "The Common Interests of Employees and Employers in the 1990s," *Report of the Economic Policy Council Panel of the United Nations Association* (New York, 1990), introductory pamphlet in possession of author.

4. Fischer, p. D–1.

5. "The Common Interests of Employers and Employees in the 1990s," p. 11.

6. Selig Perlman, *A Theory of the Labor Movement* (New York, 1928), pp. 311–12.

7. The impact of union work-place regulation on labor productivity is a different question. The data gathered by Richard B. Freeman and James L. Medoff do not suggest that unionized employers are at any disadvantage in terms of labor productivity but, on the contrary, by that measure do consistently better than nonunion employers. On the other hand, union employers earn significantly less on capital investment—19 percent less, for example, among 902 firms surveyed during the 1970s—than comparable nonunion firms. See Richard B. Freeman and James L. Medoff, *What Do Unions Do?* (New York: Basic Books, 1984), p. 183, table 12–1, and for a full treatment of the union impact on wages, productivity, and profits, chaps. 3, 11, and 12. This holds cross-nationally as well: the costs of collective bargaining are substantially higher in the United States than in other advanced industrial countries (David G. Blanchflower and Richard B. Freeman, "Unionism in the United States and Other Advanced OECD Countries," *Industrial Relations* 31 [Winter 1992], pp. 80–94). In a basic sense, these findings sustain Perlman's notion of American job-consciousness as maximalist trade unionism, i.e., in extracting for workers through collective bargaining a larger share of the returns of capitalist enterprise. The other side of the coin, however, is the abiding anti-unionism of American employers: from the standpoint of profit maximization, anti-unionism is an entirely rational choice.

8. These details are drawn from Louis Bloch, *Labor Agreements in Coal Mines . . . of Illinois* (New York, 1931) and apply to the UMWA Illinois district.

9. Sumner Slichter, *Union Policies and Industrial Management* (Washington, DC, 1941), pp. 1–3.

10. *Welcome, Fellow Workers*, booklet, UAW Local 7, January 1949, Box 3, Nick DiGaetano Collection, Walter Reuther Archives, Wayne State University, Detroit, Michigan.

11. See, e.g., John Bodnar, Roger Simon, and Michael P. Weber, *Lives of Their Own: Blacks, Italians, and Poles in Pittsburgh, 1900–1960* (Urbana, IL, 1982).

12. Gary Gerstle, *Working-Class Americanism: The Politics of Labor in a Textile City, 1914–1960* (Princeton, NJ, 1989), chap. 4.

13. Sanford M. Jacoby, *Employing Bureaucracy: Managers, Unions, and the Transformation of Work in American Industry, 1900–1945* (New York, 1985), chap. 6.

14. David Brody, "Workplace Contractualism in Comparative Perspective," in *Industrial Democracy in America: The Ambiguous Promise*, ed. Nelson Lichtenstein and Howell Harris (New York, 1993), pp. 190–92.

15. Christopher Tomlins, *The State and the Unions: Labor Relations, Law, and the Organized Labor Movement in America* (New York, 1985), chaps. 2, 3.

16. David E. Feller, "A General Theory of the Collective Bargaining Agreement," *California Law Review* 61 (May 1973), pp. 686–90, 700–707. On the relationship between the legal system and private law, in which the unionized work place of the 1960s serves as a paradigm, see Phillip Selznick, *Law, Society and Industrial Justice* (New York, 1969).

17. Charles Heckscher, *The New Unionism: Employee Involvement in the Changing Corporation* (New York, 1987), pp. 85, 99.

18. The AFL–CIO hopes to answer that question, in the immediate term, by offering associate memberships to individuals and through its Union Privilege program, providing them with credit cards, group insurance, mail-order pharmaceuticals, and other useful services. Some observers see in this the beginnings of a transformation of organized labor from an economic to a human-services movement. What the associate-member program surely does reveal is the uphill struggle that the unions know they face in the organizing field. For a survey of union programs, see Arthur B. Shostak, *Robust Unionism: Innovation in the Labor Movement* (Ithaca, NY, 1991), which is truly an exercise in the power of positive thinking.

19. Despite a quite volatile history, including a massive breakdown in the face of the Great Depression, the market susceptibility of "progressive" labor relations has received little systematic analysis by American scholars. For an English exploration of this problem, see Andrew L. Friedman, *Industry and Labour: Class Struggle at Work and Monopoly Capitalism* (London, 1977); and also, Andrew L. Friedman, "Management Strategies, Market Conditions and the Labour Process," in *Firms, Organization and Labour: Approaches to the Economics of Work Organization*, ed. Frank H. Stephen (London, 1984). See also the instructive introductory essay in *The Power to Manage? Employers and Industrial Relations in Comparative Perspective*, ed. Steven Tolliday and Jonathan Zeitlin (London, 1991), pp. 1–31.

20. Kochan, Katz, and McKersie, *American Industrial Relations*, pp. 246–47.

21. *The New York Times*, 16 December 1991, 16 February and 22 March 1992, and for a survey of IBM's new labor policy—aptly entitled "Pulling One's Weight at the New I.B.M."—*The New York Times*, 5 July 1992, Business Section, pp. 1, 6.

22. *The New York Times*, 24 September and 16 December 1991, 2 January 1992.

23. *The New York Times*, 15, 16 December 1991.

24. The Survey data in this paragraph are taken from Heckscher, *The New Unionism*, chap. 12; and Kochan, Katz, and McKersie, *American Industrial Relations*, pp. 214–15.

25. Heckscher, *The New Unionism*, pp. 238, 242.

26. In this discussion I am focusing on what Dorothy Sue Cobble has recently characterized as "worksite unionism," in which job rights are defined in relationship to a particular site and employer. But, as she rightly notes, an increasing portion of the service sector is made up of workers ranging from highly skilled contract computer programmers to part-time, mostly female clericals who lack that relationship. Currently more than a quarter of the civilian labor force is made up of so-called contingent workers who work part-time, are temporaries, or are contract employees. For relatively mobile workers such as these,

industrial justice would have a quite different content, arising in varying degrees from their concerns with occupational identity, control over the labor supply, portable rights and benefits, and peer determination of performance standards and work-place discipline. For such workers, the challenge to the labor movement is to come forth with a new institutional form that Cobble calls "occupational unionism." But its roots are, as she argues, already well established in the history of craft unionism, and, indeed, Cobble's insights derive from her historical study of organized waitresses. Dorothy Sue Cobble, "Organizing the Postindustrial Workforce: Lessons from the History of Waitress Unionism," *Industrial and Labor Relations Review* 44 (April 1991), pp. 419–36. Both Cobble and Heckscher offer imaginative prescriptions for the labor-law and institutional changes needed before the white-collar private sector can be organized. Whether the existing unions are incapable of transformation, as Heckscher is inclined to believe (p. 237), seems to me something of an open question: after all, old-line AFL unions like the Teamsters, Machinists, and Meat Cutters proved extraordinarily resilient once challenged by the CIO, and current unions are much more flexible jurisdictionally than those of the 1930s. But it does not actually matter very much whether established unions do it, or whether new institutions emerge, or, as happened in the public sector, professional associations evolve into unions so long as the end result is trade unionist in function.

Beyond Industrial Unionism

Alice Kessler-Harris and Bertram Silverman

American trade unions have historically been adaptive institutions responding vigorously to changing circumstances. If sometimes rather belatedly, they have over the past 100 years transformed themselves from craft-centered organizations with guild-like characteristics to powerful enterprises for organizing mass-production and semiskilled workers into huge industrial unions. But now they seem to have stumbled. Faced with dramatic reductions in the proportion of workers who produce goods, trade-union leaders are confronted with the task of bringing a new generation of service-sector workers into their ranks. So far, the results have not been auspicious. Although the highest rate of growth is among service workers and some of the largest unions are in the service sector, private-sector trade-union membership has declined to 13 per cent of the labor force—its lowest level since the early 1930s.[1] And public sympathy with trade unionism is at a low ebb.

How are membership and confidence to be restored? It is time for another metamorphosis. Once again trade unions are called upon to transform themselves into institutions that speak to the needs and interests of an evolving work force. Formidable obstacles lie in the way. These include an unsympathetic government and increasing hostility from business as well as the continuing transformation of the American economy and the structure of the labor force. But labor has faced, and overcome, all of these obstacles before. It can overcome them again if it gives voice to a coherent set of values and programs capable of reaching the new service worker and commanding the support of the larger society.

As a class-based institution, the unique role of the trade union in American society has been to articulate a concept of solidarity. Where the dominant American ideology confidently assumed that unending abundance and opportunity justified faith in self-reliance and individual advancement, the trade-union movement postulated limited job options and unequal power in the work place. Only solidarity and collective action, trade unionists believed, could protect and improve the quality of life of ordinary people and ensure them a fair share of opportunity. Yet in recent years trade unionists have backed away from the collective values they once nurtured in an effort to promote individual well-being instead.

Alice Kessler-Harris is a professor of history and the director of Women's Studies, Rutgers University. Bertram Silverman is a professor of economics and the director of the Center for the Sudy of Work and Leisure, Hofstra University.

An earlier version of this paper appeared in *Dissent*, Winter 1992

The great historical swings in the labor movement illustrate why and how this happened. When the American labor movement consolidated its resources in the late nineteenth century and started its career as a continuing part of the American scene, its goals and directions were guided by the interests of skilled, white, male craft workers who saw themselves as independent artisans. Threatened by a loss of autonomy at work and then by the advance of mass-production techniques, craft workers struggled to protect their dignity at work, their jobs, and their communities. They banded together in an effort to control the pace of change and to maintain some influence in new manufacturing processes. To do so, they shed ideas of self-employment and began to associate themselves with the new American Federation of Labor.

The AFL's constituent unions saw workers in the various crafts, trades, and skills as wage workers. To ensure that opportunities to pursue their trades and skills with dignity were not diminished, unions sought to control hiring, training, and standards of quality. Many of these craft unions were tied to immigrant communities, where they bridged the work interests of members and the interests of the larger community. They occupied a male-dominated world and focused on male pride in the work place and male support of the home. And because they excluded most of the new semiskilled operatives as well as virtually all of the unskilled working population, they included few women or people of color.

In the end, the labor movement they created could not protect the craft workers' traditional work habits or their control over the process of work, but it fought successfully to maintain the craft worker's sense of dignity. It struggled for a "family" wage sufficient to support a household, a limit on the number of hours in the working day, and the ability to confront irrational work rules. Faced with a rapidly consolidating industrial sector, AFL president Samuel Gompers adopted a two-pronged strategy. He agreed that the purpose of business was to make profits and insisted on the right of workers to a share that was consistent with a reasonable standard of living. Though many have criticized this historic compromise, Gompers's acknowledgment that the dignity of workers was rooted in the capacity to stretch the limits of industry's willingness to share profits provided the foundation for the first sustained national labor movement in the United States.

By the 1930s, as industry developed new techniques for maximizing production and efficiency, the issues and the workers changed. Mass-production technology created new groups of industrial workers whose skills were easily replaceable but whose numbers gave them a certain amount of power. Still predominantly white and male, the industrial and manufacturing work force now boasted a greater share of immigrants and their children, of women, and of people of color. Less concerned with skill or craft issues in their increasingly routinized work places, this new generation of workers demanded job security through seniority, wanted protection against being driven on the job, and sought wages sufficient to purchase an increasing variety of consumer goods.

Propelled to meet these needs, the labor movement split. Goaded by the new Congress of Industrial Organizations (CIO), the AFL slowly altered a long-standing hostile attitude to government intervention on behalf of workers and, at first reluctantly and then with increasing enthusiasm, supported programs that would protect all Americans from the vagaries of unemployment, old age, disability, and desertion. A broad range of depression-buffeted people who had experienced the perils of limited opportunity applauded these new efforts. Trade-union pressure, as historian Richard Hofstadter noted, gave the Democratic party a social-democratic flavor never before felt in American politics.[2] The transformative nature of these economic objectives was not immediately apparent partly because they were consistent with a growing popular Keynesian consensus that linked workers' higher wages and job security with sustained economic growth and prosperity. But in the end they enabled the labor movement to develop what UAW president Walter Reuther later called "a whole new middle class." Through the 1960s the wages of unionized workers outpaced those of the nonunionized. They provided workers with access to a middle-class world of consumption and life-style, including suburban housing, paid vacations and old-age pensions, and options for educating their children. Success rekindled the possibility that this opportunity might, after all, be unlimited. The search for higher standards of living seemed to open opportunity to women as well, encouraging them to enter the labor force in support of family life.

This generation of workers sought the satisfactions of work outside the work place, hoping that their enhanced incomes would buy for them and their families a measurable improvement in the quality of their lives. If work became more routinized and less intrinsically satisfying, more-affluent working-class families could nevertheless believe that outside of work and in their communities they were participating in the American dream of unbounded individual opportunity. In effect, they rejected the labor-movement theme song, "Solidarity Forever," for the strident individualism of Frank Sinatra's "I Did It My Way." Paradoxically, then, the very success of trade unions in winning higher wages led workers to interests that transcended the work-place concerns on which trade unions had thrived. Unions increasingly found that they were losing touch with their members once they left the factory gates. The decline of the labor movement had begun.[3]

The tensions internal to trade unionism increased in the 1960s and 1970s. Continuing to seek a middle-class lifestyle for their members, trade unions tried to achieve the appearance of upward economic mobility within a job context that was still circumscribed by limits. In the skilled craft unions the result was job protectionism that subjected them to attack by a growing civil-rights movement and reduced the credibility of the entire labor movement as a moral voice for less-privileged workers.

By the 1970s, protectionism seemed to dominate the nonwork lives of union members as well. Increasingly, white workers worried more about the "new immigrants," frequently Black and Hispanic, who threatened the stability of their neighborhoods. Having created a "private" welfare system that provided social benefits equivalent to Western European standards, they resented the poor whose welfare seemed to promise higher taxes that would undermine their fragile living standards. Well-paid male unionists resisted changes in lifestyle called forth by the need for dual incomes and working wives.

The problem this created became apparent by the 1980s. Having lost touch with the larger sense of collective responsibility that had given trade unions their moral voice, union leaders found themselves unable to mobilize a working class. Instead, they bewailed the appearance of an increasingly unequal society whose more-privileged members resisted sharing their good fortune with the working and nonworking poor. Industrial unionism, which remained job centered, could no longer speak to the concerns and interests of a new and more diverse cohort of organized workers whose political passions were more readily mobilized outside rather than inside the work place.

The 1984 election pointed up the trade union's loss of moral voice. A generation after Walter Reuther announced the advent of the middle-class worker, his successor as UAW president, Douglas Fraser, lamented the conservative middle-income automobile worker who voted for Ronald Reagan. Forty-five percent of white male unionists in that election voted for Reagan, compared to only 5 per cent of black male workers.[4] The shifting political perspectives of these workers restricted trade-union leaders from advancing a social-democratic agenda. As Douglas Fraser commented resignedly, trade-union leaders could not move too far ahead of their membership. But just as the transformation of the work place from craft to industrial production challenged the trade-union movement to organize in new ways, to seek new goals, and to form new political alliances, so postindustrial capitalism requires a new direction for trade unions. To understand that new social reality, unions must come to grips with what has changed and can no longer be recaptured. Fundamental to these changes are shifting notions of family and community.

First, class consciousness provides a poor basis for organizing workers. In an earlier period, despite racial, ethnic, and gender divisions, workers shared a common economic experience that reinforced class identity. Most workers were poor, and they tended to live together or in contiguous neighborhoods. Even those who were somewhat better off found their life chances limited because their world was segregated by residence, education, and income from the "middling sort." Today the majority of workers are not poor, and many share neighborhoods and schools with middle-class professionals. Husbands and wives in two-income families and partners in nontraditional families frequently represent different occupational standings.

Recent stagnation of real family income has not changed this new social reality. Workers are an integral part of the consumer society and have accommodated to its values. Consequently, work no longer defines a worker's class identity in such a way as to encapsulate all other major social and political issues. Like the unemployed white auto workers who voted for Ronald Reagan in 1984, most workers now are likely to construct their political attitudes and behavior in response to life experiences outside the work place.[5]

The increasingly female composition of the postindustrial work force and the accompanying growth of female membership in unions constitutes a second factor in the changing social world in which trade unions now function. In the 1970s and early 1980s, an increase in trade-union membership among women partially compensated for the decline among men. By some estimates, about two-thirds of new members are female, and women now account for 37 percent of all members—up from 24 percent in the mid-seventies.[6] Though women have been in the work place for some time, bringing the family and its issues and problems with them, their increasing presence in unions in the past decade has encouraged attention to the connection between work and family life. The dual-income family poses crucial questions of how to care for children, of pregnancy and parenting, and of the quality of leisure time that have a direct impact on the work place and that frequently require local or national governmental action to resolve them.

Women who moved from unpaid household work to paid work fueled the shift from an industrial to a service economy. These were not, by and large, women who moved from industry to services. Rather, they were married women or single parents entering the labor force for the first time. Dependence on the wages of the female wage earner, partner, or single has permitted many working-class families to enter the middle-income world and find greater economic security. But dependence on the incomes of female wage earners also ties work more closely to family. Total family time devoted to wage work has increased dramatically. Indeed, families are working as much today as they did during the nineteenth century, and the women in them are facing time pressures that reopen questions about work and family life.[7]

Third, the service economy raises new issues about the quality of life and particularly about the capacity of individuals or families to glean satisfaction from individual consumption. As the price of mass-produced goods has fallen, they have been made available to ordinary workers. Automobiles, televisions, VCRs, and microwave ovens can be consumed individually without undermining the quality of the product. But the spread of these "democratic goods" offers only limited satisfactions.[8] The good life in a postindustrial world also requires access to good neighborhoods and to such community and social services as health care, education, recreational facilities, and sanitation. Their quality depends on how these services are collectively produced, distributed, and consumed. And this in turn increasingly rests on such values as cooperation, trust, loyalty, honestly, and generosity. These are quite different from the acquisitive values required for individual consumption. As economist Albert Hirschman has noted, marketing encourages people to exercise their option to "exit" or to be mobile if they wish to improve the quality of consumption. The service economy, in contrast, depends more and more on cooperative relations between producers and consumers of services. The buying and selling of televisions, VCRs, clothing, and food is different from transactions involving education, health care, and community services. The former is more likely to be seen as an impersonal transaction in which consumers freely move their dollars around to maximize personal satisfaction. But the exchange relationship in the delivery and acquisition of social services is a different matter. They depend on close interpersonal relationships between producers and consumers. The same women and men who distribute services like teaching, nursing, protection, and welfare also consume them as mothers, fathers, and citizens. The quality of those services depends on the interpersonal skills of the provider and client and the trust, loyalty, and responsibility created in those tie-forming relationships.

Finally, the function of the corporation and its responsibilities to the larger society have changed. As technology and international competition shift the mass-production industries to the developing countries, the significance of assembly-line workers among labor's membership recedes. At the same time, the use of computers enables industry to organize new and more flexible modes of production that utilize part-time and immigrant workers. The "human resource managers" of America's most competitive industries speak more today about the values of cooperation, participation, and trust to enhance worker productivity and innovation. In their view, much of the distinction between management and labor no longer applies, and traditional trade unions have become irrelevant. The resulting changes encourage new forms of managerial control that threaten to marginalize unions in the modern work place.

The postindustrial corporation is international in scope and reach and is not easily constrained by national economic policies. Technology based on information and knowledge rather than natural resources and physical capital cannot be restricted to national borders. Highly mobile capital pushes corporations to seek low-wage environments that threaten the hard-won fringe benefits that constituted the private insurance systems of more-fortunate workers. When corporations pursue a low-wage strategy, they frequently ignore their social responsibilities and undermine the stability of communities, weakening the social service on which the quality of life increasingly depends. These issues loom ever larger as government reduces its social-welfare functions and the family, church, and other voluntary associations struggle vainly to fill the gap.

If the changes we have outlined are correct, spontaneous unionism ignited by class identity will not work. Nor can traditional collective bargaining as it emerged in the 1940s meet the challenges of the service economy. Work may still be the place where unions organize to defend workers' rights and dignity, but in the new reality the only way forward for unions is through politics. For only through politics can the problems of postindustrial America be addressed, and only through politics can trade unions reach the larger constituency they need to change their fortunes and their public image. At the very least, politics is the only way that the public can learn about the connection between unionism and democracy and therefore change the legal environment to one that nurtures unionism.

What needs to be done? The central issue for labor in the postindustrial era is the ability once again to become the voice of the majority of working people. If the old craft union responded to the needs of a skilled and relatively insular male worker for job security and the industrial union spoke to the desire of the mass-production worker for a higher and more secure standard of living, the unionism of the 1990s has little choice but to address the "quality-of-life" issues that are raised by a heterogeneous group of twentieth-century workers. Trade unions were strategically decisive in the development of the New Deal and post–New Deal programs because their goals touched the concerns and interests of the larger society. Today unions need to assess their new constituency in the light of the economic and social changes of the past generation and open-mindedly to explore the kinds of social policies that will meet the new needs of a transformed working class. Around these new social policies—around the construction of a new welfare state, if you will—trade unions have the opportunity to win a broader constituency and to connect once again to the issues that concern large numbers of working people. This is not a radical proposal. Rather, it builds on the initiatives that some unions and union leaders have already begun to take. Reclaiming the moral authority of labor's voice will require trade unions to involve themselves in new areas. Primary among these is the task of providing support for the modern family and particularly of designing services for it that have long been abandoned to impersonal bureaucracies and politicians. Unions have already responded to the influx of women by placing such issues as parental leave, flexible benefits, pay equity, and reduced hours of work on their agendas. In 1988–89, the Coalition of Labor Union Women featured family issues in a year-long campaign to encourage unions toward imaginative solutions. But the demand for new benefits, whether provided by the government or employers, is only part of the issue raised by the increasing participation of women in the work force. Unions must mediate between family and employer, providing members with such necessities as child care, counseling services, and access to social services. Recognizing that what constitutes a "family" is a work-force issue, they will participate in redefining it. For example, they might renegotiate benefit packages tailored to married couples to acknowledge the existence of some three million gay and lesbian parents as well as countless nonmarried couples with and without children.

Unions must also turn their attention more fully to the communities in which workers reside. This will become increasingly essential as the expansion of the service sector, where women are most often employed, moves the terrain of struggle from the work place to the community. Unlike the old worker who dealt primarily with machines, the new one deals with people and the public. Her sense of dignity resides not only in the conditions under which she works but in her ability to service her clients effectively. As in her work life the emphasis moves from the quantity of goods produced to the quality of the services she can provide, so in her private life the emphasis shifts from the quantity of goods she can buy to the quality of her life and that of her family. The disturbing questions faced by the new worker involve not only how to increase income or resolve work-related disputes but how families will survive the hurdles of schooling, health care, environment, and sometimes the violence and drugs that endanger neighborhood life.

All workers depend on a variety of neighborhood and community amenities and supports to sustain their quality of life and ultimately on government support to provide economic security. How to improve the quality of those services and distribute them fairly must become one of the central problems of trade unions if they are to thrive in postindustrial capitalism. Though these problems cannot be resolved by collective agreements negotiated at the bargaining table, failure to address them makes trade unions largely irrelevant to millions of actual and potential members. It also impoverishes a large sector of the public whose voice trade unions could effectively represent.

Dissolving the artificial barrier between the public and the worker must become one of the trade union's major tasks. Unions that can link workers who provide social services with consumers of those services create a natural alliance. To do so, unions must be closely involved with their members in such issues as education, housing, poverty, and crime. Some unions are beginning to do more of this—for example, teachers who link wages and working conditions to the improvement of education and health care and social-service workers who seek to link their organization more closely to their poor and underprivileged clients. Others, such as the International Ladies Garment Workers Union (ILGWU) and the Amalgamated Clothing and Textile Workers Union (ACTWU), have begun to set up community offices to address workers' nonwork concerns directly.

The process of community involvement requires that unions participate in creating what the historian Eric Hobsbawm called "social fronts," which link workers and their unions to community groups and institutions that address their family and community problems.[9] Transcending the private insurance system that trade unions helped create over the last fifty years, unions should make efforts to reach the unorganized. The now-defunct Progressive Alliance attempted in the late 1970s to address such social issues as plant closings. More recently, the AFL–CIO has begun to offer individuals who do not belong to bargaining units alternative ways of identifying with a union. In the spirit of these proposals, community involvement accepts responsibility for a broader range of issues than those encompassed by the work place. This approach offers the unions a credible voice in healing racial divisions and in bridging the gulf that isolates the poor from the mainstream of society.

Finally, trade unions need to challenge narrow definitions of corporate profitability and responsibility, insisting that governments treat corporations as social institutions whose activities loom well beyond their immediate economic domain. Daniel Bell suggested this notion in his 1973 *The Coming of Post-Industrial Society*. The corporation, he argued, consisted of "the management and the board of directors, operating as trustees for members of the enterprise as a whole—not just stockholders, but workers and consumers too—and with due regard to the interests of society as a whole."[10] The model comes close to that of most West European nations, which typically hold managers and boards of trustees responsible for negotiating social issues. It finds its resonance in the activities of some political and social institutions, such as municipal governments, colleges, foundations, and churches, that have already begun to use their positions as stockholders to influence corporate economic and social policies. Trade unions have successfully used pressure on trustees to settle major strikes. Within the AFL–CIO Executive Council, a subcommittee led by the president of the ACTWU, Jack Sheinkman, has begun to develop a theory of "stake holders' " rights within a corporation. The stake-holder theory holds that job holders and residents of communities where plants are located have a stake in the corporation no smaller than that of shareholders. This conception is consistent with the long-term interests of modern corporations, which are discovering that a high-wage, high-performance economy depends on the effectiveness of local schools and on family and community stability.[11]

The voice of the trade union is threatened with silence if unions fail to take account of new realities. Industrial unionism earned attention by conceding managerial prerogatives in exchange for rising real wages and good fringe benefits for workers. The trade-off worked reasonably well in the 1940s, 1950s, and 1960s for unionized workers. But to cling to it today will place unions in increasingly marginal positions. Already many liberals seem to have tacitly accepted their absence from social debate. The authors of *The Good Society*, for example, offer a prescription for change that includes no reference to the role of trade unions.[12]

To regain national influence, trade unions need to establish a louder and more comprehensive voice. They can play an important role in reshaping the welfare state by moving beyond traditional collective-bargaining and private insurance schemes to become more responsive to the diverse needs of local communities and families. Doing so will help reawaken workers' interest in politics. If, as social commentator E.J. Dionne argues, "ordinary Americans believe that local communities and institutions can meet their needs more effectively and compassionately than big institutions run from far away,"[13] then trade unions with their capacity to reach into local arenas can play major roles.

The key to a new trade-union strategy consists in articulating new definitions of social responsibility that mediate between community and individual rights; between family responsibility and women's rights; between corporate social responsibility and property rights; between fairness and individual merit. Trade unions that take on these challenges leave the industrial-union phase behind. Working with groups within and outside the corporations, they free themselves to develop a new conception of the welfare state that will once again connect the labor movement to the larger society.

Notes

1. Michael A. Curme et al., "Union Membership and Contract Coverage in the United States, 1983–1989," *Industrial and Labor Relations Review*, October 1990, pp. 5–33.

2. Richard Hofstadter, *The Age of Reform* (New York: Vintage Books, 1955), p. 308.

3. Commentators who noted this decline in the late 1950s include Solomon Barkin, *The Decline of the Labor Movement* (Santa Barbara, CA: Center for the Study of Democratic Institution, 1961), and Daniel Bell, "The Capitalism of the Proletariat," *Encounter*, February 1958.

4. Douglas Fraser, "New Directions in Trade Unionism," unpublished talk presented at a Symposium on the Changing World of Work and Workers, Hofstra University, UAW-District 65, New York, 9 May 1987; A.H. Raskin, "In Search of a Mission," in *Unions in Transition: Entering the Second Century*, ed. Seymour Martin Lipset (San Francisco: ICS Press), p. 31.

5. It would be a mistake to view workers' recent concerns about the decline in high-wage blue-collar jobs as a signal for the revival of traditional class politics. The widening wage gap between less-educated blue-collar workers and more-educated professional employees has intensified workers' feelings of unfairness. But those sentiments also have sharpened the division between working-class families who must work more to maintain their middle-income living standards and the poor who are increasingly isolated from traditional Democratic Party and trade-union political activity.

6. U.S. Department of Labor, Bureau of Labor Statistics, *Employment and Earnings* 36 (January 1988), p. 225.

7. Juliet Schor, *The Overworked Americans: The Unexpected Decline of Leisure* (New York: Basic Books, 1991).

8. Roy Harrod, "The Possibility of Economic Satiety," in *Problems of United States Economic Development* (New York: Committee for Economic Development, 1958), vol. 1, pp. 207–13; Fred Hirsch, *Social Limits to Growth* (Cambridge, MA: Harvard University Press, 1976). For a different perspective, see Albert O. Hirschman, *Shifting Involvements* (Princeton, NJ: Princeton University Press).

9. Eric Hobsbawm, "Labor and Politics," unpublished paper presented at A Symposium on Labor and Politics, Hofstra University, UAW-District 65, New York, 8 October 1988.

10. Daniel Bell, *The Coming of Post-Industrial Society: A Venture in Social Forecasting* (New York: Basic Books, 1976), p. 296. Richard Freeman has suggested that the model of a Japanese firm maximizing a weighted average of the interests of all its "stake holders," including workers, may come closer to the mark for capitalist firms in general than profit maximization does. Such a model, if it in fact included the active participation of trade unions, workers, and community organizations, would help slow down the movement of business and enhance economic and social stability. Richard Freeman, "Getting Here from There: Labor in the Transition to a Market Economy," in *Labor and Democracy in the Transition to a Market System*, ed. B. Silverman, R. Vogt, and M. Yanowitch (Armonk, NY: M.E. Sharpe, 1992).

11. For a fuller discussion of a high-wage, high-performance strategy, see Ray Marshall and Marc Tucker, *Thinking for a Living: Education and the Wealth of Nations* (New York: Basic Books, 1992).

12. Robert N. Bellah et al., *The Good Society* (New York: Knopf, 1991).

13. E.J. Dionne, Jr., *Why Americans Hate Politics* (New York: Simon and Shuster, 1991).

Index

About the Editors

Bertram Silverman is a professor of economics and director of the Center for the Study of Work and Leisure at Hofstra University. He has worked as a trade union economist and has organized and directed a joint university–trade union college degree program for working adults. Silverman has written about labor problems in the United States, Latin America, and Europe and is co-editor with Murray Yanowitch of *The Workers in "Post-Industrial" Capitalism*.

Robert C. Vogt has served as Dean of the College of Liberal Arts and Sciences at Hofstra University since 1977. He holds a Ph.D. in Political Science with a specialization in Comparative Politics. Since 1981 he has directed several programs and projects relating to U.S. technology transfer and economic development and investment policy in China, Eastern Europe, and post-Soviet republics.

Murray Yanowitch is professor emeritus of economics at Hofstra University. He is the author of numerous works about Soviet social, economic, and labor issues including *Controversies in Soviet Social Thought: Democratization, Social Justice, and the Erosion of Official Ideology*; *Social and Economic Inequality in the Soviet Union: Six Studies*; and *Work in the Soviet Union: Attitudes and Issues*. He is also the editor of two journals of translations of Russian social scientific writings: *Sociological Research* and *Problems of Economic Transition*.

Professors Silverman, Vogt, and Yanowitch are the editors of the companion volume to this book, *Labor and Democracy in the Transition to a Market System: A U.S.–Post-Soviet Dialogue* (Armonk, NY: M.E. Sharpe, 1992).